20th International Conference on WWW/Internet and 18th International Conference Applied Computing 2021 (ICWI AC 2021)

Online
13-15 October 2021

Editors:

Pedro Isaías
Hans Weghorn

ISBN: 978-1-7138-3938-5

Printed from e-media with permission by:

Curran Associates, Inc.
57 Morehouse Lane
Red Hook, NY 12571

CURRAN ASSOCIATES INC. proceedings .com

Some format issues inherent in the e-media version may also appear in this print version.

International Association for Development of the Information Society (IADIS)
Rua Sao Sebastiao Da Pedreira
No. 100, 30, 1050-209
Lisbon, Portugal

Phone: 351 21 3151373
Fax: 351 21 3151244

secretariat@iadis.org

Additional copies of this publication are available from:

Curran Associates, Inc.
57 Morehouse Lane
Red Hook, NY 12571 USA
Phone: 845-758-0400
Fax: 845-758-2633
Email: curran@proceedings.com
Web: www.proceedings.com

TABLE OF CONTENTS

20th International Conference

on

WWW/Internet 2021

and

18th International Conference

Applied Computing 2021

(ICWI AC 2021)

13-15 October 2021

Online Event

IMPACT OF PROMOTIONAL SOCIAL MEDIA CONTENT ON CLICK-THROUGH RATE – EVIDENCE FROM A FMCG COMPANY

Maria Madlberger[1] and Jiri Jizdny[2]
[1]*Webster Vienna Private University, Praterstrasse 23, 1020 Vienna, Austria*
[2]*AG FOODS Group a.s., Škrobárenská 506/2, 617 00 Brno, Czech Republic*

ABSTRACT

Social media are a key communication channel between businesses and their customers and an effective means to induce customer engagement. However, there is little empirical evidence on the impact of social media marketing on the click-through rate which ultimately contributes to profitability and financial success. This paper investigates impacts of different attributes of social media content, i.e., image, text-based features, and a retargeting campaign, on the click-through rate by analyzing data obtained from an e-commerce company's A/B testing. The findings show that image posts outperform text-based posts in terms of engagement, but not for the click-through rate. Retargeting outperforms social media campaigns in respect of the click-through rate. On the other hand, text-based features such as emojis and seasonal vocabulary do not show a significant impact on the click-through rate. The findings allow conclusions on an optimized allocation and design features of social media content.

KEYWORDS

Social Media Marketing, Click-Through Rate, Retargeting, Engagement

1. INTRODUCTION

The rapid development of information technologies allows businesses to be closer to their customers and better understand their needs and wants. One particularly effective communication channel are social media as they facilitate a bidirectional interaction between businesses and customers. The use of social media is still rising. For example, the number of Instagram users has increased from 2019 to 2020 by 22.9 percent and reaches a level close to 1 billion users worldwide. This development has been further accelerated by the COVID-19 pandemic (Enberg, 2020). Companies are adjusting their marketing communication according to these developments. Likewise, e-commerce continues to be on the rise. In 2018, there were global retail sales through e-commerce of $2.84 trillion, increasing to expected $4 trillion in 2020, and in 2021 they are anticipated to reach $4.88 trillion (Clement, 2019).

Whereas there is ample research on social media marketing and drivers of user engagement on social media (Zahay, 2021), business practitioners are still concerned with the extent of the economic effectiveness of social media communication. Communication through social media can become successful only when it is combined with measurable communication and marketing goals (Kumar et al., 2016). In particular, the causality paths from social media communication to sales and ultimately profitability are not fully clarified. Two key indicators in this respect are the conversion and the click-through rate. The conversion rate is defined as the number of conversions, e.g., to a purchase, in relation to the number of clicks. The click-through rate is determined as the number of clicks on a specific content, e.g., an advertisement, divided by the number of impressions of this content (Ghose and Yang, 2009). Hence, in order to achieve a conversion and therefore a purchase, the click-through rate is a key prerequisite.

The contribution of social media communication to the click-through rates has not yet been sufficiently examined. The study at hand seeks to address this research gap by empirically investigating how various features of social media communication are associated with the click-through rate. Based on extant evidence from literature, we address design features of different social media marketing campaigns in the form of images as well as text-based features and retargeting campaigns. For this purpose, data of a Central European online retailer in the fast-moving consumer goods (FMCG) sector is analyzed.

The research questions of this study are the following:

RQ1: How are text- and image-based design features of social media content associated with the click-through rate?

RQ2: How effective are social media campaigns compared with retargeting campaigns in respect of the click-through rate?

The paper is organized as follows: In the subsequent section, a review of literature on social media marketing and social networks is provided. Section 3 proposes the hypotheses. Section 4 discusses the research methodology, data collection, and results of the hypothesis tests. Finally, the research and managerial implications are discussed in section 5.

2. SOCIAL MEDIA MARKETING

Social media provide the technological platform for social interactions to co-create value and content (Strauss and Frost, 2014). Social networks integrate the functions of different social media and are characterized by several features: (1) Users desire communication, hence they are searching for social networks to communicate directly with others, (2) users typically act under their true identity, (3) the vast majority of content is created by the users themselves on private and corporate profiles, (4) social network operators have limited control over communication and content creation between individuals, (5) users, especially companies choose the addressees of their communication, and (6) bidirectional and persistent communication requires companies to be alert and continuously respond to questions or complaints from users (Strauss and Frost, 2014).

Marketing on social media and social networks can be conducted in three basic ways: owned media pass the advertiser's communication messages to the users through its own channels which is the corporate page or profile on social networks. Paid media consist of communicative messages conveyed by another organization, i.e., the operator of the social network, that is being paid by the advertiser to do so. Earned media denotes messages that are disseminated by actors other than the advertiser without any compensation. In social networks, earned media is provided by users who are communicating marketing-relevant messages, which is referred to as engagement (Strauss and Frost, 2014). In order to maximize effectiveness of social media marketing, advertisers need to use both owned and paid media in order to motivate customers to engage with them positively in the form of earned media. Therefore, the purpose of communicative messages and advertisements is of high relevance. It needs to be based on the goal the advertiser seeks to pursue. Social networks adapt to such requirements and offer the delivery of advertisements accordingly to users who are most likely to accomplish the respective advertising purposes. For instance, Facebook offers three basic advertising purposes, i.e., awareness ads that are delivered to users who are likely to be interested in the product or business itself as well as related advertising, consideration ads which are provided to users who are expected to start searching for information about the advertised product, and conversion ads which are targeting users who are, compared to others, frequently clicking on the ad or even making a purchase (Lee et al., 2018).

Literature has identified various ways of how user engagement, conversion, and click-through rates can be stimulated on social networks. Social media advertising has a positive impact on purchase intention and brand trust (Fuguitt, 2015). The provision of entertaining and informative content about a brand shows a significant and high impact on user engagement on social networks. Users are also mostly engaged in watching videos and pictures that are brand-related and reading reviews of products that are linked with visual content (Kujur and Singh, 2020). Engagement is further triggered by the placement of call-to-action which results in doubling the likes, multiplying comments by three, and multiplying sharing by seven (O'Brien, 2019). A popular instrument to increase conversion and click-through rates on the Internet is retargeting, a personalized advertisement based on the previous browsing history on the advertiser's website which recommends users on external websites to return to that website. Retargeting has turned out to impact significantly the number of website visits as well as sales (Lewis and Reiley, 2014, Lobschat et al., 2017).

In retargeting campaigns, users often do not recognize retargeting advertising and mistakenly interpret it as a regular campaign. If users do not complete a customer journey by making a purchase or any other requested action, retargeting can turn out to effectively increase conversion (Veszelszki, 2018), especially when the user has just visited the advertiser's online store and the banner has a high degree of content personalization (Bleier and Eisenbeiss, 2015). Personalization and targeting small segments in general result in a higher tendency towards conversion (Srinivasan et al., 2016). Furthermore, personalization has a substantial positive impact on customer retention (Bojei et al., 2013).

3. HYPOTHESES DEVELOPMENT

In the following, the research hypotheses are elaborated in order to shed light on factors that drive user engagement as well as the click-through rate as a proxy of conversion. The hypotheses examine the impact of various popular design features in social media marketing.

A majority of the people consume content visually. At present, 91% of consumers favor content that is interactive and visual over static content. Visual content such as photos and infographics are making a brand's posting on social networks more valuable and diversified for users (Dayan, 2018). Social media content should be visually appealing. To further enhance the appeal of a post, the advertiser should combine different content types, such as text with photos or videos. The degree of visual quality affects user engagement, i.e., the number of likes, comments, shares, and clicks (Syrdal and Briggs, 2018). An analysis of 100 brands and more than 1,300 posts of these brands revealed that posts need to be visually appealing in order to be recognized by the audience on crowded news feeds of social media (Brubaker and Wilson, 2018). Hence, the following hypothesis has been developed to address the visual appeal on the audience.

H1: Image posts on social media show higher engagement than text posts.

A higher engagement rate is also positively associated with a higher click-through rate (Yang et al., 2016) because higher engagement as a response to an ad results in a more positive attitude which itself drives the intention to click on the respective ad (Calder et al., 2009). This relationship has been found in the consumer goods sector (Yang et al., 2016) as well as in the tourism sector (Lin et al., 2018). Since we consider images to stimulate engagement, we conclude that the presence of images will also be positively associated with the click-through rate. Industry research has shown that such a direct relationship between images in social media content and the click-through rate does exist (Bercovici, 2014). Therefore, we propose the following hypothesis:

H2: Images on social media posts a show higher click-through rate than text posts.

Emotional content in social media marketing shows a positive impact on user engagement as well as the conversion and click-through rate. Liu et al. (2019) discuss the influence of emojis for branding effect, download willingness, and product purchase intention. Their study reveals that emojis help to increase brand awareness for low frequency users and they can boost download willingness. Similarly, emojis result in higher engagement rates in the form of retweets on the social media platform Twitter (Pancer et al., 2017, Quesenberry and Coolsen, 2019). Although download willingness does not show to significantly impact purchase intention, it increases the conversion of website visits. Emojis show an indirect impact on engagement by conveying humor and emotions. Combining such affective content with informative content, such as a promoted deal, enhances users' conversion rate (Lee et al., 2018). Thus, the following is proposed:

H3: Emojis in the text of a social media advertisement increase the click-through rate.

The large number of contents provided on social networks results in a high degree of distraction (Zhang et al., 2020). As users scroll through their news feed quickly, it is challenging for advertisers to grab their attention, make them focus on the published content, and engage with the content (Brubaker and Wilson, 2018). One effective characteristic of text-based content known from research on online consumer reviews is relevance of the vocabulary (Tao and Zhou, 2020). Reviews that contain more relevant terminology are considered more helpful (Qazi et al., 2016). Therefore, we conclude that if an advertiser provides posts or ads that direct users towards topical areas, such a strategy may help to raise user reactions. We refer to seasonality as a context that is considered more topical during the respective season. To investigate whether a larger emphasis on a seasonality-related concept shows a larger impact than a smaller one, we propose:

H4: Seasonality-related words at the beginning of a social media advertisement increase the click-through rate.

Digital channels offer various opportunities for retargeting campaigns. Evidence on the effectiveness of retargeting in this context is mixed. Users can have trust issues with the brand, if they are receiving continuously very specifically targeted advertisements as they perceive their privacy to be threatened (Stevens, 2014). On the other hand, retargeting is turning out effective especially among users who spend more time on the advertiser's website and thus demonstrate surfing behavior by browsing through the product categories and products. Hence, retargeting performs best if being personalized to the respective audience (Lambrecht and Tucker, 2013). Despite a certain degree of personalization of social media content delivery through the platform operators, we assert that retargeting shows a higher degree of personalization and thus is more effective in stimulating click-through, so that we propose:

H5: Retargeting campaigns achieve a higher click-through rate than social media content.

4. RESULTS

4.1 Data Collection

Data collection has been conducted within a Central European fast moving consumer goods (FMCG) online shop operator. The company offers high-quality tea in teabags for the retail, gastronomy, hospitality, and food service markets and sells its products to consumers via its online store. For hypotheses tests, data has been retrieved from the company's ERP system over a period of several weeks as well as data retrieved from Google Analytics and Facebook Insights. At the end of November and at the beginning of December 2019, the company launched social media campaigns for the Christmas season. For the study, a total of eight campaigns on Facebook and Mailchimp have been specially designed for A/B testing and subsequent analysis. They consist of two posts as owned content to test H1 and H2, four Facebook advertisements to test H3 and H4, and two retargeting campaigns (one on Facebook and one by email newsletter) to test H5. In collaboration with the company's graphic designer, one of the co-authors created the texts and images for the social media contents in order to create the stimuli necessary for the hypothesis tests, using Facebook Ad Manager and Mailchimp. The analyzed campaigns lasted from December 9 until December 18, 2019.

4.2 Hypothesis Tests

To test H1 and H2, two types of posts have been created of which the engagement and the click-through rates have been retrieved. The first post consisted of the following text, translated into English: "Who did not solve Christmas gifts yet? Solve your Christmas gifts from the comfort of home – do not forget that Santa Claus comes in 20 days." The second post includes a picture of the product, i.e., a tea box, with the already made tea in a cup, and a Christmas rose, accompanied by a shorter text: "Christmas is here in 12 days".

The test of H1 shows that the post with the image content [image] shows a higher engagement than the post with the text-only content [text]. The image content has been delivered to a larger audience and achieved a significantly higher proportion of likes, shares, comments, and clicks than the text-only content (n [text] = 1,147, n [image] = 1,617, p [text] = 1.221%, p [image] = 2.600%, z = 2.5314, $p < .01$). Thus, hypothesis 1 is supported.

When it comes to H2, the findings show that the proportion of clicks on the image content is similar to that of the text-only content. The small difference is not significant (n [text] = 1,147, n [image] = 1,617, p [text] = .959%, p [image] = .989%, z = .0802, $p > .05$), so that H2 is rejected.

For H3, two social media advertisements have been created and published. One ad shows an image of gift tea boxes, the text "Gift that warms up", and an emoji of a heart at the end of the text [emot]. The second ad displays the same image, the text "Taste real teas", and no emoji in the text [no_emot]. The z test displays no significant difference in the click-through rate (n [emot] = 8,182, n [no_emot] = 7,328, p [emot] = 3.52%, p [no_emot] = 3.33%, z = .6499, $p > .05$) so that H3 is rejected.

For H4, the A/B testing took place for two ads with varying usage of a specific word in a specific seasonality, i.e., the Christmas season. The chosen specific Christmas season word is "gift". The first ad displays the word "gift" at the beginning of the sentence [beg] whereas the second ad shows the word "gift" at the end of the sentence [end]. There was a higher number of exposures to the ad with the season-related word in the beginning. The z value shows that the click-through rate does not differ significantly between the two ads (n [beg] = 8,182, n [end] = 5,688, p [beg] = 3.52%, p [end] = 3.446%, z = .2338, p > .05) so that H4 is rejected.

For H5, a retargeting campaign through the service of Mailchimp has been done. The campaign was connected to the online store. When users visited it, the campaign displayed them a retargeting post with the product, which they were looking at and allured them to return to the online store. For the hypothesis test, all December campaigns on Facebook [FB] have been compared with a newsletter-based retargeting campaign during the same time period [retarget]. The difference between the click-through rates of both campaigns is significant (n [FB] = 46,719, n [retarget] = 1,042, p [FB] = 3.881%, p [retarget] = 6.24%, z = 3.8732, p < .001), supporting H5.

Table 1 summarizes the results of the hypothesis tests.

Table 1. Summary of hypothesis tests

Hypothesis	Proposed impact	Result
H1	**Image posts on social media show higher engagement than text posts**	Supported
H2	**Images on social media posts a show higher click-through rate than text posts**	Rejected
H3	**Emojis in the text of a social media advertisement increase the click-through rate**	Rejected
H4	**Seasonality-related words at the beginning of a social media advertisement increase the click-through rate.**	Rejected
H5	**Retargeting campaigns achieve a higher click-through rate than social media content**	Supported

5. DISCUSSION

5.1 Research Implications

This study provides insights into consumer reactions to various social media contents. Within the context of owned media, i.e., social media posts, it could be shown that the presence of an image significantly raises engagement. This result is consistent with the findings by Brubaker and Wilson (2018) as well as Syrdal and Briggs (2018) who contend that promotional content has to be visually appealing for the audience. Visual content is also largely preferred over static content and results in a higher engagement of the reached audience (Dayan, 2018). A key issue in this respect is the need of brands to catch the audience's attention in an overloaded social media news feed (Buchanan et al., 2018). However, the presence of the image shows no positive impact on the click-through rate so that it cannot be concluded that image content is more effective in terms of conversion than text-based content. This finding challenges the widely assumed, but barely demonstrated relationship between engagement and the click-through rate and therefore calls for a further investigation of possible mediating variables in the long chain of causality between social media engagement and economic profitability.

With the paid advertisements, the findings show that variations in the text features do not impact the click-through rate. In contrast to the findings of Liu et al. (2019), our study could not show that emojis in an ad lead to a higher click-through rate. Although emotions and especially humor show a positive impact on engagement (Lee et al., 2018) as well as brand attachment behavior (Arya et al., 2018), this effect is not achieved for the click-through rate by the inclusion of emojis in a social media ad. Also, the placement of season-related vocabulary in different positions of social media ads did not increase the click-through rate.

These findings suggest that they are another possible indicator of a weak relationship between engagement and actual click-through behavior. Within the context of emotions as well as topicality of vocabulary, more evidence is needed to understand the potentially mediated effects of emojis, emotional content in general, and relevance of vocabulary in promotional social media content.

Comparing the effectiveness of different communication channels, our findings support the assertion that a personalized retargeting campaign results in a higher click-through rate than social media content. This result is in line with the findings obtained by Lambrecht and Tucker (2013) who found that if customers spend some time on a website, associated retargeting campaigns achieve significantly higher user resonance. The previous visit of a company's website is a stronger trigger for being receptive to a retargeting campaign. This implies that social media content should be considered being complementary to retargeting campaigns. The click-through rate achieved by social media content forwards users to the company website from where users can be further addressed more effectively by retargeting.

5.2 Managerial Implications

The research design has employed an A/B testing approach implemented by a FMCG company. This procedure shows that A/B testing can yield useful and actionable results with little additional effort, especially if complemented with statistical analyses. The findings provide various implications for the creation of content on social media and a reliable assessment of their potentials to ultimately influence the click-through rate which is a prerequisite of social media marketing profitability.

Firstly, the findings clearly show that the connection between engagement and click-through rate is not overly strong and therefore should not be overestimated. Particularly in terms of goal-setting it is important to clearly distinguish between communicative goals related to engagement and economic goals of conversion, click-through rate, or purchase. Firms may not take measures to increase engagement if they intend to pursue economic goals. Second, the role of design features in social media content in terms of their impact on the click-through rate is low, hence it may not be over-estimated. The use of emojis and seasonality terms can possibly increase engagement in the form of likes, shares, or comments, but is not influential for the click-through rate so that it should not be used to support profitability goals. Third and finally, companies are recommended to use a mixture of different social media contents as well complement social media marketing with retargeting campaigns. This is in line with the assertion of an integrated marketing communications approach that aims at a holistic and consistent design of the communicative mix across a variety of media.

6. CONCLUSION

The focus of this study is to investigate the role of marketing communication on social media in the conversion of customers in FMCG e-commerce by addressing their impact on the click-through rate. The results which were collected from a FMCG company's ERP system, Google Analytics, Facebook Manager, and Mailchimp show that the presence of images can stimulate engagement, but text-based modifications and images show no significant impact on the click-through rate. Further, newsletter-based retargeting results in a higher click-through rate than social media contents.

The findings of the research ought to be acknowledged in the light of several limitations. Data collection was based on social media data from one company that is specializing in one product category. Hence, the results cannot be generalized to other companies and industries with different customer target groups as well as the whole FMCG industry. The applied social network was Facebook. Other social networks or social media could show different user reactions, for example, text-based posts could show a different impact on Instagram or Twitter. Likewise, the study took place in one country among a target group that is largely concentrated in urban areas so that a geographical bias may exist. Finally, data has been collected during the Christmas season. Hence, dissimilarities can appear in the results if the study was conducted within a more extended period of time.

Future research may address a more comprehensive investigation of reasons for the rejected hypotheses as well as further potential drivers of the click-through rate and conversion. On the one hand, insights from consumer behavior during the various stages of the purchase funnel could shed more light on the effectiveness of omni-channel management approaches that seek to integrate different communication and distribution channels (Verhoef et al., 2015). On the other hand, the effect of product categories may be revisited in this context, as this variable turned out to show a moderating impact in other e-commerce application areas, e.g., online consumer reviews (Ren and Hong, 2019). Finally, the causality path from exposure to promotional social media content, engagement, click-through rate, and conversion, needs to be further examined for a better understanding of this complex phenomenon.

REFERENCES

Arya, V. et al., 2018. Are Emojis Fascinating Brand Value More Than Textual Language? Mediating Role of Brand Communication to Sns and Brand Attachment. *Corporate Communications: An International Journal,* Vol. 23, No. 4, pp. 648-670.

Bercovici, J., 2014. Using a Network of Instagrammers as a Virtual Creative Agency. *Forbes,* Vol., No. 4/28, pp. 20.

Bleier, A. and Eisenbeiss, M., 2015. Personalized Online Advertising Effectiveness: The Interplay of What, When, and Where. *Marketing Science,* Vol. 34, No. 5, pp. 669-688.

Bojei, J. et al., 2013. The Empirical Link between Relationship Marketing Tools and Consumer Retention in Retail Marketing. *Journal of Consumer Behaviour,* Vol. 12, No. 3, pp. 171-181.

Brubaker, P.J. and Wilson, C., 2018. Let's Give Them Something to Talk About: Global Brands' Use of Visual Content to Drive Engagement and Build Relationships. *Public Relations Review,* Vol. 44, No. 3, pp. 342-352.

Buchanan, L. et al., 2018. A Thematic Content Analysis of How Marketers Promote Energy Drinks on Digital Platforms to Young Australians. *Australian and New Zealand Journal of Public Health,* Vol. 42, No. 6, pp. 530-531.

Calder, B.J. et al., 2009. An Experimental Study of the Relationship between Online Engagement and Advertising Effectiveness. *Journal of Interactive Marketing,* Vol. 23, No. 4, pp. 321-331.

Clement, J. 2019. *Global Retail E-Commerce Market Size 2014-2023.* https://www.statista.com/statistics/379046/worldwide-retail-e-commerce-sales/.

Dayan, Z. 2018. *Visual Content. The Future of Storytelling.* https://www.forbes.com/sites/forbestechcouncil/2018/04/02/visual-content-the-future-ofstorytelling/#28410b5f3a46.

Enberg, J. 2020. *Global Instagram Users 2020.* https://www.emarketer.com/content/global-instagram-users-2020.

Fuguitt, G., 2015. Arf David Ogilvy Awards. *Journal of Advertising Research,* Vol. 55, No. 3, pp. 339-352.

Ghose, A. and Yang, S., 2009. An Empirical Analysis of Search Engine Advertising: Sponsored Search in Electronic Markets. *Management Science,* Vol. 55, No. 10, pp. 1605-1622.

Kujur, F. and Singh, S., 2020. Visual Communication and Consumer-Brand Relationship on Social Networking Sites - Uses and Gratifications Theory Perspective. *Journal of Theoretical and Applied Electronic Commerce Research,* Vol. 15, No. 1, pp. 30-47.

Kumar, A. et al., 2016. From Social to Sale: The Effects of Firm-Generated Content in Social Media on Customer Behavior. *Journal of Marketing Research,* Vol. 80, No. 1, pp. 7-25.

Lambrecht, A. and Tucker, C., 2013. When Does Retargeting Work? Information Specificity in Online Advertising. *Journal of Marketing Research* Vol. 50, No. 5, pp. 561-576.

Lee, D. et al., 2018. Advertising Content and Consumer Engagement on Social Media: Evidence from Facebook. *Management Science,* Vol. 64, No. 11, pp. 5105-5131.

Lewis, R.A. and Reiley, D.H., 2014. Online Ads and Offline Sales: Measuring the Effect of Retail Advertising Via a Controlled Experiment on Yahoo! *Quantitative Marketing and Economics,* Vol. 12, No. 3, pp. 235-266.

Lin, S. et al., 2018. Value Co-Creation on Social Media. *International Journal of Contemporary Hospitality Management,* Vol. 30, No. 4, pp. 2153-2174.

Liu, S.-F. et al., 2019. Analysis of a New Visual Marketing Craze: The Effect of Line Sticker Features and User Characteristics on Download Willingness and Product Purchase Intention. *Asia Pacific Management Review,* Vol. 24, No. 3, pp. 263-277.

Lobschat, L. et al., 2017. What Happens Online Stays Online? Segment-Specific Online and Offline Effects of Banner Advertisements. *Journal of Marketing Research,* Vol. 54, No. 6, pp. 901-913.

O'Brien, J. 2019. *Facebook Ads & Facebook Marketing Mastery Guide 2019.* https://stackskills.com/courses/348500/lectures/5333933.

Pancer, E. et al., 2017. Part F: Digital Marketing, Social Media, and Entertainment Marketing: Signed, Sealed, Delivered - Examining User Generated Content: Emoji and Brand Engagement on Social Media. AMA Summer Educators' Conference Proceedings. pp. F25-F26.

Qazi, A. et al., 2016. A Concept-Level Approach to the Analysis of Online Review Helpfulness. *Computers in Human Behavior,* Vol. 58, No., pp. 75-81.

Quesenberry, K. and Coolsen, M., 2019. Twitter Posts That Are Engaging: A Content Analysis of Twitter Brand Post Text Thatn Increases Retweets, Replies and Favorites in Twitter Brand Posts to Influence Organic Viral Reach. American Academy of Advertising Conference Proceedings. pp. 120.

Ren, G. and Hong, T., 2019. Examining the Relationship between Specific Negative Emotions and the Perceived Helpfulness of Online Reviews. *Information Processing & Management,* Vol. 56, No. 4, pp. 1425-1438.

Srinivasan, S. et al., 2016. Paths to and Off Purchase: Quantifying the Impact of Traditional Marketing and Online Consumer Activity. *Journal of the Academy of Marketing Science,* Vol. 44, No. 4, pp. 440-453.

Stevens, A.M., 2014. What Is Creepy? Towards Understanding That Eerie Feeling When It Seems the Internet Knows 'You'. *Academy of Management Annual Meeting Proceedings,* Vol. 1, No. 1, pp. 1.

Strauss, J. and Frost, R., 2014. *E-Marketing,* Pearson, Essex, UK.

Syrdal, H. and Briggs, E., 2018. Engagement with Social Media Content: A Qualitative Exploration. *Journal of Marketing Theory & Practice,* Vol. 26, No. 1/2, pp. 4-22.

Tao, J. and Zhou, L., 2020. A Weakly Supervised Wordnet-Guided Deep Learning Approach to Extracting Aspect Terms from Online Reviews. *ACM Transactions on Management Information Systems,* Vol. 11, No. 3, pp. 1-22.

Verhoef, P.C. et al., 2015. From Multi-Channel Retailing to Omni-Channel Retailing: Introduction to the Special Issue on Multi-Channel Retailing. *Journal of Retailing,* Vol. 91, No. 2, pp. 174-181.

Veszelszki, Á., 2018. Like Economy: What Is the Economic Value of Likes? *Society and Economy,* Vol. 40, No. 3, pp. 417-429.

Yang, S. et al., 2016. Brand Engagement on Social Media: Will Firms' Social Media Efforts Influence Search Engine Advertising Effectiveness? *Journal of Marketing Management,* Vol. 32, No. 5-6, pp. 526-557.

Zahay, D., 2021. Advancing Research in Digital and Social Media Marketing. *Journal of Marketing Theory & Practice,* Vol. 29, No. 1, pp. 125-39.

Zhang, X. et al., 2020. The Influences of Information Overload and Social Overload on Intention to Switch in Social Media. *Behaviour & Information Technology,* pp. 1-14.

USING NEURAL MACHINE TRANSLATION FOR DETECTING AND CORRECTING GRAMMATICAL ERRORS

Dongqiang Yang, Xiaodong Sun and Pikun Wang
School of Computer Science and Technology, Shandong Jianzhu University, Jinan 250101, China

ABSTRACT

Computer assisted language learning can help ESL/EFL learners facilitate their writings in multiple ways such as spell checking, grammar checking, and style checking. Owning to the complexity of various linguistic errors intertwining in a sentence, it is still a challenging task to detect and correct grammatical errors automatically. Different from previous studies on using pattern matching or statistical language models on this task, we design a Transformer-based neural sequence transduction model to detect and correct grammatical errors. Neural language models are often data-hungry and their performance is also data-dependent. Given the limited size of standard learner corpora and its enormous annotating cost, we employ another Transformer-based encoder-decoder structure to back-translate an error-free sentence into an erroneous one, automating data augmentation for training neural models. We first design some artificial rules to produce a noisy learner dataset to train the back-translation model. The model can then generate more synthesized learner data for training the Transformer-based correction model. In addition to that we also propose an iterative training scheme that unifies the process of error generation and correction. Our state-of-the-art model can reach $F_{0.5}$, the harmony vale of precision and recall, at 64.3% in the shared task of CoNLL-2014, surpassing all the participating systems.

KEYWORDS

Transformers, Grammatical Error Detection, Grammatical Error Correction, Neural Machine Translation

1. INTRODUCTION

Grammatical error correction (GEC) has long been regarded as a challenging task in natural language processing (NLP). Although there have been some commercialized GEC systems in use such as auto-checking spelling and grammar in Microsoft's Office® and Grammarly®, we still have a long way to approach a human level of accuracies on assisting language learners such as spell checking, grammar checking, and style checking (Dale 2016, Dale and Viethen 2021), amongst others. The earlier studies on GEC mainly employed pattern matching or manually constructed rules to detect and correct very limited error type, whereas statistical language models have now evolved into a mainstream technology for identifying and correcting grammatical errors. Especially with the advent of deep learning (Collobert and Weston 2008) and Transformer (Vaswani et al. 2017) in NLP, neural language models such as BERT (Devlin et al. 2018) and GPT-1/2 (Radford et al. 2018a, Radford et al. 2018b) have revitalized GEC, and have transformed the GEC task from a traditional sentence editor to a sentence composer (Dale and Viethen 2021).

In the paper we propose an iterative training scheme for GEC on the neural machine translation (NMT) architecture, where GEC is treated as a language translation task, translating an erroneous sentence into a correct one that fully fits in the grammatical requirements of authentic English. NMT strongly depends on the quality and quantity of training data. Given the enormous cost of manually collecting and tagging learner corpora for GEC, it is natural to generate artificial data automatically to facilitate in training NMT. Instead of applying rule-based data augmentation directly on GEC (Bryant et al. 2017, Grundkiewicz et al. 2019), we suggest to first generate artificial learner data to train a NMT-based grammatical error generation (GEG) model, then training another NMT-based GEC with the synthesized learner data from GEG. Through unifying GEG and GEC with iterative training, our model achieves state-of-the-art results in the shared task of CoNLL-2104.

2. RELATED WORK

2.1 Grammatical Error Types

Note that ESL/EFL language learners often encounter various error types in their writings, caused by violating spelling, morphological, syntactic, or semantic rules customized and legitimized in native English. We generally refer to them as grammatical errors in the paper, following the practice in the shared GEC tasks of CoNLL-2014 (Ng et al. 2014) and BEA-2019 (Bryant et al. 2019). Apart from the common lexical and orthographic (spelling and punctuation) error types, along with the syntactic (word order and tense) ones, CoNLL-2014 also covered semantic errors such as disobeying collocation and idiom usages, which contains 28 error types in total annotated in NUCLE (Dahlmeier et al. 2013). BEA-2019 collected more learner corpora than CoNLL-2014, consisting of FCE (Yannakoudakis et al. 2011) , W&I+LOCNESS (Granger 1998, Bryant et al. 2019), Lang-8 (Mizumoto et al. 2011, Tajiri et al. 2012), and NUCLE, which were re-tagged with 25 error types under 3 editing operations including missing (M), replacement (R), and unnecessary (U). Since lexical semantic errors were not specifically identified in BEA-2019, we use NUCLE in CoNLL-2014 as the only resource to evaluate our GED and GEC models.

2.2 NMT-based GED and GEC

Recent developments on Transformer-based (Vaswani et al. 2017) NMT have achieved significant progress on correcting grammatical errors. In the typical neural sequence transduction for GEC task (Ji et al. 2017, Chollampatt and Ng 2018), an encoder often works for deriving a distributional representation for an erroneous sentence, which is then injected into a decoder to restore its original and correct form with one word output at each time step. Using multiple attention mechanisms and positional embeddings on the input and output streams, Transformer can avoid the long-distance dependency issue commonly existed in the sequential processing of recurrent neural networks such as LSTM and GRU, in which a contextualized token or span embedding can be learned in both encoder and decoder to better comprehend local surroundings. As an improvement on unified word embeddings (Mikolov et al. 2013a, Mikolov et al. 2013b) and their semantic composition for span or sentence embeddings, it can greatly benefit the GEC task in detecting and correcting errors (Junczys-Dowmunt et al. 2018, Grundkiewicz et al. 2019, Kiyono et al. 2019, Zhao et al. 2019, Kaneko et al. 2020).

To better mine the pattern of word co-occurrences in context through the attention mechanism, Transformer needs a large volume of parallel learner data for GEC to work effectively in building up correlations between an erroneous sentence and its original and correct counterpart. Most studies manually construct artificial rules to generate noisy data in complementing the shortage of learner corpora in training NMT-based GEC, whereas others use back-translation, i.e., another NMT-based grammatical error generation (GEG) model, to transduce an original error-free sentence into an erroneous one. Since neural language models can grasp latent dependencies between linguistic units better than the artificial rules, GEG can leverage back-translation NMT for data augmentation to enrich learner data resources. We suggest to first harvest noisy or erroneous data using the artificial rules to train GEG, then utilizing the back-translation synthesized data from GEG to train GEC. To further improve accuracies of GEC, we can feed the candidate sentence outputs from GEC into the training process of GEG. Therefore, the iterative training on GEG and GEC can continue until the system's goal is fulfilled.

2.3 Evaluation

The performance of GEC tasks is often evaluated with the traditional IR metrics of precision and recall, which are commonly adopted in the toolkits of MaxMatch scorer M^2 (Dahlmeier and Ng 2012) and ERRANT (Bryant et al. 2017). GLEU, a variant of BLEU for machine translation, calculates a n-gram based matching score to measure up the fluence of correction results. Since we use the CoNLL-2014 shared task to investigate our GEC models, we take the M^2 scorer in the evaluation. We also report $F_{0.5}$, the harmony value of precision and recall, which assigns twice weights on precision as much as recall, given that a precise correction is more helpful for language learners.

3. GEC WITH DATA AUGEMENTATION

The basic training procedure of our proposed system is shown in Figure 1, where both GEG and GEC employs an identical Transformer structure.

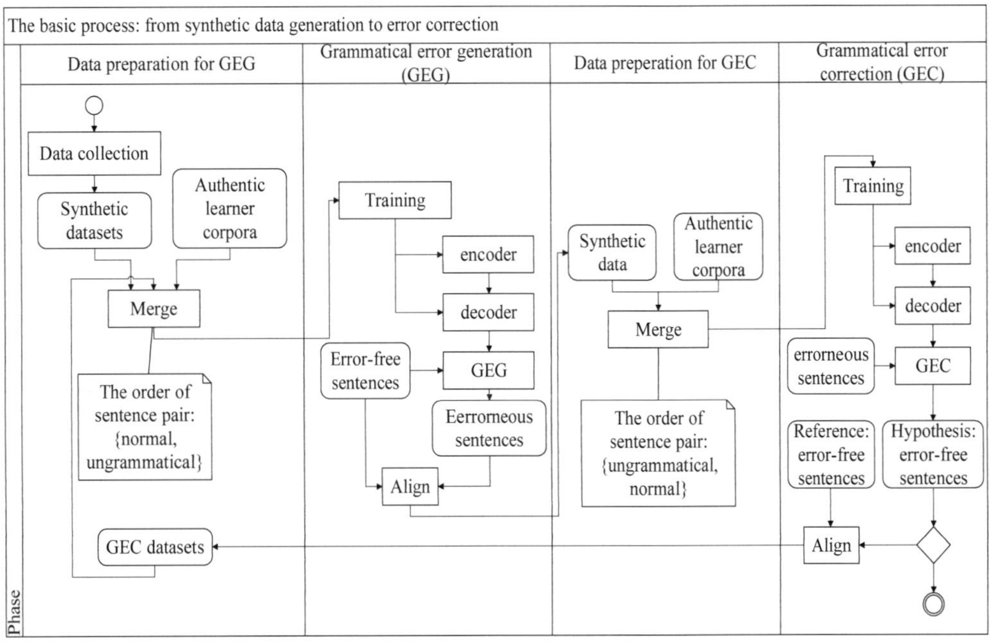

Figure 1. A schematic diagram for iteratively training NMT-based GEG and GEC

3.1 Artificial Rules

Given the enormous cost of annotating learner corpora, Levenshtein distance on the character and word level is often used to create artificial data. For example, Grundkiewicz et al. (2019) employed a spelling checker to automatically construct a confusion set for any target word in a sentence, then replacing the target word with a word in the confusion set can yield a corresponding spurious sentence.

To thoroughly cover errors that ESL/EFL learners frequently commit, we first analyze the error distribution in NUCLE. We find that misusing errors on articles, prepositions, spelling, morphological forms of verbs and nouns, and punctuations commonly exists. We specifically construct confusion sets for these error types. There are 2 to 3 errors on average in a 10-word long sentences in NUCLE. For a grammatically correct sentence, we randomly perform insertion/deletion/substitution/swap on 25% of its tokens. We can therefore produce aligned learner data on character/token-level. Table 1 shows a sample of producing an erroneous sentence with the substitution operation. The whole process of generating spurious sentences with the substitution operation is depicted as follows:

1) For a verb, we retrieve its morphological or inflected forms from a verb form dictionary. If a target verb has no inflected form available, we substitute it randomly with any token in its spelling confusion set.
2) For a countable nouns, we first match its singular and plural forms from a noun form dictionary; for an uncountable noun, we add *s/es* after each noun to construct its confusion set.
3) The confusion set for an article consists of a fixed size of {*a, an, the, Ø*}.
4) The confusion set for prepositions or punctuations consists of a group of commonly used tokens.
5) For a spelling variant, we use a spelling error dictionary to construct its confusion set.

Table 1. A sample of substitution operation for data augmentation

Error type	Target token	Confusion set
Verb	*accelerate*	*accelerates/accelerated/accelerated/accelerating*
Noun	*accommodation*	*accommodations*
Article	*a*	*an/the/Ø*
Preposition	*to*	*for/in/as/from/of/among/into/on/about/at/from/by/with*
Punctuation	,	*. /!/:/?/;/'/"/Ø*
Spelling	*cooking*	*coking/chocking/kooking/cocking*

3.2 GEG and GEC

Since both GEG and GEC work similarity in terms of neural sequence transduction, we employ the Transformer structure with the identical hyper-parameter setting, given the training objective for reducing cross-entropy between the intermediate output of decoder and a reference sentence. We use the open-source toolkit of *fairseq* on seq2seq transduction. The encoder and decoder individually consist of 6 stacks of Transformer blocks, each of which has a multi-head attention layer of 8 heads, followed by a feed forward layer of 4,096 units. In addition, the decoder block, functioning as an autoregressive model, is also equipped with a multi-head attention layer to calculate the attention or correlation between all the output tokens of encoder and each input token of decoder. Its masked multi-head attention layer also guarantees that each output token only depends on its forward context in an autoregressive way. As for the scheduled learning rate, we set up the initial value as 0.002 with the warming steps of 16,000. The dimensionality of encoder and decoder embeddings is 512. We use the Adam optimizer with $\beta_s = (0.9, 0.997)$ and $\epsilon = 10^{-9}$. The drop-out rate is 0.2, applied on both attention and feed forward layers. The maximum length of input tokens is 2,048.

We train GEG with both artificial and authentic leaner corpora. We then train GEC with GEG-generated synthesized data, together with the authentic learner corpora. To further improve correction quality, we can repeat the GEG to GEC process through feeding the output of GEC, trained with the authentic learner corpora, to the next round of GEG training.

3.3 Ranking GEC Outputs

To improve the quality of hypothesis sentences in GEC outputs, we set up a beam (12) search output for the decoder of GEC, which implies that GEC preserves its top 12 candidates while decoding with the current input token at each time step, together with its forward contextual tokens that have been explored. We design a rescoring algorithm (Chollampatt and Ng 2018) to rank the 12 candidate sentences, which functions as a grammatical error detector to maximize possibility of recovering the original sentence. We mainly run 4 metrics for each candidate, including the probability of encoder-decoder output, editing distance, statistical language model, and BERT-based GED:

1) The probability of encoder-decoder output. Given an erroneous sentence, the final score of each candidate sentence after GEC is the sum of log probabilities of each token during beam search. Instead of accepting the top 1 as the desirable result, we take the output probability as a feature for rescoring.
2) Editing distance. We match each token-level editing operation with a feature, indicating the number of changes between the original erroneous sentence and its corresponding GEC-generated candidate. We calculate 3 editing operations including insertion, deletion, and substitution.
3) Statistical language model (SLM). Language model is still an effective tool in detecting grammatical errors (Bryant and Briscoe 2018). We first train a 5-gram SLM with the KenLM (Heafield, 2011) on the One Billion Word corpus (Chelba et al. 2013). In line with the beam search of GEC, we sum up the log probabilities of 5-grams in a candidate sentence as the feature.
4) GED. Using transfer learning on BERT (Devlin et al. 2018), another Transformer-based masked NLM, we fine-tune a binary classifier on the CoLA dataset (Warstadt *et al.*, 2019) that only anticipate if a sentence is grammatically correct. We take the GED classification result as a feature in ranking.

Overall, after collecting 6 features from above 4 metrics, we train a linear regression formula with the features on the training dataset of NUCLE to re-rank the 12 candidate sentences.

4. DETECTING AND CORRECTING GRAMMATICAL ERRORS

We first apply the artificial rules on the corpus of One Billion Word (Chelba et al. 2013) to generate noisy training data for GEG. Apart from that, we also incorporate some publicly available authentic learner corpora, including NUCLE (Dahlmeier et al. 2013), FCE (Yannakoudakis et al. 2011), W&I+LOCNESS (Granger 1998, Bryant et al. 2019), Lang-8 (Mizumoto et al. 2011, Tajiri et al. 2012). Table 2 lists their statistics as follows:

Table 2. Corpora statistics for training GEG

Corpus	Sentence	Token
NUCLE	57.2K	1.2M
FCE	28.4K	455K
W&I+LOCNESS	34.3K	628K
Lang-8	1.0M	11.9M
One Billion word（subpart）	1.7M	19M

4.1 Effectiveness of Artificial Rules on GEC

We first used the aforementioned rules to generate different size of artificial learner data. We varied the size from 20M to 200M with a step of 60M to investigate their effectiveness. Note that 20M data in term of file size is equal to about 190K number of sentences. Figure 2 shows the correction results on the test part of NUCLE while training with different datasets. Note that we added the GEC results that were acquired from exclusively using the authentic learner corpora for comparison in Figure 2, where we denote $F_{0.5}$ with F.

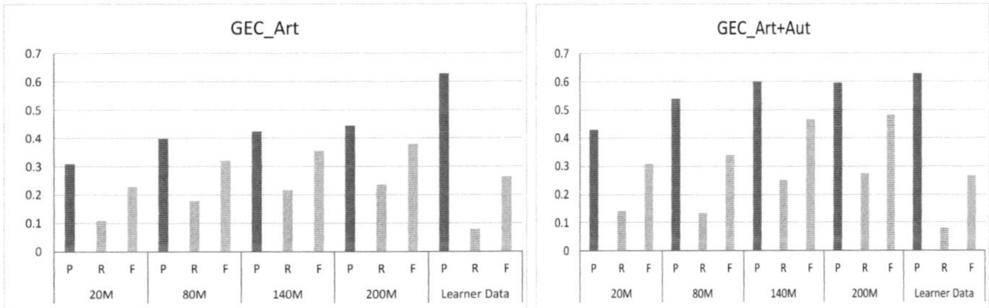

Figure 2. Test results of using different learner corpora to train GEC. Left (GEC_Art) is the results of training only with the artificial data, and right (GEC_Art+Aut) the results with both artificial and authentic learner data

The results of GEC_Art in Figure 2 (left) clearly show that as the growth of artificial data from 20M to 200M, both precision and recall increased significantly. Although training with the authentic data GEC_Aut can achieve a high precision, its recall rate was significantly lower than GEC_Art. GEC_Art with 200M can achieve $F_{0.5} = 37.9\%$, outperforming GEC_Aut ($F_{0.5}$=26.5%).

We then combined both authentic and artificial (from 20M to 200M) data to train GEC_Art+Aut with results shown in Figure 2 (right). It indicates that in comparison with GEC_Art, GEC_Art+Aut significantly improved precision and recall, but the growth of precision attempted to level off after training with 140M data, although recall may continue to increase with more artificial data available.

To sum up, our artificial rules are effective in generating erroneous sentences to train GEC. Subject to lack of computing resources, we did not attempt to produce more artificial data in training GEC.

4.2 Back-Translation of GEG

After evaluating the effectiveness of artificial rules with GEC, we tested methods of using back translation to generate synthetized data in training GEC. We trained GEG with the authentic learner data with/without the artificial one, and then used different size of synthesized data, generated from GEG, to train GEC. As shown in Table 3, in contrast with training GEC only with the authentic data, the back-translation model, GEG_Aut→GEC_Syn, significantly outperformed GEC_Aut in Figure 2 on the recall rate. With more data injected into GEG, $F_{0.5}$ on GEC can improve by 6.2% on average and arrived at 33.5% in Table 3. When we added the hypothesis sentence outputs from GEC_Syn into the training datasets for GEG_Aut+Art, $F_{0.5}$ on GEC was improved by 4.1% on average, with the highest one of 38.4%. Our results demonstrated that both iterative training of unified GEG and GEC, together with the synthesized data, can attain an improvement on GEC.

Table 3. Results of using back-translation on GEC. GEG_Aut denotes training GEG with authentic learner data, and same as GEG_Aut+Ar with both authentic and artificial data. GEC_Syn denotes training GEC with the synthesized data yielded from GEG. '→' refers to data transformation from the previous model's output to the next model's input

	Synthesized data from GEG											
	20M			80M			140M			200M		
	P	R	$F_{0.5}$	P	R	$F_{0.5}$	P	R	$F_{0.5}$	P	R	$F_{0.5}$
GEG_Aut →GEC_Syn	27.5	13.5	22.8	29.1	18.4	26.1	30.4	19.3	27.3	31.9	20.1	28.6
GEG_Aut+Art →GEC_Syn	35.9	15.3	28.2	36.0	23.2	34.3	37.2	24.3	33.5	37.1	24.0	33.5
GEG_Aut+Art →GEC_Syn→GEG	44.5	12.3	29.2	44.3	21.2	36.4	41.7	27.2	37.7	42.7	27.3	38.4
GEG_Aut+Art →GEC_Syn+Aut→GEG										72.8	38.9	62.0
GEG_Aut+Art →GEC_Syn+Aut→GEG	Rescoring									73.9	42.1	64.3

4.3 Rescoring

The synthesized learner data generated from our GEG model can have a similar effect of the authentic learner data on training GEC, as shown in Table 3. The performance of GEC on NUCLE may gain further improvement if we continue to augment the synthesized data volume. However, the authentic learner data GEC_Aut can achieve higher precision in contrast with the artificial learner data GEC_Art, as shown in Figure 2. We therefore combined both synthesized (200M) and authentic learner data to train GEC_Syn+Aut after back translation. In Table 3, we applied the combined data on GEC with iterative training, which achieved $F_{0.5} = 62\%$. We further used the rescoring algorithm in Section 3.4 to rank the beam-search output of GEC and chose the top one as the final correction result, and gained an improvement on $F_{0.5} = 64.3\%$. Our model surpassed all the participating teams in the shared task of CoNLL-2014 (Ng et al. 2014).

4.4 Analysis of Error Types

Table 4. Error type distribution for GED and GEC

	Grammatical Error Detection			Grammatical Error Correction				Grammatical Error Detection			Grammatical Error Correction		
Category	**P**	**R**	**F_0.5**	**P**	**R**	**F_0.5**	**Category**	**P**	**R**	**F_0.5**	**P**	**R**	**F_0.5**
M:ADJ	0.500	1.000	0.556	0.000	0.000	0.000	R:PART	0.917	0.550	0.809	0.909	0.526	0.794
M:ADV	0.667	0.500	0.625	0.444	0.500	0.455	R:PREP	0.775	0.399	0.652	0.676	0.368	0.579
M:CONJ	1.000	0.250	0.625	0.000	0.000	0.000	R:PRON	0.857	0.143	0.429	0.714	0.114	0.347
M:DET	0.744	0.480	0.670	0.646	0.411	0.580	R:PUNCT	0.615	0.186	0.421	0.615	0.182	0.417
M:NOUN	0.667	0.105	0.323	0.000	0.000	0.000	R:SPELL	0.875	0.090	0.318	0.750	0.075	0.268
M:NOUN:POSS	1.000	0.400	0.769	1.000	0.400	0.769	R:VERB	0.818	0.170	0.464	0.667	0.100	0.313
M:OTHER	0.600	0.081	0.263	0.500	0.091	0.263	R:VERB:F(	0.857	0.632	0.800	0.733	0.611	0.705
M:PART	0.500	0.333	0.455	0.250	0.167	0.227	R:VERB:IN	1.000	0.500	0.833	1.000	0.500	0.833
M:PREP	0.667	0.556	0.641	0.628	0.519	0.603	R:VERB:S'	0.838	0.735	0.815	0.755	0.728	0.749
M:PRON	0.546	0.400	0.509	0.500	0.333	0.455	R:VERB:TI	0.792	0.268	0.569	0.617	0.210	0.445
M:PUNCT	0.733	0.129	0.379	0.688	0.133	0.374	R:WO	0.571	0.421	0.533	0.571	0.400	0.526
M:VERB	0.647	0.478	0.604	0.588	0.455	0.556	U:ADJ	1.000	0.111	0.385	0.250	0.125	0.208
M:VERB:FORM	1.000	0.500	0.833	0.667	0.500	0.625	U:ADV	0.625	0.263	0.490	0.500	0.158	0.349
M:VERB:TENSE	0.882	0.577	0.798	0.588	0.400	0.538	U:CONJ	0.667	0.250	0.500	0.667	0.286	0.526
R:ADJ	0.667	0.083	0.278	0.500	0.044	0.161	U:DET	0.709	0.559	0.673	0.674	0.542	0.642
R:ADJ:FORM	1.000	0.333	0.714	1.000	0.333	0.714	U:NOUN	0.750	0.158	0.429	0.667	0.118	0.345
R:ADV	0.000	0.000	0.000	0.000	0.000	0.000	U:NOUN:P	0.667	0.667	0.667	0.667	0.667	0.667
R:CONJ	0.000	0.000	0.000	0.000	0.000	0.000	U:OTHER	0.533	0.119	0.315	0.533	0.131	0.331
R:CONTR	1.000	0.000	0.000	1.000	0.000	0.000	U:PART	1.000	0.800	0.952	1.000	0.800	0.952
R:DET	0.696	0.395	0.604	0.596	0.364	0.528	U:PREP	0.811	0.717	0.790	0.746	0.651	0.724
R:MORPH	0.878	0.457	0.741	0.804	0.446	0.693	U:PRON	0.800	0.267	0.571	0.600	0.214	0.441
R:NOUN	0.857	0.273	0.600	0.577	0.181	0.401	U:PUNCT	0.714	0.357	0.595	0.714	0.357	0.595
R:NOUN:INFL	0.714	0.714	0.714	0.714	0.714	0.714	U:VERB	0.619	0.464	0.580	0.476	0.370	0.451
R:NOUN:NUM	0.787	0.670	0.760	0.792	0.674	0.766	U:VERB:F(	0.600	0.750	0.625	0.600	0.750	0.625
R:NOUN:POSS	0.500	0.111	0.294	0.333	0.111	0.238	U:VERB:TI	0.625	0.417	0.568	0.588	0.417	0.544
R:ORTH	0.882	0.417	0.721	0.824	0.400	0.680	UNK	1.000	0.100	0.357			
R:OTHER	0.688	0.219	0.482	0.359	0.094	0.229	**TOTAL**	**0.759**	**0.386**	**0.636**	**0.669**	**0.350**	**0.565**

Using ERRANT (Bryant et al. 2017), an improved version of MaxMatch scorer M^2 (Dahlmeier and Ng 2012), we analyzed the distribution of error types in the final results after rescoring on GED and GEC, as shown in Table 4. Note that the results in Table 4 were slightly different from them in Table 3 as we evaluated our models with M^2 in the previous sections. Overall, GED and GEC can achieve $F_{0.5}$ at 63.6% and 56.5%, respectively, which implies that some errors that our model can successfully detect could not be corrected correspondingly. For example, although our model can find the error type of M:ADJ, missing an adjective in a sentence, with $F_{0.5}$ of 55.6%, it can not correct it properly with GEC. Results in Table 4 also imply that GEC is a much more challenging task than GED.

5. CONCLUSION

We systematically investigated different data augmentation techniques for the task of GEC. We mainly employed Transformer to design an encoder-decoder NMT for data generation and error correction. Instead of using artificial data directly on GEC, we used them on the NMT-based GEG to generate synthesized learner data for training GEC, which can improve the recall rate of correction. We also proposed an iterative training scheme to unify GEG and GEC, where the hypothesis sentences after GEC were continually injected into GEG until the system performance was satisfactory. Since we only studied the NMT-based GEG and GEC with quantitative generation of learner data, and our results were also subject to the lack of computing resources, we will study the effect of more data resources on GED and GEC in the future.

ACKNOWLEDGEMENT

This research was supported by the Humanity and Social Science Foundation of China Ministry of Education (Grant No. 15YJA740054).

REFERENCES

Christopher Bryant and Ted Briscoe (2018). Language Model Based Grammatical Error Correction without Annotated Training Data. *Proceedings of the Thirteenth Workshop on Innovative Use of NLP for Building Educational Applications*, New Orleans, Louisiana. pp. 247–253.

Christopher Bryant, Mariano Felice, Øistein E. Andersen and Ted Briscoe (2019). The Bea-2019 Shared Task on Grammatical Error Correction. Proceedings of the Fourteenth Workshop on Innovative Use of NLP for Building Educational Applications, Florence, Italy. pp. 52-75.

Christopher Bryant, Mariano Felice and Ted Briscoe (2017). Automatic Annotation and Evaluation of Error Types for Grammatical Error Correction. *Proceedings of the 55th Annual Meeting of the Association for Computational Linguistics (Volume 1: Long Papers)*, Vancouver, Canada. pp. 793-805.

Ciprian Chelba, Tomas Mikolov, Mike Schuster, Qi Ge, Thorsten Brants and Phillipp Koehn (2013). "One Billion Word Benchmark for Measuring Progress in Statistical Language Modeling." *Proceedings of the Annual Conference of the International Speech Communication Association, INTERSPEECH.*

Shamil Chollampatt and Hwee Tou Ng (2018). A Multilayer Convolutional Encoder-Decoder Neural Network for Grammatical Error Correction. *Proceedings of the Thirty-Second AAAI Conference on Artificial Intelligence.* pp. 5755-5762.

Ronan Collobert and Jason Weston (2008). A Unified Architecture for Natural Language Processing: Deep Neural Networks with Multitask Learning. Proceedings of the 25th international conference on Machine learning, Helsinki, Finland. pp. 160-167.

Daniel Dahlmeier and Hwee Tou Ng (2012). Better Evaluation for Grammatical Error Correction. *Proceedings of the 2012 Conference of the North American Chapter of the Association for Computational Linguistics: Human Language Technologies*, Montreal, Canada. pp. 568–572.

Daniel Dahlmeier, Hwee Tou Ng and Siew Mei Wu (2013). Building a Large Annotated Corpus of Learner English: The Nus Corpus of Learner English. *Proceedings of the Eighth Workshop on Innovative Use of NLP for Building Educational Applications*, Atlanta, Georgia. pp. 22-31.

Robert Dale (2016). "Checking in on Grammar Checking." *Natural Language Engineering* 22(3): 491-495.

Robert Dale and Jette Viethen (2021). "The Automated Writing Assistance Landscape in 2021." *Natural Language Engineering* 27(4): 511-518.

Jacob Devlin, Ming-Wei Chang, Kenton Lee and Kristina Toutanova (2018). Bert: Pre-Training of Deep Bidirectional Transformers for Language Understanding. *Proceedings of the 2019 Conference of the North American Chapter of the Association for Computational Linguistics: Human Language Technologies*, Minneapolis, Minnesota. pp. 4171-4186.

Sylviane Granger (1998). *The Computerized Learner Corpus: A Versatile New Source of Data for Sla Research*. Learner English on Computer. Addison Wesley Longman, London and New York.

Roman Grundkiewicz, Marcin Junczys-Dowmunt and Kenneth Heafield (2019). Neural Grammatical Error Correction Systems with Unsupervised Pre-Training on Synthetic Data. *Proceedings of the Fourteenth Workshop on Innovative Use of NLP for Building Educational Applications*, Florence, Italy. pp. 252-263.

Jianshu Ji, Qinlong Wang, Kristina Toutanova, Yongen Gong, Steven Truong and Jianfeng Gao (2017). A Nested Attention Neural Hybrid Model for Grammatical Error Correction. *Proceedings of the 55th Annual Meeting of the Association for Computational Linguistics*. pp. 753-762.

Marcin Junczys-Dowmunt, Roman Grundkiewicz, Shubha Guha and Kenneth Heafield (2018). Approaching Neural Grammatical Error Correction as a Low-Resource Machine Translation Task. *Proceedings of the 2018 Conference of the North American Chapter of the Association for Computational Linguistics*. pp. 595-606.

Masahiro Kaneko, Masato Mita, Shun Kiyono, Jun Suzuki and Kentaro Inui (2020). Encoder-Decoder Models Can Benefit from Pre-Trained Masked Language Models in Grammatical Error Correction. *Proceedings of the 58th Annual Meeting of the Association for Computational Linguistics*. pp. 4248–4254.

Shun Kiyono, Jun Suzuki, Masato Mita, Tomoya Mizumoto and Kentaro Inui (2019). An Empirical Study of Incorporating Pseudo Data into Grammatical Error Correction. *Proceedings of the 2019 Conference on Empirical Methods in Natural Language Processing and the 9th International Joint Conference on Natural Language Processing*, Hong Kong, China. pp. 1236–1242.

Tomas Mikolov, Kai Chen, G. s Corrado and Jeffrey Dean (2013a). Efficient Estimation of Word Representations in Vector Space. *Proceedings of the 1st International Conference on Learning Representations (ICLR) Workshop Track* Scottsdale, Arizona, USA. pp. 1301-3781.

Tomas Mikolov, Ilya Sutskever, Kai Chen, Greg Corrado and Jeffrey Dean (2013b). Distributed Representations of Words and Phrases and Their Compositionality. *Proceedings of the 26th International Conference on Neural Information Processing Systems (NIPS)*, Lake Tahoe, Nevada. pp. 3111-3119.

Tomoya Mizumoto, Mamoru Komachi, Masaaki Nagata and Yuji Matsumoto (2011). Mining Revision Log of Language Learning Sns for Automated Japanese Error Correction of Second Language Learners. *Proceedings of the 5th International Joint Conference on Natural Language Processing*, Chiang Mai, Thailand. pp. 147-155.

Hwee Ng, wu siew mei, Ted Briscoe, Christian Hadiwinoto, Raymond Susanto and Christopher Bryant (2014). The Conll-2014 Shared Task on Grammatical Error Correction. *Proceedings of the Eighteenth Conference on Computational Natural Language Learning: Shared Task*, Baltimore, Maryland. pp. 1-14.

Alec Radford, Karthik Narasimhan, Tim Salimans and Ilya Sutskever (2018a) "Improving Language Understanding by Generative Pre-Training." Technical report, OpenAi.

Alec Radford, Jeffrey Wu, Rewon Child, David Luan, Dario Amodei and Ilya Sutskever (2018b) "Language Models Are Unsupervised Multitask Learners." Technical report, OpenAi.

Toshikazu Tajiri, Mamoru Komachi and Yuji Matsumoto (2012). Tense and Aspect Error Correction for Esl Learners Using Global Context. *Proceedings of the 50th Annual Meeting of the Association for Computational Linguistics (Volume 2: Short Papers)*, Jeju Island, Korea. pp. 198-202.

Ashish Vaswani, Noam Shazeer, Niki Parmar, Jakob Uszkoreit, Llion Jones, Aidan N. Gomez, Lukasz Kaiser and Illia Polosukhin (2017). Attention Is All You Need. *Proceedings of the 31st International Conference on Neural Information Processing Systems*, Long Beach, California, USA. pp. 6000-6010.

Helen Yannakoudakis, Ted Briscoe and Ben Medlock (2011). A New Dataset and Method for Automatically Grading Esol Texts. *Proceedings of the 49th Annual Meeting of the Association for Computational Linguistics: Human Language Technologies*, Portland, Oregon, USA. pp. 180-189.

Wei Zhao, Liang Wang, Kewei Shen, Ruoyu Jia and Jingming Liu (2019). Improving Grammatical Error Correction Via Pre-Training a Copy-Augmented Architecture with Unlabeled Data. *Proceedings of the 2019 Conference of the North American Chapter of the Association for Computational Linguistics: Human Language Technologies, Volume 1 (Long and Short Papers)*, Minneapolis, Minnesota. pp. 156-165.

TRANSPARENCY IN SPANISH TOWN COUNCIL WEBSITES: A STUDY OF MUNICIPALITIES WITH BETWEEN 5001 AND 10,000 INHABITANTS

Antonio Muñoz-Cañavate[1], Melisa Pérez Cebadero[1] and María José Tena Mateos
[1]*Departamento de Información y Comunicación, Facultad de Ciencias de la Documentación y la Comunicación, Universidad de Extremadura, Plazuela Ibw Marwan s/n, 06071 Badajoz, Spain*
[2]*Consultoría de I+D Vector Arram Innizia (VAI)s, Pº. Fluvial, 15. Edificio Badajoz Siglo XXI. Planta 12, 06011, Badajoz, Spain*

ABSTRACT

During the last few decades, there has been a very important change within Public Administrations, fundamentally in countries with a liberal economy. Since the end of the 20th century, the need to reduce costs while improving services has led to a new concept of a more open and transparent Administration, which has undoubtedly been helped with the arrival of information and communications technologies. Administrations are made up of two spheres that work inseparably – the political and the administrative – both of which have been affected by this new culture of transparency and accountability. Thus, it is the World Wide Web together with legislation that has appeared over the last two decades which have lain the foundations of the new relationship that citizens and firms have with the Administrations, creating a new paradigm in Public Administration. This work presents the results of a study carried out on a sample of the town councils of Spanish municipalities with populations ranging from 5001 to 10,000 – in total 82 town councils. The study used questionnaires from two of the six areas already applied by Transparency International Spain to large Spanish municipalities. The results show a disparity between municipalities, since, while some meet all or almost all the indicators, others barely meet any. The implication is that political willingness or its absence is the main cause for the differences between otherwise similar municipalities. However, some indicators are met by the majority as they are those of obligatory fulfilment, being required by law.

KEYWORDS

World Wide Web, Transparency, Local Administration, Town Hall, Spain

1. INTRODUCTION

Public Administrations around the world, and especially in Western countries with a liberal economy, have seen a substantive change over recent decades aimed at always offering better services to citizens and firms (in short, improving every aspect of quality), introducing accountability (such as the obligation to report on economic-financial activities) or making information generated by the public bodies themselves more transparent. In particular, the goal pursued is a results-oriented Public Administration, where evaluation processes must measure what is done, how it is done, and what the result is.

In this way, Transparency emerges as a star concept that seeks to leave behind the more opaque moments in the history of Administrations. And Transparency laws emerge as one of the pillars of political action, seeking to make known the action of public officials, the criteria under which decisions are made, the management of public funds, and the very information generated by the Administrations themselves.

Transparency policies in Administrations and Governments are closely linked to attempts to fight corruption (Bertot et al., 2010; Schlæger & Wang, 2017; Nam, 2018). This has led to many studies and methods being used to measure Transparency in Administrations, by using ICTs and even exclusively social networks (Bosón, et al. 2012; DePaula et al. 2018), or in the case of Twitter to reach more citizens and interact with them (Faber et al., 2020). Jiménez & Albalate (2018), who researched the causal relationship between local government transparency and political corruption in a sample of the 110 largest municipalities in Spain, reached the conclusion that the lack of transparency hides corrupt activities and that the absence of a willingness to provide information is a good indicator of the probability of corruption.

Studies about Transparency have had a notable growth in local governments (Krah & Mertens, 2020). As indicated by Rodriguez-Navas & Breijo (2021), the methods used to assess the Transparency of local administrations present notable differences that are influenced by the national legislation and the administrative characteristics, so there is no international procedure that is valid for every countries.

Transparency International has conducted studies in different countries to measure corruption and transparency. In the case of Spain and its local Administrations (the subject of this study), Transparency International Spain (TIE, its Spanish acronym) has established a questionnaire of 80 indicators, structured into six blocks. They include the requirements of Spanish legislation in this regard, the last law having been applied in 2017 to the 110 largest municipalities in Spain (Transparencia Internacional España, 2017). For Spain, Garrido-Rodríguez et al. (2019) have carried out studies on town councils in municipalities with more than 20,000 inhabitants, and Cañizares-Espada et al. have designed a model to measure the transparency of social services in municipalities with more than 10,000 inhabitants (Cañizares-Espada, et al. 2021).

In other countries, studies have also been carried out to determine the levels of transparency at local level through ICTs, and from many parameters, as is the case of Korea (Park, 2001), the United States of America (Feeney & Brown, 2017), Chile (Piña & Avellaneda, 2019), Italy (Pernagallo & Torrisi, 2020) Indonesia (Yuniarta & Gusti, 2020), Philippines (Gabriel & Castillo, 2020), and even in several European countries (Alcaraz-Quiles et al., 2020).

1.1 Spanish Legislation

As is evident, Public Administrations are governed by laws that define their legal framework and functions. The processes of modernization of the Spainsh Public Administrations began in the 1980s, although it was the Law of the Legal Regime of Public Administrations and the Common Administrative Procedure of 1992 (BOE, 1992) that laid the foundations for the introduction of information and communication technologies in administrative procedures. The said Law, now repealed, was the beginning of a rapid introduction of regulations to which many others would later be added, such as those referring to electronic signatures (BOE, 1999; BOE, 2003; BOE, 2020a), the Law 11/2007 of electronic access of citizens to Public Services (BOE, 2007a), or Law 37/2007 of November 16 on the Reuse of Public Sector information (BOE, 2007b).

Today, there are three laws that are fundamental to the relationships that citizens and firms have with the Public Administrations through telematic means. These are: Law 19/2013, of December 9, on Transparency, Access to Public Information and Good Governance (BOE, 2013), which obliges Administrations to have a transparency portal on the Internet (although regional governments have also published transparency and good governance laws, which complement the State Law); Law 39/2015, of October 1, on the Common Administrative Procedure of Public Administrations (BOE, 2015a); and Law 40/2015, of October 1, on the Public Sector Legal Regime (BOE, 2015b), which regulates the electronic headquarters within the website of each Administration that can be accessed through secure certificates.

2. OBJECTIVE

The general objective of this study was to determine the level of transparency and relationships with their citizens of the Spanish town councils of municipalities with a population ranging from 5,001 to 10,000. The type of information involved is very broad, and therefore transparency can be applied to a multitude of aspects in which the information that these institutions deal with is externalized. This work therefore focuses on just two of the six blocks applied by Transparency International Spain to the 110 largest town councils in Spain regarding the active transparency and information about the municipal corporation, its website, its relationships with citizens and society, and citizen participation.

3. METHODS

To carry out this descriptive study, a series of stages were established: a) the selection of the study units, in this case the Spanish town councils in the aforementioned population range; b) the definition of the items from the studies applied by Transparency International Spain to this study; c) the design of the Excel tool, to upload the data obtained; d) the procedure for obtaining and scoring the information obtained; d) and the analysis of the results. Below we explain the different phases.

3.1 The Selection of the Municipalities

For this study, the data from the 2020 Municipal Register were collected. The study was carried out on town councils corresponding to municipalities with populations ranging from 5,001 to 10,000. The municipal registers of 1 January 2020 total 8131 municipalities in Spain, of which 545 are municipalities within this range, representing 6.7% of all Spanish municipalities.

Royal Decree 1147/2020 of December 15 (BOE, 2020b), by which the population figures resulting from the revision of the Municipal Register referring to 1 January 2020 are declared official, establishes the official Spanish population at 47,450,795. The 545 municipalities that are the object of this study have 3,844,677 inhabitants, and represent 8.1% of the Spanish population.

To select the sample from the total population of 545 municipalities with populations ranging from 5,001 to 10,000, a sample calculator[1], available on the Internet from the firm Agencia Estadística de Mercados S.C., also identified as AEM Research (http://www. aemresearch.com), was used. Thus, for this population of 545 municipalities, with a margin of error of 10% and a confidence level of 95%, a sample of 82 municipalities was established.

The list of Spanish municipalities with their updated number of inhabitants from the latest available Register was obtained from the website of the National Institute of Statistics through an Excel file with the national data ordered by province[2]. Later, the municipalities were ordered by number of inhabitants, from highest to lowest. From the final file, the populations corresponding to the studied range, 5,001 to 10,000 inhabitants, were extracted and ordered in rows from the first municipality (row 1) to the last (row 545). For the selection of the 82 municipalities, simple random sampling was used. Through the application that Excel offers, 82 numbers were randomly obtained between 1 and 545. In this way, the final sample was obtained.

3.2 The Questionnaire

As indicated in the Objective section, two of the six blocks applied by Transparency International Spain to the 110 largest town councils in Spain were used. Table 1 presents these two blocks, together with the sections and the indicators assigned to each of them. It has to be noted that the authors of the present work have included a new section in Block B of Transparency International, with Indicator 33 of the TIE referring to the existence on the Web of discussion forums, or the existence of active profiles of the town council on social networks, but without specifying either of them. Thus, we have included this new section (B.3) with 7 indicators (online forum for citizen participation, Facebook, Linkedin, Twitter, town council blog, YouTube channel, and Instagram profile).

The data was collected in the months of March and April 2021, obtaining 3524 indicators for all 82 municipalities of the sample.

For each municipality, as can be seen in Table 1, 43 indicators were obtained, and the score was determined as follows: 1 if it contains updated information; 0.5 if it contains information but it is not updated; and 0 if no information was found.

The data was collected in an Excel file. They were placed individually for each municipality, and the aggregated data of all the units studied were obtained through the Excel sheets, that served for the corresponding statistical treatment.

[1]AEM Research. Sample calculator. Retrieved from: https://www.corporacionaem.com/tools/calc_muestras.php

[2]Official population figures resulting from the revision of the Municipal Register as of 1 January. Retrieved from https://www.ine.es/dynt3/inebase/es/index.htm?padre=517&capsel=525

Table 1. Areas of transparency and number of indicators

Areas of transparency		Nº of indicators
A) Active transparency and information about the municipal corporation	1) Active publicity about positions, staff, and remuneration of the Town Council	8
	2) Active publicity about the planning, organization, and heritage of the Town Council	6
	3) Active publicity about municipal government bodies, reports, and judicial decisions	7
B) Website, relationships with citizens and society, and citizen participation	1) Website of the Town Council and municipal services	8
	2) Citizen participation and information of interest for the citizen	7
	3) Presence on social media	7
Total		43

4. RESULTS

Table 2 and Figure 1 present in percentage terms the results of the two areas of transparency evaluated for the 82 municipalities of the sample. Along with the data of the two blocks are those of the corresponding sections (three for each area). These results indicate that there is still a certain deficit regarding the information presented by the municipalities, although there is a predisposition to improve. It can also be observed that some municipalities (echoing the transparency indicators such as those of TIE) have created spaces with the titles of the indicators on their municipal websites that announce a future inclusion of the corresponding information. Although Table 2 and Figure 1 reflect the aggregate data of the 82 municipalities, it is necessary to emphasize that some (few) municipalities do comply with all or almost all of the indicators, while others barely comply with any. This disparity, for town councils with similar characteristics, indicates that economic problems are not responsible for the lack of information and data (which on the other hand are easy to obtain) but rather a willingness or absence of willingness of the political leaders to offer good information and communication systems for their citizens. It also indicates a resistance to change of some politicians, who only respond when the law requires them to do so.

Area A, which is dedicated to active transparency and information about the municipal corporation, has an importance of 36.1% in all of its 21 indicators, compared to 59.1% in area B which is dedicated to the website, the relationships with citizens and society, and citizen participation. In this second area, there are some indicators (of the 22 evaluated) that stand out from the rest. Thus, indicator number 22 makes explicit reference to the existence of a specific section about transparency: 77 of the 82 municipalities had this section which is required by the Spanish transparency law (BOE, 2013). The existence of the said section or website, however, does not imply that all the information desired is actually found, as many of the directories, of numerous municipalities, are empty. The electronic headquarters within the website of each Administration has also become a reality since the electronic administration law of 2007 (BOE 2007) and the subsequent Law of Juridical Regime of the Public Sector (BOE, 2015b), mentioned in the section on legislation require Spanish Administrations to have that secure relationship channel between the Administration and the administered. This circumstance has allowed some Spanish ICT firms to have started helping town councils manage these websites, within which transparency portals are included, with the same structure, but with content, obviously, that must be managed by each respective town hall. The most paradigmatic case, since it has been the commonest among the 82 municipalities evaluated, is that of the company Auloce SA, dedicated to offering services to local Administrations, that has created the same information and content model under the domain "sedeelectronica.es". Therefore the name of the municipality is a third level domain. This electronic headquarters includes the section dedicated to Transparency.

Table 2. Percentages obtained by areas of transparency

Areas of transparency		%
A) Active transparency and information about the municipal corporation		36.1%
	1) Active publicity about positions, staff, and remuneration of the Town Council	36.4%
	2) Active publicity about the planning, organization, and heritage of the Town Council	35.3%
	3) Active publicity about municipal government bodies, reports, and judicial decisions	36.6%
B) Website, relationships with citizens and society, and citizen participation		59.1%
	1) Website of the Town Council and municipal services	73.6%
	2) Citizen participation and information of interest for the citizen	45%
	3) Presence on social media	58.7%

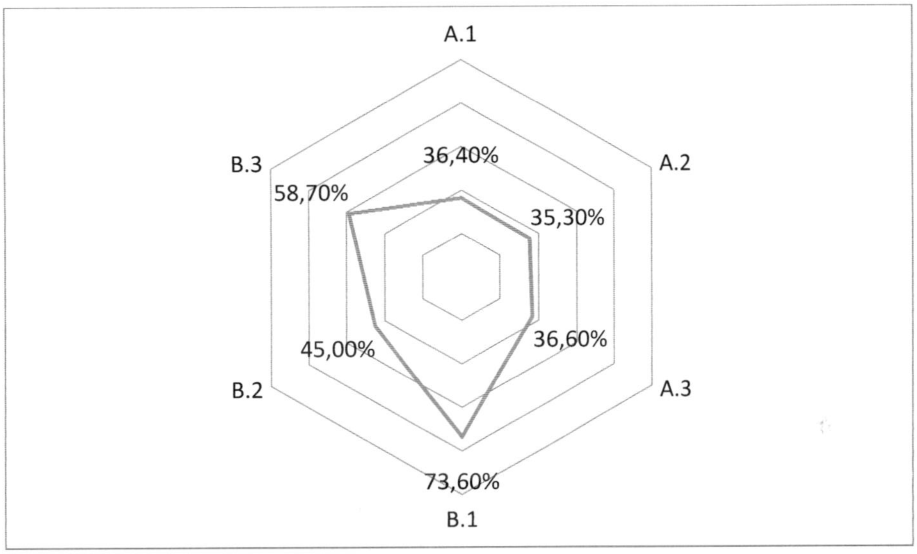

Figure 1. Chart with the Percentages Obtained in the Six Sub-Areas of Transparency

5. CONCLUSIONS

In Spain, active policies to bring about a change in the strategies of Public Administrations, with the objective of creating services for citizens through websites, have been accelerated with the Electronic Administration law of 2007 (2007a), although subsequent legislative changes through specific transparency laws in the central government and regional governments are those actually driving the change, in addition to the existence of the Council for Transparency and Good Government (http://www.consejodetransparencia.es) whose function is to promote the transparency of public activity.

This study has shown an uneven development of municipalities within the same population range, which indicates that financial problems do not drive the lack of transparency of some municipalities, but rather the absence of political willingness in some cases. There also exists external technological support for transparency (as is contracted by many municipalities) that can help the municipalities to have the appropriate technological environment for their staff to only have to upload the information. In any case, there does seem to be a predisposition to comply with the transparency indicators on the websites. Although a transparency portal is mandatory in all town council websites, in many cases it appears to be hidden and is not accessible from the main page. This may be due to the fact that it often contains little information.

It is paradigmatic that, among the still inactive spaces, there are those destined to presenting the proposals of the political parties and neighbourhood associations, with contents that could make the governing political party uncomfortable. In this sense, the results are similar to the study carried out by Simelio-Solà et al. (2021) on a sample of Spanish town councils with more than 10,000 inhabitants where the authors point out that the websites of those town councils publish very little information about the activity of the political opposition.

REFERENCES

Alcaraz-Quiles, F.J., Navarro-Galera, A., Ortiz-Rodríguez, D.2020. The contribution of the right to information laws in Europe to local government transparency on sustainability. *International Environmental Agreements: Politics, Law and Economics*, 20(1), pp. 161-178.

Bertot, J.C., Jaeger, P.T., Grimes, J.M. 2010. Using ICTs to create a culture of transparency: E-government and social media as openness and anti-corruption tools for societies. *Government Information Quarterly*, Vol. 27, No. 3, pp. 264-271.

BOE, 1992. *Ley 30/1992, de 26 de noviembre, de Régimen Jurídico de las Administraciones y del Procedimiento Administrativo Común*. Disponible en: https://www.boe.es/buscar/act.php?id=BOE-A-1992-26318.

BOE, 1999. *Real Decreto Ley 14/1999 de firma electrónica*. Disponible en: https://www.boe.es/buscar/doc.php?id=BOE-A-1999-18915

BOE, 2003. *Ley 59/2003, de 19 de diciembre, de firma electrónica*. Disponible en: https://www.boe.es/buscar/act.php?id=BOE-A-2003-23399

BOE, 2007a. *Ley 11/2007, de 22 de junio, para el acceso electrónico de los ciudadanos a las Administraciones Públicas*. Disponible en: https://www.boe.es/buscar/act.php?id=BOE-A-2007-12352.

BOE, 2007b. *Ley 37/2007, de 16 de noviembre, sobre reutilización de la información del sector público*. Disponible en: https://www.boe.es/diario_boe/txt.php?id=BOE-A-2007-19814.

BOE, 2013. *Ley 19/2013, de 9 de diciembre de Transparencia, Acceso a la información Pública y Buen Gobierno*. Disponible en: https://www.boe.es/buscar/doc.php?id=BOE-A-2013-12887.

BOE, 2015a. *Ley 39/2015, de 1 de octubre, del Procedimiento Administrativo Común de las Administraciones Públicas*. Disponible en: https://www.boe.es/buscar/act.php?id=BOE-A-2015-10565

BOE, 2015b. *Ley 40/2015, de 1 de octubre, de Régimen Jurídico del Sector Público*. Disponible: https://www.boe.es/buscar/act.php?id=BOE-A-2015-10566

BOE, 2020a. Ley 6/2020, de 11 de noviembre, reguladora de determinados aspectos de los servicios electrónicos de confianza. Disponible en: https://www.boe.es/buscar/act.php?id=BOE-A-2020-14046

BOE, 2020b. Real Decreto 1147/2020, de 15 de diciembre, por el que se declaran oficiales las cifras de población resultantes de la revisión del Padrón municipal referidas al 1 de enero de 2020. Disponible en: https://www.boe.es/diario_boe/txt.php?id=BOE-A-2020-17332

Bonsón, E., Torres, L., Royo, S., Flores, F. 2012. Local e-government 2.0: Social media and corporate transparency in municipalities. *Government Information Quarterly*, Vol. 29, No. 2, pp. 123-132.

Cañizares-Espada, M., Muñoz-Colomina, C.I, Pérez-Estébanez, R. Urquía-Grande, E. 2021. Transparency and Accessibility in Municipalities: The Case of Social Services in Spain. *Central European Journal of Public Policy*, Vol. 15, No.1, pp. 1-24.

DePaula, N., Dincelli, E., Harrison, T.M. 2018. Toward a typology of government social media communication: Democratic goals, symbolic acts and self-presentation. *Government Information Quarterly*, Vol. 35, No. 1, pp. 98-108.

Faber, B., Budding, T., Gradus, R. 2020. Assessing social media use in Dutch municipalities: Political, institutional, and socio-economic determinants. *Government Information Quarterly*, Vol. 37, No. 3, art. no. 101484,

Feeney, M.K., Brown, A. 2017. Are small cities online? Content, ranking, and variation of U.S. municipal websites. *Government Information Quarterly*, Vol. 34, No.1, pp. 62-74.

Gabriel, A.G., Castillo, L.C. 2020. Transparency and Accountability Practices of Local Government Units in the Philippines: a Measurement from the Ground. *Public Organization Review*, 20 (3), pp. 437-457.

Garrido-Rodríguez, J.C., López-Hernández, A.M., Zafra-Gómez, J.L. 2019. The impact of explanatory factors on a bidimensional model of transparency in Spanish local government. *Government Information Quarterly*, Vol. 36, No. 1, pp. 154-165.

Jiménez, J.L., Albalate, D. 2018. Transparency and local government corruption: What does lack of transparency hide? European Journal of Government and Economics, 7(2), pp. 106-122.

Krah, R.D.Y., Mertens, G. 2020. Transparency in Local Governments: Patterns and Practices of Twenty-first Century. *State and Local Government Review*, 52 (3), pp. 200-213.

Nam, T. 2018. Examining the anti-corruption effect of e-government and the moderating effect of national culture: A cross-country study. *Government Information Quarterly*, Vol. 35. No. 2, pp. 273-282.

Park, H. 2001. Reform on administrative transparency in local government: The case of Korea. *International Journal of Urban Sciences*, Vol. 5, No. 1, pp. 57-69.

Pernagallo, G., Torrisi, B., 2020. A logit model to assess the transparency of Italian public administration websites. *Government Information Quarterly*, 37 (4), art. no. 101519,

Piña, G., Avellaneda, C. 2019. Central Government Strategies to Promote Local Governments' Transparency: Guidance or Enforcement? *Public Performance and Management Review*, 42 (2), pp. 357-382.

Rodríguez-Navas, P.M., Breijo, V.R. 2021. Evaluating and fostering transparency in local administrations. *Analise Social*, 54 (233), pp. 828-862.

Schlæger, J., Wang, Q. 2017. E-monitoring of public servants in China: higher quality of government? *Journal of Chinese Governance*, Vol. 2, No. 1, pp. 1-19.

Simelio-Solà, N., Ferré-Pavia, C., & Herrero-Gutiérrez, F.-J. 2021. Transparent information and access to citizen participation on municipal websites. Profesional De La Información, Vol. *30*, No. 2. https://doi.org/10.3145/epi.2021.mar.11

Transparencia Internacional España (2017). Índice de Transparencia de los Ayuntamientos. https://www.boe.es/diario_boe/txt.php?id=BOE-A-2020-17332https://transparencia.org.es/ita-2017/

Yuniarta, G.A., Gusti Ayu Purnamawati, I.2020. Key elements of local government transparency in new public governance. *Problems and Perspectives in Management*, 18(4), pp. 96-106.

FINDING SYNONYMS IN A SYNTACTICALLY CONSTRAINED VECTOR SPACE MODEL

Dongqiang Yang, Xiaodong Sun and Pikun Wang
School of Computer Science and Technology, Shandong Jianzhu University, Jinan 250101, China

ABSTRACT

Distributional semantics in a vector space model plays an important role in natural language engineering. Apart from the word co-occurrences in plain context, the role of syntactic dependencies in deriving distributional semantics has not yet been fully investigated. We systematically investigate the salience of syntactic dependencies in accounting for distributional similarity. We first categorize the syntactic dependencies of words into four raw co-occurrence matrices that are respectively transformed into the second-order compressed matrices, then we systematically evaluate them in the TOEFL synonym test. Our results show that the semantic features of nouns mostly consist of their modifiers and their head nouns, whereas the semantic features of verbs are mostly explained by verb-modifiers and verb-objects. The syntactically conditioned contexts can interpret lexical semantics better than the unconditioned one.

KEYWORDS

Syntactic Dependencies, Distributional Similarity, Vector Space Model, Semantic Similarity

1. INTRODUCTION

Word meaning, represented in the distributional vector space model (VSM), usually employs co-occurrences in contexts, with the hypothesis of similar words sharing similar contexts (Harris 1985). To abstract distributional characteristics of words, Lowe (2001) proposes a VSM with quadruple operands (*B, A, S, M*), where (1) *B* consists of *basis elements* to form the dimensionality of a semantic space, which can be a group of words (Sahlgren 2006), syntactic dependencies (Curran 2003, Weeds 2003), and the like; (2) *A* transforms raw co-occurrence frequencies between words and the *basis elements* using functions such as Pointwise Mutual Information (PMI) and log-likelihood ratio; (3) *S* stands for similarity methods predicting semantic similarity through distributional context similarity, which often includes the *cosine* similarity and *Euclidean distance*; (4) *M* performs dimensionality reduction on a semantic space through Singular Value Decomposition (SVD) (Schütze 1992), Random Indexing (RI) (Kanerva et al. 2000), and the like. There are some comprehensive surveys on VSM in the literature. For example, Bullinaria and Levy (2006) mainly investigated the factors affecting distributional similarity in an unconditioned (a bag of words) setting such as the size of context window and similarity measures in the evaluations of multiple-choice synonym judgements, semantic and syntactic categorization, and the like; Padó and Lapata (2007) compared the difference between syntactically conditioned (syntactic dependencies) or unconditioned dimensionality of VSM.

However, the salience of syntactic dependencies in VSM has not been fully investigated in a consistent way. Previous studies on the topic (Pantel and Lin 2002, Curran 2003, McCarthy et al. 2004) failed to distinguish nuances of grammatical relations, and simply assembled different syntactic dependencies into one unified representation, which are similar to deducing distributional semantics with an unordered bag of words. Although Padó and Lapata (2007) attempted to investigate the role of each syntactic dependency in VSM through a predefined weighting scheme, they have not clearly shown to what extent one single type of syntactic dependency can contribute to distributional semantics. Observing the syntactically conditioned representation in VSM can provide more helpful clues for distributional semantics (Hirschman et al. 1975, Hindle 1990) than the unconditioned one, we in the paper focus on studying the salience of major types of grammatical relations in regulating distributional semantics. Note that we employ traditional corpus statistics rather than neural language models (Bengio et al. 2003) to investigate syntactically constrained VSM. Neural embeddings, such as the unified (Mikolov et al. 2013, Pennington et al. 2014) and contextualized ones

(Devlin et al. 2018, Howard and Ruder 2018, Peters et al. 2018, Radford et al. 2018), have achieved significant progress in NLP. However, it is out of scope of this paper to cover neural embeddings as we aim to exclude the inference of various neural network architectures and an enormous volume of social media data on deriving distributional semantics.

2. SYNTACTICALLY CONSTRAINED VSM

To deduce distributional semantics with grammatical relations in VSM, we usually conduct the following procedures: (1) pre-processing sentences in the corpora with shallow/complete parsing; (2) extracting and/or categorizing syntactic dependencies into distinctive subsets or vector spaces according to head-modifier (including adjective-noun and adverb or the nominal head in a prepositional phrase to verb) and grammatical roles (including subject-verb and object-verb); (3) applying the transformation of Singular Value Decomposition (SVD) (Schütze 1992) on the dependency sets to create the latent semantic representations; and (4) determining distributional similarity using similarity measures such as the Jaccard coefficient and *cosine*, or probabilistic measures such as KL divergence and information radius.

2.1 Syntactic Dependency Contingency

Word sense disambiguation can leverage syntactic dependencies in context, where the semantic requirements are bi-directional in the form of head-modifier and head-complement (Cruse 1986). As shown in Table 1, in the semantic traits of a construction, the dominant role of the selector is prevalent in the determination requirement, which is also facilitated with the additional dependency requirements (Cruse 1986). In one of Cruse's examples on head-modifier, for example *pregnant cousin*, the modifier *pregnant* dominates the female attributes of *cousin*, whereas *pregnant*, as the depender in the dependency restriction, also adds some features absent from *cousin*. To thoroughly study the syntactic dependencies in VSM, we mainly cover four types of grammatical relationships (i.e., **RV**, **AN**, **SV**, and **VO**), as listed in Table 1.

Table 1. The relation types in dependency construction

	determination		*dependency*	
	selector	*selectee*	*depender*	*dependee*
constructions	*modifier*	*head*	*modifier*	*head*
	head	*complement*	*complement*	*head*
RV	verb modifiers: {adverbs|head nouns}→ verbs			
AN	Noun modifiers: {adjective| pre/post-modification}→nouns			
SV	{subjects}→{predicates}			
VO	{predicates}→{objects}			

2.2 Syntactic Dependency Matrix

Following similar works on using syntactic parsers in distributional semantics, e.g., shallow parsers (Grefenstette 1992, Curran 2003) and a full parser MINIPAR (Lin 1998), to collect distributional information, we propose to construct VSMs for the 4 types of syntactic dependencies through the Link Grammar parser (Sleator and Temperley 1991). Similar to Yang and Powers (2010) in automating thesaurus construction with grammatical relations, we employed the Link Grammar parser to proceed the 100 million-word British National Corpus (BNC). After filtering out non-content words and conducting morphology and lemmatization pre-processing, we separately retrieved four types of grammatical relationships in Table 1 to construct four corresponding raw matrices, denoted as X_{RAW}: X_{RV}, X_{AN}, X_{SV}, and X_{VO}.

Consider X_{SV} a *m* by *n* matrix representing subject-verb dependencies between *m* subjects and *n* verbs. We illustrate the **SV** relation using the rows (X_{Sv} or $\{X_{i,*}\}$) of X_{SV} corresponding to nouns conditioned as subjects of verbs in sentences, and the columns (X_{sV} or $\{X_{*,j}\}$) to verbs conditioned by nouns as subjects. The cell $X_{i,j}$ shows the frequency of the ith subject with the jth verb. The ith row $X_{i,*}$ of X_{SV} is a profile of the ith subject in terms of its all verbs and the jth column $X_{*,j}$ of X_{SV} profiles the jth verb *versus* its subjects.

Our matrices are very sparse with zeros in over 95 percent of the entries. For each matrix, we transformed each cell frequency $freq(X_{i,j})$ into its information form using $log(freq(X_{i,j})+1)$ while retaining matrix sparsity. Apart from the logarithmic $freq(X_{i,j})$, Landauer and Dumais (1997) also divided it by the entropy of the column vector $X_{*,j}$ to adjust the association between words and documents, where the maximum of entropy occurs when every word in the row vector occurred evenly in one document, and the minimum is when one word is represented in the document. It can be formulated as:

$$freq(X_{i,j}) \Rightarrow \log(freq(X_{i,j})+1) \Big/ -\sum_{k=1}^{|X_{*,j}|} P(X_{k,j}) \log(P(X_{k,j}))$$

where $|X_{*,j}|$ is the size of $X_{*,j}$, and $P(X_{k,j})$ is the probability of the cell $X_{k,j}$ with respect to the sum of $X_{*,j}$. The entropy in this formula functions similarly to the Inverse Document Frequency (IDF) to the Term Frequency (TF) in IR. As an alternative, Rapp (2003) proposed to multiply by the entropy in calculating distributional similarity for clustering word senses, which was based on a word by word association matrix. Landauer and Dumais (1997) and Rapp (2003) employed the context of a bag of words, say, word co-occurrences in a fixed-size window, so that data sparseness was not as severe as in our syntactic dependency matrices. We did not apply the dampening factor of IDF-like entropy on co-occurrences acquired under the condition of syntactic dependencies as our matrices are much sparser than a typical bag-of-word VSM, and it would be superfluous to regularize the matrices repeatedly.

2.3 Finding Principal Components

To further reduce the dimensionality of these matrices, we applied SVD/LSA (Deerwester et al. 1990, Landauer and Dumais 1997) on them to transform syntactically constrained VSMs into their latent semantic space models. In the investigation of using LSA to find synonyms, Landauer and Dumais (1997) claimed that the optimal performance was subject to variation on the number of single values or principal components. The components in the compressed space reflect mainly semantic features, attributes, or concepts that are reminiscent of the human semantic memory model (Quillian 1968). In Roget's Thesaurus ver. 1911, there are nearly 1,000 semantic categories, which organize over 40,000 words. We fixed 1,000 as the default size of each word vector in the semantic space, and reduced all matrices to 1,000 singular values or eigenvectors with respect to the expensive computation of SVD on these sparse matrices. To further select the appropriate number of singular values out of 1,000, we defined the selection probability P_i of the single value S_i with respect to the relative variance it can stand for, $P_i = S_i^2/\Sigma(\text{diag}(S^2))$, where $\Sigma(\text{diag}(S^2))$ is the sum of squares of 1,000 singular values. Among the singular values, the first 20 components account for around 50% of the variance, and the first 250 components for over 75%. We established 250 as a fixed size of the compressed semantic space. In the following sections we will denote the syntactically conditioned co-occurrences or raw matrices as X_{RAW}, in contrast to the SVD compressed ones X_{SVD}.

To measure the effectiveness of syntactically-conditioned X_{RAW}, together with X_{SVD} on mining latent semantic components, we employ the *cosine* similarity of word vectors as used in LSA and commonly adopted in assessing distributional similarity.

3. MULTIPLE-CHOICE SYNONYM JUDGEMENTS

Landauer and Dumais (1997) evaluated SVD/LSA in lexical knowledge acquisition through the synonym test part of TOEFL, in which each examinee was presented with 80 questions designed for assessing his/her ability in standard written English. Each question comprises a target word followed by its four alternative words, one of which is the semantically closest answer or synonym to the question word. People from non-English speaking countries on average achieved 51.6 correct answers or 64.5% correct rate, which was taken as a baseline for this task by Landauer and Dumais (1997). Since TOEFL benchmarks the evaluation of distributional similarity (Landauer and Dumais 1997, Rapp 2003, 2004, Bullinaria and Levy 2006, Padó and Lapata 2007), we employ it to evaluate the salience of the four syntactic dependency sets and their corresponding compressed counterparts after SVD in regard to semantic knowledge acquisition.

3.1 A Walk-Through Example

To demonstrate the quality of our syntactically constrained VSMs, we listed top 10 similar words for verbs and nouns after calculating and ranking their distributional similarity (*cosine*) respectively in the SVD-compressed X_{RV} and X_{AN}, as shown in Table 2. We selected a target verb or noun (in bold) with its frequency in BNC ranging from over 10,000 times (high frequency), between 10,000 and 4,000 times (medium frequency), and below 4,000 times (low frequency).

Table 2. Top 10 similar words after computing distributional similarity in X_{SVD}

	X_{RV}	X_{AN}
High frequency	**drink**: *sip pour slop bottle spill swill slurp smoke decant eat*	**branch**: *tree twig department bureau college shrub leaf faculty outlet institute*
Medium frequency	**decline**: *decrease dwindle deteriorate diminish shrink expand wane refuse multiply wither*	**recession**: *slump downturn drought crisis depression inflation boom upheaval shortage unemployment*
Low frequency	**deter**: *discourage penalize punish dupe tempt restrain justify coerce constrain nerve*	**jewel**: *necklace sari jewellery silver brooch scarlet livery scarf diamond braces*

3.2 An Answer Finder in TOEFL

In line with Yang and Powers (2006), we first manually divided the 80 questions into four sub-question sets according to common PoS tags between a target or question word and its options or answers. They were evenly distributed on PoS tages, namely 23 adjectives (29%), 20 verbs (25%), 19 nouns (24%), 18 adverbs (23%). Secondly, with respect to each subset of the same PoS, after separately calculating the cosine similarity of the target word and its one of four options within X_{RAW} and X_{SVD}, we selected the option word with the highest similarity score as the correct answer or synonym to the target. Thirdly, to finalize the total number of answers found in X_{RAW} and X_{SVD}, we avoided simply averaging the sum of the number of answers X_{AN}, X_{RV}, X_{SV}, and X_{VO} in each sub-question set. Rather, we calculated Ans_i, the answer score to the ith question Que_i (the target word), to be equal to 1, indicating a correct answer to Que_i, if and only if (1) $TF_{i,m}$, the term frequency (*TF*) of Que_i, holds maximum in the mth matrix of {X_{An}, X_{aN}, X_{Rv}, X_{rV}, X_{Sv}, X_{sV}, X_{Vo}, and X_{vO}} and (2) $Ans_{i,m}$, the answer score to Que_i in the mth matrix is also equal to 1; otherwise $Ans_i = 0$. This can be formulated as follows: $Ans_i = 1$, if $Max(TF_{i,m}) > 0$ and $Ans_{i,m} = 1$; otherwise $Ans_i = 0$. This function implies that the final correct answer to each question is credited only if there is a correct answer in the matrix where the term frequency of the question word is maximum across all matrices. The total number of correct answers in X_{RAW} and X_{SVD} that distributional similarity (*cosine*) can work out, is the sum of $Ans_{i,m}$ across the four sub-question sets.

Consider 1 of 80 questions in TOEFL: finding the synonym of *hasten* from a group of words including *accelerate, permit, determine,* and *accompany* for example. The distributional similarity (*cosine*) was first calculated in each subset, as shown in Table 3, where the figure in parentheses is the term frequency of *hasten* in each raw co-occurrence matrix.

Table 3. Finding a synonym of the verb *hasten* in the English synonym test of TOEFL

hasten	X_{rV} (226)		X_{Vo} (235)		X_{sV} (148)	
	X_{RAW}	X_{SVD}	X_{RAW}	X_{SVD}	X_{RAW}	X_{SVD}
accelerate	0.070	**0.247**	**0.620**	**0.606**	0.143	0.353
permit	0.082	0.071	0.123	0.109	0.102	0.086
determine	**0.085**	-0.047	0.073	-0.041	0.107	-0.014
accompany	0.061	0.049	0.195	0.365	**0.176**	**0.383**

Note that there is no occurrence of *hasten* as a noun in X_{AN}. Furthermore, the word *hasten* occurred 235 times with its objects in X_{Vo}, more frequently than with its modifiers in X_{rV} (226) and subjects in X_{sV} (148), whereas *accelerate* had the highest distributional similarity with *hasten* in the raw co-occurrence matrix X_{RAW} and the compressed matrices X_{SVD}. So *accelerate*, the synonym of *hasten*, is the correct response on the assumption that the higher distributional similarity among words implies higher semantic similarity.

3.3 The Answer Distribution on Dependency Sets

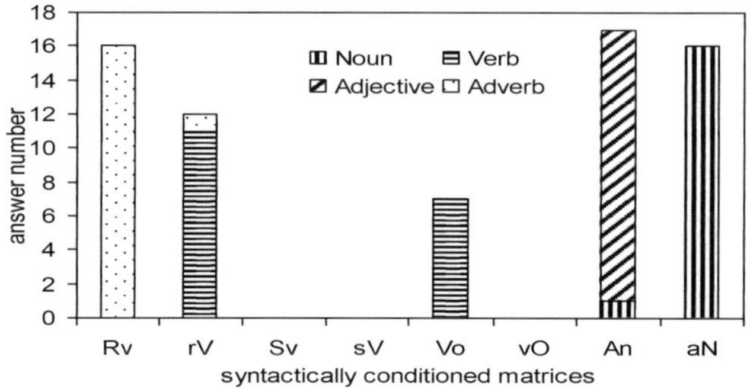

Figure 1. The total number of answers found in each dependency matrix

We correctly addressed 58 and 68 out of the 80 questions respectively using X_{RAW} and X_{SVD} in the TOEFL test. In the 68 correct answers from X_{SVD}, nearly all adverb questions (94%) were elicited correctly from X_{Rv}, where X_{RV} is the syntactic set containing the relations between verbs and their modifiers, as shown in Figure 1. All correct adjective answers came from X_{An} that mainly specifies modifiers such as adjectives with the modified nouns. Almost all correct noun answers were achieved in X_{aN}, which indicates their corresponding modifiers specifying the dominant distributional features of nouns. The total number of correct verb answers was 11 in X_{rV} and 7 in X_{Vo} respectively. This implies that both the modifiers and objects of the verbs could affect the semantic prediction of the verbs. Overall, the modifiers of nouns are likely to play an important role in accounting for their semantic features through distributional similarity; and most semantic features of verbs depend on their modifiers consisting mainly of adverbs, head nouns in the prepositional phrases, along with their objects.

3.4 A Comparison to other VSMs

The synonym test of TOEFL is widely adopted in evaluating statistical semantics acquired in the syntactically conditioned and unconditioned VSMs (Bullinaria and Levy 2006, Padó and Lapata 2007). We further compared distributional similarity (*cosine*) on the X_{RAW} and X_{SVD} (cos_{RAW} and cos_{SVD}) with other state of the art methods in this test, as shown in Figure 2.

For these comparisons, the baseline of people taking English as the Second Language (BL-ESL) denotes the average level of non-native English speakers in the test, which contains 51.6 correct answers. The methods using unconditioned word co-occurrences mainly include:

- LSA: Landauer and Dumais (1997) first created a word-by-document matrix (60,768 by 30,473) from an encyclopaedia of 4.6 million words, which was then normalized with logarithms where each cell frequency was divided by the entropy of a word across all its documents. To find synonyms, *cosine* on the SVD compressed matrix (reduced to 300 dimensions), achieved 64.4% accuracy on TOEFL.
- PMI-IR: Turney (2001) used the algorithm of Pointwise Mutual Information-Information Retrieval (PMI-IR) that mainly retrieved word occurrences within a 10-word window through the *NEAR* query from the Alta Vista search engine and then calculated word association strength with mutual information to predict answers. 73.8% of TOEFL questions were correctly addressed.
- LC-IR: Higgins (2004) proposed a similar algorithm to PMI-IR, Local Context Information Retrieval (LC-IR), using the Alta Vista search engine. Instead of the *NEAR* query that retrieving word co-occurrences in a ±10 window, he collected words absolutely adjacent to each other within one-word distance to compute word distributional similarity. LC-IR reached 81.3% accuracy on TOEFL.
- Paradig: In the investigation into word space model, Sahlgren (2006) divided plain contexts into syntagmatic and paradigmatic. The syntagmatic context provides word association for computing distributional similarity, which holds a similar assumption to PMI-IR and LC-IR, whereas the paradigmatic representation focuses word interchangeability in the same environment of surrounding words, which is analogous to LSA. With two different versions of corpora, BNC and the Touchstone

Applied Science Associates (TASA) comprising 10 million words and a collection of high-school level of English texts over a number of topics such as science and health, his results in TOEFL showed a greater number of correct answers was acquired using the paradigmatic context (75% accuracy in TASA vs 72.5% in BNC) than the syntagmatic one (67.5% in BNC vs 52.5% in TASA).

- Rapp: Rapp (2003) reported an excellent result of 92.5% accuracy in TOEFL. Apart from lemmatization and functional words filtration of BNC and SVD reduction on the dimensionality of semantic space (300 dimensions), he also normalized word co-occurrence using entropy-based transformation and removed lemmas with frequencies less than 20 times, which further lessened data sparseness and lowered the amount of noise in VSM. Without SVD, his approach using *cosine* arrived at 69% accuracy.

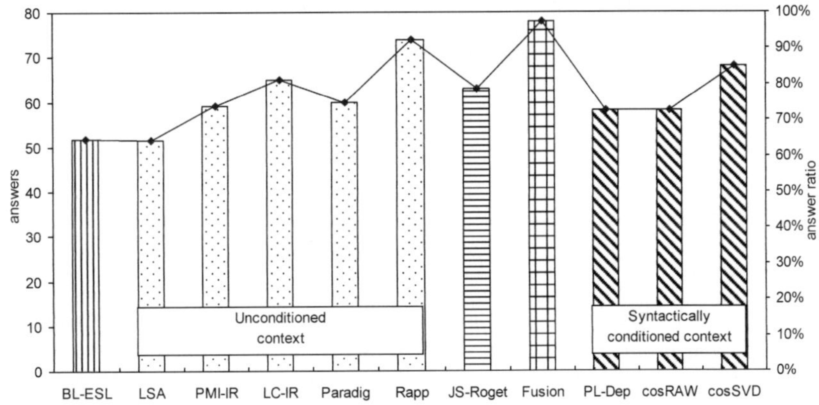

Figure 2. A performance comparison of different methods in the English synonym test of TOEFL

With respect to the VSM conditioned on syntactic dependencies, Padó and Lapata (2007) (PL-Dep) implemented a platform of comparing different syntactic dependencies, normalization methods, and similarity methods. Their optimal dependency-based model features weighting dependencies, concatenating at most three dependencies, and mapping and reducing word dimensions into 2,000 basic ones. They correctly address about 73.0% of TOEFL questions using the information theoretic similarity measure (Lin 1998).

In addition to these methods using the syntactically conditioned and unconditioned contexts, Turney et al. (2004) proposed a fusion scheme (Fusion) based on the product rule, merging LSA, PMI-IR, Roget's Thesaurus based method (Jarmasz and Szpakowicz 2003) (JS-Roget), and Connector using summary snapshots from Google querying (a similar technique to PMI-IR). Note that instead of computing distributional similarity, JS-Roget measured taxonomic similarity using the simple edge-counting of Roget's Thesaurus. Fusion achieved 97.5% accuracy on the 80 TOEFL questions, but it is not clear that is a generalizable approach. Note that in Figure 2 the methods using unconditioned context include LSA, PMI-IR, LC-IR, Paradig, and Rapp, whereas PL-Dep, cos_{RAW}, and cos_{SVD} employ syntactically conditioned context.

The synonym test of TOEFL is designed to examine lexical knowledge of non-native English speakers, and it was no surprise that JS-Roget outperformed LSA, PMI-IR, and LC-IR due to the effective organization of Roget's Thesaurus. The reason that it failed to reach 100% of the correct answers is probably attributed to the lexical knowledge coverage of the machine-readable Roget in the experiment. The improvement of PMI-IR and LC-IR over LSA could be attributed to the usage of terabyte-sized corpora that greatly reduced data sparseness in extracting synonyms. In contrast to LSA (64.4%), except for the same similarity measure (*cosine*), our competitive performance, cos_{SVD} (85.0%) and cos_{RAW} (72.5%) on TOEFL, could be partly due to the word representation with syntactic dependencies rather than plain word co-occurrences in LSA, and partly due to the division of the syntactic dependencies into the four different subsets dedicated on one of the four dependencies.

Although the correctness of cos_{SVD} (85.0%) and cos_{RAW} (72.5%) in addressing the multiple-choice synonym questions is lower than Rapp, it is worth pointing out that without SVD reduction, Rapp only arrived at 69% accuracy. Therefore, the SVD compression on word co-occurrence space contributed much more in Rapp than cos_{RAW} to cos_{SVD}. Note also that Rapp filtered out lemmas with frequency less than 20, and we did not set up a threshold to filter out the low frequency cells. We assumed that all triples for the syntactic dependency yielded from the parser could contribute to the prediction of semantic similarity through distributional similarity, even if the parse was formally incorrect or represented an unlikely reading in the context.

On the other hand, Bullinaria and Levy (2006) conclude that corpus size and quality are important factors in deciding performance of VSMs. More reliable statistics of word co-occurrences can be derived from larger and better corpora with less unusual and noisy words. In their systematic experiments of distributional similarity on VSMs, Padó and Lapata (2007) observed the VSM based on syntactically conditioned co-occurrences had significantly outperformed the VSM based on plain co-occurrences. Since our raw co-occurrence matrices, as a collection of word dependencies, are much sparser than simply counting neighboring words in a $\pm n$ window without filtering out low frequency word co-occurrences, there is still room to improve our syntactically conditioned VSM.

There is no doubt the Fusion model that combines distinctive techniques has almost perfectly tackled the synonym test of TOEFL. Due to the encouraging results of cos_{SVD}, our method might be another important resource to be merged with those in Fusion, which are mainly based on unconditioned contexts.

4. CONCLUSION

We mainly investigated the syntactically constrained VSM in deducing distributional semantics. In the task of detecting synonyms in the TOEFL synonym test, we employed distributional similarity to choose an answer from one of four options to quantify the effectiveness of syntactically constrained VSM in predicting semantic similarity. We achieved encouraging results compared to other syntactically conditioned and unconditioned VSMs. Our results showed that distributional similarity (*cosine*) can retrieve more synonyms in the compressed matrices $X_{\mathbf{SVD}}$ than in the original syntactic dependency matrices $X_{\mathbf{RAW}}$. We can tentatively conclude that head-modifier and verb-object may bear semantic restrictions on verbs, and head-modifier dependencies may regulate the meaning of nouns.

ACKNOWLEDGEMENT

This research was supported by the Humanity and Social Science Foundation of China Ministry of Education (Grant No. 15YJA740054).

REFERENCES

Yoshua Bengio, jean Ducharme, Pascal Vincent and Christian Janvin (2003). "A Neural Probabilistic Language Model." *J. Mach. Learn. Res.* 3: 1137-1155.

John Andrew Bullinaria and Joseph P. Levy (2006). "Extracting Semantic Representations from Word Co-Occurrence Statistics: A Computational Study." *Behavior Research Methods* 39: 510-526.

David A. Cruse (1986). *Lexical Semantics*, Cambridge University Press.

James R. Curran (2003). From Distributional to Semantic Similarity. Ph.D thesis, University of Edinburgh.

Scott C. Deerwester, Susan T. Dumais, Thomas K. Landauer, George W. Furnas and Richard A. Harshman (1990). "Indexing by Latent Semantic Analysis." *Journal of the American Society of Information Science* 41(6): 391-407.

Jacob Devlin, Ming-Wei Chang, Kenton Lee and Kristina Toutanova (2018). Bert: Pre-Training of Deep Bidirectional Transformers for Language Understanding. *The 2019 Conference of the North American Chapter of the Association for Computational Linguistics: Human Language Technologies*. pp. 4171-4186.

Gregory Grefenstette (1992). Sextant: Exploring Unexplored Contexts for Semantic Extraction from Syntactic Analysis. *The 30th Annual Meeting of the Association for Computational Linguistics*, Newark, Delaware. pp. 324-326.

Zellig Harris (1985). *Distributional Structure*. The Philosophy of Linguistics. Oxford University Press, pp. 26-47.

Derrick Higgins (2004). Which Statistics Reflect Semantics? Rethinking Synonymy and Word Similarity. *The International Conference on Linguistic Evidence*, Tübingen, Germany. pp. 265-284.

Donald Hindle (1990). Noun Classification from Predicate-Argument Structures. *The 28th Annual Meeting of the Association for Computational Linguistics*, Pittsburgh, Pennsylvania. pp. 268-275.

Lynette Hirschman, Ralph Grishman and Naomi Sager (1975). "Grammatically-Based Automatic Word Class Formation." *Information Processing and Management* 11: 39-57.

Jeremy Howard and Sebastian Ruder (2018). Universal Language Model Fine-Tuning for Text Classification. ACL. Association for Computational Linguistics.

Mario Jarmasz and Stan Szpakowicz (2003). Roget's Thesaurus and Semantic Similarity. *Recent Advances in Natural Language Processing (RANLP 2003)*, Borovets, Bulgaria. John Benjamins Publishing Company pp. 212-219.

Penti Kanerva, Jan Kristoferson and Anders Holst (2000). Random Indexing of Text Samples for Latent Semantic Analysis. *The 22nd Annual Conference of the Cognitive Science Society*, Mahwah, NJ, USA. pp. 1036-1036.

Thomas K. Landauer and Susan T. Dumais (1997). "A Solution to Plato's Problem: The Latent Semantic Analysis Theory of Acquisition, Induction, and Representation of Knowledge." *Psychological Review* 104: 211-240.

Dekang Lin (1998). Automatic Retrieval and Clustering of Similar Words. *The 17th International Conference on Computational Linguistics*, Montreal, Quebec, Canada. pp. 768-774.

Will Lowe (2001). Towards a Theory of Semantic Space. *The 23rd Annual Conference of the Cognitive Science Society*, Edinburgh, UK. pp. 576-581.

Diana McCarthy, Rob Koeling, Julie Weeds and John Carroll (2004). Finding Predominant Senses in Untagged Text. *The 42nd Annual Meeting of the Association for Computational Linguistics (ACL-04)*, Barcelona, Spain. Association for Computational Linguistics, pp. 267-287.

Tomas Mikolov, Ilya Sutskever, Kai Chen, Greg Corrado and Jeffrey Dean (2013). Distributed Representations of Words and Phrases and Their Compositionality. *The 26th International Conference on Neural Information Processing Systems (NIPS)*, Lake Tahoe, Nevada. Curran Associates Inc., pp. 3111-3119

Sebastian Padó and Mirella Lapata (2007). "Dependency-Based Construction of Semantic Space Models." *Computational Linguistics* 33(2): 161-199.

Patrick Pantel and Dekang Lin (2002). Discovering Word Senses from Text. *The Eighth ACM SIGKDD International Conference on Knowledge Discovery and Data Mining*, New York, NY, USA. pp. 613-619.

Jeffrey Pennington, Richard Socher and Christopher D Manning (2014). Glove: Global Vectors for Word Representation. *The 2014 Conference on Empirical Methods in Natural Language Processing (EMNLP)*. pp. 1532-1543.

Matthew E. Peters, Mark Neumann, Mohit Iyyer, Matt Gardner, Christopher Clark, Kenton Lee and Luke Zettlemoyer (2018). Deep Contextualized Word Representations. *The 2018 Conference of the North American Chapter of the Association for Computational Linguistics: Human Language Technologies*. pp. 2227-2237.

M. Ross Quillian (1968). *Semantic Memory*. Semantic Information Processing. The MIT Press, pp. 227-270.

Alec Radford, Jeffrey Wu, Rewon Child, David Luan, Dario Amodei and Ilya Sutskever (2018) "Language Models Are Unsupervised Multitask Learners."

Reinhard Rapp (2003). Word Sense Discovery Based on Sense Descriptor Dissimilarity. *The 9th Machine Translation Summit*, New Orleans, Louisiana, USA. pp. 315-322.

Reinhard Rapp (2004). Mining Text for Word Senses Using Independent Component Analysis. *The Fourth SIAM International Conference on Data Mining*, Lake Buena Vista, Florida, USA.

Magnus Sahlgren (2006). The Word-Space Model: Using Distributional Analysis to Represent Syntagmatic and Paradigmatic Relations between Words in High-Dimensional Vector Spaces. Ph.D thesis, Stockholm University.

Hinrich Schütze (1992). Dimensions of Meaning. *The 1992 ACM/IEEE Conference on Supercomputing*, Minneapolis, Minnesota, USA. pp. 787-796.

Daniel Sleator and Davy Temperley (1991). Parsing English with a Link Grammar.

Peter D. Turney (2001). Mining the Web for Synonyms: Pmi-Ir Versus Lsa on Toefl. *The Twelfth European Conference on Machine Learning (ECML2001)*, Freiburg, Germany. Springer, pp. 491-502.

Peter D. Turney, Michael L. Littman, Jeffrey Bigham and Victor Shnayder, Eds. (2004). Combining Independent Modules in Lexical Multiple-Choice Problems. *Recent Advances in Natural Language Processing III*: Selected Papers from Ranlp 2003.

Julie Elizabeth Weeds (2003). Measures and Applications of Lexical Distributional Similarity. Ph.D thesis, University of Sussex.

Dongqiang Yang and David Powers (2010). "Using Grammatical Relations to Automate Thesaurus Construction." *Journal of Research and Practice in Information Technology* 42(2): 105-122.

Dongqiang Yang and David M. W. Powers (2006). Distributional Similarity in the Varied Order of Syntactic Spaces. *2006 International Conference on Innovative Computing, Information and Control (ICICIC 2006)*, Beijing, China. pp. 406-409.

BUILDING A SEARCH-BASED ARCHITECTURE TO ENHANCE PRODUCT CERTIFICATE VERIFICATION AND REDUCING COUNTERFEIT

Eduard Daoud and Martin Gaedke
Technische Universität Chemnitz, Germany

ABSTRACT

The overall growth in the share of online sales has grown in comparison to total sales intensively. Online shopping is comfortable for consumers, but it also raises specific challenges in terms of product safety. For this, the European Commission published a notice on market surveillance of products sold online on August 1, 2017, to support authorities' work (European Commission, 2017). In addition, the Product Safety Pledge (European Commission, 2020) is a voluntary responsibility beyond product safety legal obligations. It helps to remove dangerous non-food consumer products for sale online rapidly. Furthermore, it sets out activities by online marketplaces to enhance product safety, such as offering a simplified way for customers to report potentially hazardous products. OECD wrote in their report 2016 that up to 5% of imports are counterfeited goods. The report estimated this damage at EUR 85 billion (OECD/EUIPO, 2019). This paper proposes a search-based architecture that closes the unilateral published digital product certificate information gaps, European RAPEX System, and online marketplaces. The new search-based architecture used information access technology to empower consumers and authorities by easily verifying a product within its labelled certificate. This could be one of the important steps in the direction to reduce counterfeiting. This paper aims to create a new category of applications in which the end-user identifies the counterfeit product and contributes to the fight against product piracy.

KEYWORDS

E-commerce, Information Access, Certification Industry, Counterfeiting, RAPEX

1. INTRODUCTION AND THE CURRENT PROBLEM

Detection of counterfeit products is, in certain cases, a challenge for the consumers and can sometimes even be very dangerous when it comes to medical products or toys for children, for example. ResearchAndMarkets wrote in their report on May 15, 2018, that up to 1.2 trillion USD in 2017 are counterfeited goods. Furthermore, the report estimated this damage globally at 1.82 trillion USD in 2020 (RESEARCH AND MARKETS, 2018).

In March 2020, the European Commission published its report (Directorate-General for Justice and Consumers (European Commission), 2019) on the so-called "rapid alert system", with which the Commission aims to prevent or restrict the sale of dangerous and often counterfeit products on the market. The report shows that the number of regulatory actions taken due to an alert increases year on year. For example, the number of alerts issued in 2019 was 4477, compared to 4050 alerts in 2018. The most significant conclusions of the report are that in 2019. This represents a 10% increase from the previous year and a 63% increase since 2015. Policies range from recalling unsafe products from the market or destroying products directly by the retailer. These products have not reached the consumers. From all products, toys were the product category with the highest number of alerts (29% of all alerts), second were motor vehicles (23%) and e-appliances and accessories (8%), according to the report. In addition, cosmetics, clothing, textiles and fashion items, baby products, and children's supplies also had a high number of alerts. The most frequently reported risks were related to products that pose a risk of injury (for example, fractures or concussions) (27%), followed by chemical components in products (23%) and choking hazards for children (13%). New alerts have been registered since the start of the coronavirus pandemic. For example, by July 1 2020, there had been 63 alerts on face masks, three alerts on protective suits, three alerts on hand sanitisers and three alerts on UV lamps. The rapid alert system does not give out more accurate information on how much of the listed product is fake.

The number of counterfeits reported products is extremely low concerning the number of counterfeit products imported into the EU. OECD wrote in their continuous updated report from 2016 until 2019 that up to 5% of imports are counterfeited goods. The report estimated this damage at EUR 85 billion (OECD/EUIPO, 2019). The EU relies on intervention as an essential instrument, and the directive provides for ex-post intervention by the authorities. E-commerce platform product sellers should guarantee that no unlawful and non-safe products are available on the EU market (European Commission, 2020). An independent body's prevention through product testing is more effective (Anti-Counterfeiting Committee, 2020) & (IFIA & CEOC, 2018). However, this means more product certificates, and this raises many questions.

The essential ones are: How can consumers gain more confidence in certification marks and certificates? How can the market surveillance authorities efficiently detect counterfeits in e-commerce and ensure that they are no longer on the commercial market? Certification agencies and inspection companies publish their certifications in databases accessible as a web service on their websites (produktpiraterie.org, 2020). However, whether online or in-store, end consumers cannot access quickly and without barriers to a certificate to check the validity and understand their value before buying. A results of a representative survey of 2500 Germans between 18 and 69 years of age on the awareness, trust and target groups of quality marks and certificates as well as the influence on purchase decisions and price ranges from splendid research GmbH in Hamburg, Germany in the year 2019 (SPLENDID RESEARCH GmbH, 2020) show that 44% of those questioned agree to buy a product with a quality mark as one without a mark and 51% will buy a product with a quality mark and are ready to pay 15% plus the price. Among all organisations awarding quality marks, private testing institutes to make a profit enjoy the least confidence. More than half of the Germans classify such awarding bodies as not trustworthy. The selling companies and private business associations enjoy a similarly low level of trust. In contrast, the quality marks or their awarding bodies, supposedly independent, enjoy special trust. Organisations with a state/governmental background are at the top of the list of favoured German organisations, according to a study by Hamburg-based splendid research GmbH.

The main research question is how to build an approach as a single point of trust to enable end consumers, authorities, and third parties to retrieve information about a product certificate without media breaks. All this should be done without any violation of property rights and economic interest and at the same time support authorities to detect counterfeit product e-commerce and ensure that counterfeit products are taken down from the commercial online market.

In the next section, we will highlight the subject of counterfeit domains and focus on the area where IT technology can make a positive contribution. After introducing the related works, we will outline the solution concept and technical architecture and then focus on implementing and evaluating such solutions and discussing their challenges. Finally, we will review the results of our work and consider an outlook for the future.

2. RELATED WORKS

The literature on Information Retrieval in the context of fighting counterfeited products deals mainly with ensuring data access within a central database like the RAPEX system of the European Union. However, this discussion of related work focuses on empowering consumers and authorities to detect counterfeit products by verifying the labelled product certificate and quality mark. **The requirements that we want to check** from a dedicated solution are: To have the technical capability to aggregate multiple data sources such as eBay, Amazon, the certificate databases of the certification industry, and the RAPEX database into one index (**accessibility**) and to make them publicly available to help query tools of consumers and regulatory authorities (**public verifiability**).

Therefore, we will compare our approach, the search-based architecture and the central database one. Our approach is a search-based application. It is a subordinate to Search-Based Software Engineering (SBSE) (Harman, et al., 2012) and a user-centred interactive web interface built on a platform capable of decoupling data with connectors from its source and uses a search engine index at its core. However, the typical software applications (database-based applications) can only query one data source. In contrast, the search-based application (index-based applications) can query multiple data sources and return the results in a harmonised form to the end-user (Feldman & Sherman, 2011). Furthermore, the issue of data ownership in the database is complicated since, in a central database, there is always one administrator with full access to the database, which is not the case in the search-based approach - due to the cross-system and flexible indexing possibilities – the ownership is reserved to the owner of the original data sources.

The search-based application is comparatively faster and less expensive to establish an information delivery endpoint where a large number of users participate in information access than the typical database-based application because the search-based application only performs "read" operations and the shifting of queries from one or more databases to a single index significantly saves the cost of additional services (Gregory & Laura, 2011); (Harman, et al., 2012). Since the 1982s, relational database technologies have been the primary means of storing information for businesses (Gregory & Laura, 2011).

In a traditional database application model, users access data via predefined SQL (Structured Query Language) queries. These are potential savings for IT when it comes to limiting costs and complexity. However, this single-source, heavy hit-or-miss model no longer reflects the modern information environment (Gregory & Laura, 2011).

As related work in the context of "traditional" database application does not sufficiently fulfil the requirements of aggregating multiple data sources and providing query tools for deferent perspectives, the following section presents a distinct approach to enhancing transparency while using a product certificate.

Before we proceed with the design of our new solution approach, we will briefly address two concepts:

The concept of applying authentication technologies to the fight against counterfeiting is a classic problem of identification and authentication of an entity from another based on specific features. Counterfeit products may be distinguished from valid products by some proprietary or applied characteristics. The term "counterfeit" has been associated with different categories of goods, copied, modified, or re-branded differently. In our work, we focus, according to (Guin, et al., February 2014), on the categories Overproduced, Out-of-Spec/Defective, Remarked and Tampered. Furthermore, **the concept of consumer empowerment**, which is not a new principle in itself. The need to empower the consumer to make informed choices in the market has already been presented by various sources, including (European Commission, 2011), even if the focus was not on the fight against counterfeiting but more on detecting fraud the customers. Besides, the ISO Strategic Plan 2011-2015 ISO (ISO, 2015), recognises that the advice and involvement of consumer stakeholders are essential to ISO's overall performance and success. By the term "empowerment of the consumer", the consumer can use all available tools (authentication techniques) to prevent the purchase of counterfeit products or prevent economic and health threats. Moreover, consumer empowerment focuses on the detection phase rather than the forensic phase, in which consumers are expected to identify counterfeit items using simple means, such as their smartphones.

After the related work, we continue our work with the design of the new approach.

3. DESIGN

While designing the architecture and considering the principles of web engineering (Nora, et al., 2008), we contemplate three reusable artefacts that build on each other. Each artefact represents a specific state of the design through a specific, i.e. conceptual, logical, and physical model.

3.1 Conceptual Model

To help consumers and authorities to improve the capacity to retrieve, verify product certificates and report abuse, as indicated in the related work, involves hiding the complexity of query capabilities by combining multiple data sources that address accessibility and public verifiability under one information endpoint.

These interdependent service/concepts include crawling, filtering, processing, indexing, query parser, and tagging service, among other things, a product certificate. We focus on the first line on verifying a product certificate as a central point concerning compliance aspects (fraud prevention and detection). Primary, we need to design the index structure conceptually. The conceptual structure of our index associates a triple with a document. There are properties associated with a field of a document and the triple's object (a literal) related to the field's value in the document. The triple subject is then represented as another field of the document to return due to a search hit. In this way, it is possible to identify what was found. As stated before, an inverted index is then created. This inverted index maps query string hits to subject URIs. A certificate-indexed dataset is then configured with a description of which properties are to be indexed and given a mapped URI.

It is also necessary to configure the certificate-indexed dataset to update index entries when the corresponding triples are dropped or changed from the RDF - Resource Description Framework - store. We will implement the tagging service based on Lucene index implementation (Biancalana & Micarelli, 2009). Using the standard query language of Lucene (Hatcher, et al., 2005) or Elasticsearch (Radu, et al., 2015), the certificate index can be queried. Our approach offers the possibility to create queries via the query API of Apache Lucene, which uses Java to implement a suitable query parser syntax. A query is sub-divided into terms and operators. There are two categories of terms: Single and phrases. A single term is a single word such as "certificate" or "XY". A phrase is a group of words encompassed by double inverted commas, such as "certificate xy". To extend a query, several terms or subqueries can be used in combination with Boolean operators (Hatcher, et al., 2005).

The following is a simplified tabular presentation of a certificate as an index document that KP will create and request to index:

Table 1. A tabular presentation of a certificate as an index document

Attribute Name / URI	Formatted Value	Type	Description
https://URL/certificate#address	0xaF7eD4e8e423F8	property:string	Address
https://URL/certificate#expiryDate	Dec 31, 2021, 12:00:00 AM	property:datetime	Expiry date
https://URL/certificate#holder	Test Cert.holder	property:string	Certificate holder
https://URL/certificate#issuedDate	Nov 7, 2020, 12:00:00 AM	property:datetime	Issued date
https://URL/certificate#issuer	TÜV XY	property:string	Issuer
https://URL/certificate#model	Test Model	property:string	Model
https://URL/certificate#number	CERT ABC123	property:string	Number
https://URL/certificate#product	Test product	property:string	Product
https://URL/certificate#standards	EN 50291	property:string	Standards
https://URL/certificate#valid	true	property:string	Validity

After defining the basic principles of the index structure and the query possibilities in this conceptual step, we dedicate ourselves to data collection. The so-called crawling processes. After that, we define the conceptual design basics for the further necessary steps, namely for the filtering and processing steps.

In a search-based application, the crawlers' task is to index data from various certificate databases, different eCommerce platforms and RAPEX and classify them into content, metadata and preview image. This order is essential for mapping to the predefined RDF triple after the processing steps. Then, the crawler passes the pure, unmodified data from the data source to the filtering process. As part of the processing, the filtering process is responsible for a) text extraction from the pure data, b) formatting of metadata, c) generation of a thumbnail. The formatted and recognised text is then processed by tasks such as Text Annotation and Entity recognition, followed by mapping the text and metadata to the RDF triple (index document) and then tokenised and normalised and written to the index.

To sum up the design of our approach from the conceptual point of view, we could establish the following: the architecture crawls content from the data source(s) (Crawling). The number of data formats of the underlying data sources does not matter in our approach, as we decouple the data attributes from the applications by building an index. We need to use semantic technologies like entity recognition to identify filters from the data resources and enrich them with new attributes (Processing). The unified data layer described in our approach is directly available to users, web services or third-party applications (access).

It can be accessed through standard services such as HTTP(s), SOAP, REST API and RSS (Eetu, et al., 2007).

Building on this conceptual model, the next subsection proceeds with specifying the logical flow.

3.2 Logical Model

From a logical point of view, the search-based architecture offers a Web API for the user. A user can be a consumer, a certification body user or a user of surveillance authority. The Web API provides the communication endpoint (query capabilities) in conjunction with the index. To our approached architecture also belongs a data aggregation framework responsible for the data aggregation from different data sources, especially certificates databases and other data sources like eCommerce platforms or the RAPEX platform of the EU, and administration database acts as an internal data storage for user-profiles and their activities. The architecture within the isolated processes, the indexing process and the query processing, were started as proposed to allow a more detailed consideration. For reasons of clarity, the flowchart is simplified according to Lucene structure.

The indexing process is one of the hub functionalities implemented by our search-based architecture. Figure 1 illustrates the indexing process using a flow diagram. Steps (4) index writer is the most important and core component of the indexing process. Following is a list of commonly-used steps (Hatcher, et al., 2005) during the indexing process:

Table 2. Commonly-used steps during the indexing process

Step Nr.	Description
1	Loading raw data from the data source is one of the responsibilities of the crawler
2	Filtering the text by extracting text from binary data and format the metadata to overhanding the text to the processing step (3)
3	Processing steps are text annotation, entity recognition and metadata mapping.
4	The Tokenisation is responsible for analysing a document and getting the tokens/words from the text to be indexed. Text normalisation is responsible for converting text into a single canonical form that it may not have had before. This ensures consistency of input before operations are performed on it.

After having simplified the Index process and its associated processes and described them from a logical point of view, we describe the "query processing" process in the same principle and according to the standard of Lucene. Once a user requests to search the indexed data sources, our approach prepares a query object using that text to inquire the index database to get the relevant results. As shown in the simplified Figure 1, the process of query processing consists first of a query parser (5) to detect the language of the entered text, then this text is tokenised and either the text is stemmed (6) or not. A stemmed text allows the user to perform a fuzzy search (approximate string matching) (8)(9); otherwise, the index is matched precisely (exact string matching). The search results can be sorted according to specific metadata, such as the date of the issue. The results can also be grouped or further refined through the use of filters. Possible filters are certificate holder, model, product manufacturer and most importantly, a certificate's validity.

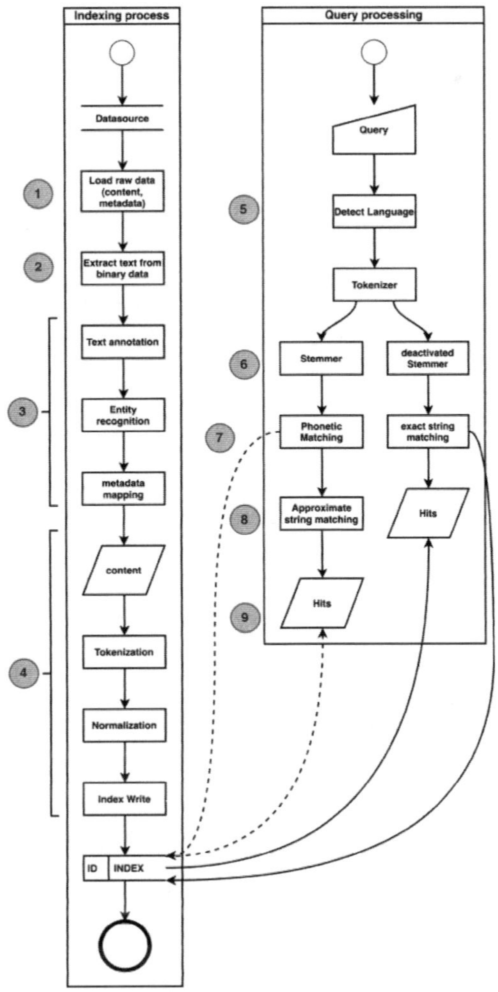

Figure 1. Indexing process and query processing flowchart (simplified according to Lucene structure)

Having built the logical model based on the conceptual model, we proceed to the technical details of the approached architecture in the next subsection.

3.3 Physical Model

From a physical point of view, our search-based approach offers four sub-services A) an HTML implemented web client runs as a service in a standard web delivery component with a light logical layer to manage the interactions (like queries) of the users with the search index. B) a query Analyser (Processing), C) an inverted index, and D) a Crawling framework. Figure 2 illustrates these services while we describe them in detail below:

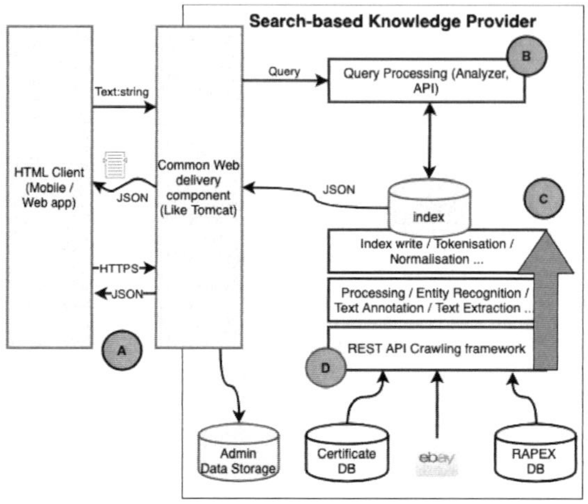

Figure 2. Physical Model Search-based knowledge provider

An end-user uses the web client anonymously or could create a user profile to profit from personalisation functionality like tagging and alerting service. The user sends a query in a textual form using a search field in the web client or web app (A); the string turns into a query after the processing step (analyser) (B).

Unlike traditional query database applications (cf. Related Work), our approach can not only provide query content in one database, instead can query the index (which is built from three data sources) and can return the results of the query in a single, unified view as suggested by (Feldman & Sherman, 2011). A REST API Crawling framework crawls (D) the content from the certificate databases (cf. Physical Model), eBay as an example for the eCommerce data and RAPEX database of the EU. The number of data formats of the underlying data sources does not matter in our approach, as we decouple the data attributes from the applications by building an index. Based on semantic technologies, the service (C) takes over the following tasks: Matching data structures of different formats, identifying relationships between the data objects, recognising entities and enriching the data with new attributes where necessary (content processing).

As mentioned, we used in our approach Lucene (Hatcher, et al., 2005) to build up the content pipeline starting with the crawling, followed by content processing and closed with the index writer. This API endpoint provides easy and secure access to end-users and other web services (Access). This access is provided in standard web formats and protocols like REST over HTTP(S) (Eetu, et al., 2007). Now that all artefacts relating to our targeted architecture have been described, the following subsection outlines the design's implementation.

4. IMPLEMENTATION

This implementation includes all design artefacts from the conceptual, logical and physical model phases to put them in the praxis (COK Project, 2020). The end-user can search the index without logging in. The following Figure 3 shows the HTML output of the (view) of the consumer logic (controller) where the end-user can submit a query according to the "Query processing" (cf. Physical Model).

For example, the consumer can search by manufacturer name such as "Toshiba" or by a specific certificate "ABC". An extended search form is available to supplement the search query with more detailed inputs via the metadata. In addition to the end-user (consumer) search option as a stakeholder, we have provided an additional privilege and functionality for the registered user. Registered users like the certification bodies or surveillance authorities' users search all data sources in full text, such as the EU's RAPEX database, eBay or certain certificate databases. We will now outline these points and their implementation. The visual representation of the search result shown in

Figure 4 below is the leading advancement to the search client of the logged-in users, recognising facets, personalisation options, data export and alerting functionality.

Figure 3. Search field GUI

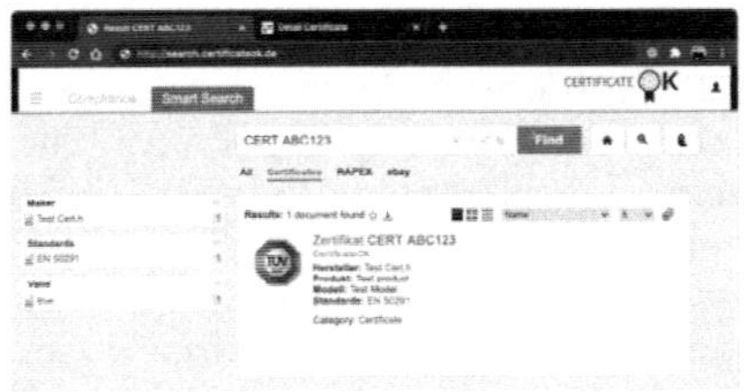

Figure 4. Search Client (GUI) for Registered Users

Cross-source indexing (Certificates from different inspections organisations, eBay and RAPEX) by the crawling framework, as described in the previous sections, allows the user to plan and execute cross-source search campaigns. For example, searching for all smoke detectors on eBay that advertise with a TÜV certificate, and these certificates and product information are automatically checked for validity/accuracy according to their existence in the index to detect and report fraud or abuse. After completing development, the next section is about the evaluation of our approach.

5. EVALUATION

To evaluate our approach to building a search-based architecture, we need first to evaluate the two requirements defined in related work. Based on this, we can systematically build and implement the related work and the architecture implementation to evaluate the requirements – accessibility and public verifiability – from the relevant evidence. To assess our approach to the degree to which our approach has fulfilled the two requirements criterion, we used the four-level rating system based on (Holger, et al., 2009). Building on the discussion of the individual evaluation criteria, the conclusion with the rating is carried out.

Accessibility: Our approach has the qualities of enabling stakeholders to access needed information using standard protocols like HTTP and JSON (cf. Figure 2). Furthermore, the architecture used a user-friendly search approach to find better and retrieve certificate information, increasing verifiability. To conclude, our approach completely fulfils the accessibility criterion.

Public verifiability: Certificate issuer specifies the scope of a certificate in the context of validity and other data like issuing date, valid until. Besides accessibility, public verifiability of certificates is provided by the search concept (Sigle Point of Information access). A certificate could be publicly verified using the search client as implemented in (cf. Figure 2). Every user could verify a certificate's validity by requesting the information behind using a Certificate ID or search terms like product name, model name, or other saved metadata. To conclude, our approach completely fulfils the public verifiability criterion.

6. CONCLUSION AND FUTURE WORKS

With the search-based architecture, all actors involved can verify certificates securely and transparently, and these certificates are neither manipulated on the systems nor during transmission. By providing a search-based architecture of certificate data provided by the certification bodies, we contributed to reducing the lack of transparency. Using a single point of certificate access, consumers lead faster or more effectively the detection and reporting process of forged or tampered certificates (reducing counterfeit). Through the search-based approach (integration API), integration between RAPEX, certification bodies and authorities are possible for better verification and data exchange. From the perspective of consumer safety and the reduction of counterfeit products, this would be an important contribution. Based on the requirements and to systematically build and implement the analysis of related work and component development. The two main requirements, accessibility and public verifiability, support conceptually, logically, and physically designing the contribution for search-based architecture. By focusing on more empowering individuals and consumers, we enabled the verification without requiring prior knowledge, except smartphones and access to the internet. To prove the concept of a search-based approach, we transferred the design artefacts into a self-contained service, which we then exemplarily integrated into the CertificateOK platform (COK Project, 2020). From the results obtained by evaluating the service, we concluded an overall completely fulfilment of the requirements. We plan to explore and research more about integrating machine learning applications to classify certificate marks and logos of certification bodies to unleash the potential of search-based certificate retrieving possibilities in future work. Shortly we intend to provide a better way of giving information by scanning the products themselves and using AI-based image recognition. This would combine two state-of-the-art technologies, machine learning and search technology, in one application. That will bring great convenience and a better experience for the consumer. However, we trust that our approached technology architecture will change the role and empower consumers to drive the market for more transparency and safety.

REFERENCES

Anti-Counterfeiting Committee, 2020. *Falsified: Test Reports & Certificates,* Brussel: TIC Council , Anti-Counterfeiting Committee.

Biancalana, C. & Micarelli, A., 2009. Social Tagging in Query Expansion: A New Way for Personalized Web Search. s.l., IEEE, pp. 1060-1065.

COK Project, 2020. *CertificateOK.* [Online] Available at: https://www.certificateok.de/_[Accessed 21 07 2021].

Directorate-General for Justice and Consumers (European Commission), 2019. *Results of the EU rapid alert system for dangerous non-food products,* Brussels: European Commission.

Eetu, M. et al., 2007. Enabling the semantic web with ready-to-use web widgets. In Proceedings of the First International Conference on Industrial Results of Semantic Technologies, Aachen, Germany: Volume 293 (FIRST'07), Lyndon Nixon, Roberta Cuel, and Claudio Bergamini (Eds.).

European Commission, 2011. *Consumer Empowerment in the EU.* [Online] Available at: https://ec.europa.eu/info/sites/info/files/consumer_empowerment_eu_2011_en.pdf [Accessed 05 2021].

European Commission, 2017. NOTICE on the market surveillance of products sold online. *Official Journal of the European Union,* C(250), pp. 2-18.

European Commission, 2020. *Communication from the Commission to the European Parliament,* City of Brussels: European Commission.

European Commission, 2020. *Product Safety Pledge, Voluntary commitment of online marketplaces..* [Online] Available at: https://ec.europa.eu/info/sites/info/files/voluntary_commitment_document_2020_2signatures_v2_003.pdf [Accessed 29 03 2021].

Feldman, S. & Sherman, C., 2011. *The High Cost Of Not Finding Information,* Framingham, Massachusetts, USA: International Data Corporation (IDC).

Gregory, G. & Laura, W., 2011. Search-Based Applications. At the Confluence of Search and Database Technologies.. Paris: Morgan & Claypool Publishers.

Guin, U., Daniel, D. & Mohammad, T., February 2014. Counterfeit Integrated Circuits: Detection, Avoidance, and the Challenges Ahead. *Journal of Electronic Testing,* 30(1), p. 9–23.

Harman, M., Mansouri, S. A. & Zhang, Y., 2012 . Search Based Software Engineering: A Comprehensive Analysis and Review of Trends Techniques and Applications, New York, NY, USA: ACM Computing Surveys (CSUR).

Hatcher, E., Gospodnetić, O. & McCandless, M., 2005. *Lucene in action.* Greenwich: Manning.

Holger, R., Stefan, F., Christoph, M. & Diana, P., 2009. *Ein Kriterienkatalog zur Bewertung von Anforderungsspezifikationen.* s.l., Softwaretechnik-Trends.

IFIA & CEOC, 2018. *TIC Federations Consumer Product Market Survey,* City of Brussles: IFIA & CEOC.

ISO, 2015. *2011-2015 ISO Strategic Plan.* [Online] Available at: https://www.iso.org/files/live/sites/isoorg/files/archive/pdf/en/iso_strategic_plan_2011-2015.pdf [Accessed 04 2021].

Nora, K. et al., 2008. *Model-Driven Web Engineering.* s.l., Upgrade - The European Journal for the Informatics Professional 9.2, p. 40–45.

OECD/EUIPO, 2019. Trends in Trade in Counterfeit and Pirated Goods, Illicit Trade., Paris: OECD Publishing.

produktpiraterie.org, 2020. *Datenbanken Geprüfter Produkte.* [Online] Available at: http://www.produktpiraterie.org/out.php?idart=70 [Accessed 21 07 2021].

Radu, G., Hinman, M. L. & Russo, R., 2015. *Elasticsearch in action.* s.l.:Manning.

RESEARCH AND MARKETS, 2018. *Global Brand Counterfeiting Report,* s.l.: RESEARCH AND MARKERTS.

SPLENDID RESEARCH GmbH, 2020. *Gütesiegel Monitor 2020,* Hamburg: SPLENDID RESEARCH GmbH.

SAASPORT MODEL: EXPLORING PROTOCOL PORTABILITY, RESOURCE ELASTICITY AND MICROSERVICE ARCHITECTURE IN THE EFFICIENT EXECUTION OF IOT APPLICATIONS

Maria Gisele Flores da Silveira[1], Wagner da Silva Silveira[1], Rodrigo da Rosa Righi[2], Cristiano André da Costa[2] and Dalvan Griebler[1,3]

[1]*Graduate Program in Cloud Computing: Infrastructures, Platforms and Services. Faculdade Três de Maio (SETREM) – Três de Maio – RS – Brazil*

[2]*Applied Computing Graduate Program – Unisinos University, Av. Unisinos 950 – São Leopoldo – RS – Brazil*

[3]*Pontificial Catholic University of Rio Grande do Sul (PUCRS), Av. Ipiranga 6681 – Porto Alegre – RS – Brazil*

ABSTRACT

Despite the high growth of the Internet of Things and the multitude of applications that use the information generated, it is estimated that 90 % of these data are not yet fully used. This is because IoT systems are based on heterogeneous networks and devices with resource restrictions, which cannot execute significant processing. So one of the alternatives that have been addressed is the use of cloud applications, where the data can be appropriately processed, stored, and analyzed. In the cloud, applications can then employ resource elasticity and be developed in microservice architectures. In state-of-the-art, the main efforts to provide portability and efficient treatment of IoT applications are described. However, a platform that provides protocol portability, resource elasticity using microservices architecture for the efficient execution of IoT applications has not yet been implemented. In this context, this work presents SaaSport, which among its contributions, will allow the efficient treatment of data generated by IoT devices that use the MQTT and CoAP protocols. The final result of this work demonstrates that the model provides an efficient treatment of the data generated in IoT environments.

KEYWORDS

IoT, Cloud Computing, MQTT, CoAP, Portability

1. INTRODUCTION

As described in [Pierleoni et al. 2020], the Internet of Things (IoT) aims to connect the real world composed of devices, sensors, and actuators to the virtual world to interconnect devices, generating information from the collected data. However, the devices, in general, have the computational power and limited storage capacity. Cloud computing allows access to a set of shared and configurable resources offered as services, with an almost unlimited capacity in terms of storage and computing. One of the main challenges faced in IoT is the high degree of heterogeneity in terms of the communication resources of the devices, protocols, technologies, and hardware [Yacchirema Vargas and Palau Salvador 2016], users and applications, to interpret the data of the devices need to know details of each protocol, which is not trivial, as it requires time. With each launch or upgrade of a protocol, there is a new learning effort.

With the continuous development and evolution of IoT, monolithic applications have become much more extensive and even more complex. This leads to low scalability, extensibility, and maintainability. In response to these challenges, the microservice architecture must be introduced in IoT applications due to its flexibility, light, and flexible coupling [Sun et al. 2017]. Still, there is a concern with software engineering and scalability so that the number of users and IoT devices do not interfere with the system's quality of service. As [Bansal and Kumar 2020] describe, the main concerns and research areas on IoT platforms are scalability, personalization, and security.

Studies carried out in the area focus on implementing gateways for the interconnection of devices with cloud environments that do not implement elasticity and have a monolithic architecture. These works explore the Message Queuing Telemetry Transport (MQTT), Constrained Application Protocol (CoAP) protocols, or specific application domains. Among the works, it is possible to mention [Dizdarevic´ et al. 2019], [Khaled and Helal 2019], and [Lai et al. 2019]. However, it is noted that the related works do not deal with the interoperability and interconnection of heterogeneous devices at the device, protocol, and data level. Moreover, as described [Lai et al. 2019], traditional centralized architectures do not have the necessary flexibility to deal with heterogeneous devices efficiently.

Among the gaps that the work seeks to fill are the efficient and high-performance treatment of communication portability for devices that use the protocols defined in the context of IoT networks. In this context, the SaaSport model was developed, a new middleware for IoT and cloud computing, which offers an abstraction layer of communication between devices using the MQTT and CoAP protocols, with Elasticity and Microservices so that through an API, it is possible for users to have access to information generated by devices and sensors, in the cloud. Thus, the objective of this work is to develop a model to allow the portability of the MQTT and CoAP protocols used in IoT. With this, it will be possible for users to access the data collected by the devices through an API available in the cloud, using microservices and elasticity.

This work is organized in a way. Section 2 presents related works. Subsequently, in section 3, the SaaSport model is described. Right after, in section 4, the model evaluation methodology is treated, where the aspects related to methods applied for model validation are specified. Furthermore, in sections 5 and 6, we present the experiments, conclusions, and perspectives of future works, respectively.

2. RELATED WORK

In this section, we present some initiatives, works, and solutions related to the proposed model. The works were selected based on the criteria: (I) origin IEEE1, ScienceDirect2, ResearchGate3, and ACM4, (II) publications in the period from 2016 to 2020, (III) search result for the keywords "Cloud Computing", "IoT", "MQTT", "CoAP", "Portability", "Interoperability" and "Microservices".

In the work of [Yacchirema Vargas and Palau Salvador 2016] a new Smart IoT Gateway was implemented, designed to allow interconnection and interoperability between heterogeneous devices in the IoT. The proposed gateway offers advantages such as: connectivity of different protocols and traditional communication technologies (Ethernet) and wireless (ZigBee, Bluetooth, Wi-Fi); uses a flexible protocol that translates all the data obtained from the different sensors into a uniform format, performing the analysis of the data obtained from the rules based on the environment related to the different types of sensors; uses a lightweight and ideal protocol for using devices with limited resources to provide an information environment; and provides local data storage for later use and analysis.

In [Martins et al. 2017] RAISe middleware was reengineered, proposing a new architecture with microservices and the use of cloud computing. The change envisaged an increase in the availability and reliability of the application. The authors point out that the resources offered by the cloud are practically unlimited and using load balancing and client redirection strategies, it is possible to provide middleware services around the clock for intelligent objects. Infrastructure automation is an essential tool to provide service elasticity. The infrastructure can be scaled to meet the specific needs of each microservice without affecting another microservice. The use of containers ensures the reproducibility of the software in the way the environment was defined. Another interesting aspect is that it allows the standardization of the service execution environment since aggregating other images construct the images.

[Sun et al. 2017] a general structure of the microservices system is proposed for the IoT application, which is a better scalable, extensible and sustainable architecture, the authors present the system design and related microservices and emphasize the leading service and communication of the device, from the service layer to the physical layer. It has a better ability to support interoperability and accommodate heterogeneous objects. In addition, this structure can quickly achieve more application integration, such as automation, intelligence, geographic service and Big Data.

The proposal by [Righi et al. 2018] includes a literature review, where the gap in addressing extensibility and interoperability in the IoT scenario is observed. The authors explored extensibility by providing an independent IoT protocol model, working with different communication models, including synchronous and asynchronous semantics. The scientific contribution appears in not providing another API but in maintaining the current ones, thus allowing communication between different technologies effortlessly. A prototype was developed that includes HTTP, MQTT, and CoAP technologies. The tests revealed a small overhead of IoT++ in the translation and forwarding of messages between the aforementioned protocols.

The structure proposed by [Pratik et al. 2018] provided a solution to the challenge of interoperability between objects that use the MQTT, CoAP protocols, and OIC data models. A client outside the network can obtain data from the sensor and actuator arriving at CoAP and sending GET and POST requests. In contrast, local clients (or actuators in the network) can obtain data from the MQTT broker through a topic subscription for taking local decisions. Since MQTT and CoAP have built-in security features, such as authentication, encryption, etc., they can add security and make the structure secure. Furthermore, as the data is stored in a tuple store database, SPARQL queries can be sent via CoAP requests in the future, assisting in troubleshooting.

In [Khaled and Helal 2019], the authors describe that systems research in the IoT is changing priorities to explore the explicit "architecture of things" that promote and allow friction-free interactions. They introduce the Atlas IoT communication structure, allowing interactions between things that speak similar or different communication protocols. The translator allows continuous communication between the CoAP, REST, HTTP, and MQTT protocols. A framework has been designed to facilitate interoperability between devices without taxing the performance of communicating homogeneously. The framework uses the concept of the topic and uses a meta-topic hierarchy to map and guide translations. The work described the architecture and a detailed benchmarking study measuring energy consumption and the characteristics of different aspects of the structure on real hardware platforms.

In the work of [Lai et al. 2019], the authors describe how microservice architectures can be adopted to create IoT services for multi-mobility in a smart city. Microservice architectures implement small, limited resources in a running process; Independent microservices can be deployed separately in a distributed system. An architectural draft has been proposed for general-purpose Internet of Things applications. Thanks to the choice of the microservice paradigm, the architecture can interact with a wide range of heterogeneous IoT devices while implementing scalability by design. On this basis, a Web application has been developed with a set of mobility services in mind for the multi-mobility of citizens in a smart city.

As described [Pamboris et al. 2020], due to the heterogeneity of devices, the complexity of developing applications requiring the collection and sharing of data across multiple IoT devices is high, as developers need to be familiar with a diverse set of services and supported APIs. The authors developed a flexible and lightweight middleware that offers a unified API to help develop applications that use multiple heterogeneous IoT devices. It abstracts much of the complexity involved in orchestrating different devices at run time. At the same time, it avoids the aforementioned warnings of existing approaches through a simple and efficient design, but one that offers a rich set of resources to developers.

This section presented the works related to the research, several possible solutions were verified. However, as described [Dizdarevic et al. 2019], current solutions are far from ideal, which creates challenges and exciting opportunities in new architectures that will undoubtedly need to combine IoT, Fog, and Cloud Computing systems to meet the requirements of future applications. In Table 1, it is possible to perceive a summary view of them, encompassing items such as capacities, protocols, and target architecture. Making a comparative analysis concerning the works related to this project, a gap is observed where there is still no proposal for portability of the MQTT and CoAP protocols using the elasticity of cloud resources and microservice architecture.

Table 1. Comparative analysis of related works

Ref.	Authors	MQTT	CoAP	Cloud	Elasticity	Arch
a	Y. Vargas e P. Salvador	Yes	Not	Yes	Not	Monolithic
b	Martins et al.	Not	Not	Yes	Not	Microservices
c	Sun et al.	Yes	Yes	Yes	Not	Microservices
d	Righi et al.	Yes	Yes	Not	Not	Monolithic
e	Pratik et al	Yes	Yes	Not	Not	Monolithic
f	Khaled e Helal	Yes	Yes	Yes	Not	Monolithic
g	Lai et al.	Yes	Yes	Yes	Not	Microservices
h	Pamboris et al.	Yes	Not	Não	Not	Monolithic

3. SAASPORT MODEL

This section introduces the SaaSport model, which will explore the portability of protocols, resource elasticity, and microservice architecture for efficient execution of IoT applications. To describe it adequately, this section has been divided into three other subsections. Section 4.1 presents the project decisions, in section 4.2, the proposed architecture is presented, which has as a legacy the models described in the section of related works, which incorporated the concept of microservices and scalability, and the description of the other definitions of configuration in the development of the work. Finally, section 4.3 demonstrates how the model works.

3.1 Project Decisions

It is relevant that the data collected by IoT devices are available for general purposes. However, a platform that provides protocol portability, resource elasticity using microservices architecture for the efficient execution of IoT applications has not yet been implemented. With this it is expected to contribute by modeling the SaaSport platform in which the data collected by the IoT devices are made available in the cloud through an API, which in order to break the structural paradigm of monolithic systems, using microservices, which are an architectural and organizational model of development in which software is composed of small independent services, in architecture with a high level of interoperability and elasticity, to develop an advanced model and significantly add to the studies and proposals for the integration of IoT and Cloud Computing.

The model is a SaaS, as it will provide a service that explores the portability of IoT protocols, resource elasticity, and microservice architecture for the efficient execution of the data processing generated in IoT applications. The MQTT Broker and CoAP server are expected to send all messages collected on their networks to the cloud using a Gateway. The Gateway will subscribe to the MQTT topics and use the CoAP Observer (RFC 7641), to get the messages and relay them to the cloud via the HTTP protocol. The data will be received in the cloud through the API Gateway, responsible for forwarding the data through the MQTT-messages and COAP-messages queues, processed and translated by the MQTT Translator and CoAP Translator microservices. After being processed, the data is sent to the store-messages queue, where the Store Messages microservice will receive and persist such messages in the InfluxDb database. Then the messages will be available so that users and external applications can read data from different IoT environments through a single REST API.

3.2 Architecture

Microservices form the basis of the architecture, are the managers of the business data and provide a REST API to other services interested in consuming information made available by them. Among the functions that the architecture will perform are: (a) collecting the messages exchanged by the IoT devices, (b) forwarding the messages, (c) processing and translating the data, (d) making the data available through an API. In order to illustrate how the communication between microservices will be implemented, Figure 1 was designed, highlighting the main components present in the model, as well as which actions each of them will trigger. In Figure 2, the most detailed architecture of the proposed solution can be seen. In which the IoT devices, allocated in their respective environments, will send the data to the Gateway, which will therefore handle the data in the cloud architecture, and make the data available through the model API for users and applications. The cloud architecture implements elasticity, replicating the instances according to the use of the service.

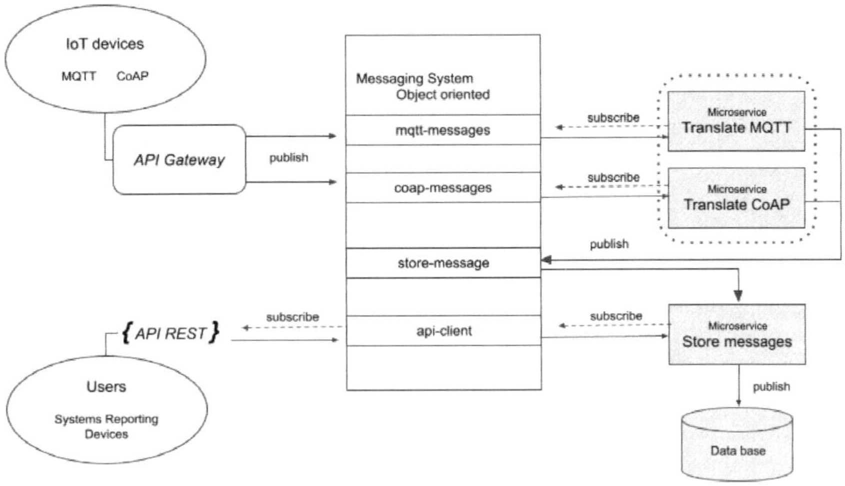

Figure 1. Proposal communication model

3.3 Operation

Data processing consists of performing tasks in the SaaSport model. The platform is designed to abstract the capture of messages through a Gateway, which makes publications in a queue, and will forward the data of each of the queues to be processed by the microservice that implements its due treatment. The components for communicating the model are detailed below:

1. API Gateway - responsible for transmitting messages collected to the cloud, using the HTTP protocol.
2. RabbitMQ - an open-source messaging server, which will control requests in queues during processing. There are 5 queues on the server, which are:
    a. mqtt-messages - stores the messages that will be consumed by the MQTT message translation microservice.
    b. coap-messages - stores the messages that will be consumed by the CoAP message translation microservice.
    c. store-messages - queue containing messages normalized to the key-value pattern, which will be consumed by the microservice responsible for storage.
    d. api-client - queue containing Rest API requests.
3. Translate CoAP - microservice responsible for processing data received by CoAP devices.
4. Translate MQTT - microservice responsible for processing data received by MQTT device.
5. Store Messages - microservice responsible for recording messages handled by Translates.
6. API Rest - responsible for making the data treated by the model available.

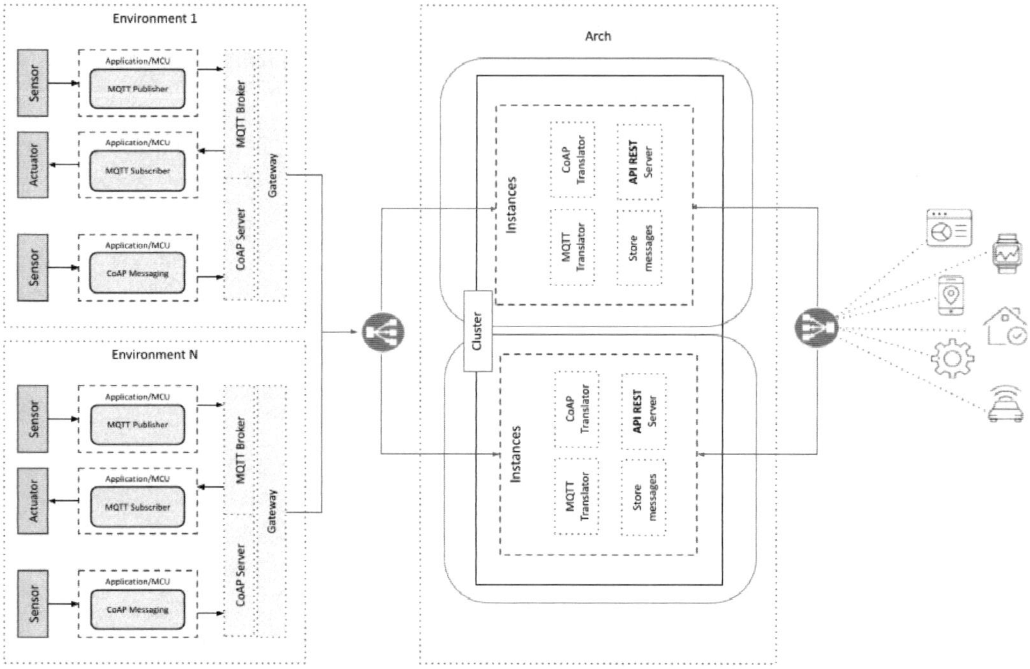

Figure 2. Architecture of the proposed solution

In order to represent the best functioning, the sequence diagram of the functioning of the model was drawn in Figure 3. In which "IoT devices" will trigger HTTP POST requests to the "gateway", which will add the request to "queue", the records in the queue will be processed and translated by "translation", will be returned to the "queue" and then stored in the "store". API Clients users will make HTTP GET requests for "endpoint", which will immediately go to the "queue" that will communicate with the database ("store") and return to the user.

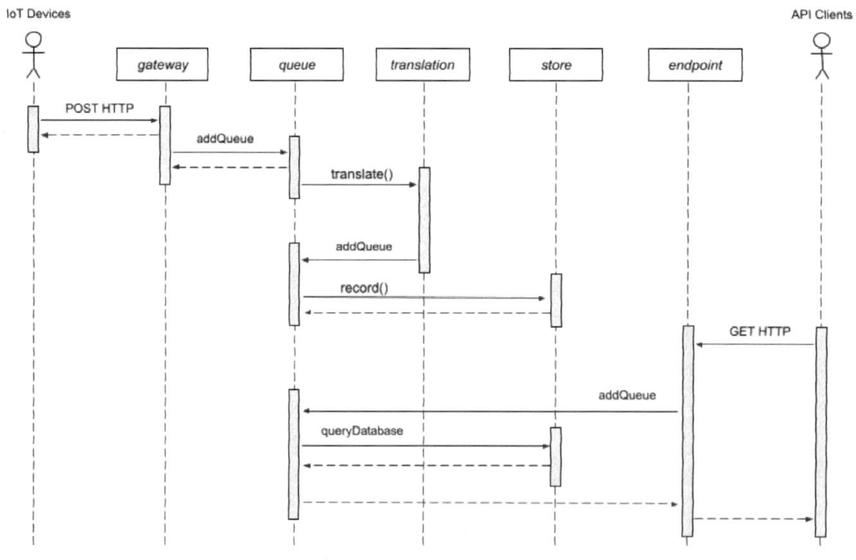

Figure 3. Sequence diagram referring to the message exchanges of the SaaSport model

4. EVALUATION METHODOLOGY

In this section, the evaluation method of the SaaSport model was documented. The section was divided into 5 parts. Where in section 5.1 the prototype is presented, in section 5.2 the infrastructure used in the tests was detailed. In section 5.3, the input data was segmented, in the sequence in section 5.4, the metrics for evaluating the model were defined. And to limit the scope of the test, the test scenarios were defined in section 5.5.

4.1 Prototype

The SaaSport model was implemented in the JavaScript language, in the multiplatform Node.js, according to details described in the model description section. The prototype had its implementation definitions made based on the technologies that have been widely used in the implementation of services in the cloud. A public Git repository was created for this work and made available at the URL <https://github.com/wagnerdevel/tcc-cloud-computing>, containing: (i) readme explaining the repository; (ii) The file structure with the source code of the architecture and experiments; (iii) Presentation (slides) of the work; (iv) Other links and support material.

4.2 Infrastructure

The model was implemented in the public cloud provider Amazon Web Services (AWS), which like [Pierleoni et al. 2020] describes one of the end-to-end Cloud-IoT platforms that currently lead the global market. Using Amazon Elastic Compute Cloud (Amazon EC2), configured with 1 instance of type T2.micro, which has 1 CPU and 1 GB of RAM, with a storage size of 8 GB. To monitor the services and generate the results, Amazon CloudWatch was used, which collects monitoring and operations data in logs, metrics and events, offering a unified view of the AWS resources, applications, and services executed. Communication between microservices uses the RabbitMQ messaging system through Amazon MQ. The data will be stored in InfluxDB, an open-source time-series database developed by InfluxData. This is optimized for fast, high availability storage and retrieval of time series data in monitoring operations, application metrics, sensor data, and real-time analysis.

ECS Auto Scaling provided the elasticity from AWS. Such service was configured using scalability policies in stages and also two CloudWatch alarms. The alarms observe a single metric of CPU utilization and send messages to EC2 Auto Scaling when the metric violates the defined threshold, thus determining when to scale the group. For example, to expand the auto-scaling group's capacity, a threshold higher than 60% of the average CPU utilization was considered. When this 60% is exceeded, an alarm will be generated for EC2 Auto Scaling, which will execute the expansion policy, adding two units of capacity to the group. The reduction in the capacity of the auto-scaling group, on the other hand, was considered a threshold below 40% of the average CPU utilization. When the CPU usage is less than 40%, an alarm will be generated for EC2 Auto Scaling, which will execute the reduction policy, removing a unit of capacity from the group.

4.3 Input Data

To validate the model, experiments were performed simulating a network of IoT devices. In which the exchange of messages is carried out, of the MQTT and CoAP application layer protocols. For testing purposes, loads were generated using scripts developed in Python with the Locust library, which represented the test scenarios, and executed in the clustered environment created on the Google Cloud Platform.

4.4 Evaluation Metrics

Metrics are ways of measuring variables and trends in behavior over a period of time, using the data collected to assess the performance of a model. In order to evaluate the SaaSport model, the metrics referring to the input data, CPU utilization, latency and average throughput were considered, observing the quality of the service with the exponential increase of the environments.

4.5 Test Scenarios

The test scenarios were designed to generate upward, downward and undulating loads. The parameters regarding the number of requisitions and scale were modified in each scenario in different periods. The following are highlighted the scenarios created to validate the model:

1. Ascending scenario where the number of requests was gradually increased during the test period.
2. Descending scenario - where the number of requests was gradually reduced during the test period.
3. Ripple scenario - where the number of requisitions was gradually increased and reduced during the test period.

5. RESULTS

To obtain the results, the SaaSport model was implemented and subjected to a battery of tests simulating IoT environments through scripts, as described in the evaluation methodology section. The data flow in the architecture was monitored with a simple load and verified through the logs if the information was following what was expected. The API Gateway abstracts the acquisition of raw data from the IoT networks to the cloud. It then sends the formatted data to the translator microservice queue, according to the application layer protocol of the request. The data is then translated and stored. The input data are created arbitrarily by each test user to simulate the data generated by IoT sensors in JSON format obtained by the gateway.

According to Auto Scaling Group policies, the prototype was configured to use a limit of up to 8 EC2 instances. The test scenarios submitted to the model obtained the results described below. The graphs of each test contain the Input data, CPU utilization, and Total instances, where it is possible to observe the behavior typical to the scenarios submitted. The X-axis of the graphs represents the interval at which the test was performed. In the Data Entry and Return Return Data graphs, the Y axis represents the number of Bytes of the loads, for which the blue line in the center traces the exact number of Bytes in each instant, which increased and decreased respectively. In the CPU Utilization graph, the Y-axis represents the percentage of usage. Moreover, in the Total Instances graph, the Y-axis represents the number of instances.

To compare the proposed model, tests were also carried out in an environment with no elasticity, composed of only one instance of type T2.micro. With the test load generated in this environment, it was possible to visualize that the latency increased according to the number of requests per second. When reaching the number of 2447 requests per second, downtime occurred. The tests performed with the scenarios previously defined in an environment configured with elasticity are presented below.

1 - Ascending scenario - the scenario that reached 10,000 users by firing requests simultaneously was configured. The test started with one user, and ten new users (spawn rate) were added per second. The result of the execution of this test scenario can be seen in Figure 4. The graphs of CPU Utilization and Total instances indicate that as the percentage of CPU utilization increased, new instances were added according to the expansion policy. Furthermore, as the CPU usage dropped, the reduction policy was implemented, reducing the number of instances by one unit.

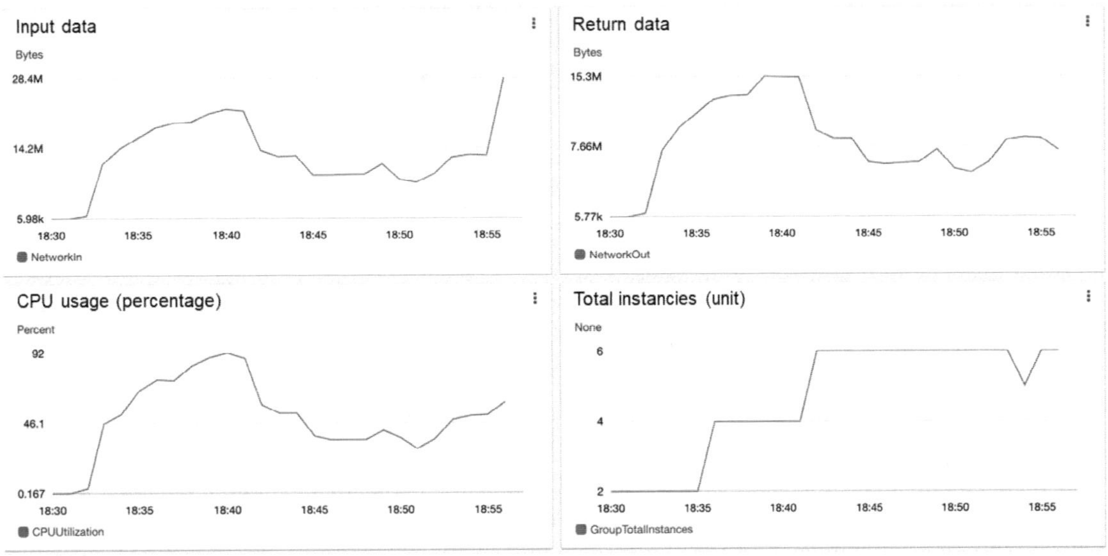

Figure 4. Bottom-up scenario: Input data, CPU usage and Total instances

2 - Descending scenario - the scenario that started with 10,000 users firing requests simultaneously was configured. This scenario gradually reduced the number of users during the test period until there were no more users. As shown in Figure 5, as the number of users was reduced, the CPU usage was also freed up, and, consequently, the number of instances was reduced by the reduction policy. At the end of the test, the auto-scaling group contained only one EC2 instance.

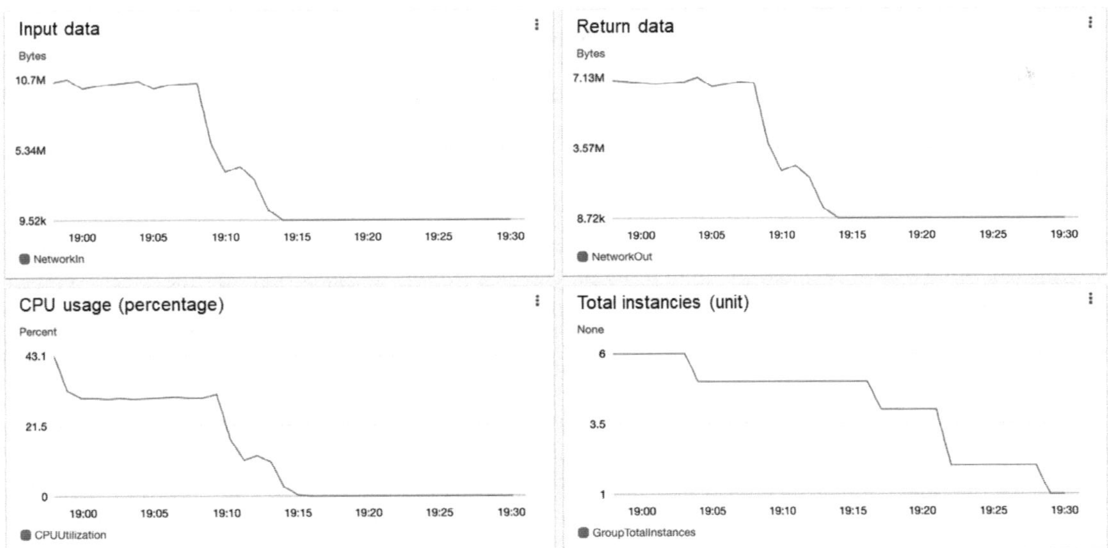

Figure 5. Descending scenario: Input data, CPU usage and Total instances

3 - Ripple scenario - where the number of requests was gradually increased and reduced during the test period, always starting from 1 user, increasing up to 5,000 users and reducing again to 1 user. Figure 6 shows the variation of loads in a wavy shape, where it is possible to observe the increase and reduction of CPU and, in parallel, the increase and reduction in the number of instances.

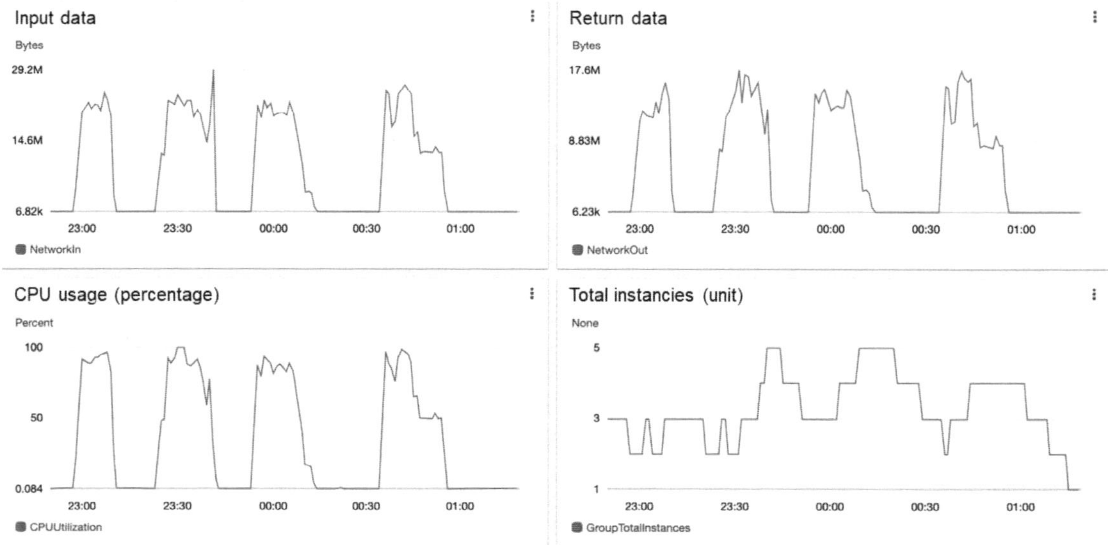

Figure 6. Ripple scenario: Input data, CPU usage and Total instances

As requests increased, the response time also increased, and the Auto Scaling Group added new instances. The creation of a new instance takes about 300 seconds. With that, some periods had requests without sufficient resources to attend them. Then, from the total number of requests made, an average of 1.67% of these failed was calculated due to packet losses in the interval in which the EC2 instances were created. Even with the increase in the number of requests, there was also an increase in latency. With 200 requests per second, the average latency was 42 milliseconds, and with 500 requests per second, the latency increased to 91 milliseconds, disregarding the failed requests.

The final result of this work demonstrates that the model provides efficient treatment of data generated in IoT environments, which use the MQTT and CoAP application layer protocols. However, the cloud environment could be improved using a proactive elasticity approach to predict the need for resource allocation to better meet requests.

6. CONCLUSION

This work aimed to present a proposal to allow messages from IoT devices that use the MQTT and CoAP protocols to be processed and made available through a cloud API so that the portability of the information collected by the model is provided. The existing technologies to be developed in this context have a high level of complexity, and the integration of these technologies requires several validation tests. The analysis and evaluation of these are possible through real implementations, mathematical models, and simulators.

Given the specificities, this work carried out the implementation and control of the MQTT and CoAP protocols, which have been mentioned in studies and widely used in IoT systems, whether in devices with limitations, with low power consumption and in general-purpose devices, with higher processing power and higher energy consumption. The microservice model supports the addition of new services to the architecture without compromising other functions, scalability of the solution, and a high level of resilience.

Concerning research, it is noted that much is being done to boost the implementation of IoT applications. As future work, the knowledge obtained through the development of this work can be considerably expanded through the implementation of other application layer protocols that have been used in IoT devices, the scalability of the scenarios where the experiments were carried out can be further explored a security policy was developed for accessing information.

ACKNOWLEDGEMENT

The authors would like to thank to the following Brazilian agencies: CNPq, CAPES and FAPERGS.

REFERENCES

Alphonsa, M. (2021). A review on iot technology stack, architecture and its cloud applications in recent trends. In Kumar, A. and Mozar, S., editors, ICCCE 2020, pages 703–711, Singapore. Springer Singapore.

Bansal, S. and Kumar, D. (2020). IoT Ecosystem: A Survey on Devices, Gateways, Operating Systems, Middleware and Communication. International Journal of Wireless Information Networks, 27(3):340–364.

Castro, T. F. S., Vale, F. G. M., and Sousa, F. H. F. (2021). Microsserviços/microservices.

Brazilian Journal of Development, 21829.

Chandrasekaran, K. (2014). Essentials of Cloud Computing. Chapman & Hall/CRC, 1st edition.

Dizdarevic´, J., Carpio, F., Jukan, A., and Masip-Bruin, X. (2019). A survey of communication protocols for internet of things and related challenges of fog and cloud computing integration. ACM Comput. Surv., 51(6).

Kavis, M. (2014). Architecting the Cloud: Design Decisions for Cloud Computing Service Models (SaaS, PaaS, and IaaS). Wiley CIO. Wiley.

Khaled, A. E. and Helal, S. (2019). Interoperable communication framework for bridging restful and topic-based communication in iot. Future Generation Computer Systems, 92:628 – 643.

Lai, C., Boi, F., Buschettu, A., and Caboni, R. (2019). Iot and microservice architecture for multimobility in a smart city. In 2019 7th International Conference on Future Internet of Things and Cloud (FiCloud), pages 238–242.

Martins, L. M. C. e., Filho, F. L. d. C., Júnior, R. T. d. S., Giozza, W. F., and da Costa,

J. a. P. C. (2017). Increasing the dependability of iot middleware with cloud computing and microservices. In Companion Proceedings of The10th International Conference on Utility and Cloud Computing, UCC '17 Companion, page 203–208, New York, NY, USA. Association for Computing Machinery.

Nast, M., Rother, B., Golatowski, F., Timmermann, D., Leveling, J., Olms, C., and Nissen, C. (2020). Work-in-progress: Towards an international data spaces connector for the internet of things. In 2020 16th IEEE International Conference on Factory Communication Systems (WFCS), pages 1–4.

Pamboris, A., Kozis, C., and Herodotou, H. (2020). Cuttlefish: A flexible and lightweight middleware for combining heterogeneous iot devices. In 2020 IEEE 17th Annual Consumer Communications Networking Conference (CCNC), pages 1–6.

Pierleoni, P., Concetti, R., Belli, A., and Palma, L. (2020). Amazon, google and microsoft solutions for iot: Architectures and a performance comparison. IEEE Access, 8:5455– 5470.

Pratik, T., Lenka, R. K., Nayak, G. K., and Kumar, A. (2018). An architecture to support interoperability in iot devices. In 2018 International Conference on Advances in Computing, Communication Control and Networking (ICACCCN), pages 705–710.

Righi, R. (2013). Elasticidade em cloud computing: conceito, estado da arte e novos desafios. Revista Brasileira de Computação Aplicada, 5(2):2–17.

Righi, R. R., Suad, F., Costa, C. A. d., and Bertoldi, M. M. G. a. L. R. (2018). Exploring extensibility and interoperability in the internet of things landscape. pages 339–343.

Rubí, J. N. S. and Gondim, P. R. L. (2020). Iot-based platform for environment data sharing in smart cities. International Journal of Communication Systems, e4515.

Sun, L., Li, Y., and Memon, R. A. (2017). An open iot framework based on microservices architecture. China Communications, 14(2):154–162.

Villaca, L., Azevedo, L., and Jr, A. (2018). Construindo Aplicações Distribuídas com Microsserviços. pages 1–40.

Yacchirema Vargas, D. C. and Palau Salvador, C. E. (2016). Smart iot gateway for heterogeneous devices interoperability. IEEE Latin America Transactions, 14(8):3900–3906.

IMPROVING KNOWLEDGE MANAGEMENT USING WIKI TOOL THROUGH EXPERIMENTAL STUDIES

Bruno A. Bonifacio, Raquel Cunha, Franciney Lima, Luis H. P. Albuquerque, Marcelo S. Ayres, Fernanda Souza, Ana M. Moreno and Erika S. Muniz
Sidia Institute of Science and Technology
Manaus – Amazonas, Brazil

ABSTRACT

Nowadays, companies are paying more attention to the importance of knowledge creation and sharing. In this sense, the use of information systems to assist knowledge management has been widely adopted by organizations. In this paper, we present an experience report on how, by using Wiki, we were able to assist in knowledge sharing and also ease of acquiring knowledge, especially for onboarding employees. Before this study was conducted, company already used Wiki as a means of knowledge sharing. However, employees still faced difficulties in acquiring knowledge shared through Wiki, such as a lack of a definite structure for creating and sharing content. After conducting this study, we were able to define main difficulties faced by employees and propose a new solution. From results obtained, it was possible to facilitate knowledge creation and exchange among employees by re-designing how information was shared through Wiki. This work has an important contribution in how the company can rapidly accumulate knowledge capital and enhance the quality of staff, and as such, enhance its competitiveness.

KEYWORDS

Transfer Technology, Sharing Technology, Wiki, Experimental Studies

1. INTRODUCTION

In current technological market environments, knowledge is a valuable resource for competitive advantage of an organization. Despite companies' efforts to retain employees, in recent years, the number of job offers for professionals of any field is increasing (Bauer *et al.* 2010). It is common that from massive demands on software projects, there is the need to incorporate new team members. In this scenario, companies that able to properly manage knowledge and become cost-effective or innovative can survive in the long run. For this reason, companies have been giving great importance to knowledge generation and sharing, using social media technologies in parallel to training and education (Zanatta *et al.* 2017). However, newcomers usually need more time to become acquainted with projects.

Although training can be the fasted and most effective way to improve employee performance, newly hired usually still encounter difficulties such as process misunderstanding, low learning curve, and other issues that cause expectation breakdowns (Mansour *et al.* 2011). The onboard period needs to be most effective to improve new employees' performance aiming to acquire job skills as fast as possible.

In this context, Wiki usage, as social media technology approach, has introduced an effective way of collaboration, communication, and knowledge sharing, especially in distributed environments (Cunha *et al.* 2020). Due to collaborative features, Wiki technology can offer users the opportunity to deconstruct and reconstruct expertise in a manner that allows for organic knowledge growth and self-correction (Biswas, *et al.* 2017). Furthermore, the social engineering principles of Wiki combined with training can reduce onboarding period, reduce costs and mistakes, and maximize productivity.

Inspired by this, we present how we improved the knowledge management and sharing process through experimental studies from our Sidia Institute of Technology, using Wiki. At first, we executed an exploratory study to identify difficulties and usability issues faced by newcomers during interaction with Wiki. Afterward, we conducted an observational study to identify learning process of newcomers and we use their feedback to group by knowledge categories during re-designing the wiki's structure. The aim of this paper is share how we re-designing of Wiki pages used by our team by grouping knowledge in categories that we believe can have a direct and indirect effect on participation of newcomers on collaboration process. We hope this experience report can encourage companies to adopt social media technologies to improve the knowledge management process and also to contribute to a better onboarding process.

This paper is structured as follows: Section 2 provides some related works and description of our company Sidia. Section 3 describes studies realized to identify improvements and understand users' interaction with wiki. In Section 4, we present results achieved and re-designing proposed using the new Wiki version. Section 5 concludes and shows some future directions.

2. IMPROVING WIKI THROUGH EXPERIMENTAL STUDIES

To some extent, newcomers usually need to learn social and technical aspects by themselves, exploiting existing information in mailing lists, source code repositories, and issue managers (Mahmood, 2015). Furthermore, newcomers may not receive enough training or may not have intimate knowledge of the practices they are normally trained to follow (Heredia *et al.*,2017).

In this context, tools are essential for collaboration among team members, enabling communication, and knowledge management with more effectiveness (Kanakis, 2019). For this reason, some tools can support as much communication, coordination, documentation as knowledge management, especially in Global Software Development (GSD) environment.

In this sense, several investigations have focused on understanding how tools can improve collaboration, communication and knowledge management. Due to cost reduction, companies have been adopting Wiki as alternative for knowledge management (Avram *et al.* 2017; Bao *et al.* 2019; Portillo-Rodriguez, 2012). According to related works, Wiki is an important resource for knowledge management. However, when Wiki has several information, users can face difficulty to use and this scenario can be a problem during the onboarding process.

Sidia is a R&D Institute, responsible for improvements on the Android Platform of Samsung products in all Latin America. As we work in a distributed environment, we have been adopting Wiki as an alternative for knowledge management. In Wiki, we provide information about project processes, tools used, focal points of each telephony partner, stages of the software development process etc. However, we observed that novice project leaders (PLs) faced great difficulty in using the Wiki due to a large amount of information, and difficulty to use and explore information access.

For this reason, we performed experimental studies to identify difficulties faced by our newcomers and another study aimed to understand how they solve problems. We use results from these studies to group knowledge in categories that we believe can have a direct and indirect effect on the participation of newcomers on collaboration process. In the next section we describe two studies already realized showing how these studies were useful to re-design Wiki pages' structure used by the team.

2.1 First Experimental Study

The first study, detailed in Cunha *et al.* (2020), we aimed to identify difficulties faced by our team. During newcomer onboarding process, new members received basic trainings related work activities and we used the first version of all activities described in Wiki as reference. However, they reported several difficulties to find information, tutorials related to process and PL activities.

In this sense, we designed our first experimental study to evaluate Wiki content used for knowledge transfer from the perspective of new project leaders by Sidia. In this scenario we designed the study, to collect data using an online questionnaire.

Table 1. First study results (Cunha et al. 2020)

Experimenta Design	Summary Results
Participants	We chose 24 volunteer participants of the PL team by convenience. These participants were composed of only newcomers and only had initial experience with Sidia project processes.
Indicators	To evaluate the quality of use and acceptance when participants interacted with wiki, we analyzed perceived usefulness and perceived ease of use indicators within the Technology Acceptance Model – TAM (Davis, 1989). This model is focused on aspects that are strongly correlated to user acceptance of a given technology.
Results	We decide to collect information about frequency of usage Wiki to understand if information provided in Wiki is adequate and useful to assist newcomers. Considering **ease of use**, 42% reported that they had difficulty with Wiki content presentation, and another 32% considered Wiki easy to find information. Considering useful perception, 76% of users reported as positive results.

The results were useful to identify usability issues, outdated content, gaps in training that affecting their onboarding process. We used results to resolve usability issues and update some wiki contents. As contributions of this study we create a Wiki template content, based on 5H2W model. This new approach was useful to help newcomers associated Wiki content to work process.

Other important contribution of this study was training program. During pandemic period, we adopted a platform that allows online training can be recorded to access any time. Since hence, we decided to realize a qualitative study regarding the participants' interaction with Wiki and their learning process strategy. We took such decision aiming to obtain a more accurate result. Thus, we can combine quantitative and qualitative data to better understand the identified problems.

2.2 Second Experimental Study

Despite results from first study, we decided to collect qualitative opinions to understand which features could be improved to facilitate knowledge transfer, as well as which problems could be compromising learnability. In addition, we aimed to collect learning strategies adopted by newcomers during the onboarding period. During study execution, we applied a questionnaire asking for subjects' opinions regarding their improvement. The questionnaire was made available for a week.

Table 2. Second study results (Lima et al. 2020)

Experimenta Design	Summary Results
Participants	By convenience we use same 24 volunteer participants of the PL team.
Indicators	To analyze the data collected we used Grounded Theory procedures - GT (Mills, 2006). We used this method to build knowledge about improvements in Wiki and to identify relationships between subjects reported and some items. We extracted qualitative data and coding using data reported by PLs. Then, codes found in questionnaires were grouped according to their properties, thus forming concepts that represent categories. For the analysis of inspector's interaction with technique, the following categories were defined: Learning Strategies, Wiki Issues, Improvements and Ideas.
Results	Considering learning strategies, we can observe that despite trainings and content, new PLs prefer asking experienced colleagues. Related to Wiki issues, we identified some problems that affect learning experience by new PLs, such as duplicated pages, dropped processes, some terms not clear and others related issues. Considering improvement and new ideas, the most important contribution of this study was related usability improvements.

The findings of second study, detailed in Lima *et al.* (2020), were important to improve our training methods during the integration phase of newcomers. Also, we adopted a mentoring program, where experienced members have been responsible to assist new members during onboarding process. We improved Wiki training section creating a quick start guide, specific for newcomers. Based on the results obtained, we created categories divided by: process, tutorials, FAQs and useful information.

Results were important to create an approach for redesigning Wiki content. Thus, we developed a proposal for a new Wiki version. In next section we present 2nd Wiki version, based on contributions and show that collaboration was maximized. Also, we present improvements applied on previous studies.

3. CONTRIBUTIONS OF EXPERIMENTAL STUDIES

Understanding obstacles that affect sharing and transfer of knowledge is the first step in identifying potential solutions. We used experimental studies to identify and understand difficulties faced by new team members. The main difficulty reported by newcomers was related Wiki organization. For this reason, as contribution of first study, we also proposed a template with good practices and content structure, following the 5W2H method to facilitate learning, importance of each page and process related to that page. Other improvements, as second study results, were improving training programs, using online platform.

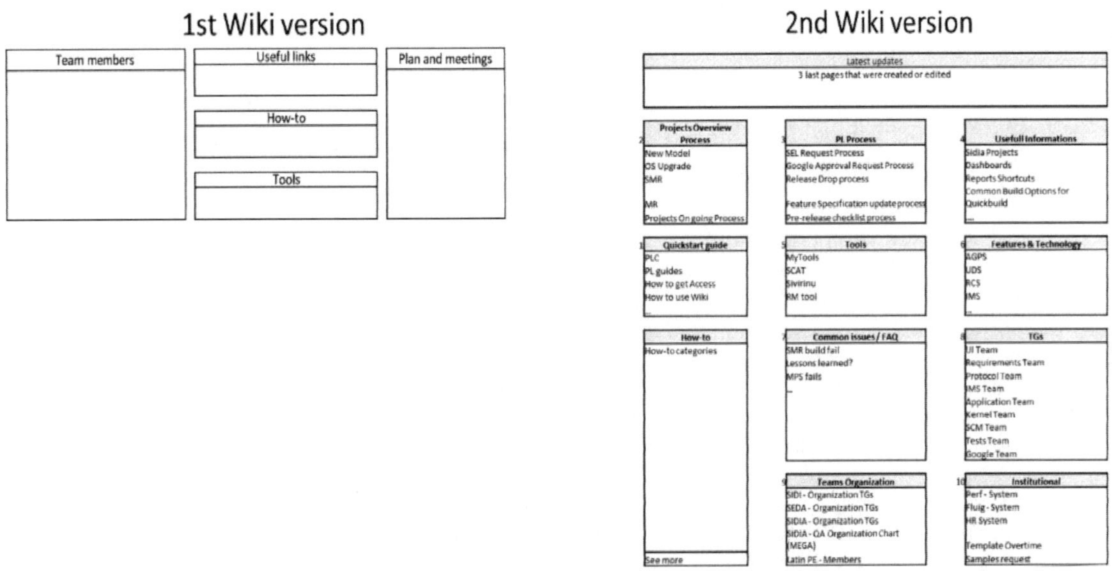

Figure 1. Changes applied from version 1 to version 2

Despite this organization, new members still had difficulties finding the desired information. For this reason, we organized content by considering knowledge groups during the re-designing of Wiki. We organized considering 10 categories, as shown in Figure 1.

Figure 1 shows difference between Wiki versions. In the first Wiki version information was grouped into following categories: useful links, how-to, quickstart guide, tools, team members and plan & meetings. Useful links category presented information related to software process, roles and responsibilities, organizational charts, glossary, trainings, reports shortcuts and others. How-to category presented information related to tutorials and others rules to process execution by PLs. Quickstart guide is a specific category created to newcomers, in this section we grouped contents related to documentation, glossary, organizations, common issues, trainings and others recommending tasks that are appropriate for newcomers. Tools category presented information, tutorials and some FAQs related to automation tools used by PL team members. Plan and meetings presented information related projects schedule and some milestones.

Based on the difficulties reported by new members, we categorized them by considering knowledge groups, process, tutorials, useful information and quick start guide for newcomers, as showed in Figure 2. These modifications improved access and search for content. In the first version, PLs related difficulty to find specific contents.

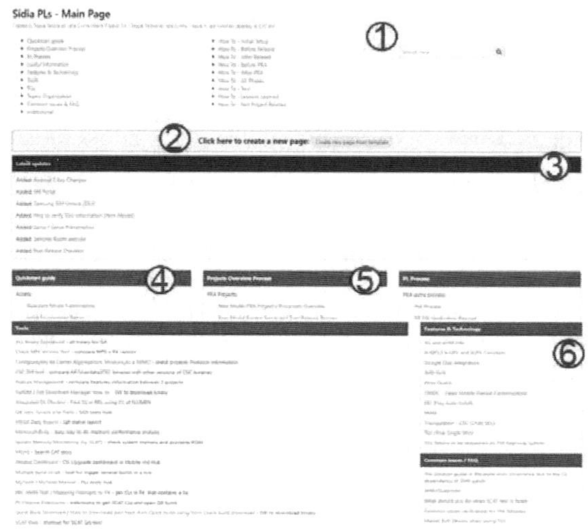

Figure 2. Overview of new Wiki page version

In the second version, grouping knowledge by common content made it easy to find specific content because we grouped the information by considering: process, how to do, useful links for each content (See point 2.1 from Figure 2). This field assists to search new contents and others that were not indexed by the main page. Also we create a template for new pages (See point 2.2 from Figure 2) to help newcomers create or update Wiki content. In addition, we created two extra sections: latest modification to help PLs to identify recent pages updated and a search field (Figure 2.3).

This grouping was useful to define learning pattern where newcomers can see from a macro perspective, considering process overview to understand how we work on projects scope. After that we present tutorials with steps to perform each activity for each process chosen by the new PL (Figure 2.4). To finish, we present information and details related to each process such as FAQs, lessons learned, known issues and quick start showing how to resolve each issue (Figure 2.5-2.6).

As important contribution was related to views and collaboration to improve new Wiki pages. After releasing new Wiki version, we collected log information to check how the new Wiki design can substantially influence collaboration and engagement. We extracted logs from March 2020 to December of 2020, see Figure 3.

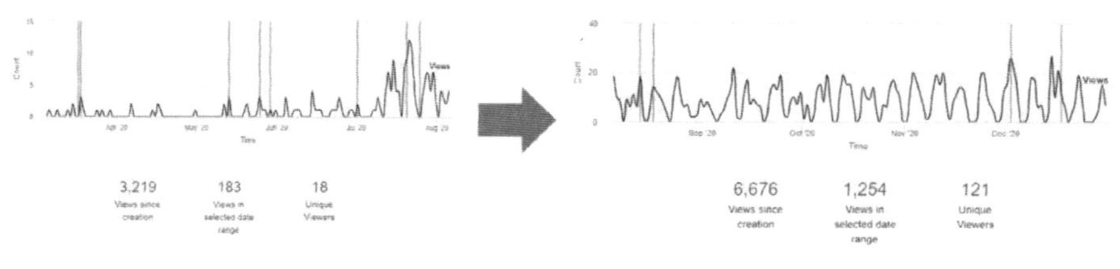

Figure 3. Rate of collaboration by newcomers after new Wiki version released

We observe that collaboration was maximized. Some factors can influence collaboration such as: learning process. As the new PLs learn a particular process or activity, they can also collaborate by updating information related to process, pages and tutorials. We can observe increasing rate of collaboration by unique viewers. This rate can be explained by modifications related improvements done by newly PLs. Despite newcomers have to depend on others to guide or train them to execute their duties, it is too important to have a main knowledge repository, such as Wiki. However, this process can be effective only if the knowledge content is well structured. Thus, the results can be considered an indicator that during onboarding process, newcomers can collaborate more efficiency with repository well organized.

4. CONCLUSION

This paper presented an extension of studies performed on Wiki, where we collected information about how newcomers learned as relates to working process at Sidia R&D Institute. Previous works, described in detailed at Cunha et al. (2020) and Lima et al. (2020), presented quantitative and qualitative results related Wiki usage by newcomers. In the first study we presented an overview about difficulties faced by new PLs during onboarding process at Sidia, specifically about knowledge transfer. In the second study, we presented a qualitative analysis, results and improvements made as contribution of the quantitative analysis.

Considering Wiki issues, we observed that most issues are related to usability and content structure. As improvement we restructured content by dividing them into sections by common knowledge (Cunha et al. 2020). Considering learning strategies, we can assume see that new PLs learned most effectively with experienced colleagues (Lima et al. 2020). In this case, we proposed recorded training sessions and shared specific pages to new PLs. Considering Improvements, we created a team which is in charge of controlling and managing Wiki content and as future work, we are planning new actions such as games and workshops to improve integration by newly PLs thus, promoting more contribution by these newcomers in Wiki content presentation.

Based on these results we are redesigning the Wiki content. However, another interesting aspect to be investigated as future work is how to minimize the impact of newcomers misunderstanding during integration in the company. In our case, we applied Wiki, but it is possible to recommend a set of data analytics based on the learning of developer profiles. However, it is an aspect that still needs further investigation.

Thus, we will replicate this study after improvement and compare the results with this work. We expect that with this experience report, we have shown, through practical examples, that it is possible to improve the learning process of newcomers in a GSD environment. In addition, we intend to encourage software development industry to improve knowledge transfer to improve newcomers' onboarding to better support difficulties faced by them.

ACKNOWLEDGEMENT

Our thanks, in the terms of the Informatics Law N° 8387/91.

REFERENCES

Avram, G. 2017. "Knowledge Wok Practises in Global Software Development," inECKM2007- Proceedings of the 8th European Conference on Knowledge Management, Barcelona, Spain, p 87-97.

Bauer, T. N. 2010. Onboarding New Employees: Maximizing Success. In The Society for Human Resource Management Foundation (SHRM), VA, USA (2010), p 234-245.

Bao, L. et al., 2019. "A large scale study of long-time contributor prediction for GitHub projects," in: IEEE Transactions on Software Engineering. 1 – 22, Vol 1.

Biswas, S. 2017. Adoption of Knowledge Management Systems: A Study on How Wiki Systems Should Be Adopted by Minimizing the Risk of Failure. In Journal of Information and Knowledge Management 7 (7), 1-7.

Cunha. et al. 2020. How do newcomers learn work process in Global Software Development (GSD)? A survey study from the perspective of newly project leaders. in Proceedings of the 15th International Conference on Global Software Engineering, 2020, pp. 117–121.

Davis. 1989. Perceived usefulness, perceived ease of use, and user acceptance of information technology. MIS Quaterly, 319-339.

Heredia, A. et al., 2017. "Tool-supported continuous business process innovation: a case study in globally distributed software teams" European J. International Management, pp. 388 - 405.

Kanakis, 2019. "Supporting a flexible grouping mechanism for collaborating engineering teams" in: Proceedings of the 14th International Conference on Global Software Engineering. p 20-31.

Lima, et al. 2020, Identify Difficulties in the Knowledge Transfer Process in Global Software: A qualitative Analysis. XIX International Conference WWW/Internet – ICWI 2020, p 20-28.

Mansour, M. Abu Salah, and L. Askenäs, 2011. "Wiki Collaboration in Organizations : An Exploratory Study", presented at the 19th European Conference in Information Systems, Helsinki, Finland. p 20-31.

Mahmood Niazi et al., 2015. "Empirical investigation of the challenges of the existing tools used in global software development projects" IET software, vol. Vol 9, p. 135 – 143.

Mills, J., Ann, B., Karen, F. 2006. The development of constructivist grounded theory. In: International Journal of Qualitative methods. Cap 5, Vol. 1, 25-35

Zanatta, A. et al. 2017. Barriers Faced by Newcomers to Software-Crowdsourcing Projects. IEEEE Software in press 2017.

THAI IMMIGRANTS' PERCEPTIONS AND ATTITUDES TOWARDS SOCIAL MEDIA USE IN CHINESE LEARNING IN TAIWAN

Nalatpa Hunsapun[1] and Chao-Chen Chen[1,2]
[1]*Graduate Institute of Library and Information Studies, National Taiwan Normal University, 162, Section 1, Heping E. Rd., Taipei City 10610, Taiwan*
[2]*Center for General Education, Chung Yuan Christian University, 200, Chung Pei Rd., Chung Li District, Taoyuan City 32023, Taiwan*

ABSTRACT

The primary purposes of this study were to explore the social media of new immigrants for Chinese learning and to investigate perceptions and attitudes of new immigrants towards social media use in Chinese learning. A total of one hundred new Thai immigrants in Taiwan who registered for marriage to a Taiwanese and requested to be residents were majoring in this study. The participants were divided into three groups based on the cluster analysis of the elements that influence Chinese learning. The three clusters were used to interpret the differences between the internal and external factors after a series of post hoc tests (Scheffé tests). The main results indicated that first, Thai new immigrants would use social media platforms to master the Chinese language and will use "YouTube," "Facebook," and "Line" as an online platform for Chinese learning. Second, Thai new immigrants were almost agreed on an internal factor – personal. Third, for internal factors, Thai new immigrants in cluster 2 (fashionable) have statistically higher scores than those in cluster 1 (self-confident) and cluster 3 (society-centered). Further, all items in external factors, Thai new immigrants in cluster 2 (fashionable) also have statistically higher scores than those in cluster 1 (self-confident) and cluster 3 (society-centered).

KEYWORDS

Perceptions, Attitudes, Social Media, Chinese Learning, New Immigrants

1. INTRODUCTION

Humans require language as a tool of communication to express their thoughts to others and comprehend their requirements. Learning a foreign language is a crucial part of the process of developing language abilities, which are utilized as a tool for communicating with foreigners. In doing so, not only do new immigrants enhance their language skills, but they also improve their cultural attitudes. There is additional evidence of the advantages of studying cultural information as part of learning a new language (Alhassan and Kuyini, 2013). At present, there are a lot of new immigrants in Taiwan. One of the most prominent reasons is Taiwan's New Southbound Policy, which began in 2016 for cooperation with 18 nations in various areas. Language barriers and complex challenges that new immigrants have faced since arriving in Taiwan. As a result, new immigrants will undoubtedly need to learn or enhance Chinese skills in order to interact effectively and adjust to new social and cultural. The Ministry of Education (MOE) of Taiwan holds basic adult education classes to support the language learning of new Immigrants in the primary and secondary schools organized by the city government. Furthermore, the Ministry of Education has also established a website titled "Learning Chinese in Taiwan" on the Office of Global Mandarin Education (OGME) (2020), which provides a variety of free online learning courses in collaboration with various agencies such as educational institutions in order to build and develop online learning tools which in turn aid Chinese learning anywhere and anytime.

The rapid development of technology leads to the changes in way of teaching, such as the construction of online teaching platforms (Jones and Hafner, 2012; Richards, 2015), the development of applications on mobile devices (Rahmawati et al., 2021; Ng et al., 2021; Ying et al., 2021), and also the social media (Reinhardt, (2019). Learners of Chinese as a second language (CSL) benefit significantly from the language learning through online communities because they have access to realistic opportunities and scenarios of language using by engaging with native Chinese speakers (Lyu and Lai, 2020). With calls to adapt language learning for the digital age, social media have become a mediated channel for language learning, bringing new options for learner agency and motivation (Kukulska-Hulme, 2012). In education, social media is becoming increasingly popular for research, and new studies and literature have shown that social media can help students learn languages (Mitchell, 2012; Özdemir, 2017; Sun and Yang, 2015). As a result, social media platforms such as Facebook, Line, and Twitter are increasingly utilized to encourage learning and as a teaching and learning channel that focuses on the continuous pursuit of information with a wide range of skills beyond what a teacher or textbook can transmit. According to Tanpraphan (2019), Myanmar migrant workers learn Thai and improve their listening capabilities by watching Thai videos on YouTube, listening to Thai music and news, and reading language books. On the use of social media of new immigrants, The National Development Council of Taiwan (2017) once again conducted the "Survey on the Current Situation and Needs of New Immigrants' Digital Opportunities" in 2017. According to the report, 91.5 percent of new immigrants have utilized the Internet and rely on their mobile phones the most (92.0 percent). The survey revealed that a total of 8.8% of new immigrants go online every day to look for information or videos to learn new skills, and a total of 35.9% of new immigrants participate in online self-learning, while 61.6 percent do not participate and 2.5 percent do not respond. According to the Hootsuite and We Are Social report (2020), Thais use the Internet and social media more than 52 million times in January 2020. Facebook, YouTube, and Line are the most popular and well-known social media networks. Statistics on Thai people's use of social media were employed in this study.

There are various studies showing the factors that influence the learning of a foreign language as a second language. Language learning is influenced by a variety of attitudes and variables: content, teaching strategies, instructional activities, medium of instruction, learning and teaching environment, and evaluation measurement. According to the literature review, social media has been used for teaching and learning for quite some time, particularly for language learning. Tu and Chen (2011) present a model for developing cloud-learning solutions that incorporates cloud computing with a learning network. This study created and developed a Chinese language cloud-learning system for new immigrants based on gamification model and researched the features of game-based cloud-learning systems, with the goal of assisting an increasing number of new immigrants in Taiwan. Lai and Tai (2021) mentioned social media has a deeper potential for language learning because language learning and sociability are so tightly linked. Language learning is now changing and having an impact on learners, owing to the rapid advancement of technology. Social media is one alternative for learning. Primarily, the purpose of this study is to explore the social media that new immigrants commonly use in Chinese learning as well as to investigate perceptions and attitudes of new immigrants towards social media use in Chinese learning. Based on the literature review above, the following questions are explored in this study:

1. What are the Thai new immigrants' perceptions on the relevant factors of social media use in Chinese learning?
2. What are the Thai new immigrants' attitudes towards social media use in Chinese learning?
3. What are the underlying patterns derived from the Thai new immigrants' perceptions on the relevant factors of social media use in Chinese learning?
4. What are the associations between the Thai new immigrants' identified patterns and their attitudes towards social media use in Chinese learning? Are there any differences in attitudes towards social media use in Chinese learning according to the different patterns?

2. METHOD

2.1 Sample

One hundred new Thai immigrants in Taiwan who registered for marriage to a Taiwanese and requested to be residents were selected as the subjects of this study. The subjects consisted of 3 males and 97 females. Most of the Thai new immigrants were aged more than 41 years (n=31) and followed by aged 26-30 years old and 36-40 years old (n=24). Their occupations are mostly unemployment (n=50), followed by factory worker/laborers (n=16) and startups (n=15). Their period of settling in Taiwan is mostly between 1 and 3

Years (n=42), followed by more than 7 Years (n=27), and between 4 and 6 Years (n=24). Most Thai new immigrants never study the Chinese language before living in Taiwan (n=53). 88 % of Thai new immigrants don't know that the Taiwan government offers Chinese language courses through social media (online) for new immigrants. Unfortunately, the gender of the subjects consisted of only three men, making it impossible to find gender differences in perceptions on the factors and attitudes relevant towards social media use in Chinese learning.

2.2 Data Collection

Google Form platforms were used to collect data through online questionnaires and sent to participants in January 2021. The questionnaire was only available in Thai to make Thai new immigrants understand clearly. Then it was translated into English and communicated amongst the experts and the researcher in order to reach a common understanding. Nevertheless, the completeness of the questionnaire responses was assessed in order to choose the most appropriate and comprehensive questionnaire for data analysis.

2.3 Instrument

The instrument used in this study was Closed-Ended Questions. The estimation of Cronbach's alpha was employed to confirm the reliability of each dimension as well as the overall reliability of the instrument. The questionnaire consisting of 34 questions divided into four sections:

- The demographic and situational of respondents include four questions, for instance, gender, age, occupation, and length of staying in Taiwan with Checklist items.
- The basics knowledge and perception of new immigrants related to social media use in Chinese learning include five items with Checklist items. Levels of Chinese skills were presented in a 1–5 Likert scale, ranging from "Excellent" = 5, "Very good" = 4, "Good" = 3, "Fair" = 2, and "Poor" = 1. There are also items about social media using of new immigrants with a 1–5 Likert scale ("Frequently" = 5, "Almost every time" = 4, "Sometimes" = 3, "Almost never" = 2, and "Never use" = 1).
- The factors that affect the Chinese learning of new immigrants include 30 questions divided into two parts; internal factors (Personal) and external factors (Instructor, Peer member, and Learning environment) with a 1–5 Likert scale, ranging from "Strongly agree" = 5, "Agree" = 4, "Neither agree nor disagree" = 3, "Disagree" = 2, and "Strongly disagree" = 1
- New immigrant's attitudes towards social media used for Chinese learning include 26 items. It consists of 5 areas: General aspect with four items, Instructor with three items, Course with ten items, Communication with four items, and Tools with three items, with a 1–5 Likert scale ranging from "strongly disagree" to "strongly agree."

2.4 Data Analysis

This study's data analysis approach comprised descriptive and inferential statistics. Descriptive statistics were used to examine the distribution of data relating to respondents' demographics and situations. The statistics used in the study was Frequency. For some questions, a score value was assigned to each level. Frequency, Mean, and Standard Deviation were the statistics employed, i.e. the basic knowledge and perception of new immigrants related to social media use in Chinese learning, social media using of new immigrants, the factors that affect Chinese learning of new immigrants, and new immigrant's attitudes towards social media use in Chinese learning. For Inferential Statistics, the statistics used in the classification are Cluster Analysis. Cluster analysis was used to understand their perception patterns of the relevant internal factor and external factor of social media use in Chinese learning as indicators. As a result, the Ward Method was used to do a Hierarchical Cluster Analysis to estimate the proper number of clusters based on Dendrogram. The use of hierarchical cluster analysis was beneficial in identifying characteristics of groups of Thai new immigrants' perception of relevant social media use in Chinese learning. One-way variance analysis (ANOVA) with Scheffe tests were conducted to examine whether significant differences existed in the three groups' Thai new immigrants' perceptions on the factors and attitudes relevant towards social media use in Chinese learning.

3. FINDING

3.1 The Perception of New Immigrants Related Social Media Use in Chinese Learning

The majority of Thai new immigrants have a decent to good level of listening and speaking skills. They also need to enhance their reading and writing skills. In addition, they had never studied Chinese before moving to Taiwan (n=53). 88% of Thai new immigrants are unaware that the Taiwan government offers Chinese language training for new immigrants through online courses. Of course, 98% of Thai new immigrants do not study Chinese through online courses held by the Taiwan government. They frequently utilize "YouTube," "Facebook," and "Line". In addition, 80% of Thai new immigrants expressed interest in engaging in social media-based Chinese classes and also use social media platforms to master the Chinese language. As a consequence, they were practically unanimous on the things used, which were "YouTube," "Facebook," and "Line" with an average of 4.25, 4.16, and 3.69, respectively. This indicates that the items with a mean score between 3.50 and 4.49 are consistent in terms of the level of satisfaction.

3.2 The Factors that affect Chinese Learning of New Immigrants

Table 1 illustrates factors that will affect the Chinese learning of Thai immigrants. As a result, it can be observed that the Thai new immigrants were almost agreed on an internal factor - Personal with an average of 3.83. Considering in level of satisfaction, by items in internal factor - personal which is labeled as "To improve their Chinese language skills" and "To pursue a career, such as finding a job to earn a higher salary or position" which records a value of an average 4.33. For the external factor, label it as "To communicate with the family member", "Support from a family member" in the Peer member context, which records a value of an average of 4.06 and 3.67, respectively. This indicated that the items ranged from the mean score between the values of 3.50 to 4.49 are consistent in terms of the level of satisfaction.

Table 1. The factors that affect Chinese learning of Thai new immigrants

The factors that affect Chinese learning of Thai new immigrants	Mean	S.D.
Internal Factors	3.83	0.768
Personal	3.83	0.768
External Factors	2.94	0.714
Instructor	2.91	0.926
Peer member	3.32	0.813
Learning environment	2.63	0.767
Total	3.32	0.631

3.3 Thai New Immigrant's Attitude Towards Social Media Use in Chinese Learning

Table 2 illustrates Thai new immigrant's attitudes towards social media use in Chinese learning. As a result, it can be observed that the Thai immigrants were almost consistent in the Course, General context, and communication with an average of 4.09, 4.07, and 3.92, respectively. When considering items of "Learning anytime", "Save time and costs", and "Learning anywhere," it records a value of an average of 4.24 and 4.21 respectively. This indicated that the items ranged from the mean score between the values of 3.50 to 4.49 are consistent in terms of the level of satisfaction.

Table 2. Thai new immigrant's attitude towards social media use in Chinese learning

Attitude towards social media use in Chinese learning	Mean	S.D.
General context	4.07	0.557
Instructor	3.58	1.005
Course	4.09	0.679
Communication	3.92	0.686
Tools	3.52	0.714
Total	3.93	0.576

3.4 Grouping and Characterizing Groups from Variables

Table 3 shows the number of participants, mean values, and standard deviations of new immigrants' characteristics that affect Chinese learning in each cluster, as well as post hoc comparisons. The internal factor - Personal (F=40.034, p<0.005), as well as external factors including Instructors (F=130.895, p<0.005), Peer members (F=28.336, p<0.005), and Learning environments (F=40.401, p<0.005), showed significant differences between clusters in the ANOVA analysis. The participants were divided into three groups based on the cluster analysis of the factors that influence Chinese learning. It is clear that the three clusters were used to interpret the differences between the internal and external factors after a series of post hoc tests (Scheffé tests).

The optimal number of groups to be divided into groups based on the Hierarchical Cluster Analysis approach. As the result, there are three groups considering the classification of Agglomeration Schedule and Ward Method. This appears to be a condition for combining numerous subgroups of information into a single group. The computation tool is Dendrogram. Using variables to define three group classifications can accurately represent the nature of the group. Each group likewise has a suitable number of samples.

Table 3. The clusters of the new immigrants' factors affect the use of social media for Chinese learning

	Internal Factors	External Factors		
	Personal	Instructor	Peer member	Learning environment
(1) self-confodent (N=27) mean/SD	3.52 (0.862)	1.82 (0.455)	2.56 (0.900)	1.78 (0.513)
(2) fashionable (N=40) mean/SD	4.45 (0.442)	3.77 (0.554)	3.77 (0.537)	3.08 (0.745)
(3) society-centered (N=33) mean/SD	3.33 (0.397)	2.76 (0.417)	3.41 (0.531)	2.79 (0.425)
F (ANOVA)	40.034*	130.895*	28.336*	40.401*
Post hoc test (Scheffé tests)	1>3 2>3	2>1 3>1	2>1 3>1	2>1 3>1

*p<0.005

After grouping, the mean square between clusters was analyzed (Agglomeration Schedule and Ward Method) by examining the statistics of the three groups with distinct features through One-way ANOVA. According to the study aims, the researcher named the three groups in table 3 to assess the characteristics of Chinese learning through social media among Thai new immigrants in Taiwan. First, as shown in Table 3, cluster 1 includes a 27 participant study sample. The participants in this cluster reflect significantly higher on the internal factor - Personal (M=3.52) than those in cluster 3. While scores on external factors include Instructor (M=1.82), Peer member (M=2.56), and Learning environment (M=1.78) were significantly lower than the scores of the other clusters. The participants classified into this cluster tend to view Chinese learning as affecting and related with themselves than other factors. Therefore, for this reason, the participants in cluster 1 were defined as Self-confident, highlighting their emphasis on internal factors - Personal. Behaviors related to language learning are driven by human beings who are also born with various potentials such as curiosity, creativity, and the need for self-development.

The second cluster consisted of 40 participants who scored significantly higher scores on the internal factor - Personal (M=4.45), and external factors include Instructor (M=3.77), Peer member (M=3.77), and Learning environment (M=3.08) than those in the other two clusters. The new immigrants in cluster 2 are the fashionable groups. They emphasized utilizing social media useful for Chinese learning as understanding internal factors and external factors which will affect Chinese learning because both are driven factors for language learning. The elements within the human being and the environment influence each other in such a way that the individual elements must be interrelated harmoniously, with the environment sometimes more significantly a greater role in the behavior than the intrapersonal component. At other times, the individual's internal components may influence the behavior of humans more than the environment.

Finally, 33 participants had significantly lower scores on the internal factor - Personal (M=3.33) than the other two clusters. However, this cluster had significantly higher scores on the external factors include Instructor (M=2.76), Peer member (M=3.41), and Learning environment (M=2.79), than cluster 1. Thus, the participants in this cluster, defined as society-centered, emphasized language learning as what makes people learn languages may be due to learning that is governed by external factor conditions rather than personal needs such as Instructor, Peer member, and Learning environment.

As shown in Table 4, it revealed the results of testing for difference between the mean of each variable when the cluster was different with significantly at 0.00. For both factors, p-values are *p*<.005. Therefore, there is a statistically significant difference in the Chinese learning of Thai new immigrants.

Table 5 revealed the results for testing the difference between the mean of each variable when the cluster was different significantly. For both factors, the significance value shows that Course, Communication, and Tools (p = 0.001, 0.003, 0.005, respectively), which is below 0.005. As a result, there is a statistically significant difference in the Thai new immigrant's attitude towards social media use in Chinese learning. On the other hand, General context and Instructor have a significance value higher than 0.005. It means no significance in Thai new immigrant's attitude towards social media use in Chinese learning.

Table 4. A comparison of factors that will affect Chinese learning of new Thai immigrants using one-way ANOVA

Factors that will affect Chinese learning	Group	Sum of Squares	df	Mean Square	F	Sig	Post hoc test (Scheffé tests)
Internal Factors							
Personal	Between Groups	26.386	2	13.193	40.034	.000	1>3 2>3
	Within Groups	31.965	97	.330			
	Total	58.351	99				
External Factors							
Instructor	Between Groups	61.896	2	30.948	130.895	.000	2>1 3>1
	Within Groups	22.934	97	.238			
	Total	84.830	99				
Peer member	Between Groups	24.157	2	12.078	28.336	.000	2>1 3>1
	Within Groups	41.346	97	.426			
	Total	65.502	99				
Learning environment	Between Groups	28.555	2	14.277	40.401	.000	2>1 3>1
	Within Groups	34.279	97	.353			
	Total	62.833	99				

*p<0.005

Table 5. A comparison of Thai new immigrant's attitude towards social media use in Chinese learning using one-way ANOVA

Attitude towards social media use in Chinese learning	Group	Sum of Squares	df	Mean Square	F	Sig	Post hoc test (Scheffé tests)
General context	Between Groups	2.427	2	1.214	4.155	.019	2>3
	Within Groups	28.333	97	.292			
	Total	30.760	99				
Instructor	Between Groups	9.644	2	4.822	5.172	.007	1>2
	Within Groups	90.439	97	.932			
	Total	100.083	99				
Course	Between Groups	4.737	2	2.368	5.617	.005	1>3 2>3
	Within Groups	40.899	97	.422			
	Total	45.636	99				
Communication	Between Groups	6.573	2	3.286	7.958	.001	2>3
	Within Groups	40.059	97	.413			
	Total	46.632	99				
Tools	Between Groups	5.771	2	2.886	6.258	.003	2>1
	Within Groups	44.730	97	.461			
	Total	50.501	99				

*p<0.005

4. CONCLUSION

First of all, it should be emphasized that this study was limited by its narrow scope and small sample, which might explain the lack of significance of the findings. It's possible that they performed equally between groups, with little variation, and may have influenced the results. The majority of Thai new immigrants have a decent to a good level of listening and speaking skills. On the other hand, they need enhance their reading and writing skills. In addition, they had never studied Chinese before moving to Taiwan. 80% of Thai new immigrants expressed interest in engaging in social media-based Chinese classes. Thai new immigrants will use social media platforms to master the Chinese language. As a consequence, the Thai immigrants were practically unanimous on the things used, which were "YouTube," "Facebook," and "Line".

As a result, it can be observed that most Thai new immigrants agreed on internal factors – personal that affects their Chinese learning. The goal of language learning was "To improve their Chinese language skills" and "To pursue a career, such as finding a job to earn a higher salary or position". According to Peng (2014), internal factors about life planning affect Chinese learning to have a better life about jobs in the future. For external factors, a study by Peng (2014) found Institute factors are the main factors that affect Chinese learning, while this study found "To communicate with the family member" and "Support from a family member" in the Peer member context influencing Thai immigrants to learning Chinese. It may be observed they are new Thai immigrants in Taiwan who registered for marriage to a Taiwanese. Thus, Communicate and support by family members will be the main factors to affect language learning.

Social media may give beneficial language learning possibilities. However, it is important to investigate the factors towards social media uses for language learning. In addition, the type of social media must be taken into account in order to be able to apply it in language learning appropriately. However, language learning through social media should focus on learning and interaction between learners and instructors, including access to information and knowledge without barriers.

ACKNOWLEDGEMENT

This work was supported by Professor Chin Chung Tsai.

REFERENCES

Abidin, M. J. Z., Ahmad, N., and Kabilan, M. K., 2010. Facebook: An online environment for learning of English in institutions of higher education. *Internet and Higher Education,* Vol.13, No.4, pp 179–187.

Aichner, T. and Jacob, F., 2015. Measuring the Degree of Corporate Social Media Use. *International Journal of Market Research,* Vol.57, No.2, pp 257–275.

Alhassan, A. M., and Kuyini, A. B., 2013. Teaching immigrants norwegian culture to support their language learning. *International Education Studies,* Vol.6, No.3, pp 15-25.

Brick, B., 2011. Social networking sites and language learning. *International Journal of Virtual and Personal Learning Environments,* Vol.2, No.3, pp 18-31.

Derakshan, A. and Hasanabbasi, S., 2015. Social Networks for Language Learning. *Theory and Practice in Language Studies,* Vol.5, No.5, pp 1090-1095.

Dogoriti, E., Pange, J. and Anderson, G.S., 2014. The use of social networking and learning management systems in English language teaching in higher education. *Campus-Wide Information Systems,* Vol.31, No.4, pp 254-263.

Gong, Y., Gao, X., and Lyu, B., 2020. Teaching Chinese as a second or foreign language to non-Chinese learners in mainland China (2014–2018). *Language Teaching*, Vol.53, No.1, pp 1–19.

Ho, W. Y. J., 2018. Mobility and language learning: A case study on the use of an online platform to learn chinese as a foreign language. *London Review of Education,* Vol.16, No.2, pp 239-249.

Hootsuite and We Are Social, 2020. *Digital 2020: Thailand*, Retrieved January 15, 2021, from https://datareportal.com/reports/digital-2020-thailand

Jones, R.H. and Hafner, C.A., 2012. Understanding Digital Literacies: A practical introduction. London: *Routledge.*

Kietzmann, J.H., Hermkens, K., McCarthy, I.P. and Silvestre, B.S., 2011. Social media? Get serious! Understanding the functional building blocks of social media. *Business Horizons*, Vol.54, No.3, pp 241-251.

Kommers, P. A. M., 2011. *Social media for learning by means of ICT.* Moscow, Russia: UNESCO Institute for Information Technologies for Education.

Kosaiyawat, S., 2000. A develparticularapproach for a special policy school in Chon Buri: A case study of a Chinese language teaching school. *Journal of Education,* Vol.15, No.2, pp 77-95. (in Thai).

Kukulska-Hulme, A., 2012. Language learning defined by time and place: A framework for next generation designs. In Left to My Own Devices: Learner Autonomy and Mobile Assisted Language Learning. Innovation and Leadership in English Language Teaching, 6. edited by Díaz-Vera, Javier E., Bingley, 1–3. U.K.: *Emerald Group Publishing Limited.*

Lai, Chun; Tai, Chung-Pui, 2021. *Types of social media activities and Hong Kong South and Southeast Asians Youth's Chinese language learning motivation. System,* Vol.97, pp *102432.*

Liu Y., 2021. Chinese Culture Penetration in Teaching Chinese as a Foreign Language in the Era of Mobile Internet. In: MacIntyre J., Zhao J., Ma X. (eds) The 2020 *International Conference on Machine Learning and Big Data Analytics for IoT Security and Privacy*. SPIOT 2020. Advances in Intelligent Systems and Computing, Vol.1283.

Lyu, B., and Lai, C., 2020. Interacting with native speakers of chinese through online learning communities: A case study with east asian learners. *Global Chinese,* Vol.6, No.2, pp 215-235.

Mitchell, K., 2012. A social tool: Why and how ESOL students use Facebook. *CALICO Journal, 29*(3): 471–493.

New Southbound policy portal., 2020. *MOE launches Chinese learning platform for foreigners, lauded widely.* Ministry of foreign affairs, Republic of China (Taiwan). Retrieved January 15, 2021, from https://news.immigration.gov.tw/PH/NewsPost.aspx?NEWSGUID=efae2a35-6e36-454f-a07b-3840fb689001andutm_source=mofa_nspp

Ng, C. H., Koh, N. K., and Ling, H. L., 2021. Incorporating new literacies in designing a mobile learning application for secondary/middle school students. *Education and Information Technologies,* Vol.26, No.2, pp 1485-1504.

Obar, Jonathan A. and Wildman, Steve, 2015. Social media definition and the governance challenge: An introduction to the special issue. *Telecommunications Policy*, Vol.39, No.9, pp 745–750.

Özdemir, E., 2017. Promoting EFL learners' intercultural communication effectiveness: A focus on Facebook. *Computer Assisted Language Learning,* Vol.30, No.6, pp 510–528.

Peng L., 2014. Factors Affecting Students' Motivation in Studying Chinese at Siam University. *Journal of Cultural Approach.* Vol.15, No.28, pp 27-38.

Poore, M., 2016. *Using social media in the classroom: A best practice guide (2nd ed.).* Washington DC: SAGE.

Rahmawati, E., Nur Ismiyasari, F., Etika Rahmawati, L., and Abidin, Z., 2021. The different google classroom and edulogy platform e-learning on HOTS problem for elementary students in the corona pandemic period. Paper presented at the *Journal of Physics: Conference Series,* Vol.1806, No.1.

Reinhardt, J., 2019. *Social media in second and foreign language teaching and learning: Blogs, wikis, and social networking. Language Teaching,* Vol.52, No.1, pp *1–39.*

Richards, J.C., 2015. The changing face of language learning: Learning beyond the classroom. RELC Journal, Vol.46, No.1, pp 5–22.

Sanguannam, K., 2013. *The study of the use of foreign language curriculum (Chinese language) in schools under Bangkok affiliation.* Master of arts' thesis, Chulalongkorn University. (in Thai)

Sittiwong, T., 2015. The study of undergraduate students Opinion towards the use of Facebook in Graphics Design and Production for Education in Field of Educational Communications and Technology Faculty of Education, Naresuan University. *Journal of Education Naresuan University.* Vol.17, No.3. (in Thai).

Suchonvanich, J., 2018. Teaching Chinese as a Foreign Language with Information and Communication Technology (ICT): A Case Study of the People's Republic of China. *KKU Research Journal of Humanities and Social Sciences (Graduate Study,* Vol.6, No.2. (in Thai).

Sun, Y., and Yang, F., 2015. I help, therefore, i learn: Service learning on Web 2.0 in an EFL speaking class. *Computer Assisted Language Learning,* Vol.28, No.3, pp 202–219.

Tanpraphan, P., 2019. Communication Competency of Myanmar Workers in Thailand. *RSU National Research Conference 2019. April 23, 2019.* (in Thai).

The Education Department of New Taipei City Government. 2020. New Taipei City International Education website. Retrieved January 15, 2021, from https://www.international-education.ntpc.edu.tw/ischool/publish_page/316/

The National Development Council of Taiwan, 2017. Survey on the Current Situation and Needs of new immigrants' Digital Opportunities in 2017. [Chinese]

The Office of Global Mandarin Education (OGME), 2020. Online Learning. Retrieved January 15, 2021, from https://ogme.edu.tw/lc/learning

Tu, C.-C. and Chen, A.-P., 2011. Building a learning games network in cloud learning platform based on immigrant education. *Advances in Social Networks Analysis and Mining (ASONAM), 2011 International Conference on, 2011,* pp. 746–750

Wagner, R., 2011. Social Media Tools for Teaching and Learning. *Athletic Training Education Journal.* Vol.6, No.1, pp 51 – 52.

Wang, S., and Luo, H., 2021. Exploring the meanings and grammatical functions of idioms in teaching Chinese as a second language. *International Journal of Applied Linguistics (United Kingdom).*

Wang, T., and Li, Y., 2019. An investigation on Chinese Teaching and learning situation of schools in Northern Thailand. *Panyapiwat Journal,* Vol.11, No.2, pp 244-256.

Xue, S. and Churchill, D., 2020. Educational affordances of mobile social media for language teaching and learning: A Chinese teacher's perspective. *Computer Assisted Language Learning.*

Yang, Chia-chen; Lee, Yen, 2018. *Interactants and activities on Facebook, Instagram, and Twitter: Associations between social media use and social adjustment to college. Applied Developmental Science,* Vol.24, No.1, pp *1–17.*

Ying, Y., Susilo, P. M., Mei, F. R., and Rahardjanti, T., 2021. The role of the mandamonic games in supporting mandarin learning at elementary school. *Journal of Physics: Conference Series,* Vol.1764.

GRAPH BASED TEMPORAL AGGREGATION FOR VIDEO RETRIEVAL

Aprameya Bharadwaj, Arvind Srinivasan, Aveek Saha and Subramanyam Natarajan
PES University, India

ABSTRACT

Large scale video retrieval is a field of study with a lot of ongoing research. The work that has been done in this field either uses image queries from within the video dataset or iterates through videos frame by frame. These approaches are not generalized for queries from outside the dataset and do not scale well for large video datasets. To overcome these issues, we propose a new approach for video retrieval through image queries where an undirected graph is constructed from the combined set of frames from all videos to be searched. The node features of this graph are used in the task of video retrieval. Experimentation is done on the MSR-VTT dataset by using query images from outside the dataset. To evaluate this novel approach P@5, P@10 and P@20 metrics are calculated.

KEYWORDS

Video Retrieval, Graph, Ranking, Cosine Similarity, MSR-VTT

1. INTRODUCTION

Video Retrieval is one of the most eminent and challenging problems in the digital world today. It is the task of ranking videos in a database based on their relevance to user input queries. While most practical applications use video meta-data to convert the problem into a straight-forward page ranking problem, there are vast databases of videos with no labeled meta-data. The next big challenge that hasn't been solved yet is to tap into the temporal information contained in video data. While image classification and object detection tasks in images have been proven to work really well in the last few years, simply searching for objects in the frames of a video would fail to make use of the temporal information contained in videos.

In this paper, we propose a novel approach to solve this problem. We first pre-process a video database to extract key features from video frames. These features are clustered, such that similar frames end up in the same cluster. We generate the embeddings for these clusters by aggregating the embeddings of their constituent frames. To account for temporal information in videos, we model these clusters as nodes in a graph. Then, the cluster embeddings are augmented by including neighboring cluster information. These augmented cluster embeddings are stored and used in our video ranking process.

2. RELATED WORK

The paper (Araujo, et al., 2015) introduces a new retrieval architecture, in which the image query can be compared directly with database videos - significantly improving retrieval scalability compared with a baseline system that searches the database on a video frame level. However, this paper only uses query images which are frames of the videos in the dataset and does not work with out-of-dataset images. The paper (Li, et al., 2019) introduces a method of integrating the spatial temporal neighbourhood information using an attention mechanism that focuses on useful features on each frame. The Neighborhood Preserving Hashing method creates a learned hashing function that can easily map similar videos. Another approach for representation learning for videos is to create hierarchical graph clusters built upon video-to-video similarities. This is explored in the paper (Lee, et al., 2020) using two different methods, the first is to create smart triplets and the second is to create pseudo labels. When videos are represented as individual frames it makes the modeling of long-range semantic dependencies difficult. The paper (Shao, et al., 2021) solves this issue by incorporating long range temporal features at the frame level using self attention. For training on video retrieval datasets they propose a supervised contrastive learning method that performs automatic hard negative mining and utilizes the memory bank mechanism to increase the capacity of negative samples. The paper (Dong, et al., 2019) tackles the challenging problem of zero example video retrieval. This paper takes a concept-free approach, proposing a dual deep encoding network that encodes videos and queries into powerful dense representations of their own. As experiments on three benchmarks, i.e. MSRVTT, TRECVID 2016 and 2017 Ad-hoc Video Search show, the proposed solution establishes a new state-of-the-art for zero-example video retrieval. The authors of (Miech, et al., 2018) use heterogeneous data sources to learn text-video embeddings. They propose a new model called Mixture-of-Embedding-Experts (MEE). The proposed model shows considerable improvements and beats previous text-to-video retrieval and video-to-video retrieval methods.

The paper (Hu, et al., 2007) introduces a semantic-based video retrieval framework. Motion trajectories are detected using clustering based methods. These clusters are structured hierarchically to obtain activity models. A hierarchical structure of semantic indexing and object retrieval is then proposed. Here, each individual activity gets all the semantic descriptions of the activity model from its parent activity. This is then used to access individual objects semantically. (Zhang, et al., 2019) proposes an efficient method for video retrieval using image queries. The authors propose the Visual Weighted Inverted Index algorithm to improve the accuracy and efficiency of retrieval and evaluate the approach on the Youtube-8M and Sports-1M datasets. GraphSAGE (Hamilton, et al., 2017) is an algorithm for inductive learning and representation on large graphs. It generates low dimensional vectors for the nodes of the graphs. Existing models before this had to be re-trained when a new node was added to the graph. GraphSAGE uses node information and neighbour information and aggregates them to generalize the features of the unseen node. Aggregators take the neighbourhood as input and combine the embeddings with certain weights to create embeddings for the neighbourhood. The initial embedding of each node is set to its node features. Till the 'K' neighbourhood depth, the neighbourhood embedding is created using the aggregator function for each node and it's concatenated with the node features. This is then passed through a neural network to update the weights and features. The CLIP4Clip method in (Luo, et al., 2021) also experiments on the MSR-VTT dataset however they also train the CLIP model on the dataset to finetune the hyperparameters. The major differences in our proposed model are - the text data is not needed for our model and there is no training on the testing dataset that needs to be done. This makes our proposed method more lightweight and scalable for web-applications. The proposed model in this paper can be used on any dataset without needing it to be trained on that dataset. The CLIP4clip paper also does not talk about the retrieval of videos when it comes to frames that are not contained in any videos. However, our proposed pipeline has been designed to work for any images as it works on cosine similarity. Another use of the CLIP model (Portillo, et al., 2021) for video retrieval is for getting video representations without annotations.

The multi-modal transformer (MMT) proposed in (Vedaldi, et al., 2020) is used to tackle the task of video retrieval from captions and vice versa. However this method also requires a captioned video dataset for training like the previous CLIP model. The method proposed in (Dzabraev, et al., 2021) builds on the MMT architecture and uses a deeper and wider transformer with more aggressive dropouts to achieve better performance. However this approach also suffers from the same drawback as the previous MMT model in that it requires a captioned dataset to perform text to video retrieval. (Bain, et al., 2021) is a paper that proposes a state-of-the-art method for video retrieval through textual queries. They have developed an architecture that builds on top of transformers to learn joint text-video representations. The method proposed in (Liu, et al., 2019) also works on learning efficient representations for videos for the purpose of retrieval through text queries. Both these methods have been tested on popular retrieval benchmarks including the MSR-VTT dataset. K-NN (Zhang, et al., 2007) is an unsupervised machine learning algorithm to cluster data points. Euclidean distance is used as the comparison metric. Euclidean distances of the incoming point with the centres of all the clusters are calculated. The shortest distance is found and the incoming data point is assigned to that particular cluster. Residual networks are a class of deep neural networks proposed in (Szegedy, et al., 2017). In theory deeper networks should have the same training error as the shallow ones, but this paper shows the inability to approximate identity mappings by many nonlinear layers. However, with residual learning, the solvers make the weights of the non-linear layers almost zero to approach identity mappings.

3. PROPOSED METHOD

The database of videos is first pre-processed. To create a memory-efficient and useful means of representing the videos, smart video embeddings were created.

3.1 Representing Video Frames

In our proposed pipeline, the only input to our model is a database of videos. Although videos are rich in information when observed by a human being, computers require alternate methods to process videos. The first step is to analyze videos at the level of their component frames. Once we have extracted frames from the video, we can use image embedding generation techniques to represent them. The input videos are sampled at 2 frames per second. Each frame is passed through an image embedding generation model. In our method, we have chosen to use pre-trained Residual Networks which are trained on the Imagenet dataset to generate frame embeddings. These networks produce embeddings of length 2048. Their residual connections allow features at lower layers to be preserved in deeper layers. We experimented with two variants of the residual network - ResNet50 and ResNet152. These networks are 50 and 152 layers deep respectively.

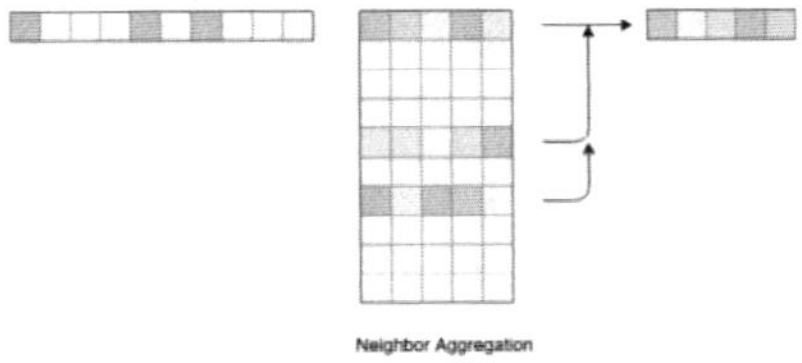

Figure 1. Neighbor Aggregation in Graph Convolutional Networks

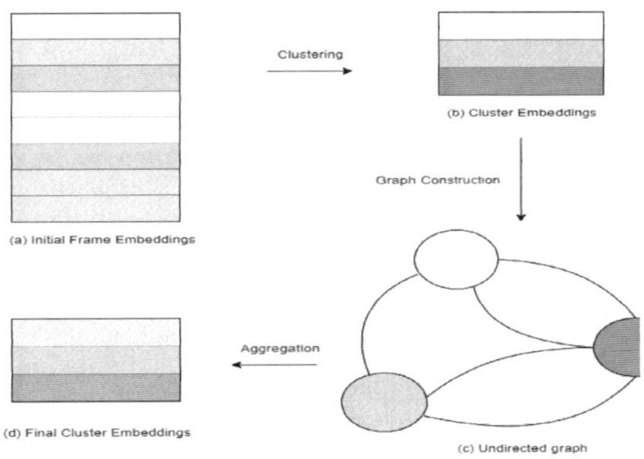

Figure 2. Augmented Embedding Generation

3.2 Representing Videos

Videos are generally represented as a concatenation of their component frame embeddings. In our approach, we have chosen to represent the entire dataset of videos together, instead of generating individual video representations, as seen in Figure 2 (a). This will allow us to improve the retrieval speed of the model.

Once we have generated embeddings for all sampled frames in the dataset, we cluster them (Figure 2 (b)). We use the K-Nearest Neighbors algorithm as a light-weight clustering algorithm that can be used for large-scale clustering applications. To find the optimal number of clusters the elbow method was used and the number of clusters was fixed at 175. The change in MAP@10 for some categories with varying numbers of clusters can be seen in Figure 4. Frames across videos in the dataset are assigned into 175 clusters. These clusters are represented by the mean of their component frame embeddings. In this clustering process, we lose out on the important temporal information that is inherently present in videos. To preserve this information, we use a graph-based aggregation technique.

An undirected graph using these clusters is created where each cluster is treated as a node. If frame Y which belongs to cluster 1 follows frame X which belongs to cluster 2 in the video, then there is an edge connecting cluster 1 and 2 (Figure 2 (c)). The edge weights in the graph are directly proportional to the number of such frame-frame (and cluster-cluster) transitions. To add temporal information to the embeddings, the cluster embeddings are aggregated with their first order neighbor cluster embeddings (Figure 2 (d)). We concatenate the mean of neighborhood features in the aggregation step as shown in Figure 1. Since a node's neighbors contain information about the common frame transitions in a video, representing that node by concatenating the mean of its neighbors' embeddings helps retain temporal information in the video. This final representation is used in retrieval.

3.3 Video Retrieval

Any query image is first processed by the image embedding generation model. We use the augmented cluster embeddings to reduce the search space for every query. The query image embeddings are first compared with the cluster embeddings. The cosine similarity is used as the similarity metric for these embeddings. The clusters are ranked based on their cosine similarities and the top 'c' clusters are chosen for further comparisons. All frame embeddings present in these top clusters are compared with the query image, and ranked based on their similarities. The 'k' number videos corresponding to the top matching frames are retrieved for each query image and Precision@k is calculated as:

$$P@k = \frac{R \cap k}{k}$$

Where 'R' is the number of videos that are the same category as the query image and 'k' is the total number of videos retrieved. After this mAP@k is calculated for all the query images for a particular category. mAP is the mean of all the P@k for all the images for a particular category. It is given as:

$$mAP = \frac{\sum_{n=1}^{k} \quad P@k}{k}$$

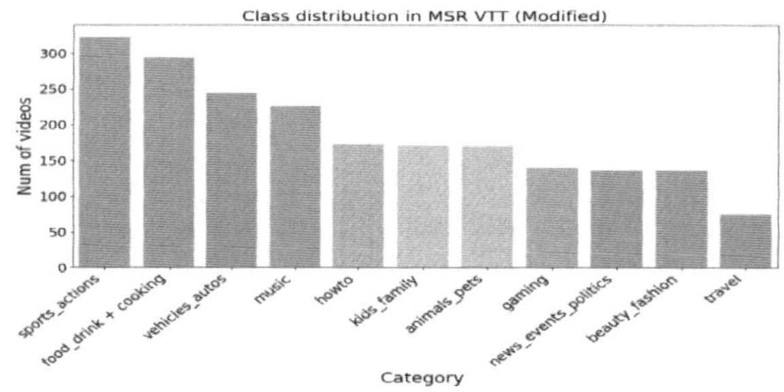

Figure 3. MSR VTT number of videos per class after modification

4. DATASET

For the evaluation of this technique experiments were performed on the MSR-VTT dataset. The dataset contains 2990 videos which are around 20-60 seconds long and belong to 20 different categories. This technique uses the video information only hence making it possible to retrieve previously unseen videos. The categories of videos in the dataset are: 1. Music 2. People 3. Gaming 4. Sports, Actions 5. News, Events, Politics 6. Education 7. TV Shows 8. Movie, Comedy 9. Animation 10. Vehicles, Autos 11. How-to 12. Travel 13. Science, Technology 14. Animals, Pets 15. Kids, Family 16. Documentary 17. Food, Drink 18. Cooking 19. Beauty, Fashion 20. Advertisement. For our testing we merged some similar categories like Food and cooking and removed others like movies, documentary, advertisement, etc due to the arbitrary nature of the classes. For example, it's difficult to tell the difference between a movie clip and a clip from a TV show or documentary without any context. Another reason for excluding some of the other classes like Science and Technology or education, is that there is often no clear visually discernible factor that puts a video in this category. For example a video of a teacher explaining a concept might be classified as education but there's no way to understand that the person in the video is a teacher or that something is being taught. The 11 relevant categories left were: 1. Music 2. Gaming 3. Sports, Actions 4. News, Events, Politics 5. Vehicles, Autos 6. How-to 7. Travel 8. Animals, Pets 9. Kids, Family 10. Food, Drink, Cooking 11. Beauty, Fashion.

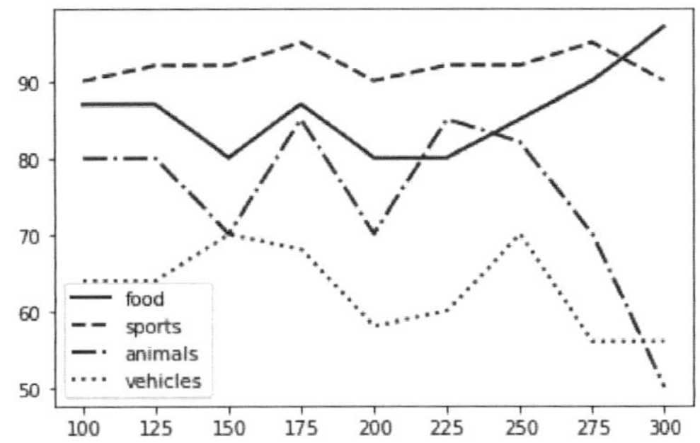

Figure 4. MAP@10 with varying number of clusters

5. RESULTS AND CONCLUSIONS

The experiments for this study were run on a system with a 2.2 GHz Intel Core i7 processor with 16 GB of RAM. The system also had an Intel Iris Pro integrated graphics with 1.5 GB of memory. In the results, P@K denotes the precision of the results in the top 'K' ranked videos. The query images selected to evaluate this model were not from the dataset. Randomly four images for a particular category were selected and this model was run. For frames in the dataset, the model perfectly selects the video that it's from. All the results depicted here are for images not from the dataset. As seen from the below tables, Resnet-152 outperforms Resnet-50. In a task that is as complex as this, we expect the larger model to work better than the smaller one. The depth of the ResNet-152 is more than three times the depth of ResNet-50. This means that there are a lot more weights to train, and consequently a lot more parameters to learn. However, ResNet-50 searches through the videos at approximately 18000 frames per second, in comparison to ResNet-152's 15000 frames per second. Although this is a considerable difference in speeds, the accuracy of search in ResNet-152 is significantly higher.

Also when the results of the proposed technique which are in tables 1 and 2 are compared to just clustering and retrieving which are given in tables 3 and 4, we see that the performance of the proposed method is better. The results in table 1 show improved mAP rates when compared with table 3 and similarly the results in table 2 show improved mAP rates when compared with table 4. This is because using this technique we can keep a track of the temporally relevant clusters due to the graph created and retrieve from those clusters as well. However, just by clustering and retrieving, there is a loss in temporal information and hence the precision of the retrieval also falls. In this model the number of temporal clusters to retrieve from can be specified and the best videos from those can be chosen. It can be seen that the results in table 1 and 2 outperform the results in table 3 and 4 respectively in almost all categories. To improve on this further a ResNet model can be pre-trained on a different task, such as scene detection. This would improve the results for certain categories where the composition of the video frames are more important for classification than the individual objects in them. Also, this model can be trained on a particular category such as sports, vehicles etc if it's known beforehand what domain the model has to work in. Even without this it is evident the proposed model outperforms the traditional model.

Table 1. Model Using ResNet152

Category	mAP@5	mAP@10	mAP@20
Music	60%	42.5%	37.5%
Gaming	50%	40%	37.5%
Sports, Actions	100%	97.5%	90%
News, Events, Politics	45%	40%	36.25%
Vehicles, Auto	85%	65%	56.25%
How-to	30%	40%	28.75%
Travel	55%	42.5%	32.5%
Animals, Pets	85%	72.5%	61.25%
Kids, Family	40%	40%	32.5%
Food, Drink, Cooking	40%	40%	50%
Beauty, Fashion	60%	52.5%	38.75%

Table 2. Model Using ResNet50

Category	mAP@5	mAP@10	mAP@20
Music	30%	35%	31.25%
Gaming	55%	47.5%	36.25%
Sports, Actions	100%	95%	88.75%
News, Events, Politics	50%	42.5%	36.25%
Vehicles, Auto	60%	57.5%	51.25%
How-to	40%	40%	31.25%
Travel	50%	47.5%	35%
Animals, Pets	90%	70%	50%
Kids, Family	45%	40%	33.75%
Food, Drink, Cooking	35%	37.5%	45%
Beauty, Fashion	45%	45%	33.75%

Table 3. Model Using ResNet152 without creating graph

Category	mAP@5	mAP@10	mAP@20
Music	45%	37.5%	33.75%
Gaming	40%	35%	38.75%
Sports, Actions	100%	97.5%	91.25%
News, Events, Politics	45%	47.5%	37.5%
Vehicles, Auto	80%	57.5%	50.25%
How-to	35%	40%	31.25%
Travel	55%	37.5%	28.75%
Animals, Pets	90%	80%	61.25%
Kids, Family	35%	32.5%	30%
Food, Drink, Cooking	40%	42.5%	45%
Beauty, Fashion	50%	42.5%	37.5%

Table 4. Model Using ResNet50 without creating graph

Category	mAP@5	mAP@10	mAP@20
Music	35%	32.5%	27.5%
Gaming	65%	55%	46.25%
Sports, Actions	100%	92.5%	83.75%
News, Events, Politics	50%	45%	32.5%
Vehicles, Auto	68%	58%	60%
How-to	40%	41.5%	31.25%
Travel	40%	37.5%	30%
Animals, Pets	90%	72.5%	62.5%
Kids, Family	35%	30%	28.75%
Food, Drink, Cooking	35%	37.5%	43.5%
Beauty, Fashion	75%	52.5%	43.5%

Table 5. Speed Comparison of Models

Model	Effective Search Speed (Video Frames / Second)
ResNet152	15000
ResNet50	18000

6. FUTURE WORK

The videos in the MSR-VTT dataset are of very short duration. If the videos are longer, another technique can be leveraged to retrieve videos as explained below. Similar to the proposed technique the videos are sampled at 2 frames per second and then the frames are passed through the chosen residual network to get the embedding of each frame. Each embedding is a vector of dimension 2048. The embeddings of each frame are clustered using K-NN. The embedding for each cluster is calculated as the average of all vectors in that cluster. To preserve the temporal information, an undirected graph using these clusters is created as explained previously but here a graph is created for each video. To also add temporal information to the embeddings as explained, the cluster embedding is also aggregated with its first order neighbor cluster embeddings. Now an incoming image is not compared with individual frames of a video but it is compared with these temporal vectors. The query image is compared to these temporal vectors using cosine similarity. The advantage of this technique is that, when new videos are introduced into the dataset, the embedding and clustering has to be done only for these videos individually. However, in the proposed method the graph might change as the cluster centres will be forced to change due to the addition of new frames. This also means that all the frame embeddings don't need to be stored as this method only works with the video embedding. Hence, the overall memory used will be lesser even though the memory access will be the same. As seen in tables 6 and 7, there isn't a big difference between creating a graph or retrieving just after clustering even when the ResNet152 was used. This can be due to the short nature of the videos in this dataset.

Table 6. Results for creating graph for individual videos using ResNet152

Category	mAP@5	mAP@10	mAP@20
Music	35%	37.5%	33.5%
Gaming	45%	35%	37.5%
Sports, Actions	100%	95%	92.5%
News, Events, Politics	50%	40%	40%
Vehicles, Auto	75%	57.5%	53.75%
How-to	30%	35%	33.75%
Travel	55%	40%	28.75%
Animals, Pets	85%	77.5%	62.5%
Kids, Family	35%	35%	30%
Food, Drink, Cooking	40%	42.5%	46.25%
Beauty, Fashion	55%	50%	40%

Table 7. Results for retrieval without creating graph using ResNet152

Category	mAP@5	mAP@10	mAP@20
Music	45%	37.5%	33.5%
Gaming	40%	35%	38.75%
Sports, Actions	100%	97.5%	91.5%
News, Events, Politics	45%	47.5%	37.5%
Vehicles, Auto	80%	57.5%	50%
How-to	35%	40%	31.25%
Travel	55%	37.5%	28.75%
Animals, Pets	90%	80%	61.25%
Kids, Family	35%	32.5%	30%
Food, Drink, Cooking	40%	42.5%	45%
Beauty, Fashion	50%	42.5%	37.5%

REFERENCES

Araujo, A., Chaves, J., Angst, R., & Girod, B. (2015, September). Temporal aggregation for large-scale query-by-image video retrieval. In 2015 IEEE International Conference on Image Processing (ICIP) (pp. 1519-1522). IEEE.

Bain, M., Nagrani, A., Varol, G., & Zisserman, A. (2021). Frozen in time: A joint video and image encoder for end-to-end retrieval. arXiv preprint arXiv:2104.00650.

Dong, J., Li, X., Xu, C., Ji, S., He, Y., Yang, G., & Wang, X. (2019). Dual encoding for zero-example video retrieval. In Proceedings of the IEEE/CVF Conference on Computer Vision and Pattern Recognition (pp. 9346-9355).

Dzabraev, M., Kalashnikov, M., Komkov, S., & Petiushko, A. (2021). Mdmmt: Multidomain multimodal transformer for video retrieval. In Proceedings of the IEEE/CVF Conference on Computer Vision and Pattern Recognition (pp. 3354-3363).

Hamilton, W. L., Ying, R., & Leskovec, J. (2017, December). Inductive representation learning on large graphs. In Proceedings of the 31st International Conference on Neural Information Processing Systems (pp. 1025-1035).

Hu, W., Xie, D., Fu, Z., Zeng, W., & Maybank, S. (2007). Semantic-based surveillance video retrieval. IEEE Transactions on image processing, 16(4), 1168-1181.

Lee, H., Lee, J., Ng, J. Y. H., & Natsev, P. (2020). Large scale video representation learning via relational graph clustering. In Proceedings of the IEEE/CVF Conference on Computer Vision and Pattern Recognition (pp. 6807-6816).

Li, S., Chen, Z., Lu, J., Li, X., & Zhou, J. (2019). Neighborhood preserving hashing for scalable video retrieval. In Proceedings of the IEEE/CVF International Conference on Computer Vision (pp. 8212-8221).

Liu, Y., Albanie, S., Nagrani, A., & Zisserman, A. (2019). Use what you have: Video retrieval using representations from collaborative experts. arXiv preprint arXiv:1907.13487.

Luo, H., Ji, L., Zhong, M., Chen, Y., Lei, W., Duan, N., & Li, T. (2021). Clip4clip: An empirical study of clip for end to end video clip retrieval. arXiv preprint arXiv:2104.08860.

Miech, A., Laptev, I., & Sivic, J. (2018). Learning a text-video embedding from incomplete and heterogeneous data. arXiv preprint arXiv:1804.02516.

Portillo-Quintero, J. A., Ortiz-Bayliss, J. C., & Terashima-Marín, H. (2021, June). A straightforward framework for video retrieval using clip. In Mexican Conference on Pattern Recognition (pp. 3-12). Springer, Cham.

Shao, J., Wen, X., Zhao, B., & Xue, X. (2021). Temporal context aggregation for video retrieval with contrastive learning. In Proceedings of the IEEE/CVF Winter Conference on Applications of Computer Vision (pp. 3268-3278).

Szegedy, C., Ioffe, S., Vanhoucke, V., & Alemi, A. A. (2017, February). Inception-v4, inception-resnet and the impact of residual connections on learning. In Thirty-first AAAI conference on artificial intelligence.

Vedaldi, A., Bischof, H., Brox, T., & Frahm, J. M. (Eds.). (2020). Computer Vision-ECCV 2020: 16th European Conference, Glasgow, UK, August 23-28, 2020, Proceedings, Part II (Vol. 12347). Springer Nature.

Zhang, C., Lin, Y., Zhu, L., Liu, A., Zhang, Z., & Huang, F. (2019). CNN-VWII: An efficient approach for large-scale video retrieval by image queries. Pattern Recognition Letters, 123, 82-88.

Zhang, M. L., & Zhou, Z. H. (2007). ML-KNN: A lazy learning approach to multi-label learning. Pattern recognition, 40(7), 2038-2048.

DEVELOPMENT OF A FOCUSED WEB PAGE CRAWLER BASED ON GENRE AND CONTENT

Marcelo Trajano Alves Júnior, Marcos Felipe Pontes Rezende and Guilherme Tavares de Assis
Department of Computing - Federal University of Ouro Preto
Ouro Preto - MG , Brazil

ABSTRACT

Focused crawlers are generally used to crawl pages that satisfy some particular property and that are relevant to a specific topic of interest and are important for a wide variety of applications. For particular situations, a focused crawling approach was proposed and developed where the topic of interest can be expressed by terms that describe the genre and content of the desired web pages. In order to improve the efficiency and effectiveness of such an original genre-aware approach to focused crawling, the following improvements have been proposed, developed and validated: relevant page location policy based on Link Context, semi-automatic seed page determination, automatic similarity threshold definition and automatic refinement of genre and content term sets. In this context, this work proposes to develop a complete and functional version of a crawler, called Yucca, following the original genre-aware approach to focused crawling and the improvements already developed and validated, so that it can be used by different users in a simple and robust way. To validate Yucca, experiments were performed involving the crawling of web pages referring to three distinct and current topics of interest. In general, Yucca presented itself as an effective focused crawler, since the levels of precision achieved by the crawling processes carried out were quite satisfactory, reaching more than 80% on average when considering 10 pages returned as relevant by the crawler.

KEYWORDS

Focused Web Crawler, Focused Crawling Processes, Genre Terms, Content Terms

1. INTRODUCTION

Currently, according to Ahlgren (2021), there are more than 1.83 billion websites on the internet and this number grows exponentially each year; with this, it becomes necessary to create new Information Retrieval techniques, in order to facilitate the crawl Web pages and, consequently, the search for information desired by users. For this, as seen in Bhatt *et al.* (2015), search engines are basic tools to search for something of interest on the internet from repositories that are generated by traditional Web crawlers: a traditional Web crawler serves to crawl Web pages starting with seed pages and following the links contained in it, thus visiting other pages until it has covered a sufficient number of pages or reached a certain objective.

However, according to Costa *et al.* (2017), general purpose search engines do not solve well the problem of locating web pages referring to a specific topic, as the page collections generated by them are quite voluminous and, generally, user queries are short involving little information. In this context, focused crawlers (Jiang *et al.*, 2013) serve to generate smaller and restricted page collections, as they have the larger purpose of crawling pages that are, in the best possible way, relevant to a specific topic or interest of the user, from a more detailed specification of what one wants to crawl.

Thus, aiming to perform effective and efficient processes of focused crawlers, an approach was proposed and developed (Assis *et al.*, 2009) aimed at meeting specific situations. In general, such an approach consists of considering the evidence of genre (the type or style of text in specific documents) and content (the subject or theme you want to crawl) present on a given page and establish a degree of similarity between such evidence and the specific topic of interest. Therefore, this work had, as its main objective, to establish a framework that allows the construction of effective, efficient and scalable focused crawlers, without the need for a priori training or any type of pre-processing. Specifically, the proposed focused crawler approach is useful in situations where a topic of interest can be expressed through two distinct sets of terms: the first describing genre aspects of the desired pages and the second referring to the subject or content described on those pages. Through experiments performed, such an approach to focused crawler based on genre presented satisfactory levels of precision, recall and F1: 85% to 100% for all topics of interest considered.

However, there is no crawler, that is, a functional tool itself, which performs focused crawling processes, following the original approach mentioned, and also includes the improvements already applied and duly validated in the approach (Mangaravite *et al.*, 2012, Mangaravite *et al.*, 2014, Siqueira *et al.*, 2016, Costa *et al.*, 2017, Assis and Souza, 2018). Thus, this work proposes to develop and validate a complete and functional version of the focused crawler based on genre and content, called Yucca, considering the original approach and the integration of components related to the already validated improvements of the approach, so that it can be used by different users in a simple and robust way. Then, the main contributions of this work are: (a) proposal of Yucca, a focused web page crawler based on genre and content of interest ; (b) improving the effectiveness (determination of relevant pages) and efficiency (faster locating of relevant pages) of the crawling processes performed by Yucca compared to the original defined approach; (c) definition of functional characteristics related to the crawling processes that users wish to perform, through the use of a friendly interface proposed for Yucca; (d) analysis of results obtained through real Yucca validation experiments, involving specific topics relevant to the current moment.

The remainder of this work is organized as follows. In Section 2, related works are presented. In Section 3, the focused crawler proposed in this work, involving its functioning architecture, characteristics and layout, is described. In Section 4, the practical experiments performed are presented and the results obtained are analyzed. Finally, in Section 5, conclusions and perspectives for future work are presented.

2. RELATED WORK

As already mentioned, this work aims to develop and validate the first complete and functional version of Yucca: a focused web crawler based on genre and content. Thus, as related works, the original genre-aware approach and its proposed and developed improvements (see Subsection 2.1) and examples of current focused crawlers guided by heuristics (see Subsection 2.2) are presented.

2.1 Original Approach to Genre-Aware Focused Crawling

The original approach to genre-aware focused crawling (Assis *et al.*, 2009) establishes a framework that allows the construction of effective, efficient and scalable focused crawlers, which take into consideration the genre and content of the desired pages. Figure 1 shows the architecture of the original approach to genre-aware focused crawling.

According to Siqueira *et al.* (2016), as you can see in Figure 1, firstly (step 01), the priority queue called Frontier is initialized with the URLs of the seed pages (a set of pages from which to start the crawling), setting the URL scores to 1. For each URL in Frontier (step 02), the corresponding page is visited (step 04) and its content analyzed (steps 05 to 09): each page is represented as a n-dimensional vector based on it's terms (vector model) and the cosine distance is used to measure the similarity between the current page and the set of terms that represent the pages of interest. This measure is calculated separately to each set of terms (steps 05, 06 and 08), generating a specific similarity score between the current page and the sets of terms that represent, respectively, the genre, the content and the URL string of the desired pages. Each URL string term is related to the page genre or to the desired content. Then, these scores are combined into a final single one (steps 07 and 09), considering different weights for the sets of genre terms and content terms, and compared with a given threshold defined by an expert. If this final score is greater or equal to this threshold (step 10), the visited page is included in the set of relevant pages. Next, if the current page is considered relevant, the scores of URLs in Frontier that correspond to the sibling pages of the current page are changed to the final score (step 11). Finally, the previously extracted links from the current page are inserted into the Frontier (step 12) having their scores set to 0.

As already mentioned, improvements were proposed, developed and validated, in order to improve the original approach described in Figure 1. As a first improvement, the use of Link Context was proposed in (Mangaravite *et al.*, 2012), which aims to use text anchor, link title, and URL to improve the process of determining the visit priority scores that define the ordering of unvisited URLs found in the crawler's

Frontier. In general, to compute such scores, we also used the cosine distance between the terms of genre and content, input parameters of the original approach, and the texts generated by using the Link Context. The application of such a technique resulted in the improvement of the crawler's visit policy, generating an increase of up to 100% of efficiency in the original genre-aware approach.

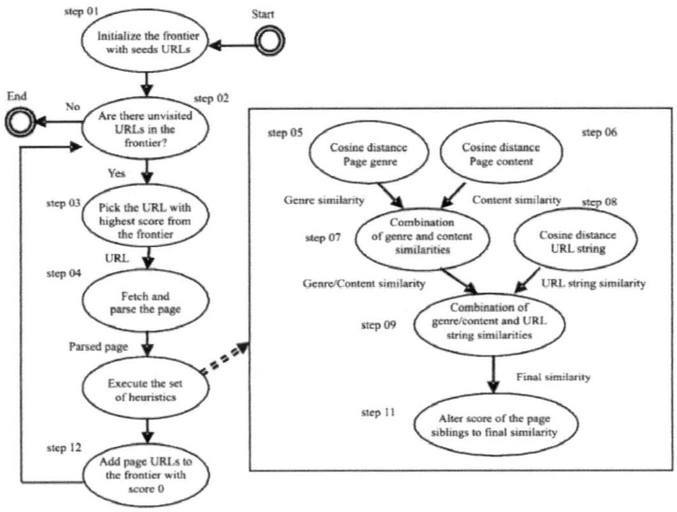

Figure 1. Architecture of the original approach to genre-aware focused crawling (Assis *et al*, 2009)

As a second improvement, Mangaravite *et al.* (2014) proposed a strategy for semi-automatic generation of seed pages, related to a certain topic of interest, so that the relevant pages to the desired topic are more quickly located by the crawler. The proposed strategy consists of using the specified terms of genre and content in a search engine, more specifically Google, to generate the seed pages. According to the experiments performed, the UnionFirst heuristic established for semi-automatic generation of seed pages, which uses only the first genre and content term in the query sent to the search engine, resulted in an improvement in efficiency in the original approach of up to 53%.

As a third improvement, in the work developed by Siqueira *et al.* (2016), three strategies were developed to automatically determine the similarity threshold used in focused crawling processes of the original approach. For each strategy developed, focused crawling processes were performed involving three distinct topics of interest. Through the results obtained, it was observed that the crawling processes, related to the strategy based on a K-Means grouping method (partitioning method), were the ones that presented the best effectiveness values, reaching very close F1 levels (difference of only 5.4%) from those obtained when the similarity thresholds were defined by specialists of the topics of interest considered.

And finally, as a fourth improvement, aiming to improve the sets of terms of genre and content, provided as input data, two strategies, for improving such sets based on association matrix and natural language processing, were proposed by Costa *et al.* (2017). Through the analysis of the results of the experiments described, it was possible to see that the strategy based on a matrix of association of terms, using the established metric Shortest Distance (calculation of the similarity sij, between two terms ti and tj, by the normalized sum of the smallest distances between these terms, considering all pages that have these terms) was the one with the best results, promoting an increase in the F1 metric of 6.29% when compared to the F1 value obtained by the crawling process, for the same specific topic, whose terms of genre and content have not been expanded.

2.2 Focused Crawlers Guided by Heuristics

In Lee *et al.* (2019), a genre-aware focused crawler was proposed and developed (in this case, genre refers only to academic texts), called SlideCrawler, aiming to crawl slide files with academic content, through Google as a crawling tool to manage queries and perform the desired downloads. The proposed crawler has: (a) a query generator to specify the desired slide format and the university to be consulted; (b) a URL extractor that is responsible for extracting URLs from slides and removing possible duplicates; and (c) a download manager that downloads the files pointed to by the extractor. In the experiments performed, SlideCrawler was able to download more than 850,000 academic slide files with diverse content. Comparing with another crawler called Apache Nutch (open source web crawling tool), SlideCrawler was able to crawl 3.7 times more slide files. However, despite the crawler being based on genre, it is limited to only a file format and a specific site, unlike the crawler proposed in this work, which aims to crawl the largest amount of pages in a given specified topic.

Not considering genre, Chen *et al.* (2012) use a recognition algorithm based on link analysis to obtain the most relevant pages to the desired topic of interest. This algorithm follows two premises: (a) if page A has a link to page B, then page B is a recommendation for page A; and (b) if there are links that connect pages A and B, then both pages can belong to a common theme. Based on this, Chen *et al.* (2012) deduced two more premises, namely: (a) if pages A and B point to the same pages, then these two pages are considered relevant, that is, the more links two pages match, the greater the degree of relevance between them; and (b) if a page has many links pointing to the same topic, it means that this page has a high chance of being relevant to the topic as well. Thus, to consider that a particular page A visited by the proposed focused crawler is relevant to the specified theme, it is necessary that the ratio between the number of links that are on such page A and the number of links that lead to it is greater than a predefined threshold. Considering medical themes in their experiments, this approach obtained a level of precision higher than 93% and recall higher than 83%, considering similarity thresholds equal to 0.5, 0.6, 0.7, 0.8 and 0.9; however, the approach does not use the semi-automatic generation of similarity threshold and seed pages, unlike the crawler proposed in this work, which has such functionalities in order to improve the effectiveness and efficiency, without the intervention of users regarding the provision of similarity threshold and seed pages, from focused crawling processes.

3. PROPOSAL AND DEVELOPMENT OF YUCCA

From the original approach to genre-aware focused crawling (see Figure 1) and its presented improvements, a functional and complete crawler, called Yucca, to focused crawling based on genre and content was proposed and developed. Figure 2 shows the functioning architecture of Yucca.

According to Figure 2, aiming at a particular crawling process to be performed for a specific topic of interest, the terms of genre (Step 01) and content (Step 02) are initially specified, these being the user's tasks. Then, in Step 03, the seed pages are semiautomatically generated using the terms of genre and content specified; such seed pages initialize the list of unvisited URLs, present in Frontier, with Yucca's visit priority score equal to 1. Considering the generated seed pages, Step 04 generates the association matrix for definition (Step 05) of terms expanded of the original terms. Continuing, in Step 06, the similarity threshold is automatically specified and determined using the terms specified by the user in Step 01 and 02 and the expanded terms in Step 05. Starting the crawling process itself, while there are unvisited URLs in the Frontier (Step 7), the one with the highest visit score is unqueued from Frontier (Step 08) and the corresponding page is visited by Yucca (Step 09); this visit consists of analyzing its relevance, through a set of similarity calculation heuristics, regarding the specific topic of interest. Thus, in Steps 10 and 11, the cosine distances between the visited page and the original and expanded terms of genre and content are calculated, respectively, combining and generating, in Step 12, the similarity of genre and content. Then, in Step 13, the cosine distance between the original and expanded terms of genre and content and the URL of the visited page is calculated, combining it, in Step 14, with the calculated similarity of genre and content (Step 12), thus generating the final similarity of the page visited in relation to the specific topic of interest. If such final similarity is greater than the automatically generated similarity threshold (Step 15), the visited page is considered relevant and, thus, it is stored in the repository of relevant pages to the specific topic of interest; in addition (Step 16), according to the queuing policy defined for Frontier, the visit score of URLs not yet visited, corresponding to the sibling pages of the visited page, is changed to the value of the calculated final similarity. Finally (Step 17), not linked to the execution of heuristics to calculate similarity, the URLs present in the visited page are added to Frontier with visit scores defined by the similarity between the terms of genre and content and the link contexts (Mangaravite *et al.*, 2012) of the URLs in question.

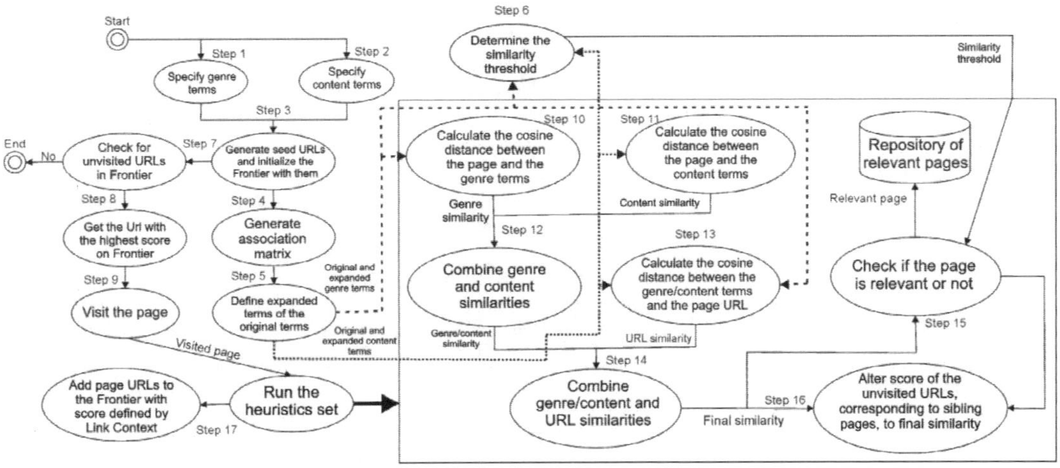

Figure 2. Yucca's functioning architecture

4. PRACTICAL EXPERIMENTATION

In this section, the Yucca evaluation experiments are presented and analyzed, following the architecture proposed in Figure 2. Subsection 4.1 describes the performed experiments and Subsection 4.2 presents and evaluates the results obtained through the performed experiments.

4.1 Experimental Setup

In order to evaluate the first functional version of Yucca, crawling processes were performed considering 3 current and distinct topics of interest, namely: (1) articles related to symptoms caused by Covid-19; (2) articles related to structural racism; (3) and articles related to global warming. Furthermore, in order to verify the importance of the content and genre terms used in the crawling processes, 3 different weight combinations were considered for the genre and content terms: Genre 0.3 and Content 0.7; Genre 0.4 and Content 0.6; and Genre 0.6 and Content 0.4. Due to the fact that the three defined topics have the same genre (articles), the same set of genre terms was specified for the topics, namely: article, introduction, conclusion, theoretical framework, abstract and result. Regarding content terms, different sets of terms were specified for each topic of interest, namely: (topic 1) covid-19, symptoms, signs and effects; (topic 2) structural racism, prejudice and racial discrimination; (topic 3) global warming, climate, climate change, ozone layer, greenhouse effect, temperature and environment. For all crawling processes performed, the following common characteristics were specified: maximum number of pages visited: 5000; maximum number of pages returned by Yucca, as relevant, to calculate precision: 60; and weight of a page's URL and genre/content combination (used in Step 14 of Figure 2): 0.5.

Furthermore, in order to analyze the pages returned as relevant by Yucca, throughout the execution of each crawling process, a log was stored containing the following information about each visited Web page: visited page identifier, automatically assigned by the crawler; URL of the visited page; HTML code of the visited page; and calculated similarity value between the page visited and the original and expanded genre and content terms for the topic of interest.

Finally, to evaluate the experiments performed, the precision metric was used. According to Brownlee (2020) and considering the context of this work, precision is a metric that establishes the fraction of pages really relevant to the desired topic of interest, which were returned by the focused crawler, in relation to all pages returned by it.

4.2 Experimental Results

Considering all the crawling processes performed, for each topic of interest defined, Table 1 presents the test case (weights associated with the terms of genre and content), the similarity threshold reached, the number of pages visited and the number of pages returned and therefore considered relevant by Yucca. Note that such values are presented for each test case performed for the same topic of interest, being: (1) "articles related to symptoms caused by Covid-19", (2) "articles related to structural racism" and (3) "articles related to global warming", varying the weight of the genre and content terms.

Table 1. Results of the test cases performed

Topic	Test Case	Similarity threshold	Number of visited pages	Number of retrieved pages
(1)	Genre: 0.3/ Content:0.7	0.3251	2838	98
	Genre: 0.4/ Content: 0.6	0.2663	2876	460
	Genre: 0.6/ Content: 0.4	0.3365	3007	63
(2)	Genre: 0.3/ Content:0.7	0.2189	3876	3037
	Genre: 0.4/ Content: 0.6	0.3796	3845	1198
	Genre: 0.6/ Content: 0.4	0.4503	3916	177
(3)	Genre: 0.3/ Content:0.7	0.1335	3646	2082
	Genre: 0.4/ Content: 0.6	0.3716	3577	201
	Genre: 0.6/ Content: 0.4	0.3716	3564	1750

Figures 3, 4 and 5 show, for each topic of interest, the levels of precision obtained considering different amounts of pages retrieved by Yucca, in descending order of similarity to the desired topic: 5 to 60 pages returned, from 5 out of 5. For instance, considering an arbitrary topic and a number of pages retrieved k, the graph points the fraction of the retrieved pages by Yucca that is relevant indeed.

As can be seen in Figure 3, related to the crawling processes associated with the topic of interest "articles related to symptoms caused by Covid-19", test case 1, associated with weights of 0.3 for genre and 0.7 for content, obtained a precision higher than the other tests, maintaining an average level of 83% when considering the 60 pages returned. However, when considering only the first 10 pages returned with greater similarity by Yucca, a common case in a search engine, test 3, associated with weights of 0.6 for genre and 0.4 for content, presents an average precision higher than the others, achieving 90% of precision. Moreover, the test case 3, associated with weights of 0.6 for genre and 0.4 for content, produces 100% of precision with 5 pages returned. However, the results of both test cases 2 and 3 get worse considering more pages.

Considering the topic of interest "articles related to structural racism", as can be seen in Figure 4, the precision curves for each test case were very similar; however, test case 1, associated with weights of 0.3 for genre and 0.7 for content, was slightly superior to the other tests, maintaining an average level of precision of 84% when considering the 60 pages returned. All tests showed satisfactory levels of precision, regardless of the number of pages returned, which can be seen in the graph with its lines very close to each other.

Regarding the topic of interest "articles related to global warming", as seen in Figure 5, test 3, associated with weights 0.6 for genre and 0.4 for content, was slightly superior to the others, maintaining an average level 82% precision when considering the 60 pages returned. When considering the first 10 pages returned with greater similarity by Yucca, tests 2 and 3 have similar averages of precision close 85%. Furthermore, with a high level of pages returned, both test cases presented a high precision close to 75%.

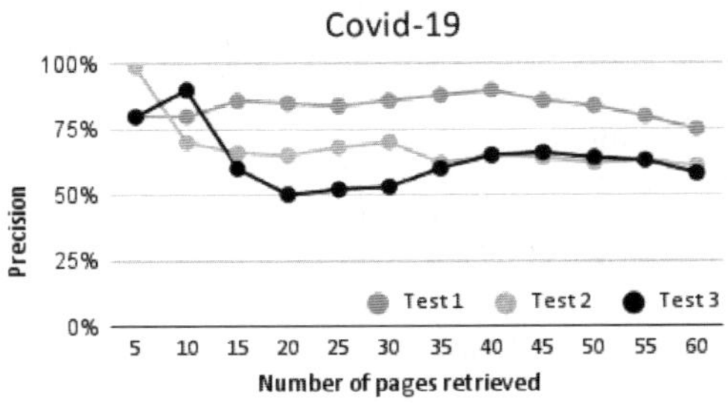

Figure 3. Precision levels – Covid-19 topic

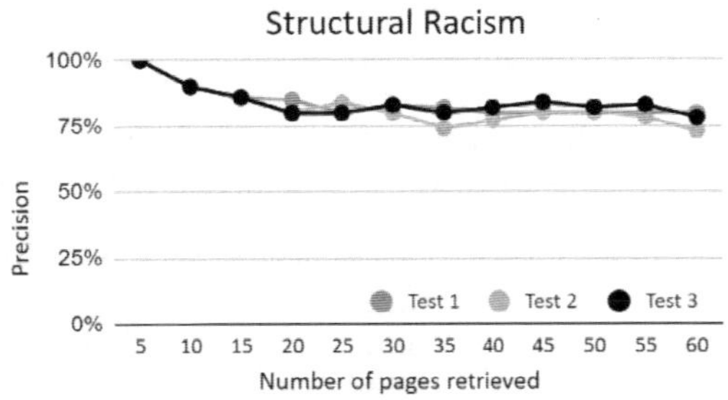

Figure 4. Precision levels - Structural Racism topic

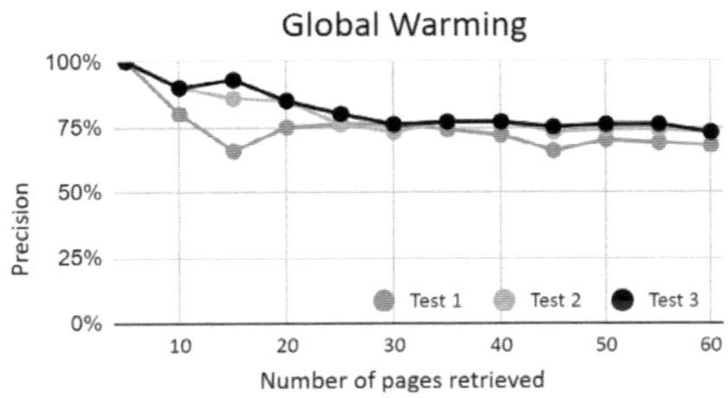

Figure 5. Precision levels - Global Warming topic

Figure 6 shows the best curve obtained by the three topics of interest using the most accurate test case for each one. Comparatively, it is observed that the generated precision curves remained very close and with good levels of precision, thus demonstrating accurate and satisfactory results for the topics considered. It is noteworthy, in this case, the crawling process related to the topic of interest "articles related to symptoms caused by Covid-19", since, despite having obtained the worst levels of precision for the first 10 pages returned, it presented about 90% precision for the first 40 pages returned as relevant by Yucca.

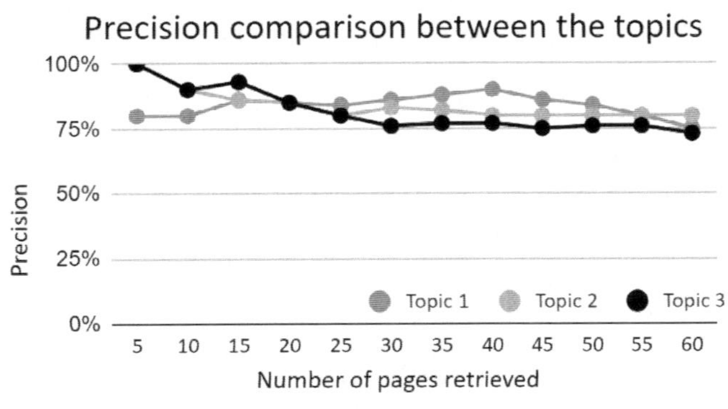

Figure 6. Precision comparison between the best results of the topics

5. CONCLUSION

As presented, this work proposes to develop a complete and functional version of a focused crawler based on genre and content, called Yucca, considering the original approach proposed in Assis *et al.* (2009) and the improvements made by Mangaravite *et al.* (2012, 2014), Siqueira *et al.* (2016) and Costa *et al.* (2017).

Seeking to evaluate the Yucca, as seen, experiments were performed considering 3 distinct topics of interest and, in all topics, the efficacy results were very satisfactory, with similar levels of precision. In particular, it was possible to observe that, depending on the weights of the terms of genre and content, the levels of precision can be different, although, regardless of such weights, the levels of precision were above 80% for up to 10 pages returned as relevant by Yucca in the three topics. This is an excellent result since, when analyzing documents linked to a specific topic, users generally check the first documents returned.

As future works, we intend to (1) propose, develop and integrate to Yucca a component for semi-automatic determination of terms of genre and content, linked to a specific topic of interest, necessary for carrying out a crawling process; (2) perform new Yucca validation experiments using, including, other metrics such as recall and F1; and (3) conduct user experience studies regarding the use of Yucca, in order to analyze its usability.

ACKNOWLEDGEMENT

This research was partially funded by research grants from PROPP/UFOP. Furthermore, it was carried out on the GAID/UFOP Laboratory.

REFERENCES

AHLGREN, M. 2021. *100 + estatísticas e fatos da internet para 2021.* Available at: <https://www.websitehostingrating.com/pt/internet-statistics-facts/>. [Accessed June 4, 2021].

ASSIS, G. T. et al. 2009. A genre-aware approach to focused crawling. World Wide Web, Springer, 12(3), p. 285–319.

ASSIS, G. T. et al. 2018. Improving the scalability of a genre-aware approach to focused crawling. *In Proceedings of the 17th International Conference WWW/Internet (ICWI)*, Budapest, Hungry, p. 159-166.

BHATT, D. et al. 2015. Focused web crawler. *In: Advances in Computer Science and Information Technology (ACSIT)*, vol. 2, 11, p. 1-6

BROWNLEE, J. How to calculate precision, recall, and f-measure for imbalanced classification. 2020. Available at: <https://machinelearningmastery.com/precision-recall-and-f-measure-for-imbalanced-classification/>. [Accessed June 4, 2021].

CHEN, Z. et al. 2012. Web page recognition algorithm based on link analysis in theme search engine. *In 2012 Second International Conference on Cloud and Green Computing.* p. 405-409. Available at: <https://doi.org/10.1109%2Fcgc.2012.42>.

COSTA, G. G. et al. 2017. Automatic improvement of terms used in focused crawling processes on web page. *In Proceedings of the 16th International Conference WWW/Internet (ICWI).*

JIANG, J. et al. 2013. Focus: learning to crawl web forums. *IEEE Transactions on Knowledge and Data Engineering*, 25(3), p. 1293–1306.

LEE, J.-G. et al. 2019. An effective approach to enhancing a focused crawler using google. *The Journal of Supercomputing, Springer US.* ISSN0920-8542,1573-0484. Available at: <http://doi.org/10.1007/s11227-019-02787-9>. [Accessed January 4, 2021].

MANGARAVITE, V. et al. 2012. Improving the Efficiency of a Genre-Aware Approach to Focused Crawling Based on Link Context. p. 17–23 of: Web Congress (LA-WEB), *2012 Eighth Latin American. IEEE.*

MANGARAVITE, V. et al. 2014. Semi-automatic generation of seed pages in genre-aware focused crawling. p. 51–58 of: *Proceedings of the 13th International Conference WWW/Internet (ICWI).*

SIQUEIRA, G. O. et al. 2016. Automatic determination of similarity threshold for focused crawling processes on Web pages. *In: Proceedings of the 15th International Conference WWW/Internet (ICWI).*

A SYSTEMATIC REVIEW ON THE IMPLEMENTATION OF BUSINESS INTELLIGENCE AT FEDERAL UNIVERSITIES

Thiago Rizzi Santos, Marcos Wagner S. Ribeiro, Weuler Borges Santos, Lucas Rodrigues Costa and Carlos Gabriel S. Stédile

Instituto de Ciências Exatas -- Universidade Federal de Jataí, (UFJ) , Jataí - GO - Brazil

ABSTRACT

Institutions (companies or organizations) due to the high level of complexity of their processes and the need to expand competitive advantages make use of Management Information Systems (MIS) to give their managers correct and immediate information for decision-making. Specifically, federal universities, that search for other objectives (quality, efficiency in their final area - education) also depend on these same MIS to achieve their management objectives. However, the lack of data systematization, lack of systems models, and a wide and complex decision-making structure make these institutions have difficulties in presenting their information correctly, unified, and standardized. From this context, this paper presents a Systematic Literature Review (SLR) on the implementation process of Business Intelligence (BI) in federal institutions of education with the premise of characterizing the information model contained in these institutions. As a methodology, a Systematic Review was established with an emphasis on three aspects: delimitation of the theme; review protocol and conducting the review. The results obtained in the analysis point towards the use of Big Data and Data Mining to support decision-making.

KEYWORDS

Business Intelligence, Information Systems, Decision-Making, Big Data, Data Mining

1. INTRODUCTION

In the current context of organizations in a highly competitive scenario, the decision-making process happens all the time and in different sectors within an institution. However, to ensure the right decisions within a business, a crucial factor is to obtain accurate information at the right time. To assist in this purpose, one of the technologies used is the Management Information Systems (MIS).

Such technologies, according to (Oliveira, 2008), allow managers to obtain, in a dynamic and practical way, the necessary information to support the decisions that guide the institutions, in internal administrative matters; in sales strategies; or other areas that need more accurate management of indicators. The same author reinforces that management information systems become indispensable because, in most companies that use computerized systems, there is a lot of data available, but this data alone cannot be used in the decision-making process without first going through a process of conversion, transformation, making them effectively become information. It is at this stage where management information systems work, compiling these data sets into processed information.

In the public sector, according to (Barros, 2016), information management is usually more complex, as the strategies are not intended to obtain competitive advantages over competitors or seek to maximize their profits, but rather, the quality, efficiency, and consequently, accountability for those who are under (community) and/or under its jurisdiction (control bodies). Furthermore, paraphrasing the same author, there are still several factors in government organizations that hinder the agility of information, such as changes in governments, with new policies and lines of action, and naturally, the already common budget restrictions.

Bearing in mind these inherent barriers to the public sector, it is still necessary to take into account that the Information Systems used by public institutions do not always comply with recommended practices to ensure greater data quality and, consequently, efficiency in the generation of information, such as: Integrated

IT; a suitable tool for data processing; standardization; investments and efforts in the area (Oliveira, 2008). And these peculiarities come down to the problem of this research, the lack of systematization of data from federal educational institutions, making it difficult to make strategic decisions in administrative and/or academic management.

Public bodies described as federal educational institutions or related entities (In Brazil), by decrees (MEC, 2021) are classified into: a) Federal Technological Education Centers (6 units); b) Universities Foundations (2 units); c) Federal University Foundations (26 units); d) Federal Institutes (38 units), and e) Federal Universities (44 units). Of interest to this research, the Federal Centers and Institutes are excluded from the previous list, the others, which are also designated as IFES (Federal Institutions of Higher Education) according to their body (ANDIFES - National Association of Directors of IFES - (ANDIFES, 2021)) of congregation and representation. These bodies (institutions) have specificity in structuring their information, not having a single model of management information system. In these, each chooses a model or a version of a more widespread system model. This lack of standardization arises from the very dynamics of the structures resulting from the university's own guiding documents (INEP, 2021) (bylaws, regulations, Institutional Development Plan, and others). These documents establish in their organizational structures peculiar forms according to the understanding of their members or participants, without differing from other institutions in the legal and formal scope, but sufficiently different to require specific informational systems. In addition to these characteristics, the federal university (a term that will be generalized in this research) as an agency linked to the Federal Government makes use of specific systems at the federal level, called Structuring/Structuring Systems (SIAFI, SIASG, SIORG, and others) of the Public Administration (Estruturadores, 2019) which are modular systems that do not always connect and also do not interact causing, in most cases, the need to create data redundancy to supply them.

That said, (Barros, 2016) states that it is important that there is a single information system that involves and enables interaction between the academic and administrative areas. This is because, at the federal university, new situations are always emerging, and an organized and updated system is increasingly necessary to meet demands in the administrative and academic spheres, in short, so that professors, technicians, students, and the whole society have access to all information needed.

Given this context, on the premise that it is natural for the institution to adapt to systems that communicate with other levels of government and considering the impossibility of exchanging all Structuring Systems for a single Information System model, the proposal of this research arises from a Systematic Literature Review that points to some paths that will be presented in the Analysis and Conclusions section.

2. METHODOLOGY

The method used to carry out this SLR was approached by (Kitchenham, 2004), highlighting the phases for implementing a review in these terms that include: a) Delimitation of the Theme; b) Review Protocol; c) Conducting the Review. The strategy was chosen to guarantee the researcher the quality of the results obtained during the process, and the reassessment until it is approved. The theme in its raw state was refined from the first results of the searches, allowing the authors, through an incremental/spiral method, to clearly obtain the object of study, the related problem, and mainly, the area of the solution. Therefore, the delimitation of the theme is already the result of the analysis of the Systematic Literature Review, giving it a broader aspect than a mapping. Also, the review protocol presented in this research is the latest version that allowed the authors to conclude the contribution they could make to the method based on the analysis of the results found in the data extraction. And they present the research questions, the search strategy, the quality criteria, and inclusion/ exclusion criteria.

2.1 Research Questions

In Table 1, four research questions were defined, which aim to guide the main hypotheses.

Table 1. Definition of Research Questions

Identification	Question
Q1	What are the main difficulties encountered in implementing BI in universities?
Q2	May the use of technologies such as BI be a means of facilitating decision-making in an academic environment?
Q3	Is the lack of systematization, standardization, and organization of data from universities and/or public higher education institutions an obstacle in the generation of data/information?
Q4	May the use of Data Mining and Big Data minimize the difficulties of managing data and information when used in conjunction with BI?

2.2 Search Strategy

At this stage, three classifications were defined for the composition of the search strategies: Research source; Search Terms, and Search Strings. Table 2 summarizes this structure. And Table 3 presents a classification of terms according to specific criteria that allow validating the research questions.

Table 2. Search Sources and Strings

Search Items	Description
Research Sources	Banco de Teses e Dissertações; ACM Digital Library; IEEE Xplore
Search Terms	"Business Intelligence", "Big Data", "Tomada de Decisão", "Dados não padronizados", "Universidades", "Non-standard Data", "Decision-Making", "Universities"
Search Strings	BDTD: "Business Intelligence" AND "Tomada de Decisão" ACM DL: "Business intelligence" AND "Big Data" AND "Decision-Making" IEEE Xplore: Universities AND "Business intelligence" AND "Decision-Making"

Table 3. Classification of Research Questions

Criterion	Term	Synonym/Similar	Translation
Population	Universidades	Academic Environment Higher education institutions Non-standard Data	Universities
Intervention	Business Intelligence	Data Mining Big Data	Data Mining
Context	Tomada de Decisão	Data/Information Management	Decision-Making
Comparation	Impactos	Contributions	Impacts
Results	Processo de Facilitar	Minimize the Difficulties	Improvement

2.3 Inclusion and Exclusion Criteria

In order to have previously defined, based on the results found, fundamentals to include or exclude an article from the research, inclusion and exclusion criteria were defined, represented in Tables 4 and 5.

Table 4. Classification of Inclusion Criteria

	Inclusion Criteria
Criteria	Description
IC1	Articles that include Business Intelligence
IC2	Articles that have at least the abstract available
IC3	Articles in which the year of publication is after 2015
IC4	Articles in which the "population" is companies/universities or similar

Table 5. Classification of Exclusion Criteria

	Exclusion Criteria
Criteria	**Description**
EC1	Articles in the abstract or expanded summary (short paper) format
EC2	Articles without full version available for web access
EC3	Articles in languages other than Portuguese and English.
EC4	Duplicate articles

2.4 Quality Criteria

At this stage of the design, a methodology was established to carry out the quality analysis of the articles. For this, four criteria and scores from 1 to 5 were stipulated, where the objective is to assess whether the work contemplates them or not. It is also important to emphasize that the proposal is not to compare the works themselves, but to verify their importance for the theme proposed in this systematic review.

Listed below are the criteria and their respective definitions:

1. **Presentation:** How the researcher presents his study including the planning that was used
2. **Methodology:** Quality related to how the work was prepared and conducted
3. **Validation:** How the analysis was performed, and the metrics used to achieve the results
4. **Survey Question:** Application of the question or research question

2.5 Conducting the Review

The pre-established research method was applied to identify potential articles related to the theme of this systematic review. Initially, 391 articles were retrieved, 28 from the main Theses and Dissertations Banks (Brazilian Library of Theses and Dissertations), 231 from ACM DL, and 132 from IEEE Xplore. Subsequently, the title, abstract, and keywords of the recovered works were read. At this stage, 356 articles were excluded and 35 were included. Finally, the inclusion and exclusion criteria were applied. At this stage, another 13 articles were excluded. The result is presented below:

Table 6. Data Extraction Results

Research Sources	Initial Results	Excluded	Included
Banco de Teses e Dissertações	28	24	4
ACM Digital Library	231	221	10
IEEE Xplore	132	124	8
Total	391	369	22

3. ANALYSIS

Q1 - What are the main difficulties encountered in implementing BI in universities?

Among the main difficulties observed in the implementation of Business Intelligence in universities, one is the organizational culture. This problem was directly cited by (Santos, 2017) and (Apraxine & Stylianou, 2017), the authors argue that it is important to take into account the data at the time of decision-making and not base it only on intuitions. Therefore, other impasses could also be overcome with the change in the institution's culture, it must embrace the idea of a BI system and be willing to learn and understand how they can benefit from its use.

Another limiting factor cited by (Neto, 2017) and (Barros, 2016) is the constant changes in the management of a university, implying the constant updating of the set of informational requirements. (Barros, 2016), cites the importance of creating a sector that is responsible for updating the system.

In addition, (Neto, 2017) reports that there were limitations regarding the development of an integrative BI, mainly due to the unavailability of data that could be used in some sectors of universities, such as the treasury. Being limited to creating only one Data Mart with academic data.

Given the above, other obstacles that were observed mostly among researchers should also be taken into accounts, such as the improvement of technological infrastructure with the investment in hardware, software, and training of employees responsible for registering data in the system and administrative techniques, such as the creation and analysis of performance indicators and the strategic use of information.

Q2 - May the use of technologies such as BI be a means of facilitating decision-making in an academic environment?

The idea that BI systems can facilitate decision-making in an academic environment is unanimous among selected articles involving BI in universities.

According to (Neto, 2017), the term Business Intelligence, created by Howard Dresner of the Gartner Group in 1989, is part of the need for competitive advantages, aiming at better business decision-making. However, with the evolution of technology, it started to be used in different types of organizations, currently widely used in educational institutions. (Apraxine & Stylianou, 2017), mentions that BI practices can lead to the desired result, providing quality and value that lead to an improvement in the decision-making process. Educational institutions have a large amount of data, which has a critical influence on the decision-making process, as it can be available across the department from a single source and analyzed to report the need for change and improvement in the internal and external environment of a university. (Gubalova, 2016), reinforces the same idea and says that BI tools allow a simplification of the analysis process, also offer government officials an integrated reporting and analysis environment to help university managers in the process of decision-making.

Q3 - Is the lack of systematization, standardization, and organization of data from universities and/or public higher education institutions an obstacle in the generation of data/information?

Considering the works analyzed, it was concluded that none of them have as their main focus the lack of data organization, but rather the cause of this problem. In short, the lack of integration between information systems used in universities. Thus, this research question is not considered in the construction of a taxonomy for the evaluation of related works. This generated a new research question related to the lack of integration between systems, which, according to the qualitative analysis, is the main obstacle in the generation of information in universities. According to (Santos, 2017), there are several explanations for the lack of information in universities, highlighting the lack of integration between data from different systems, in addition to the lack of a favorable environment and adequate tools for data processing. (Barros, 2016), shares the same idea and states that to minimize the difficulties of generating information, it is highlighted that IT needs to be integrated, to visualize the strategic objective of the organization and the services provided for her. For (Neto, 2017), there is a high need to use MIS's that provide information reliable to provide greater control over academic monitoring and improvements in the strategic and managerial decision process, with an integrated administrative, financial, and academic management.

Q4 - Can the use of Data Mining and Big Data minimize the difficulties of managing data and information when used in conjunction with BI?

The Data Mining analytical tool, according to (Santos, 2017), consists of a process that uses techniques to extract and identify useful information and, consequently, knowledge (or patterns) from large volumes of data, and these patterns can be presented as trends, business rules, correlations, or predictive models. Data Mining, for many authors (including retrieved articles) and in the literature in general, is considered essential and used as part of the basic architecture of a BI system. However, recent research points to the need for an updated BI architecture, using, in addition to the usual components, Big Data techniques to deal with the increase in the volume, variety, and speed of generated data. For (Bousty, et al., 2018), most current BI solutions are not able to keep up with the rapid evolution of data generation. (Santos & Costa, 2016), exemplify the migration from a traditional Data Warehouse to the Big Data scenario, thus supporting BI.

3.1 Quantitative Analysis

According to the established research questions, Table 7 presents the quantitative for each research question in relation to obtaining or not the answer through the selected research articles.

Table 7. Quantitative Analysis

Q1	Q2	Q3	Q4
9	9	8	17

Based on these results presented in Table 7 it is possible to state that:

1. Questions 1 and 2 returned a fair number of answers, as the topic "BI implementation to facilitate decision-making" is really relevant in the context of BI in universities.

2. Question 3 initially did not return any answer, as the research question was premised on the lack of data systematization, however, most of the works present the analysis of the consequence of this problem, which is the lack of integration between systems. Thus, the question was readjusted and also returned a number considered to be low, but sufficient for analysis.

3. Question 4 returned the highest number of answers, as this research question is more comprehensive compared to others, in which the scope was reduced to universities only. Among the 17 responses returned, 15 addressed Data Mining, 9 Big Data, and 7 both technologies. The reduced number of returns on Big Data is mainly because this term has become popular recently.

3.2 Qualitative Analysis

1. **What are the main difficulties encountered in implementing BI in universities?**
   This question, which was answered by 9 of the 22 selected works, presents as a premise, from this analysis, that the following criteria must be observed in a work in terms of BI implementation in universities:
   - Business understanding
   - Organizational culture
   - Staff training
   - Technological infrastructure (hardware and software)

   Thus, in the construction of taxonomy, this first item will be titled "Structure for BI".

2. **May the use of technologies such as BI be a means of facilitating decision-making in an academic environment?**
   This question, which, like the previous one, was answered by 9 of the 22 works retrieved, from this analysis, presents as a condition that the following criteria must be observed in a work with the purpose of facilitating decision-making in an academic environment:
   - Easy access
   - Reliability of Answers

   In taxonomic terms, this item will be titled "Data Availability".

3. **Is the lack of integration between university management information systems an obstacle in the generation of information?**
   This question, which was answered by 8 of the 22 selected papers, as a result of this analysis, shows that the following criteria should be analyzed in a paper for the purpose of integrating Management Information Systems from universities:
   - Enabling environment (unique information management system)
   - Decision support systems

   Therefore, in the construction of taxonomy, this item will be called "System Integration".

4. **May the use of Data Mining and Big Data minimize the difficulties of managing data and information when used in conjunction with BI?**
   This question that had the highest response rate, 17 of the 22 selected works, exposes as a premise, from this analysis, that some criteria must be observed in a work in terms of applying Big Data and Data Mining in a BI system.
   - DM Methodology
   - DBMSs
   - Big Data Systems

   Thus, for a taxonomic model, this last item will be titled "BI Optimization".

4. CONCLUSION

The paths found as a possible proposal to alleviate the problem presented earlier in this research, which, again emphasizing, arises from a systematic literature review, explore the use of advanced analytical technologies such as Business Intelligence (BI), Big Data, and Mining tools to support decision-making in administrative/academic environment.

In this way, the conclusion is reached that the natural path, from these technologies presented, is to be able to transform data (even if from an unknown organization) into useful information and knowledge for the important and already mentioned decision-making process, making the integration from multiple sources, and getting "a single version of the truth" for all members of an organization.

In view of this evaluation, considering the results obtained in the qualitative analysis of the articles found, the following taxonomy of work evaluation was generated that have the same theme, designated here as related articles. This taxonomy is described below:

a) Structure for BI.
b) Data Availability.
c) Systems Integration.
d) BI Optimization.

In view of this and assuming a solution to the research problem, this research presents the following contribution: **Creation of a methodology using Big Data and Data Mining to implement a Business Intelligence system in a federal institution of higher education.**

And, in addition, the following specific objectives would be introduced:

1. Analyze the structure of information systems in Federal Universities.
2. Survey the specific informational needs of managers and the respective departments of the institution.
3. Analyze the availability of information and its respective correctness in decision-making at federal universities.
4. Explore the analytical technologies necessary for the development of the Business Intelligence system.
5. Evaluate and validate a methodology for developing a BI system.

REFERENCES

ANDIFES, 2021. *Associação Nacional dos Dirigentes de Instituições Federais de Ensino Superior.* [Online] Available at: https://www.andifes.org.br [Acesso em 28 04 2021].

Apraxine, D. & Stylianou, E., 2017. *Business intelligence in a higher educational institution: The case of University of Nicosia.* Nicosia, Cyprus, IEEE Computer Society.

Barros, B. M. D., 2016. *Proposta de um Sistema de Business Intelligence para suporte a gestão dos cursos de graduação da Universidade Federal do Pampa.* Santa Maria, RS, s.n.

Bousty, H. et al., 2018. Investigating Business Intelligence in the era of Big Data: concepts, benefits and challenges. *Association for Computing Machinery.*

Estruturadores, S., 2019. *Ministério da Economia - Governo Federal.* [Online] Available at: https://www.gov.br/economia/pt-br/assuntos/sistemas-estruturadores[Acesso em 28 01 2021].

Gubalova, J., 2016. *The use of Business Intelligence Tools for leadership and university administration.* Slovakia, Institute of Electrical and Electronics Engineers Inc..

INEP, 2021. *Instituto Nacional de Estudos e Pesquisas Educacionais Anísio Teixeira.* [Online] Available at: https://www.gov.br/inep/ [Acesso em 28 04 2021].

Kitchenham, B., 2004. *Procedures for Performing.* Australia: Keele University.

MEC, 2021. *Ministério da Educação - Governo Federal.* [Online] Available at: https://www.gov.br/mec [Acesso em 28 04 2021].

Neto, J. d. L. M., 2017. *Desenvolvimento de um Sistema de Inteligência de Negócios para Apoio da Gestão Acadêmica.* Itajubá: Universidade Federal de Itajubá.

Oliveira, D. D. P. R. D., 2008. *Sistemas de Informações Gerenciais: Estratégias, Táticas, Operacionais.* 12ª ed. São Paulo: Editora Atlas.

Santos, J. S. D., 2017. *BUSINESS INTELLIGENCE: Uma proposta metodológica para análise da evasão escolar em instituições federais de ensino.* s.l.:Universidade Federal do Paraná.

Santos, M. & Costa, C., 2016. Data Warehousing in Big Data: From Multidimensional to Tabular Data Models. *Association for Computing Machinery.*

A DATA-DRIVEN STUDY OF CITIZEN SCIENCE DATA QUALITY ASSESSMENT PROFILE

Jailson N. Leocadio[1] and Antonio M. Saraiva[2]
[1] *Escola Politécnica, University of São Paulo*
Av. Prof. Luciano Gualberto 158, Tv. 3, 05508-010, São Paulo-SP, Brazil
[2] *Escola Politécnica, University of São Paulo, Av. Prof. Luciano Gualberto 158, Tv. 3, 05508-010*
Instituto de Estudos Avançados, University of São Paulo, R. Praça do Relógio 109, 05508-970
São Paulo-SP, Brazil

ABSTRACT

In Citizen Science (CS) projects, data quality (DQ) has been a major concern and discussions have been held to evaluate and ensure the quality of what is produced by volunteers, but few studies have assessed how volunteers get involved and the impact of their behavior on data quality. This study aimed to study a data-driven CS profile to data quality assessment. Here, we analyzed citizen science data extracted from the iNaturalist, a platform to record species observations. We used 58,488 observations recorded in São Paulo, Brazil, and Manchester, England, to train machine learning models, using Random Forest, and to create a DQ profile to classify data according to its quality. We applied an approach that, first identifies information elements (IE) and quality dimensions to describe the data and users' behavior. The data was then cleaned, pre-processed and transformed. Three models were created: a complete model (with all features), a reduced model (with dimension reduction) and a model with only characteristics that describe the users' behavior. The precision score for the models were 0.931, 0.932 and 0.774, respectively. The results showed that data quality can be described with few features and user behavior is very important to understand the quality of what is produced by volunteers.

KEYWORDS

Data Quality Assessment, Machine Learning, Data Mining, Biodiversity Data

1. INTRODUCTION

According to the Oxford English Dictionary, citizen science (CS) is the collection and analysis of data by members of the general public, typically as part of a collaborative project with professional scientists. CS projects can engage participants in different stages of a scientific research (Wiggins and Crowston, 2011), but the most common is that volunteers contribute to the data collection. In these cases, data quality (DQ) is a very frequent concern (Wiggins et al., 2011) due to the lack of ability of participants and bias, among other issues, and efforts have been made to assess and guarantee quality and prevent problems from different sources (Wiggins et al., 2011). As a result, CS data has been proving to be reliable (Brown and Williams, 2019), comparable to specialist data (Aceves-Bueno et al., 2017) and it is a potential solution for data scarcity problems in some research fields (e.g., biological species distribution), a driver of scientific breakthroughs (Palacin et al., 2020) and an emerging data source for measuring the United Nations Sustainable Development Goals (SDG) achievement (Fritz et al., 2019). However, few studies have evaluated how volunteers engage with projects and how scientists perceive data provided by them (Ellwoodet al., 2017), although these studies could provide practical insights that can assist the design, development, and evaluation of digital CS platforms and projects in general (Palacin et al., 2020).

In data quality studies, procedures generally aim at measuring quality, improving quality or evaluating DQ impact (Ge and Helfert, 2007). In the first case, measuring DQ means to judge the data fitness for use in a given context and can be performed quantitatively or qualitatively (Veiga et al., 2017). As DQ is considered a multidimensional concept (McGilvray, 2008), diverse evaluation attributes can be applied in order to assess it, with no consensus on an ideal set of dimensions. In addition, the relevance of each dimension can be perceived according to the data use context (Veiga et al., 2017). Common quality dimensions reported are accuracy and precision, experience and ability of participants, volunteers' training, spatial and temporal data scope, among others.

To improve quality in CS, Artificial Intelligence (AI) techniques are commonly applied to support volunteer's data validation (Jones et al., 2018), performing automatic tasks, such as, organisms counting and species identifications and it is recognized as a way to deal with CS data quality issues (Wiggins et al., 2011). Machine learning (ML) algorithms, in its different approaches like supervised, unsupervised and semi-supervised learning, can also contribute to increase the knowledge about citizen scientists individuals and the data produced by them. In supervised learning, labeled datasets are used to train models that will classify new data or accurately predict results, according to the knowledge initially extracted. Classification is a subcategory of this approach, and its goal is to predict categorical class labels. One example is the the Random Forest (Breiman, 2001) (RF) algorithm (also used for regression), an ensemble method that predicts combining the results of several decision trees.

The aim of this study is to propose CS profiles to data quality assessment. A DQ profile consists of information elements (IE) and quality dimensions that, combined, create features used to model quality criteria via supervised learning algorithms of AI. The profiles intend to consider important aspects of CS, as user behavior, and be applicable to classify data according to its quality.

2. MATERIAL AND METHODS

We used the conceptual framework on biodiversity data quality (Veiga et al., 2017) as a basis to the method. It states that a DQ profile organizes the quality needs to clearly describe how DQ should be handled to enable its assessment and management in a specific use case context. To create a DQ profile, according to the framework, it is necessary to define 1. a context (used as the profile scope delimitation), 2. information elements (important pieces of data that should be evaluated in the use case context), 3. dimensions (measurement attributes), 4. criteria (the rules that states how data is considered fit for use in the use case context) and 5. enhancements (improvements to make data fitter for use in the context). This last component is not used in the present research, as our objective is only the evaluation of quality.

2.1 iNaturalist Data

We collected citizen scientist data provided by iNaturalist (www.inaturalist.org), a CS platform that hosts contributive projects for biodiversity data collection where volunteers contribute with specimen observations around the world and make suggestions of the taxon identification (ID) in any record. iNaturalist was created in 2008, and it has over a million users and over 58 million observation records available for download and scientific use. Its data is also published in the Global Biodiversity Information Facility (GBIF, www.gbif.org), an international network and data infrastructure aimed at providing open access to data about all types of life on Earth. The observations recorded inside the cities of São Paulo, SP, Brazil until September 27, 2020, and Manchester, England until October 04, 2020, were selected and downloaded. The amount of data corresponds to 63,620 observations, but only those that are not from captive specimens were used, a total of 58,488. That data was provided by 3,580 different observers (people who posted the observation) and 5,387 different identifiers (people who made suggestions of taxon names for the observations).

The quality grade provided by iNaturalist was used to define the classes that indicate if the observation had or had not quality, as this present work applies supervised learning. The iNaturalist metric defines three categories of quality: *Casual* is the initial level, but it can also be assigned for observations that have had their information questioned by users or the system; *Needs Id* indicates that the observation has date, is georeferenced, has photo or sound and is not of a human being but misses an identification of species; the *Research Grade* is applied when the users agree at the species level on the identification. This last level was used to indicate presence of quality and the other two, absence. Thus, the dataset contained 27,566 (47.1%) observations labeled as having quality and 30,922 (52.9%) as not having quality.

2.1.1 Information Elements

A total of 13 IE were defined to represent each observation: *annotation* (information about the life stage, plant phenology, alive or dead, and sex), *coordinates* (composed of longitude and latitude), *description* (text with observation details), *identifier user* (users who suggested a taxon name for identification), *observation date* (date when the observation occurred), *observer user* (user who posted the observation), *observation field* (custom detail fields), *photo* (photos provided in the observation record), *place* (location where observation was recorded), scientific name (observation current taxon), *sound* (sounds provided in the observation record) and *update date* (date when some new information was added to the observation).

Table 1. Features generation. Mechanism of evaluation for each dimension and EI

IE	Dimension	Evaluation
annotation	completeness	number of annotations
coordinate	completeness	if there is coordinate data
	appropriateness	if both, latitude and longitude values, are present
	accuracy	positional accuracy of coordinate
	latitude.completeness	if there is latitude data
	latitude.appropriateness	if the value is numeric and is in the range of -90 to 90
	latitude.precision	number of decimal places
	longitude.completeness	if there is longitude data
	longitude.appropriateness	if the value is numeric and is in the range of -180 to 180
	longitude.precision	number of decimal places
description	completeness	if there is description data
identifier user	completeness	number of unique identifier users
	ability	mean of identifier users' ability in the time of observation (number of IDs accepted as correct over the total of IDs)
	engagement	number of IDs contribution in the dataset
observation date	completeness	if there is date of observation
	appropriateness	if the value is a date
	accuracy	number of agreements of date quality metric over disagreement number
	currency	number of days since observation (related to the data collection date, informed in the second paragraph of Material and Methods)
	precision	number of items present (year, month and day)
observer user	completeness	if there is an observer user
	engagement	observation contribution number in the data set
	ability	number of observations considered correct (Needs Id and Research) over the total of observation in dataset contributions
observation field	completeness	number of custom observation fields
photo	completeness	number of photos
place	completeness	if there is a place data
scientific name	completeness	if there is taxon data
	appropriateness	number of taxon recognition[2]
	accuracy	number of agreements over the disagreement of the taxon for the observation
	precision	level of the taxon in the taxonomic classification system
	value consistency	if the taxon is in its range, regarding the common distribution observations
sound	completeness	number of sound files
update date	completeness	if there is an update date
	appropriateness	if the value is a date
	currency	number of days since observation (related to the data collection date, informed in the second paragraph of Material and Methods)
	precision	number of items present (year, month and day)

2.1.2 Dimensions

The dimensions selected to evaluate the data were *ability* (proportion of correct contributions made by the user), *accuracy* (how close a value is to the value considered correct), *appropriateness* (adequacy of the representation format and domain of values), *completeness* (presence or degree of presence), *currency* (degree of how current the assessed value is), *engagement* (number of contributions), precision (the representation of the data is sufficiently accurate to distinguish the possible values of the domain) and *value consistency* (the existence of a conflict with another element). The dimensions followed a particular evaluation sequence: when an IE was not a user, first, it was measured for *completeness*; if a minimum degree was reached, then the *appropriateness* measurement was carried out; likewise, if a minimum level of *appropriateness* was reached, any other dimension could be used. If the IE was a user, first, it was measured for *completeness*, if a minimum degree was reached, then *engagement* was calculated; likewise, if the *engagement* was greater than zero, the *ability* evaluation was performed. When a data was missing (*completeness* equals to 0) or had no *appropriateness*, subsequent dimensions were set to 0. Thus, the only dimension applied to all IE was *completeness*, the others were used when their measurement were possible to be made and could produce relevant information to assess CS data quality. The features generation produced a total of 35 connections among IE and dimensions (Table 1).

2.1.3 Modeling

To obtain the criteria model, we applied data mining techniques to pre-process and transform the data, and to the modeling. First, the data were divided, using stratified random sampling, into training set, containing 60% of the observations, validation set, with 20%, and test set, with the 20% remaining. In the pre-processing, we identified (using only training set) correlated features, features that did not show variation in their values (constant features) and features that were identical to another (features in double). These problematic features were removed from the three data sets. Still in pre-processing stage, duplicate observations were removed from the training set (a total of 523). In the transformation stage, the highly skewed features were log-transformed and all features were scaled to values ranging from 0 to 1.

The machine learning algorithm selected for study was Random Forest (RF). We predicted the classes for the test set using three different model instances: the complete model containing the features that resulted from the pre-processing and transformation; a reduced model after a feature selection based on features importance; and a model with only the features related to the citizen scientist behavior (engagement and ability derived features). For all models, the hyper-parameters tuning was carried out using randomized search with 500 iterations, cross-validation 3-fold and precision (positive predictive value) as the scoring evaluation. This metric was selected because we wanted to maximize the correct classification of positive class (have quality), reducing false positives, i.e., bad data erroneously classified as good data. We used permutation importance technique in the validation set, with precision as the scoring evaluation, to compute feature importance and to help us to make dimensionality reduction. Using the complete model configuration, we removed each feature successively, one by one, from the least to the most important, retrained the model with each cumulative removal and calculated the metrics from the confusion matrix: precision $TP/(TP+FP)$, kappa, accuracy $(TP+TN)/N$ and negative predictive value (NPV) $TN/(TN+FN)$. We used Python (3.7.10) and the package scikit-learn (0.22.2.post1) for modeling.

3. RESULTS

The data pre-processing identified and removed 1 feature, *observation-date.precision*, that presented high correlation (0.9 Pearson's coefficient) to observationdate.completeness. In the constant feature analysis, 10 features were removed: *coordinate.completeness*, *coordinate.appropriateness*, *coordinate-latitude.completeness*, *coordinate-latitude.appropriateness*, *coordinatelongitude.completeness*, *coordinate-longitude.appropriateness*, *observer-user.completeness*, *update-date.completeness*, *update-date.appropriateness* and *update-date.precision*. The features that were in double were *observationdate.appropriateness* and *observation-date.completeness* (which was maintained). After that, only 23 features remained.

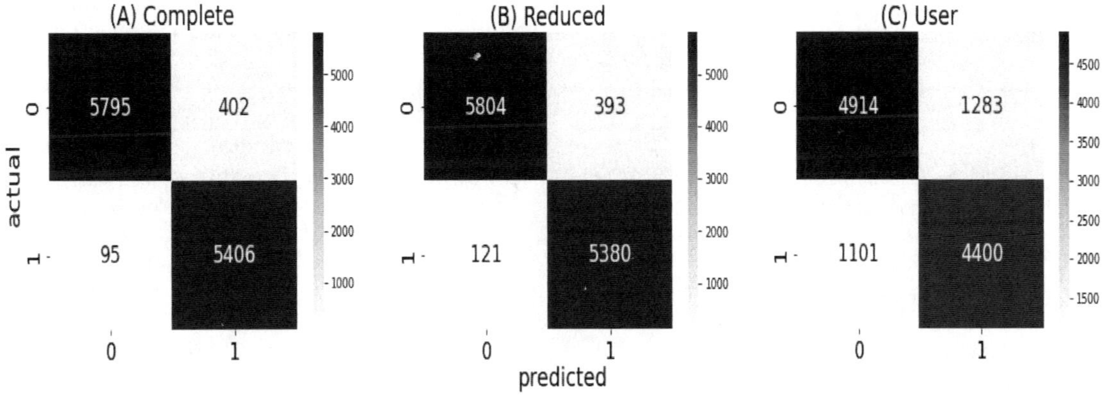

Figure. 1. Confusion matrices of three models. (A) complete, (B) reduced and (C) with only volunteer behavior features. In the Y axis are the actual values (0 for quality absence, 1 for quality presence). In X axis are the predicted values

The best hyper-parameters found in the random search for RF complete model were: maximum depth = 50 (the maximum depth of the tree), maximum features = square root of the number of features (number of features to consider for the best split), minimum samples leaf = 1 (minimum number of samples required to be at a leaf node), minimum samples split = 2 (minimum number of samples required to split an internal node) and number of estimators = 800 (number of trees in the forest). For the other not mentioned hyperparameters, their default values were used. Analyzing the confusion matrix (Figure 1 A), the model presented a precision of 0.931, kappa 0.915, accuracy 0.958 and NPV 0.984.

Table 2 presents the features in descending order of importance, obtained by means of the technique of permutation importance, along with precision, kappa, accuracy and NPV values for the trained models with features removal. For dimensionality reduction, we removed the 13 least important features. They did not impact in the precision score, when removed together: *scientific-name.appropriateness, scientificname.completeness, observation-date.accuracy, observationfield.completeness, place.completeness, sound.completeness, annotation.completeness, photo.completeness, observationdate.currency, coordinate-longitude.precision, scientificname.value-consistency, coordinate-latitude.precision* and *coordinate.accuracy*. After that, only 10 features remained for the reduced model: *observation-date.completeness, identifierusers.engagement, description.completeness' , observeruser.ability, observer-user.engagement, update-date.currency, identifier-users.ability, scientific-name.accuracy, identifierusers.completeness* and *scientific-name.precision*. The best hyper-parameters found for this reduced RF model were maximum depth = 70, maximum features = square root of the number of features, minimum samples leaf = 1, minimum samples split = 2 and number of estimators = 300. This model (Figure 1 B) presented a precision of 0.932, kappa 0.912, accuracy 0.956 and NPV of 0.98.

For the model with only the features related to the citizen scientist's behavior (engagement and ability dimensions), the best hyper-parameters found were maximum depth = 50, maximum features = square root of the number of features, minimum samples leaf = 1, minimum samples split = 2 and number of estimators = 800. This third model (Figure 1 C) presented a precision of 0.774, kappa 0.592, accuracy 0.796 and NPV of 0.817.

Table 2. Feature's importance and selection. The first columns contain the features in descending order of importance. The first row represents the complete model and its evaluation metrics. Each line removes a new feature, and the metric values are for the model with cumulative removal

Feature removed (mean of importance)	Number of features removed	Precision	Kappa	Accuracy	NPV
-	0	0.931	0.915	0.958	0.984
scientific-name.appropriateness (-0.001)	1	0.931	0.915	0.957	0.983
scientific-name.completeness (0)	2	0.931	0.914	0.957	0.982
observation-date.accuracy (0)	3	0.931	0.914	0.957	0.983
observation-field.completeness (0)	4	0.932	0.915	0.958	0.983
place.completeness (0)	5	0.931	0.915	0.958	0.983
sound.completeness (0)	6	0.932	0.916	0.958	0.984
annotation.completeness (0)	7	0.929	0.912	0.956	0.983
photo.completeness (0.001)	8	0.930	0.912	0.956	0.982
observation-date.currency (0.001)	9	0.929	0.910	0.955	0.981
coordinate-longitude.precision (0.001)	10	0.928	0.909	0.954	0.981
scientific-name.value-consistency (0.001)	11	0.928	0.910	0.955	0.981
coordinate-latitude.precision (0.001)	12	0.929	0.910	0.955	0.981
coordinate.accuracy (0.001)	13	0.931	0.912	0.956	0.980
observation-date.completeness (0.001)	14	0.931	0.910	0.955	0.979
identifier.engagement (0.001)	15	0.927	0.902	0.951	0.974
description.completeness (0.001)	16	0.928	0.901	0.951	0.973
observer.ability (0.002)	17	0.927	0.901	0.951	0.973
observer.engagement (0.002)	18	0.924	0.893	0.946	0.968
update-date.currency (0.003)	19	0.905	0.833	0.916	0.927
identifiers.ability (0.005)	20	0.892	0.873	0.936	0.984
scientific-name.accuracy (0.007)	21	0.874	0.863	0.931	0.998
identifiers.completeness (0.043)	22	0.684	0.513	0.753	0.861
scientific-name.precision (0.173)	23	-	-	-	-

4. DISCUSSION

The dataset used in this study contained only wild observations, as we decided not to include those reported as captive, in order to avoid incorporating in our models the rules of iNaturalist quality degree system, that classifies them as *casual*: the main goal of the platform is to observe wild organisms. Captive biodiversity data can contribute relevant information (Li et al., 2019), depending on the research questions, such as the protocol for citizen science monitoring of recently planted urban trees (Vogt and Fischer, 2017). According to our approach, data quality needs are defined by intent-to-use analysis and only after defining a particular context, should such rules be derived.

The dimensions used cover some of the most important aspects of citizen science data quality presented in the literature. The *Completeness* evaluation deals with missing data, common issue in DQ analysis and also present in CS data (Caruana et al., 2006), (Reed et al., 2013). As expected, we did not have much of this problem in our dataset because most of iNaturalist data is collected automatically using volunteer device information and sensors (e.g. date, time, coordinates, among other) or has data entered via auto-complete and autoformatting input. However, this can lead to constant features (all values are equal), features in double and high correlation. We found this kind of problem in features derived from dimensions such as completeness, *appropriateness* and precision, and IE of coordinate and dates data. *Completeness* along with *Appropriateness*, which defines if data is in accordance with its representation type and domain of values, are considered here as basic for further evaluations: the data must be present and be of the type expected, at least, to be analyzed.

Accuracy is a very commonly applied dimension, generally understood as how close the value is of what is considered correct. In CS, this evaluation is usually performed using expert validation, when volunteers have their data compared to data from a specialist (Kosmala et al., 2016). Here, for this purpose, sometimes we used a reference value provided by the user data (i.e. positional accuracy for *coordinate.accuracy*) or users voting (taxon agreement over taxon disagreement for *scientific-name.accuracy*), which was the third most important feature in the complete model (Table 2). Another popular dimension is *Precision*, commonly used in CS via replication approach, where a combination of different volunteers' data can improve the DQ (Swanson et al., 2016). Here, *scientificname.precision* was the most important feature for classification in complete model. We used *Currency* to define the data age and *Value consistency* to verify connections between different IE, for example: the taxon and the place to confirm species distribution (*scientific-name.value-consistency*). The *engagement* and *ability* dimensions describe the volunteer's behavior in relation to his contribution history and how many of them were considered correct. Here, we used these evaluation in different volunteer roles: observer and identifier. In CS, researchers report improvement in volunteers' skills when experience is gained (Ratnieks et al., 2016) and we try to incorporate these improvements calculating the dimension evaluation according to the observation date analyzed.

The performance of the model showed that we could classify the data with very few features and even among these lasts variables, some are much more important than others. From the complete model to the reduced, we improved the precision metric (Figure 1) with increase in False Negatives (FN). In our understanding, it is necessary to guarantee the correct "have quality" class classification and it is preferable to lose some good data than to use bad data thinking that it is good. Thus, we selected primarily the precision to make most of the evaluation and model selection. The model with only features of volunteer's behavior presented a precision of around 0.7. We consider this result as promising for further studies on the performance of volunteers and its impact on the quality of their contribution.

Future work includes the development of more dimensions to explain the behavior of citizen scientists and related problems frequently present in CS, such as temporal and space biases, and comparison of different ML techniques.

5. CONCLUSION

This work studied the Information Elements and Dimension to data quality classification in Citizen Science, using data from the iNaturalist platform. The identification of the most important features for classification can help in the development of quality measures for similar projects, which have similar variables, in addition to promoting a greater understanding of the impact of user behavior on the data.

ACKNOWLEDGEMENT

We acknowledge the citizen scientists for their contributions, iNaturalist for providing a platform to house many CS projects, Coordenação de Aperfeiçoamento de Pessoal de Nível Superior (CAPES) for the financial support to JNL (Finance Code 001, grant number 88882.333367/2019-01), and São Paulo Research Foundation - FAPESP, grant number 2018/14994-1 to AMS.

REFERENCES

Aceves-Bueno, E., Adeleye, A. S., Feraud, M., Huang, Y., Tao, M., Yang, Y., and Anderson, S. E., 2017. The accuracy of citizen science data: A quantitative review. *The Bulletin of the Ecological Society of America*, 98(4):278–290.

Breiman, L., 2001. Random forests. *Machine learning*, 45(1):5–32.

Brown, E. D. and Williams, B. K., 2019. The potential for citizen science to produce reliable and useful information in ecology. *Conservation Biology*, 33(3):561–569.

Caruana, R., Elhawary, M., Munson, A., Riedewald, M., Sorokina, D., Fink, D., Hochachka, W. M., and Kelling, S., 2006. Mining citizen science data to predict orevalence of wild bird species. *In Proceedings of the 12th ACM SIGKDD International Conference on Knowledge Discovery and Data Mining, KDD* '06, page 909–915, New York, NY, USA. Association for Computing Machinery.

Ellwood, E. R., Crimmins, T. M., and Miller-Rushing, A. J., 2017. Citizen science and conservation: Recommendations for a rapidly moving field. *Biological Conservation*, 208:1–4. The role of citizen science in biological conservation.

Fritz, S., See, L., Carlson, T., Haklay, M. M., Oliver, J. L., Fraisl, D., Mondardini, R., Brocklehurst, M., Shanley, L. A., Schade, S., et al., 2019. Citizen science and the United Nations sustainable development goals. *Nature Sustainability*, 2(10):922–930.

Ge, M. and Helfert, M., 2007. A review of information quality research—develop a research agenda. *In Paper present edat the International Conference on Information Quality 2007*. Citeseer.

Jones, F. M., Allen, C., Arteta, C., Arthur, J., Black, C., Emmerson, L. M., Freeman, R., Hines, G., Lintott, C. J., Mach´a˘ckov´a, Z., et al., 2018. Time-lapse imagery and volunteer classifications from the zooniverse penguin watch project. *Scientific data*, 5(1):1–13.

Kosmala, M., Wiggins, A., Swanson, A., and Sim-mons, B., 2016. Assessing data quality in citizen science. *Frontiers in Ecology and the Environment*, 14(10):551–560.

Li, E., Parker, S. S., Pauly, G. B., Randall, J. M., Brown, B. V., and Cohen, B. S., 2019. An urban biodiversity assessment framework that combines an urban habitat classification scheme and citizen science data. *Frontiers in Ecology and Evolution*, 7:277.

McGilvray, D., 2008. *Executing data quality projects: ten steps to quality data and trusted information TM*. Elsevier.

Palacin, V., Gilbert, S., Orchard, S., Eaton, A., Ferrario, M. A., and Happonen, A., 2020. Drivers of participation in digital citizen science: Case studies on j¨arviwiki and safe cast. *Citizen Science: Theory and Practice*, 5(1).

Ratnieks, F. L. W., Schrell, F., Sheppard, R. C., Brown, E., Bristow, O. E., and Garbuzov, M., 2016. Data reliability in citizen science: learning curve and the effects of training method, volunteer background and experience on identification accuracy of insects visiting ivy flowers. *Methods in Ecology and Evolution*, 7(10):1226–1235.

Reed, J., Raddick, M. J., Lardner, A., and Carney, K.M 2013. An exploratory factor analysis of motivations for participating in zooniverse, a collection of virtual citizen science projects. *In 2013 46th Hawaii International Conference on System Sciences*, pages 610–619.

Swanson, A., Kosmala, M., Lintott, C., and Packer, C., 2016. A generalized approach for producing, quantifying, and validating citizen science data from wildlife images. *Conservation Biology*, 30(3):520–531.

Veiga, A. K., Saraiva, A. M., Chapman, A. D., Morris, P. J., Gendreau, C., Schigel, D., and Robertson, T. J., 2017. A conceptual framework for quality assessment and management of biodiversity data. *PLoS ONE*, 12(6):1–20.

Vogt, J. M. and Fischer, B. C., 2017. A protocol for citizen science monitoring of recently planted urban trees. *Urban Forests, Ecosystem Services and Management*; Blum, J., Ed, pages 153–186.

Wiggins, A. and Crowston, K., 2011. From conservation to crowdsourcing: A typology of citizen science. *In 2011 44th Hawaii International Conference on System Sciences*, pages 1–10.

Wiggins, A., Newman, G., Stevenson, R. D., and Crowston, K., 2011. Mechanisms for data quality and validation in citizen science. In 2011 IEEE Seventh International Conference on e-Science Workshops, pages 14–19

EVALUATING YONA LANGUAGE

Adam Kövári, Alexander Meduna and Zbyňek Křivka
Department of Information Systems, Faculty of Information Technology, Brno University of Technology
Božetěchova 2, 612 00 Brno, Czech Republic

ABSTRACT

The paper evaluates a new concurrent, functional programming language Yona. Specific focus is placed on the asynchronous IO aspects of this language and its current implementation. The evaluation in the later chapter serves as the demonstration of Yona's capabilities, and it helps to set the direction of further research and development in this language by identifying significant bottlenecks.

KEYWORDS

Functional Programming, Disruptor-Inspired Ring-Buffer, Non-Blocking IO, Truffle Framework, GraalVM JVM, Benchmarks

1. INTRODUCTION

Yona is a high-level dynamic functional programming language with a strong focus on non-blocking concurrent computation. Yona has a rich runtime system, immutable data structures, concurrency model inspired by the LMAX disruptor (Thompson, et al., 2011) and JIT compilation and interoperability with other languages on the GraalVM platform (Würthinger, et al., 2013). Yona language is implemented using the Truffle framework (Würthinger, et al., 2017), provided by the GraalVM, which allows the implementation of interpreters that can use JIT capabilities on this VM. This paper explains the fundamental design decisions of the implementation and testing of this language; it also presents some initial set of results.

1.1 Design Goals

Yona hides the complexity of concurrent programming in its runtime. The concurrency system of Yona wraps future values in a Promise [1] -like structure (Liskov & Shrira, 1988), executes them in a disruptor-inspired ring-buffer, and then unwraps actual values whenever it becomes available, all this hidden on the runtime level. This optimization prevents the programmer from seeing any difference in values that have been computed or are yet to be computed in the future. It does not expose any low-level threading and since it contains only immutable data structures, nor it needs any synchronization primitives. Yona contains highly optimized immutable built-in data structures, including `Set`, `Dict` (Steindorfer & Vinju, 2015), and `Seq` (based on Finger Trees (Hinze & Paterson, 2006)), which eliminate concurrent mutation type of errors. Advanced concurrency in Yona can be implemented using the built-in Software Transactional Memory (STM) module (Fernandes & Cachopo, 2011). In addition to these features, Yona is a powerful functional language, with advanced pattern matching (Ramesh & Ramakrishnan, 1992), tail-call optimization, first-class module support, resource management, enabling programmers to write efficient programs in a very high-level style.

[1] Promise represents the eventual completion (or failure) of an asynchronous operation, and its resulting value.

1.2 Short Syntax and Semantics Guide

Full syntax and semantics of the language can be found on the language website[2]. However, we provide one example here that shows the most relevant pieces of the syntax and semantics of the language, necessary to understand the next section about the socket implementation.

```
try
  let
    keys =
      with File::open "keys.txt" {:read} as keys_file
        File::read_lines keys_file
      end

    values =
      with File::open "values.txt" {:read} as values_file
        File::read_lines values_file
      end
  in
    Seq::zip keys values |> Dict::from_seq
catch
  (:ioerror, _msg, _stacktrace) -> {}
end
```

Figure 1. Zipping keys and values read from two files concurrently in Yona

This program in Figure 1 reads two files, keys.txt and values.txt, in parallel and in a non-blocking way (no thread is blocked), zipping lines read, producing a dictionary of these keys and values as a result.

As diving deeper into this process, the following actions take place:

- Because `let` expression is used, Yona will perform a static analysis of dependencies between individual aliases[3] defined within the scope of these expressions, `keys` and `values` in this case. Since they do not depend on each other, they **may** be executed in parallel - they are put into two independent buckets of tasks.
- No other aliases are defined; thus, buckets of tasks begin their execution. The task from the first bucket begins execution - lines are being read from the keys.txt file. Function `Files::read_lines` is implemented as a non-blocking function in the standard library. It returns an underlying promise value immediately and puts a task to read lines into the runtime buffer of tasks. Promises are fully transparent to the programmer, and they do not need to be aware of this, as it is only a runtime type.
- Since `File::read_lines` returned, the next task from the second bucket may begin to be processed. Like before, this task reads lines in the values.txt file, independently in a non-blocking way, returning immediately.
- In this example, no further aliases are defined, so the body[4] of the `let` expression may be processed now. The body is processed after both aliases, `keys` and `values` become available. Function `Seq::zip` takes both of them, zipping keys with values, producing a sequence of tuples then passed to function `Dict::from_seq`, which produces the final dictionary. The `let` expression needs to wait for aliases defined within its scope to be ready but it does not mean that the thread executing this `let` expression is blocked. In fact, if this `let` expression was nested in some other expression or returned as a result of a function, there could be other computations being executed in the same thread, while waiting for the result of this particular `let` expression.

[2] http://yona-lang.org/ - Language description, standard library documentation, homepage

[3] Because there are no mutable variables in Yona, names referring to value will be called "aliases". They could be seen as "final" or "constant" variables in other languages

[4] The body of the `let` expression is an expression following the `in` keyword

This relatively simple example shows the execution model in Yona. Hopefully, it demonstrates how easy it is to write non-blocking, concurrent programs in Yona, without any explicit interaction from the programmer to make it so. The programmer only needs to use the standard library, and the runtime takes care of all the underlying concurrency implementation details.

1.3 Implementation of Files

All file operations in Yona are implemented in a non-blocking way. In the case of files, the underlying runtime uses Java NIO2 to implement read/write operations (Ganesh & Sharma, 2013). From the programmers' perspective, a file is represented as a file context manager[5], used by the read and write functions from module `File`. Function `open` creates this context manager. For example, see Figure 1.

File operations in Yona are implemented as an abstraction on top of Java NIO2 `AsynchronousFileChannel`, a callback-based API for Java, and it internally uses Java Executors to execute the non-blocking operations. Future versions of Yona intend to remove this level of indirection and bypass any use of Java Executor, which has a similar purpose to the Yona's disruptor.

1.4 Implementation of Sockets

This section describes the implementation of TCP Sockets in Yona's standard library. Socket IO implementation, same as File IO, is significant in the context of Yona, since one of the main focus areas of this language is non-blocking IO. Sockets in Yona use underlying Java NIO socket infrastructure.

Implementation of TCP Sockets consists of three modules: `socket\tcp\Server`, `socket\tcp\Client` and `socket\tcp\Connection`. These modules provide functionality for opening channels, accepting clients, making client connections, and reading and writing to sockets.

In addition to these three modules, there is additional infrastructure in the runtime that supports the non-blocking nature of the socket modules. Specifically, there is an NIO Selector thread, which polls for changes in socket states, such as that socket becomes acceptable, connectable, readable, and writable. Once any of these events happens, the runtime will look for an appropriate request[6], to fulfill and then once its work is done, that particular request gets completed, and the program is resumed to continue handling the obtained data.

1.4.1 TCP Server

Module `socket\tcp\Server` has two functions creating context managers for TCP channels and connections. Function `channel` creates new TCP channels and returns a context manager that is used when accepting new clients.

```
with socket\tcp\Server::channel (:tcp, addr port) as channel
    infi (\-> accept channel) # accept new connections in an infinite loop
end
```

Function `accept` accepts a client connection as soon as it becomes ready.

```
with daemon socket\tcp\Server::accept channel as connection
    # deal with the accepted connection
end
```

[5] Context managers are Yona's way for managing resources in a consistent way, so that resources are closed as soon as they are not needed anymore.

[6] We are using term "request" here, since it seems more proper in the context of sockets, however in reality, it is just a runtime promise, same as any other in context of Yona

The example above uses a "daemon" context manager, which causes Yona to wait only until the connection is made, but not until the whole body of this `with` expression is processed, before returning the result of the `with` expression. This allows Yona to handle connections concurrently, since as soon as the connection is accepted, its handling is moved to the background. The use of the `with` expression still makes sure that resources related to this connection are disposed after the work on this connection has finished.

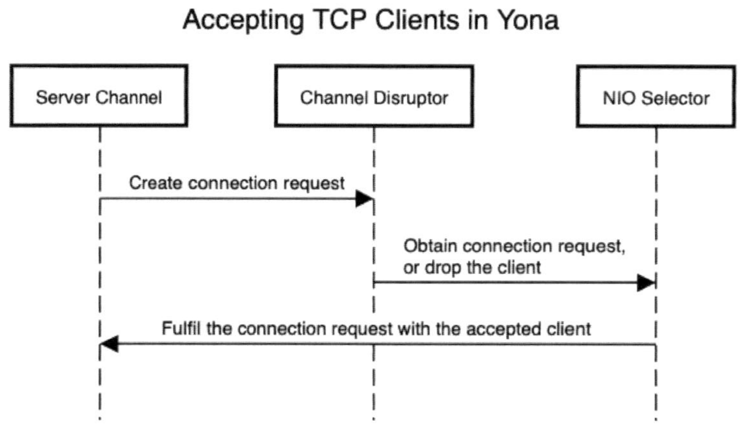

Figure 2. Flow of accepting a connection on an open TCP channel

The diagram in Figure 2 visualizes how a connection request is made and when it is fulfilled. The whole process is asynchronous, and server code creates requests, or promises, that are fulfilled once connection is ready. This way, the program is not blocked, and it can do some other processing without waiting for the result of the `accept` operation.

1.4.2 TCP Client

This module provides function `connect` that creates a TCP connection to a server, represented as a context manager.

```
with socket\tcp\Client::connect "localhost" 5555 as connection
    # read/write from and to the server
end
```

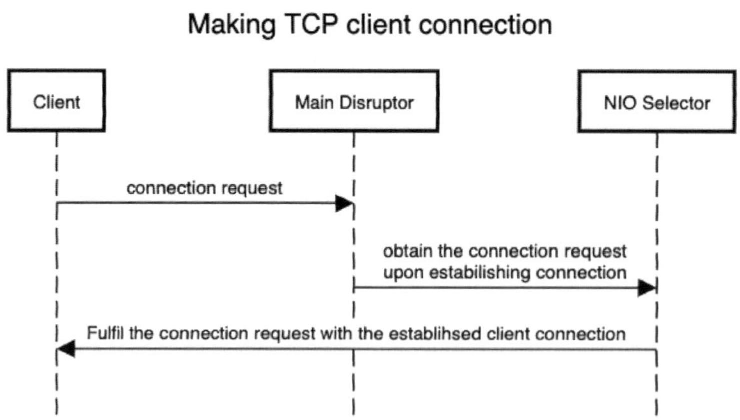

Figure 3. Flow of making a client connection to a server

Figure 3 above shows how a client connection is made in a non-blocking way. Function `connect` will produce a connection request in the background and only once the client connection is established, the connection request is fulfilled, asynchronously, by the NIO Selector thread.

1.4.3 Connection Read/Write Operations

Module `socket\tcp\Connection` contains functions for reading and writing on TCP connections. These functions work for both client and server connections.

```
socket\tcp\Connection::write connection "hello"
socket\tcp\Connection::read_until connection (\b -> b != 10b) # read until LF
```

These functions create a read or write request in the connections read or write disruptor-based queue (`NIOQueue`).

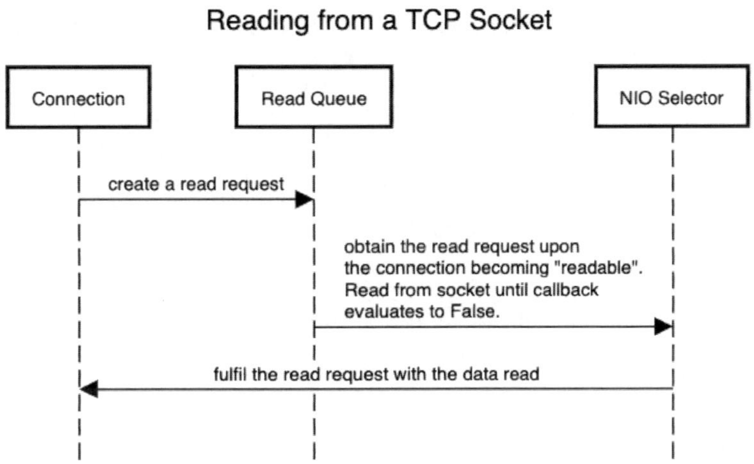

Figure 4. Reading from a TCP Socket

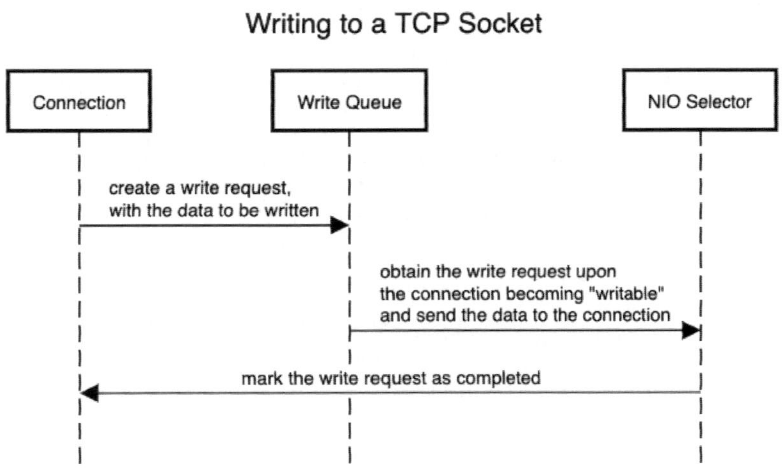

Figure 5. Writing to a TCP Socket

The read/write requests are bound to a specific connection instance (context manager), where they are buffered in their own disruptor queues. In this way Yona passes data between the NIO Selector thread and the main program.

2. EVALUATION

This chapter describes a set of benchmarks developed to discover significant bottlenecks and help drive further research and development. Yona is still under active development, including the interpreter, and runtimes, and the standard library.

Choice of the benchmarks reflects the current priorities of Yona implementation, which is the concurrency and non-blocking IO. The first three tests are well-known benchmarks, used to evaluate various languages and concurrency models, and the last benchmark is a combination of the previous ones. It provides an additional level of complexity, and its purpose is to determine if combining different types of IO (network and file), would cause any unexpected performance issues.

2.1 Method

We have measured the performance of several simple benchmarks and compared them with other major programming languages using comparable approaches[7]. Algorithms selected for these benchmarks are on purpose not the most efficient algorithms to solve a particular problem, but such algorithms that could meaningfully benchmark various implementation aspects of different languages (e.g. interpreter performance, IO performance, or standard library efficiency). Languages used to compare with Yona in these benchmarks are Python, JavaScript and Erlang. That is because Python and JavaScript are the most popular dynamic languages, while Erlang is a dynamic, concurrent and functional language and Yona as well.
Tests were performed on 64-bit Linux, Intel i5-9600K, 16 GB of memory.

2.1.1 Echo Server

Th first benchmark is a simple non-blocking TCP echo server. The purpose of this benchmark is to detect whether the implementation of non-blocking sockets in Yona's standard library has any significant bottlenecks. This benchmark is not algorithm-heavy, and it depends on the IO performance. Nevertheless, if Yona performed significantly worse than other languages, it would point to particular inefficiency in the standard library functions implemented for Yona. The results are in Table 1.

Table 1. Simple echo server benchmark

Echo Server (connections / seconds to process)	100	1000	10.000
Node 16	0.248	2.625	126.06
Python 3.9	0.254	2.61	126.06
Erlang 23	0.244	2.567	126.62
Yona 0.8.1	0.26	2.945	130.23

This benchmark tests the throughput by creating 100, 1000 and 10,000 concurrent clients connecting to a simple echo server written in respective languages. The client is a simple socket client written in Rust to minimize its system footprint. Time was measured by running the following command:

```
time parallel -n0 -j <NoC> ./echo-client ::: {1..<NoC>}
```
[8]

where `<NoC>` is the number of clients/connections 100; 1000 or 10,000. While Yona was slightly a bit slower, it was not a difference of a significant magnitude. This test suggests that the socket implementation of a TCP server in Yona has no serious bottleneck.

[7] The source code of all benchmarks performed in this paper is available at the Yona git repository: https://github.com/yona-lang/yona/tree/master/benchmarks
[8] The three colons syntax of the GNU Parallel to specify number of processes to execute. Argument `-j` specifies the number of concurrent processes, and `-n0` means that the `echo-client` process has no arguments.

2.1.2 Bubble Sort

The second benchmark is focused on algorithmic performance and can help detect potential issues with the interpreter performance. Since the algorithm implemented in this benchmark is not tail-recursive, it will suffer from stack overflow for larger inputs. Bubble sort is a well-known algorithm with the worst-case complexity of O(n2), where n is the number of items, so it can indicate performance issues in the language interpreter.

Table 2. Bubble Sort benchmark

Bubble Sort (numbers / microseconds)	10	100	200	300
Erlang 23	19	1,172	3,818	7,771
Node 16	119	6,387	19,659	55,703
Python 3.9	56	7,592	41,902	204,889
Yona 0.8.1	77,380	1,066,452	2,848,917	6,217,559

The results demonstrate the exponential complexity growing with the size of the input. The input contains a list of random integers. It is very clear from this benchmark that the performance of Yona is significantly, several magnitudes of worse than that of other languages. The exact cause of this performance issue is not yet known at the time of writing this article. Solving this bottleneck will be crucial in the next development of Yona.

2.1.3 Read Lines

This benchmark is designed to evaluate the performance of non-blocking file IO. Similar to the Echo Server benchmark, the purpose of this test is to determine whether Yona contains any bottleneck in its standard library module for reading files. Since Python does not contain this functionality in its standard library, a third-party library `aiofiles`[9] was used to achieve the same functionality as other languages. This benchmark reads a large file with 128,457 lines, working in line-by-line way.

Table 3. Read Lines benchmark

Read Lines (lines / microseconds)	128,457
Node 16	65,955
Erlang 23	533,595
Python 3.9	6,649,067
Yona 0.8.1	2,611,637

This result clearly points to an inefficiency in the Python's third-party library. While Yona's performance is slower than the one in Node and Erlang, the difference is not even one magnitude large. The result of this benchmark suggests that there is a room for improvement in Yona, the exact details of which are yet to be determined in future work.

2.1.4 SCP Server-Client

This benchmark is a combination of the Echo Server and the Read Lines tests. It is a simple server-client application, where the server reads input from the client, line-by-line and writes it to a file, and the client reads a file, line-by-line and sends it to the server. This test was chosen to detect possible issues when combining non-blocking file and socket operations in Yona. It is a more complex, real-world application testing the benefits of non-blocking IO.

[9] https://pypi.org/project/aiofiles/0.6.0/

Table 4. SCP benchmark

SCP (server language/ microseconds)	SCP (client language / microseconds)	
Erlang 23	Yona 0.8.1	8,381,385
Yona 0.8.1	Yona 0.8.1	9,589,741
Yona 0.8.1	Python 3.9	11,546,680

For the sake of comparing different server implementations as well, there is an Erlang and Yona server implementation. In this case, the client was Yona, in both runs. There is a difference between Yona and Erlang as a server, the difference is 13%. In case of using a different client implementation, Python performed about 15% worse than Yona. This benchmark shows that the non-blocking IO implemented in the standard library of Yona performs roughly similarly than that in other popular programming languages.

3. CONCLUSION

The tests performed during this evaluation were designed to test the capabilities of Yona, primarily in the scope of its concurrent and non-blocking nature. Yona's performance in these tests is in line with other mainstream programming languages. The Bubble sort test is focused more on CPU performance and clearly indicates a severe bottleneck in Yona interpreter or built-in data structures. Solving this bottleneck will likely improve performance in other areas as well, but solving it must become a top priority for the subsequent work on this programming language.

Yona provides a higher level of abstraction than all other languages it was compared with, and even though is still in its early days of development, it shows very interesting performance in key areas of concurrency, which has been the primary focus area of the development so far. Focusing on the interpreter performance and addressing the bottlenecks in the CPU-bound algorithms will be crucial to allow Yona to become competitive with other long-established and highly optimized languages and runtimes. We hope the method and results of our evaluation of Yona will push for further research and improvements to this language and can be used as a basis for future comparisons against comparable languages and platforms.

ACKNOWLEDGEMENT

This work has been supported by the Czech Science Foundation, project No. 19-24397S and the BUT grant FIT-S-20-629.

REFERENCES

Fernandes, S. M. & Cachopo, J., 2011. *Lock-Free and Scalable Multi-Version Software Transactional Memory.* New York, NY, USA, ACM, p. 179--188.

Hinze, R. & Paterson, R., 2006. Finger Trees: A Simple General-purpose Data Structure. *J. Funct. Program.,* 3, Volume 16, p. 197–217.

Ramesh, R. & Ramakrishnan, I. V., 1992. Nonlinear Pattern Matching in Trees. *J. ACM,* 4, Volume 39, p. 295–316.

Ganesh, S. G. & Sharma, T., 2013. Java File I/O (NIO.2). In: *Oracle Certified Professional Java SE 7 Programmer Exams 1Z0-804 and 1Z0-805: A Comprehensive OCPJP 7 Certification Guide.* Berkeley(CA): Apress, p. 251–280.

Liskov, B. & Shrira, L., 1988. *Promises: Linguistic Support for Efficient Asynchronous Procedure Calls in Distributed Systems.* New York, NY, USA, ACM, p. 260–267.

Steindorfer, M. J. & Vinju, J. J., 2015. *Optimizing Hash-array Mapped Tries for Fast and Lean Immutable JVM Collections.* New York, NY, USA, ACM, p. 783–800.

Würthinger, T. et al., 2013. *One VM to Rule Them All.* New York, NY, USA, ACM, p. 187–204.

Würthinger, T. et al., 2017. *Practical partial evaluation for high-performance dynamic language runtimes.* New York, NY, USA, ACM, p. 662–676.

Thompson, M. et al., 2011. *Disruptor: High performance alternative to bounded queues for exchanging data between concurrent threads.* [Online] Available at: https://lmax-exchange.github.io/disruptor/disruptor.html

PARALLEL BACKTRACKING FOR THE STUDY OF THE HYDROPHOBIC-POLAR MODEL

Ioan Sima and Daniela-Maria Cristea
Faculty of Mathematics and Computer Science, Babeş-Bolyai University, Cluj-Napoca, Romania

ABSTRACT

Proteins are the molecular machines that underlie the functioning of living organisms. Without knowing the three-dimensional structure and sequence of the proteins, their functions cannot be predicted. The protein structure prediction consists in finding one of a huge number of conformations. For that, the hydrophobic-polar (HP) model was considered. Although the backtracking algorithm is not suitable for the analysis of exponentially sized spaces, we apply it in a parallel variant. By applying techniques to reduce conformational space and decrease computational time, we obtained all conformations for several sequences known in the literature and for kappa-Hefutoxin1, a real protein in scorpion venom. The purpose of this type of research is to understand the structure of combinatorial space. The analysis of the obtained conformations shows that they are arranged in a certain order in the combinatorial hypercube.

KEYWORDS

Protein Structure Prediction, Parallel Backtracking, HP lattice model, Combinatorial Space

1. INTRODUCTION

From a chemical point of view, proteins are immense molecules, in specific jargon called biomacromolecules. They are important components of cells because are the basis of life. Proteins are built of chains of tens to thousands of amino acids (AAs). Amino acids, as their name suggests, are molecules which have opposite chemical characteristics: acid, given by the carboxyl functional group (-COOH), and alkaline, given by the amino group ($-NH_2$) (Reddy, 2020). Of the hundreds of types of AAs found in a living organism, only 20 types are proteinogenic AA, i.e., they are genetically encoded by the genetic code, which means they participate in protein formation (Garett & Grisham, 1999). With one exception, all the twenty proteinogenic amino acids have a similar structure: a central α-carbon (C) atom to which an amino group, a carboxyl group, a hydrogen atom and an organic radical (R) group are attached. Amino acids differ from each other only by the nature of the organic radical (or residue). Organic residues can be classified according to their behavior towards the water in: hydrophobic (or non-polar) AAs, which repel water molecules, and hydrophilic (or polar) AAs, which attract water molecules and form weak bonds with them (Garett & Grisham, 1999).

Proteins work in two different types of environments: aqueous and/or fat. Most of them are immersed in the cellular aqueous cytoplasmic environment, where they take on a globular shape. Globular proteins reach this shape in water, because the hydrophobic AAs (denoted by **H** letter) tend to hide from water in the center of the protein, forming the so-called hydrophobic kernel, and polar AAs (**P** letter) arrange on the surface of the protein to bind to water molecules. The globular shape of the proteins approaches the spherical shape, knowing that the sphere has the smallest surface for a given volume.

Protein folding (PF) is the process by which a protein AAs chain (or a sequence of AAs), called primary structure (1D), is transformed into a single folded shape, called native conformation or tertiary structure (3D). A protein can work only in this folded state (it has the biological function). A protein has a huge number of possible folded states, but only one is biologically functional. All the other folded states lead to a degenerate protein that leads to disease and death (Harrison, Chan, Prusiner & Cohen, 1999). Many factors contribute to the protein folding process, but it is proved that hydrophobic forces have the most weight (Dill, 1990; Dill, Ozkan, Shell & Weikl, 2008), meaning that the ability of AAs to attract or avoid water molecules is essential to understanding how proteins are folding. Determining the amino acid sequence of a protein in a given DNA sequence is a simple process. Instead, despite Alpha Fold's recent successes (Jumper, Evans, Pritzel, & al. 2021), the determination of the three-dimensional conformation of proteins is still an incompletely understood and partially solved process (Hossenfelder, 2021). The most important factor that determines the protein function is the protein conformation, also called the three-dimensional or the folded form.

The protein structure prediction (PSP) consists in predicting or finding the native conformation based on the primary structure. Because the number of possible conformations is immense, tackling this problem is a big challenge (Levinthal, 1969). For instance, the size of the conformational space of insulin, which is a relatively small protein, is $\approx 3^{300}$ ($\approx 10^{143}$) conformations number. Based on the experimental results, in the 1960s, Anfinsen advanced the thermodynamic hypothesis, which states that proteins fold into the minimum energy conformation (Anfinsen, 1973). This observation underlies most models created to simplify the protein folding problem. Of these, the hydrophobic-polar (HP) model stands out for its simplicity, which has made it perhaps one of the most used and well-known models in the computational biology world (Dill, 1985; Lau & Dill, 1989). In the HP model, PSP turns into a combinatorial optimization problem whose solution space of the modeled protein is strongly reduced compared to the solution space of the real protein. Despite drastic simplifications, solution space increases exponentially with the linear increasing number of AAs. It has been shown that the prediction of protein structure is NP-complete (Berger & Leighton, 1998). That means, for most proteins, the prediction of protein structure is infeasible by classical algorithms that scan the entire combinatorial space because computational time increases exponentially. For this reason, heuristic techniques have been most used to find native conformation on the HP model. For sequences up to 100 AA, good results were obtained with Genetic Algorithm (Unger & Moult, 1993), Particle Swarm Optimisation (Lin & Su, 2011; Mansour, Kanj & Khachfe, 2021), Ant Colony Optimisation (Shmygelska & Hoos, 2003; Shmygelska & Hoos, 2005), Reinforcement Learning (Czibula, Bocicor & Czibula, 2011), WOA (Sima & Pârv, 2019). *CPSP-Tools Server* obtains excellent results for HP sequences up to 300 AA: https://cpsp.informatik.uni-freiburg.de/HPstruct/Input.jsp (Mann, Backofen & Will, 2008).

In this paper, we go back to the old parallel backtracking that we apply to small proteins. Our main goal is not only to find the native conformation (the optimum solution in the combinatorial space), but also to study the combinatorial space structure. Then, we try to extrapolate this knowledge to the medium and large protein sequences, modeled on the HP model, for which the parallel backtracking algorithm is not applicable in a reasonable time. This work hopes to be a new beginning of the application of deterministic algorithms, in parallel variants, to combinatorial problems with spaces of exponential solutions, in particular to PSP. The paper presents the continuation of the experiments started in our previous work (Sima, 2018).

The rest of the paper is structured as follows. Chapter 2 gives background knowledge of the hydrophobic-polar model and the energy function used. Chapter 3 describes the usefulness and application of the parallel backtracking algorithm on the HP model. Section 4 presents our experimental results and in Chapter 5 we present the conclusions and future work.

2. HP MODEL

Over time, several models have been proposed for solving PSP and simulating PFP. Thus, depending on the granularity there are: i). all-atom models, in which the working units are atoms of the proteins (Wu, Zhang, Qin, Liu and Wang, 2008), ii). coarse-grained models - the units are the amino acids (Dill, 1985), and iii). intermediate models, in which each AA is represented by two units (beads) (Nunes, Galvão, Lopes, Moscato & Berretta, 2016). In another possible classification, we have: a). on-lattice models and b). off-lattice models (Rakhshani, Rahati & Dehghanian, 2016).

Based on the observation that hydrophobic forces are of the greatest importance for protein folding, in the 80's of the last century, was proposed the hydrophobic-polar model (Dill, 1985; Lau & Dill, 1989). It is the simplest model and it belongs to the category of coarse-grained models and those of the on-lattice type.

The simplifications that HP makes are: 1). the 20 types of real proteinogenic amino acids are reduced to 2 modeled types: **H** AAs and **P** AAs; 2). discretization of the continuously Euclidean space in which real proteins folding through the use of lattices; 3). by resemblance to thermodynamic free energy, a conventional parameter, called energy, is introduced, and 4). consideration of amino acids as a whole, not in complete atomic detail.

By reducing the number of AA types from 20 to 2, the number of combinations between them is reduced from 210 to 3, and real protein sequences are turned into HP sequences.

As examples of geometric lattices, used for PSP, we mention: 2D (rectangular or square) (Unger & Moult, 1993), 2D trigonal (Yang, Wu & Lin, 2018), 3D cubic or FCC (Face-Centered Cubic) type (Maher & al., 2014). In the 2D square and 3D cubic, the angles under which the amino acids can be placed, side by side, are 90 degrees, 180 degrees and 270 degrees, respectively. AAs of the HP sequence can be arranged in points of the lattice, resulting in HP conformations (note that, these HP conformations should not be confused with the real protein conformations). These conformations can be represented by an absolute or relative encoding.

In absolute encoding, in the 2D square HP model four letters (R for right; U for up; L for left, and D for down) are used to denote the four directions in which an amino acid can be arranged on the lattice in relation to the previous amino acid. We denote the HP conformation by *RULD string*. In the 3D cubic HP model, to the four letters above, we add two more: F, for the front direction and B, for the back direction.

For relative encoding, the number of letters in the alphabet decrease by one. Hence, for the 2D square lattice, we have three letters: S (straightforward), L and R, and, for the 3D cubic lattice, there are five letters: S, L, R, F, B, with the same significance as in the absolute encoding.

Conventional energy is associated with every conformation of a protein. The native conformation has the minimum energy. Thus, the search for the native conformation in the combinatorial space is reduced to the search for the conformation with the minimum energy, and the PSP on the HP model turns into a problem of combinatorial optimizations. Two AAs, Ai and Aj, are called *sequence neighbors* if they are successive in the HP sequence (i.e. $|i-j| = 1$, where $||$ denotes absolute values of a number, and i, j are AAs positions in HP sequence, respectively). Two AAs, Ai and Aj, are called *topological neighbors* if they are adjacent on the lattice, but not in the HP sequence (i.e., $|i-j| \neq 1$ and $|x_i-x_j| = 1$ or $|y_i-y_j| = 1$, where x, y are Cartesian coordinates of Ai and Aj on the lattice; the other retain their above significance).

The energy of a conformation is the sum of the energies between two H AAs (said HH contact) which are topological neighbors but are not sequence neighbors. In the classical HP model, the energy of a H..H contact is considered –1, and the energy of the other contact is zero ($E_{HH} = -1$, $E_{HP} = 0$, $E_{PH} = 0$, $E_{PP} = 0$). In this way, the energy of a conformation represents the total number of contacts between AA H, by convention, taken with a minus sign. Thereby, PSP on the HP model turns into a minimization problem, similar to protein folding in the real environment. The conformation with the lowest energy will form a hydrophobic core in the protein center, and a polar shell on the outside, the same as that of real proteins.

Berger, in 1998, showed that the protein structure prediction on the HP model is NP-complete (Berger & Leighton, 1998), and in (Bahi et al., 2011) reveals a chaotic behavior of energy function on hydrophobic-polar model.

3. METHODS

3.1 Backtracking Algorithm

Over time, deterministic and non-deterministic algorithms have been applied to predict the structure of proteins on the HP model. Artificial intelligence (AI) techniques are known to find the optimal local solutions, but there is no guarantee that they are the global optimal solutions. In addition, because the PSP on the HP model has a chaotic behavior (Bahi, Cote & Guyeux, 2011), metaheuristic techniques have difficulty in finding the optimal global solutions for this problem. Hence the need to apply deterministic algorithms that go through the whole combinatorial space solutions to find with certainty the conformation with minimum energy for any sequences of amino acids. These optimum conformations could be used for two purposes: 1) to test the quality of non-deterministic algorithms and 2) to compare them with the native conformations of real proteins.

Backtracking is one of the classic deterministic algorithms whose purpose is to find all solutions (or several solutions) in the combinatorial space of all possible solutions. Incrementally, the algorithm builds candidate solutions and abandons a candidate which cannot be completed at a valid solution (Cristea & al, 1998). By reason of the combinatorial space (that is, finite) of solutions and running time increase exponentially as the number of amino acids in the protein sequence increases, the application of the backtracking algorithm was avoided by the scientists. Therefore, the increase in computing power of processors in recent years, as well as the existence of parallel architectures, justify the application of the backtracking algorithm at least in the case of relatively short amino acid sequences. Next, we apply some methods of restricting the combinatorial space to the areas with feasible solutions (SAW – self avoiding walk), then the space is exhaustively traversed by a parallel backtracking algorithm with 3 and 9 CPU threads, respectively.

3.2 The Reducing of the Combinatorial Space

On the 2D HP square lattice, in absolute encoding of directions, the combinatorial space size of RULD sequences is 4^{n-1}, and in relative encoding, the SRL sequences space size is 3^{n-1}, where n is the RULD or SRL sequence length (number of protein amino acids). Each sequence starts with the letter "C", corresponding to the first A that is fixed in the center of the lattice. The second amino acid can be placed, relative to the first, in one of four directions: R, U, L or D. The square has a symmetric rotation axis of order four, C4, (Nemes, 2006; Vincent, 2013). Accordingly, the conformations generated in the four directions are symmetrical (in fact, it is the same conformation rotated by 90 degrees three times). Therefore, the second amino acid can be fixed at any position of the four directions, chosen arbitrarily. As shown in Figure 1, we fixed the second amino acid in the right direction (R) relative to the first amino acid. By eliminating the other three directions, the RULD conformational space is reduced 4 times, from 4^{n-1} to 4^{n-2}.

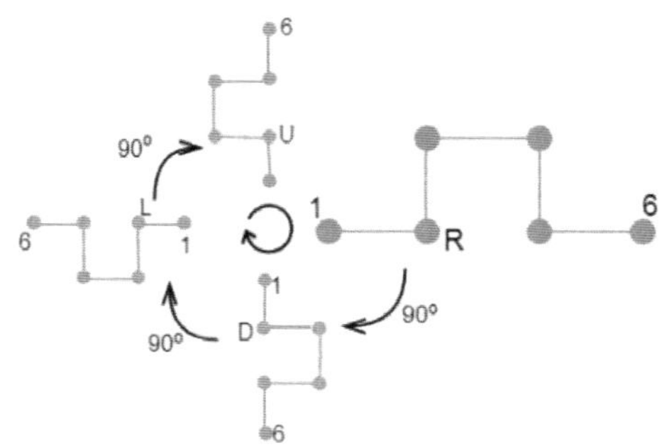

Figure 1. The elimination of the three directions of 2D HP model
Absolute directions: $4^{n-1} \longrightarrow 4^{n-2}$
Relative directions: $3^{n-1} \longrightarrow 3^{n-2}$

Because in the relative encoding of directions, the alphabet has three letters corresponding to the 3 directions (straight, right and left), the SRL conformational space is reduced from 3^{n-1} to 3^{n-2}. But the use of relative directions involves a longer processing time than the use of absolute directions. We used the directions absolute encoding for data processing on the lattice, and the directions relative encoding for the generation of a new direction during the advancement of the backtracking algorithm. In this way, we have two gains: 1). the combinatorial space is smaller (3^{n-2}), specific to the relative directions, and 2). the computing time of the energy and the verification of the topological neighbors is shorter, specific to the absolute directions.

3.3 The Parallelization of the Backtracking Algorithm

The backtracking solution is generated by adding a new direction to the existing one. Then, the lattice is checked: if the position is free the algorithm computes the energy and advances, otherwise, the algorithm eliminates the direction, returns to the previous step and chooses the next direction that has not yet been checked. If all directions lead to busy lattice nodes by the previous AAs, then the backtracking returns with one more step. If all directions lead to busy lattice nodes by the previous AAs, then the backtracking returns with one more step. Thus, the algorithm checks all possible SRL conformations, but retains (and counts) only the conformations that are SAW (we call them feasible). Because in relative encoding, three new directions can be generated at each step, the backtracking algorithm can be easily parallelized using a number of threads (or processes) with powers of three: 3, 3^2 , 3^3 , 3^4 , 3^5, etc., on CPU or GPU (Niculescu, 2005). We experimented with 3 and 9 threads, respectively. For three threads, the parallelization graph is shown in Figure 2.

4. RESULTS

In this work, a parallel backtracking algorithm was applied for sequences with the length between 4 and 22 AAs, including the sequences showed in Table 1. The 22 AAs sequence is *kappa-Hefutoxin1*, with a molecular weight of 2664.91, that is found in scorpion venom (Srinivasan et al., 2002, PDB, 2021), which we translated from the protein sequence to the HP string according to the classification AAs presented in a previous article (Telcian et al., 2020) and Ref. (Rashid, 2016). The other HP sequences were generated, and Seq 1 (20 AAs) was taken from Ref. (Unger & Moult, 1993). The software was written in Java and the experiments were run on a computer with the following configuration: CPU: Intel(R) Core (TM) i7-7700HQ CPU @ 2.80GHz, 4 cores, 8 logical processors, RAM: 16 GB, GPU: NVIDIA GeForce GTX 1060, 6 Gb RAM, OS: Windows 10 Professional 64-bit.

Table 1. Benchmark data set

No of seq and AA	Sequence	Optimal energy
1 – 20	**HPHP PHHP HPPH PHHP PHPH**	-9
2 – 21	**HHHP PPPH HPPP PHHH PHPH H**	-8
2 – 22	**HPHP HPPP HPPP PPPP PPPP PP**	0

In the 3-threads version, the 3 directions of the third AA are processed by another thread, as can be seen in Figure 2. In the 9-thread version, each thread starts at AA 4. Table 2 shows the number of feasible conformations (only SAW) obtained after running the backtracking algorithm with 3 threads on the 3 sequences.

Table 2. Total number of feasible conformations for three HP sequences

No of AA	C-R-R	C-R-D	C-R-U	Total
20	29,300,703	27,239,226	27,239,226	83,779,155
21	78,447,107	72,988,592	72,988,592	224,424,291
22	210,522,003	195,839,752	195,839,752	602,201,507

Note that the number of feasible conformations for the "C-R-D" branch is equal to the number of conformations for the "C-R-U" branch. The equality is valid for all 19 sequences analyzed (from 4 AAs to 22 AAs). This observation suggests that the conformations on the two branches are symmetrical to each other. This means that symmetrical pairs represent the same conformation. It follows that the RULD (or SRL) SAW conformational space is actually about a third smaller than previously considered. Consequently, the search in one of the branches is useless. In the future, we will eliminate the search in the "C-R-U" branch.

For the 20 AAs and the 21 AAs sequences, respectively, one of the optimal conformations is represented in Figure 3 and in Figure 4. The red units are hydrophobic AAs, and the blue units are polar AAs. It can be seen that **H** AAs forms a hydrophobic core. Due to the HP parity problem (all hydrophobic AAs are in odd positions), kappa-Hefutoxin1 has no native conformation in this model.

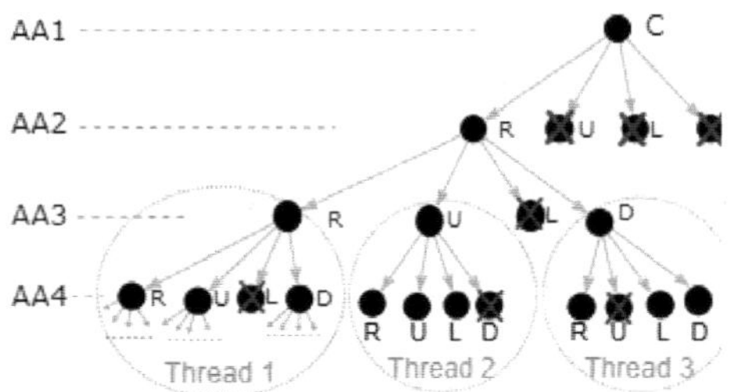

Figure 2. The graph backtracking

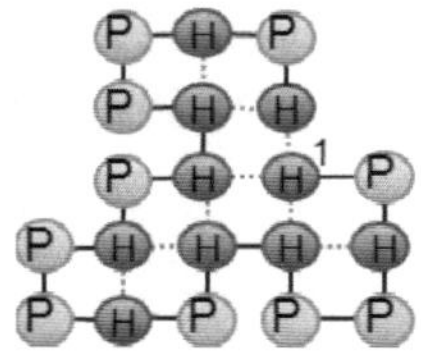

Figure 3. The optimum conformation for the 20 AAs sequence

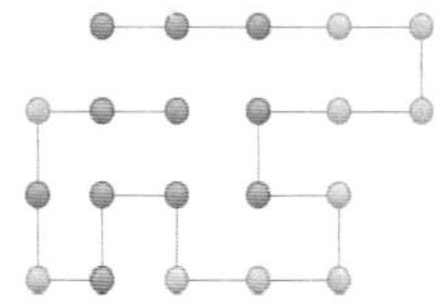

Figure 4. The optimum conformation for the 21 AAs sequence

In Table 3 are presented the number of conformations for 2D HP square lattice and computing time. In the "No RULD strings without symmetric" column is the dimension of whole combinatorial space, and "No feasible conformations" columns contains the number of SAW computed by backtracking.

Table 3. Number of conformations for 2D HP square lattice

No. of AAs	No RULD strings without symmetric (4^{n-2})	No feasible conformations	Computing time (seconds)		
			Sequential	3 threads	9 threads
2	1	1	<1	<1	<1
3	4	3	<1	<1	<1
4	16	9	<1	<1	<1
5	64	25	<1	<1	<1
6	256	71	<1	<1	<1
7	1,024	199	<1	<1	<1
8	4,096	543	<1	<1	<1
9	16,384	1,479	<1	<1	<1
10	65,536	4,067	<1	<1	<1
11	262,144	11,025	<1	<1	<1
12	1,048,576	30,073	<1	<1	<1
13	4,194,304	81,233	<1	<1	<1
14	1.7E+07	220,375	<1	<1	<1
15	6.7E+07	593,611	<1	<1	<1
16	2.7E+08	1,604,149	1	<1	<1
17	1.1E+09	4,311,333	2	1	<1
18	4.3E+09	11,616,669	4	2	1
19	1.7E+10	31,164,683	14	8	4
20	6.9E+10	83,779,155	23	15	8
21	2.7E+11	224,424,291	89	34	23
22	1.1E+12	602,201,507	98	45	28

In absolute encoding of directions, the space of RULD conformations (solutions) has the shape of a discrete hypercube with an edge length of 3 units (i.e. on each edge there are 4 points, one for each direction), while in relative encoding the values decrease by one unit. Because the first two AAs of the HP sequence are fixed on the lattice, the hypercube has 4^{n-2} dimensions for absolute encoding, and 3^{n-2} for relative encoding, respectively. Concretely, the space of the solutions of the sequences of 4 AAs is a discrete square, to those of 5 AAs, a discrete three-dimensional cube, so on.

The blue bar in Figure 4 represents the number of feasible conformations, and the whole bar, the total number of conformations. It is observed that the SAW fraction decreases with increasing number of amino acids.

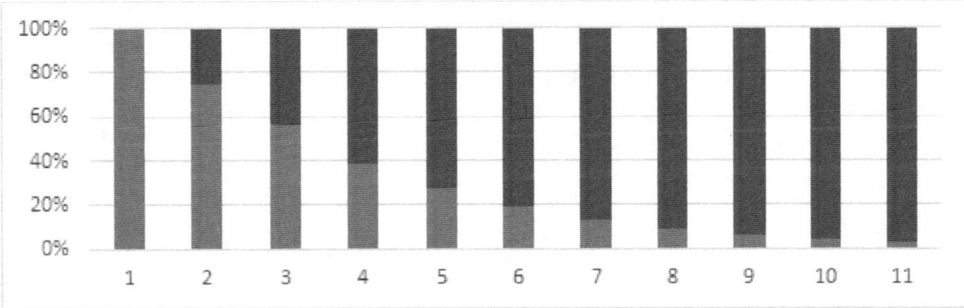

Figure 5. Feasible conformation fraction

5. CONCLUSION AND FUTURE WORK

In this paper we consider the parallel backtracking algorithm that we apply to the HP model for enumerating feasible conformations (SAW) and for studying the structure of conformational space. Due to the increase of computing power and by applying some conformation space reduction techniques, even if the conformational spaces are very large, their exhaustive verification is possible for short sequences. We found optimum conformations for known HP sequences and for kappa-Hefutoxin1, a protein from scorpion venom. Understanding the folding phenomenon, even on simplified models such as HP, may suggest new ideas for unfolding active proteins in venom and designing anti-venom serum.

In the future we propose the approach of the following targets: 1) the analysis, farther, of the number of feasible conformations for longer sequences and the finding of an analytical formula for the calculation of this number (if exist a such formula); 2) understanding the chaotic structure of the combinatorial space of solutions in order to create algorithms that avoid searching for non-feasible conformations; 3) finding a rule (if any) by which non-deterministic algorithms (GA, PSO, ACO, and so on) to search efficiently (non-chaotically) in the solution space, and 4) applying the parallel backtracking using GPU platforms.

ACKNOWLEDGEMENT

It is a pleasure to acknowledge discussions and the critical reading of the manuscript providing by Prof. Dr. Bazil Pârv. The authors thank to Simona Ispas, responsible for graphic design.

REFERENCES

Anfinsen, C. B., 1973. Principles that govern the folding of protein chains. *Science*, Vol. 181, No. 4096, pp. 223–230.

Bahi, J. M., Cote, N. and Guyeux., C., 2011. Chaos of protein folding. *Neural Networks (IJCNN),* pp. 1948–1954.

Berger, B. et Leighton, T., 1998. Protein folding in the hydrophobic-hydrophilic (HP) model is NP-complete. *Journal of Computational Biology,* Vol. 5, No. 1, pp. 27–40.

Cristea, V. et al., 1998. *Tehnici de programare (Programming Techniques).* Ed. Teora Publishing, Bucharest, Romania – in romanian

Czibula, G., Bocicor, I. et Czibula, Gergely I., 2011. A reinforcement learning model for solving the folding problem. *International Journal of Computer Technology and Applications.*

Dill, K. A., Ozkan, S. B., Shell, M. S. and Weikl, T. R., 2008. The protein folding problem. Annual review of biophysics, Vol. 37, pp. 289–316.

Dill, K. A., 1985. Theory for the folding and stability of globular proteins. *Biochemistry*, Vol. 24, pp. 1501.

Dill, K. A., 1990. Dominant forces in protein folding. *Biochemistry* Vol. 29, No. 31, pp. 7133–7155

Garett, R. H. et Grisham, C. M., 1999. *Biochemistry.* Barrosse, E. et Vondeling, J. J., second edition.

Harrison, P. M., Chan, H. S., Prusiner, S. B. et Cohen, F. E., 1999. Thermodynamics of model prions and its implications for the problem of prion protein folding. *Journal of Molecular Biology*, Vol. 286, No. 2, pp. 593–606.

Hossenfelder, S., 2021. Has Protein Folding Been Solved?. https://www.youtube.com/watch?v=yhJWAdZl-Ck. Accessed in July 15, 2021

Jumper, J., Evans, R., Pritzel, A. et al., Highly accurate protein structure prediction with AlphaFold. *Nature,* Vol. 596, pp. 583–589.

Lau, K. F. et Dill, K. A., 1989. A lattice statistical mechanics model of the conformation and sequence space of proteins. *Macromolecules,* Vol. 22, pp. 3986–3997.

Levinthal, C., 1969, How to fold graciously. *Mossbauer Spectroscopy in Biological Systems Proceedings*, pp. 22–24.

Lin, C.-J. et Su., S.-C., 2011. Protein 3D HP model folding simulation using a hybrid of genetic algorithm and particle swarm optimization. *International Journal of Fuzzy Systems*, Vol. 13, pp. 140–147.

Maher, B., Albrecht, A., Loomes, M., Yang, X.-S. et Steinhöfel, K., 2014. A Firefly-Inspired Method for Protein Structure Prediction in Lattice Models. *Biomolecules,* Vol. 4., pp. 56–75.

Mann, M., Will, S. et Backofen, R., 2008. CPSP-tools - Exact and Complete Algorithms for High-throughput 3D Lattice Protein Studies. In *BMC Bioinformatics*, Vol. 9, pp. 230.

Mansour, N., Kanj, F. et Khachfe, H., 2021. Particle swarm optimization approach for protein structure prediction in the 3D HP model. *Interdisciplinary Sciences: Computational Life Sciences,* Vol. 4, No. 3, pp.190–200.

Nemes, G. N., 2013, *Aplicatii ale teoriei grupurilor in chimie (Chemical Applications of Group Theory),* Presa Universitara Clujeana Publishing, Cluj-Napoca, Romania, – in romanian.

Niculescu, V., 2005. *Calcul Paralel. Proiectare si dezvoltare formala a programelor paralele. (Parallel Computation. Design and formal development of parallel programs).* Presa Universitara Clujeana Publishing, Cluj-Napoca, Romania – in romanian.

Nunes, L. F., Galvão, L. C., Lopes, H. S., Moscato, P. et Berretta, R., 2016. An integer programming model for protein structure prediction using the 3D-HP side chain model. *Discrete Applied Mathematics,* Vol. 198, pp. 206–214.

Rakhshani, H., Rahati, A. et Dehghanian, E., 2016. Cuckoo Search Algorithm and Its Application for Secondary Protein Structure Prediction. *Journal of Informatics and Computer Engineering*. Vol. 2., pp. 134–139.

Rashid, M.A., Khatib, F., Hoque, M.T. and Sattar, A., 2016. An enhanced genetic algorithm for ab initio protein structure prediction. *IEEE Transactions on Evolutionary Computation,* Vol. 20, No. 4, pp. 627–644.

Reddy, M. K., 2020. *Amino acid.* Encyclopaedia Britannica. https://www.britannica.com/science/amino-acid

Sima, I., 2018. Parallel Algorithm For Protein Folding Simulation On Hp Model. Experimental Study, *Symposium New Trends in Computer Science (ZAC)*, Vol. 40, No. 1, pp. 1-6.

Sima, I. and Pârv, B., 2019. Protein Folding Simulation Using Combinatorial Whale Optimization Algorithm, *International Symposium on Symbolic and Numeric Algorithms for Scientific Computing (SYNASC)*, Timisoara, Romania, pp. 159–166.

Shmygelska, A. and Hoos, H. H., 2003. An improved ant colony optimisation algorithm for the 2d hp protein folding problem. In Xiang, Y. et Chaib-draa, B. editors, Advances in Artificial Intelligence, *Springer* Berlin Heidelberg., pp. 400–417.

Shmygelska, A. et Hoos, H. H., 2005. An ant colony optimisation algorithm for the 2D and 3D hydrophobic polar protein folding problem. *BMC Bioinformatics,* Vol. 6, No. 1, pp. 30.

Srinivasan, K. N. et al., 2002. kappa-Hefutoxin1, a novel toxin from the scorpion heterometrus fulvipes with unique structure and function. *The Journal of Biological Chemistry*, Vol. 277, No. 33, pp. 30040–30047.

Telcian, A., Cristea, D. and Sima, I., 2020. Formal concept analysis for amino acids classification and visualization. *Acta Universitatis Sapientiae, Informatica*, Vol. 12, No. 1, pp. 22-38.

Unger, R. et Moult, J., 1993. Genetic algorithms for protein folding simulations. *J. Mol. Biol., Vol.* 231, No. 1, pp. 75–81.

Vincent, A., 2013. *Molecular Symmetry and Group Theory*, *Second Edition*, John Wiley et Sons, Chichester, United Kingdom.

Wu, L., Zhang, J., Qin, M., Liu, F. et Wang, W., 2008. Folding of proteins with an all-atom Gō-Model, *J. Chem. Phys.* Vol. 128, No. 235103.

Yang, C.H., Wu, K.C., Lin, Y.S. et al., 2018. Protein folding prediction in the HP model using ions motion optimization with a greedy algorithm. *BioData Mining,* Vol. 11, No. 17.

PDB - kappa-Hefutoxin1. https://www.rcsb.org/structure/1HP9. Accessed: 06/25/2021.

FEASIBILITY STUDY AND EMPIRICAL ANALYSIS OF A LOW-COST FINGERPRINT RECOGNITION FOR IMMUNIZATION TRACING

Esther Mukoya, Richard Rimiru and Michael Kimwele
Jomo Kenyatta University of Agriculture and Technology
P.O Box 62000 Nairobi-00600 Kenya

ABSTRACT

Many Fingerprint recognition systems mostly use minutiae features. Feature extraction module, a critical stage in fingerprint recognition, is mainly dependent on the image quality. Practically, the process of obtaining a good quality fingerprint image can be challenging. This is so especially with children fingerprint images collected using standard fingerprint devices. Children fingerprint recognition can be applied in immunization clinics to trace children attending the immunization. This will help to create effective follow-ups especially for children who are likely to miss their immunizations. Given that children fingerprints are of lesser quality, especially when collected via standard equipment, a system that can improve the quality and hence make the image recognizable is ideal. In this work, the authors focus on children fingerprint images which comprise of well-known distortions such as wetness, small area and blurriness. An accurate and efficient fingerprint feature extraction from children's fingerprints which are usually of poor-quality fingerprint image is a difficult task. Fingerprint enhancement technique is introduced using residual dense network to perform image Super resolution. Local features are extracted using dense connected convolutional layers. This is then followed by image filtering. The output of the processed image has a black background with the bifurcations shown in white. In this research, the image was inverted to obtain the final output with white background and black lines. Quality scores were obtained using the National Institute of Standards and Technology fingerprint Image Quality algorithm to determine the quality improvement after the image enhancement and the method provides better results.
Experimental results showed that the enhancement improved the visual clarity of the low-quality images. Thus, with ideal enhancement, children's fingerprints can be applied in follow-ups of immunization clinics.

KEYWORDS

Fingerprint Recognition, NFIQ, Residual Dense Network, Image Enhancements

1. INTRODUCTION

Children recognition by use of fingerprint has undergone a lot of research. Despite this, it still remains an unsolved challenge. This could be attributed to the fact that children fingerprint images have poor quality and suffer from nonlinear distortion.

A solution to this challenge is beneficial in areas like in identification of missing children and strengthening of health systems particularly immunization programs. The coverage of immunization programs remains suboptimal in many low and middle countries (LMICs). Generally, this could be attributed to caregiver illiteracy on child immunization status (Lahariya, 2015). Most children guardians are hardly able to know and comprehend the benefits and risks that are related with child immunization which in turn can lead to poor adherence to recommended immunization schedules. Similarly, in most LMICs, contemporary immunization status of infants is recorded in a booklet paper, which is ineffective in many ways such as the booklets may go missing, process of looking up data is tedious. Use of biometrics such as fingerprints have a great potential to accurately record immunizations and improve efficiency in searching data. Fingerprints are known to be unique, more permanent and low cost, thus an affordable technique to use for routine immunization coverage. Fingerprints play an important role in improving the immunization coverage for children who are under the care of either illiterate or ignorant caregivers. Immunization records may be captured along with fingerprint images which provide unique identification of the child.

One unique challenge in children fingerprint recognition system is that existing technologies- both hardware and software- are not proficient enough to capture children's fingerprints. A lot of research has gone into developing advanced hardware (with higher resolution) to collect these fingerprint images. (Yaseen Moolla et al, 2021), (Anil K. Jain, Sunpreet S. Arora, 2016) to improve recognition level. These technologies may not be available in low-cost areas especially in developing countries. Enhancement of the images is an important step for ease of recognition. The unified framework residual dense network method is used for the enhancement to generate better-quality fingerprints from the infant fingerprints. To demonstrate the effectiveness, we evaluate our method by measuring the quality level of the images using the NIST Fingerprint Image Quality (NFIQ) of the fingerprints. In summary, our main contributions are two-fold:

- An image enhancement algorithm using a unified framework residual dense network to improve the quality of the children fingerprint images collected using a standard scanner. We improved the algorithm by further inverting the images to obtain a white background instead of a black one.
- Assess the feasibility and acceptability of using fingerprints for children for tracking during immunization visits.

This paper is structured as follows. Section 2 summarizes the main literature and related works. Section 3 illustrates the materials and methods used in the experiments in this paper. Section 4 outlines the experiment results and quality scores obtained. Section 5 shows the Discussion while section 6 provides the conclusions.

2. RELATED WORK

A study of the state-of-the-art reveals that significant works have been published for children fingerprint recognition and its use in tracking vaccinations in recent years. These studies have led to the reduction of false-positive and negative errors in the recognition of fingerprint patterns and provides an optimal opportunity to provide fast, cheap, and safe recognition tools. The most known and available standard for fingerprint readers is one that has a standard resolution of 500 dpi (PPI) (FBI Biometrics Specifications, 2021). This a fingerprint reader is mainly targeted for adult fingerprints. Several research of developing higher resolution devices have been done and (Anil K. Jain, Sunpreet S. Arora, 2016) developed a contact-based device with a resolution of 1270PPI. They addressed the problem of identifying infants using a custom-built high-resolution fingerprint reader and applied enhancement methods to improve the visual appearance of the collected images. The enhanced images were used to identify and verify infants using a standard COTs matcher.

Since then, the study by (Joshua Engelsma, et al, 2019) also developed a higher resolution device of 1900PPI for fingerprint recognition. These readers are however scarce and not easily available for use in low- and middle-income countries (LMIC). As demonstrated by (Anil K. Jain, Sunpreet S. Arora, 2016), image enhancement algorithms are key to improvement in identification of fingerprints for children. This is true in circumstances where the high-resolution hardware equipment may not be easily available like LMIC. In the study by (Anil K. Jain et al,, 2015), the authors collected children fingerprints using standard fingerprint reader- the 500 PPI Digital Persona U.are.U 4500 HD. The Digital Persona U.are.U 4500 HD fingerprint reader is quite compact and ergonomically well designed for even small fingers. While study by (Yaseen Moolla et al, 2021) have shown that it's possible to develop a contact-less high-resolution device to acquire fingerprints from infants, with participants as young as 6 weeks of age, their main shortfall is that the images are acquired over a small area hence can result in partial fingerprints. This in essence can affect the recognition capability with matching algorithms.

Studies have shown that the good quality images require minor pre-processing and enhancement. On the contrary, low quality images require major pre-processing and enhancement. (Lin Hong et al, 1998) proposed an image enhancement technique using image using filtering technique.

Another study by (Macharia Paul et al, 2017) showed that it's possible to use infant fingerprint for unique in follow-up of HIV Exposed Infants (HEIs) after delivery. The authors were able to demonstrate that infant fingerprint can be collected using the standard and available fingerprint reader equipment. However, they did not implement an android based biometric application. Apart from tracking of HIV Exposed Infants (HEI), Fingerprint technology have been used in other health follow-up studies. For example, (J. J. Engelsma et al, 2021) used fingerprint technology for tracking nutritional supplements supply for children. VaxTrac, piloted a unique identification system of infants using fingerprints in Chad- A west African country (Anil K. Jain et al,, 2015). The system, intended to be used to track vaccination schedules of children. However, the system is reported to have low accuracy rates. Later they used mothers' fingerprints instead. Fingerprint have also been used in civil Identification. India initiated the AADHAR program to provide a unique identifier to its (Sen, Srijoni, 2019). India is not the only country that has implemented the national digital identity system.

Kenya, has prioritized the attainment of Universal Health Care (UHC) by 2022 through the expansion of health insurance coverage by the National Hospital Insurance Fund (NHIF). NHIF introduced reforms aimed at accelerating the country's progress towards UHC. These include revised premium contributions, expanded benefit cover and new provider benefits. However, there were reports of weak financial accountability that led to fraud mainly from the media. This included weak identification processes for the beneficiaries. NHIF then introduced use of biometrics for purposes of identification. However, as the exercise for biometric data collection went on, biometrics for children below five years was not done. This was attributed to the fact that fingerprint recognition of infants has some challenges. Kenya Medical Research Institute (KEMRI), a state corporation that carries out health research in Kenya initiated a research for promotion of maternal and child health programs. In this research, they evaluate the effectiveness of a biometric system within the management of kid and mother health information, which is vital for understanding the health status of local residents.

Recently, Deep learning methods on image resolution works have achieved a lot of success. Super-Resolution (SR) involves reconstruction of a high-quality image using one or more low-quality image(s). (K. Singh et al, 2015), developed a fingerprint image super resolution using ridge orientation-based collected coupled dictionaries. In this approach, the training patches are put into various groups based on the orientation of the ridges. They reported a significant improvement in terms of a Peak-to-Signal Noise Ratio (PSNR) and Structured Similarity Index Matching (SSIM) accuracy. (W. Bian et al, 2016) presented a new algorithm on Image Super resolution. Their main idea was to use to perform the reconstruction of the SR image by using sparse representation with ridge pattern prior based on classification coupled dictionaries.

3. MATERIALS AND METHODS

This research entailed development of a fingerprint image database from volunteer children attending vaccination clinic at a local health center. The parents are initially informed of the process and they sign a consent form. The fingerprint samples are provided from four fingers of the child, the left and right thumb and the left and right index fingers. The samples provided were typically used for both enrolment and verification process. Each collected image is labelled with information about the child. This includes the type of finger, the name and Date of birth of the subject. The proposed approach works in several consecutive stages:

Dataset Acquisition – this describes how the data was captured and fed into the system.

Fingerprint Enhancement– The dataset used had poor quality images. Enhancement was done to restore the clarity of the fingerprint image for ease of recognition and matching.

Fingerprint extraction and Matching – This is the final stage of decision making where the NIST fingerprint quality scores are determined for each enhanced fingerprint. a probe fingerprint template is matched against the database of fingerprint templates using an algorithm. The best and closest template is chosen from the database. This is regarded as the actual fingerprint recognition process. In this paper NFIQ scores were determined and this informed the possibility of recognition process.

3.1 Dataset Acquisition

In this study we collected fingerprint image data from children who were attending immunizations and health assessment in public hospitals. The process for data collection requires that parents be recruited individually from the immunization queues, and then informed about the research background, research goal and how the fingerprint scanner works. Parents who were willing to consent for their children to participate in data collection signed the consent form on behalf of their children. The health workers at the health centre helped the researcher in recruiting parents to participate in the exercise.

Data collection was conducted where fingerprint samples of the same subject (child) were collected using two different devices, the futronic FS 80 and the Digita Persona 4500U. An example of futronic scanner is shown in Figure. 1. (a). Both scanners were of 500 PPI resolution. The data collector assisted the parents/guardians to help the child place their fingers on the devices. For children under the age of 12-months-old, the data collector would hold the fingerprint sensor up to the child with one hand, and then with their other hand, place the infant's finger onto the device.

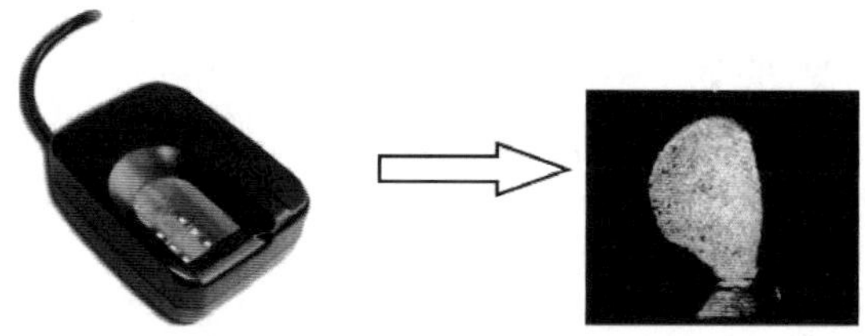

a b

Figure 1. Picture of (a) scanning device (b) sample output image

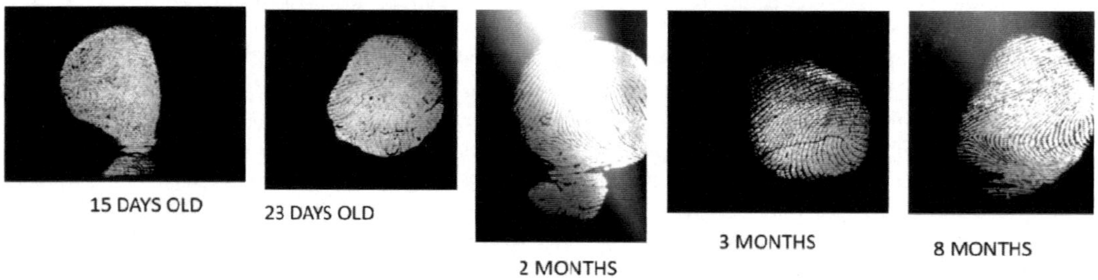

Figure 2. Sample Images collected

The dataset

This data collection consisted of 1,424 total images, collected from 215 children in the 0-3 months old group, 48 children in the 4-6 months old group, 66 children in the 7-9 months old and 24 children in the over 9months group.

Table 1, shows the statistics of the collected fingerprint data. The gender of the participants is not shown for privacy reasons. While Figure 3 demonstrates the age distribution of the collected fingerprint images. For comparison purposes a publicly available dataset for children (P Basak etal, 2017) was also used in the experiments. Even though the dataset contains images of children above 18 months, the images have the same resolution of 500 PPI as our dataset.

3.2 Fingerprint Enhancement

After image capture the next question is how do we extract and match the fingerprints. Given a fingerprint image, we can first enhance the fingerprint image then extract features for matching.

Fingerprint image enhancement is a very effective step in recognition systems. It helps improve the ridge clarity and certainly it essentially becomes a top factor for predetermination of success in matching accuracy. The major concern should be to improve a structure quality of fingerprints without interfering with the features. Enhancement also benefits in reducing spurious features and instead we get more accurate features.

In this paper, we first enhanced the resolution of the fingerprint image using super-resolution using the Residual Dense Block (RDB) technique (Y. Zhang, Y. Tian, Y. Kong, B. Zhong and Y. Fu, 2018). The RDB consists of three main components: the dense Connected layers, the local feature fusion and the local residual learning. Together they form a connecting memory mechanism where each layer is connected to all the previous layers in the network. Inspired DenseNet (G. Huang, Z. Liu, and K. Q. Weinberger., 2017), this approach extracts and adaptively uses the extracted features from all previous layers efficiently. The two major advantages of the RDN are the use of both local features and global features. This leads to a dense feature vision with deep supervision. By use of DenseNet structure, the RDN transfers features between layers such that the output of each layer is given as the input to its succeeding layers. Consider the $(y_0, y_1 \ldots y_{l-1})$ and y_l to be inputs and output of the l_{th} layer respectively such that:

$$y_l = H_l\,([y_0, y_1 \ldots y_{l-1}]). \qquad \textit{Equation 1}$$

y_l represents that concatenation of feature maps from preceding layers. The H_l function is the activation function that produces G feature maps. G is a hyper parameter that represents the growth rate such that the l_{th} layer has G_0+G_{l-1} as input feature maps. The outputs of each layer have direct connections to all subsequent layers and this helps preserve useful hierarchical features.

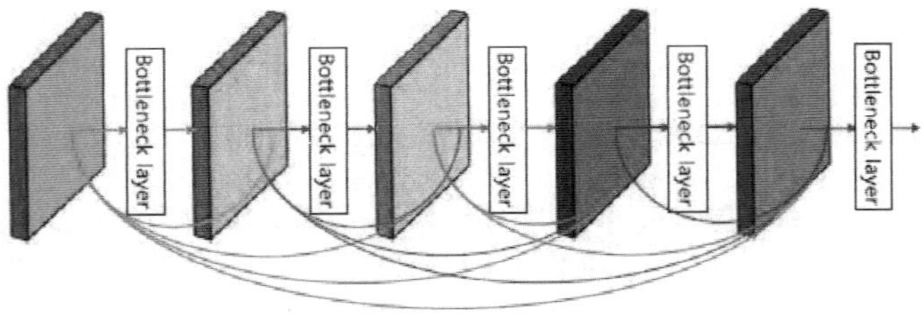

Figure 3. DenseNet structure (G. Huang, Z. Liu, and K. Q. Weinberger., 2017)

We implemented the Residual Dense Network (RDN) in this research using the python Image Super Resolution (ISR) library. To further improve the image resolution, the resultant output image was further processed to refine the bifurcation using fingerprint enhancer whose technique is shown in (Lin Hong et al, 1998). The output of the processed image has a black background with the bifurcations shown in white. In this research we additional enhanced the image by inverting the images. We inverted the image to obtain the final output with white background and black lines. This additional concept was very significant in this research because our experiments entailed recognition hence it was important that we obtain a white background.

The residual Dense Network has four main parts. The residual dense blocks (RDBs), dense feature fusion (DFF), and finally the up-scaling net (UP-Net). The residual Dense Block consists of three main parts: the dense Connected layers, the local feature fusion and the local residual learning. In the Dense Connected layers, all the features of the preceding layers form as input into the succeeding layer. This helps to preserve a good number of important features that can be used in recognition. The local feature fusion uses a 1x1 CNN layer we to control the output information in an adaptive manner.

From the results obtained, we posit that enhancement using the Residual Dense Network technique is mandatory to obtain acceptable results. Improvement of the enhanced image by inverting the image to have a white background was significant to quality measures that were obtained. Figure 4 shows the images after the enhancement procedure.

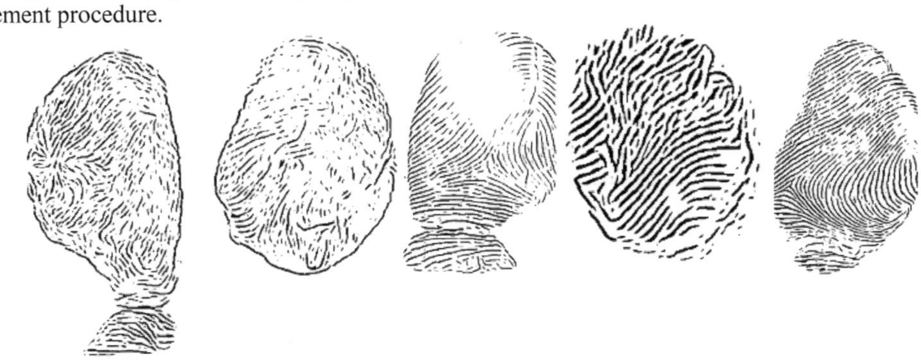

Figure 4. Fingerprints after enhancement with RDN

Table 1. Statistics of collected fingerprint data

	0 to 3 months	4 to 6 months	7 to 9 months	Above 9 months	Total
SUBJECTS PER AGE-SET	215	48	66	24	353

3.3 Fingerprint Feature Extraction and Matching

Fingerprint feature extraction is an important step in fingerprint recognition systems especially in poor quality images. The fingerprint recognition system requires accurate feature extraction for reliable classification and matching. Fingerprint matching, involves recognition of the fingerprint image from a subject against an existing database of fingerprint images.

There exist many biometric matching algorithms used for automatics recognition of persons, where the biometric features are matched against an existing database. However, its widely accepted that the performance of matching algorithms is affected by quality of images. Calculation of image quality score is thus important and is mainly provided for by the National Institute of Standards and Technology (NIST) fingerprint Image Quality (NFIQ). This NFIQ score has five levels of quality scores ranging from 1 (highest quality) to 5 (lowest quality) (Elham Tabassi, Charles Wilson, Craig Watson, 2004). The scores are intended to be predictive of the matching performance of an image in a fingerprint matching algorithm. In practice, NFIQ score 1, 2, 3 and 4 are acceptable for fingerprint matching. NFIQ score 5 is regarded as poor fingerprint image quality and fingerprint images with such quality are not recommended for use in fingerprint matching systems.

In this research, after fingerprint data collection, NFIQ scores were determined for all the collected images before enhancement. Thereafter NFIQ scores were also determined after the enhancement. The enhancement procedure improved the quality scores for the images hence they were useable in matching algorithm. This is considered quite important in this study given that the data collection was done using standard technology that was easily available to the researcher. The enhancement is significant as it improves the ridge clarity and hence the ridge spacing of the children's fingerprint images comes close to that of adults. This facilitates quality improvement as measured using NFIQ scores. A comparison of the image quality scores before and after enhancement is shown in tables 2 and 3. Table 2 shows the quality of images before enhancement using the NFIQ score matrix. While Table 3 shows the quality of images after enhancement. Taking images of 0 to 3 months we can observe an improvement of images at quality 5 from 80 images to only 9 images after enhancement. The Residual dense network Image super resolution was also applied to the children public dataset (P Basak etal, 2017). There was considerable improvement in quality measurement which implies better recognition.

Table 2. Quality Scores using NFIQ Before enhancement

NFIQ Score		0 to 3 months	4 to 6 months	7 to 9 months	Above 9 months
1	Count	15	34	27	13
	% Within group	7%	71%	41%	54%
2	Count	0	6	11	6
	% Within group	0%	12.5%	17%	25%
3	Count	9	0	20	5
	%Within group	4%	0%	30%	21%
4	Count	111	8	0	0
	%Within group	52%	17%	0%	0%
5	Count	80	0	8	0%
	%Within group	37%	0%	12%	

Table 3. Quality Scores using NFIQ After enhancement

NFIQ Score		0 to 3 months	4 to 6 months	7 to 9 months	Above 9 months
1	Count	16	39	32	13
	%Within group	7%	81%	48%	54%
2	Count	9	8	26	6
	%Within group	4%	17%	40%	25%
3	Count	111	1	4	5
	%Within group	52%	2%	6%	21%
4	Count	70	0	4	0
	%Within group	33%	0%	6%	0%
5	Count	9		0	0%
	%Within group	4%	0%	0%	

4. RESULTS

In this section we provide the experimental evaluation of the proposed technique. We primarily aimed to demonstrate the feasibility of fingerprint recognition using standard low-cost equipment. We collected a database of 1404 images from 353 subjects. All the images have a resolution of 500PPI and dimension size of 320x480 pixels. The main effort was to simulate real life scenarios in Low- and Medium-Income Countries (LMIC areas) by testing our algorithm on poor quality fingerprint images. Fingerprint images vary depending on gender, collection process, age and cooperation of the subject. Fingerprint enhancement was performed using the Residual Dense Network for Image super resolution technique. An improvement to the technique was added to invert the image such that it had a white background against the white ridges of the fingerprint image. Then the image quality was determined using the opensource National Institute of Standards and Technology (NIST) fingerprint Image Quality (NFIQ) software. The NFIQ scores range between 1 (excellent quality) and 5 (poor quality).

4.1 Fingerprint Quality Score Results

Table 2 and 3 show the results as described below.
Of the 215 child fingerprints collected for age group 0 to 3 months, 37% (80) had an NFIQ score of 5, 52 % (111) had a score of 4 while only 7% (15) had the excellent score of 1. After the enhancement procedure with our method, about 96% (206) of the fingerprint images of ages 0-3 months had a score between 1 and 4. Looking at the 4 to 6 months category, 17% of the images had an NFIQ scale of 4. After enhancement the NFIQ quality score improved such that five images improved to a score of 1, two images improved to a score of 2 while one image improved to score 3. In the category of 7 to 9 months age for the children, 12% of the images had an NFIQ score of 5. After enhancement, all the images obtained a higher score and there was no image that had an NFIQ score of 5. There was no substantive change on the image quality for category of images for children above 9 months. This could be due to fact that the images were already good enough. The scores obtained after the enhancement for both 0 to 3 months, 4 to 6 months and 7 to 9 months greatly improved in quality which in essence implied a sufficient feature extraction from the images. NFIQ scores of 1 to 4 are acceptable and suitable for fingerprint recognition tasks.

5. DISCUSSION

Tracking children through their fingerprints has the potential to greatly strengthen immunization coverage and accuracy. Fingerprint technology can be used to create children's profiles that contain immunization records. This requires an effective fingerprint matching system for the retrieval of the immunization records. In this study we lean towards feasibility and empirical analysis of a potential fingerprint system using poor quality images collected by use of standard technology.

For effective matching, the fingerprint images were enhanced using the residual Dense network for super resolution. The images were further inverted to obtain a white background for better visual form. In low- and medium-income developing countries (LMIC), there is scarcity of high-resolution hardware equipment for image recognition. The Image enhancement is thus quite helpful due to lack of this high-tech equipment. In the research, the NFIQ score improved highly after the enhancement procedure. This can improve the matching of the fingerprint hence the immunization profiles retrieval.

Advantages of the proposed method: The proposed method of image enhancement has the advantage of utilizing both local and global features which becomes a good representation of the image. In addition, since the backbone of RDN is the DenseNet Neural network, less parameters are employed in the method, hence reduction in computational costs. The inversion of the images was done such that the black pixels were converted to white and the white pixels converted to black. The inversion of the images gave the images a good visual clarity.

6. CONCLUSIONS

Many children in developing countries suffer from early mortalities due to lack of immunizations. This could be due to difficulty of accessibility of low-cost tracking systems for children as they attend clinics. A low-cost follow-up method to trace immunization for children is essential to ensure that all children attend immunization clinics as and when required. We took an initiative to conduct an empirical analysis of recent methods/techniques in using fingerprint recognition to track immunization of children as a contribution to solving this problem.

A low-cost fingerprint recognition approach for children assists in tracking their movements from one health service facility to another for immunization. It enables infants to be followed across different regions. The need for an affordable biometric solution is paramount in contexts where the high-resolution equipment is scarce. Given that children fingerprints collected with standard equipment are generally of poor quality, a solution that adapts to this is key. This was the key objective of this study. Fingerprint images were collected from children below one year of age who were attending immunization clinics. We performed image enhancement using residual dense network technique. The dense network ensures re-use of features from all the dense layers. This helps to achieve a good resolution with less loss of information. The image was further enhanced by inverting such that it had a white background. NFIQ score experiments were conducted to compare quality of the image before and after the enhancement procedure. There was considerable improvement of the quality scores. The quality improvement measure shows that it's feasible to recognize children's fingerprints.

For future work, we recommend performing further studies that include the collection of more fingerprint data with the use of various capture devices, and potential applications in diverse areas.

ACKNOWLEDGMENT

The authors of this paper would like to acknowledge the public hospital that allowed the researcher to collect data from the children visiting the clinics.

We also thank the parents and caregivers of children who gave consent on behalf of their children to help achieve the goal of this research.

REFERENCES

Anil K. Jain et al,. (2015). *Biometrics for Child Vaccination and Welfare: Persistence of Fingerprint Recognition for Infants and Toddlers.* Department of Computer Science and Engineering Michigan State University.

Anil K. Jain, Sunpreet S. Arora. (2016). Giving Infants an Identity: Fingerprint Sensing and Recognition. *8th conference on Information and communications technologies and development)ICTD.* Anne Arbor Michigan.

Elham Tabassi, Charles Wilson, Craig Watson. (2004). *Fingerprint Image Quality.* National Institute of Standards and Technology.

FBI Biometrics Specifications. (2021). *https://www.fbibiospecs.cjis.gov/Certifications/FAQ.* (FBI) Retrieved from https://www.fbibiospecs.cjis.gov: https://www.fbibiospecs.cjis.gov/Certifications/FAQ

G. Huang, Z. Liu, and K. Q. Weinberger. (2017). Densely connected convolutional networks. *In IEEE Conference on Computer Vision and Pattern Recognition.*

J. J. Engelsma et al. (2021). "Infant-ID: Fingerprints for Global Good. *IEEE Transactions on Pattern Analysis and Machine Intelligence.*

Joshua Engelsma, et al. (2019). Infant-prints: Fingerprints for reducing infant mortality. *arXiv preprint.*

K. Singh et al. (2015). Fingerprint image super-resolution via ridge orientation-based clustered coupled sparse dictionaries. *Journal of Electronic Imaging.*

Lahariya, C. (2015). Health system approach" for improving immunization program performance. *Journal of family medicine and primary care, 4*(4), 487-494.

Lin Hong et al. (1998). Fingerprint Image Enhancement: Algorithm and Performance Evaluation. *IEEE Transactions on Pattern Analysis and Machine Intelligence*, vol. 20, no. 8, pp. 777-789.

Macharia Paul et al. (2017). The feasibility of using an android-based infant fingerprint biometrics system for treatment follow-up. *2017 IST-Africa Week Conference, IST-Africa 2017.* IST-Africa 2017.

P Basak etal. (2017). Multimodal biometric recognition for toddlers and pre-school children. *IEEE International Joint Conference on Biometrics (IJCB)*, 627-633.

Sen, Srijoni. (2019, MAY). *A Decade of Aadhaar: Lessons in implementing a foundational ID system.* Retrieved from A Decade of Aadhaar: Lessons in implementing a foundational ID system: https://www.orfonline.org/research/a-decade-of-aadhaar-lessons-in-implementing-a-foundational-id-system-50464/

W. Bian et al. (2016). Fingerprint image super resolution using sparse representation with ridge pattern prior by classification coupled dictionaries. *IET Biometrics, vol. 6, no. 5*, 342-350.

Y. Zhang, Y. Tian, Y. Kong, B. Zhong and Y. Fu. (2018). Residual Dense Network for Image Super-Resolution. *IEEE/CVF Conference on Computer Vision and Pattern Recognition*, 2472-2481.

Yaseen Moolla et al. (2021). Biometric Recognition of Infants using Fingerprint, Iris, and Ear Biometrics. *IEEE ACCESS*, 38269-38285.

IMPROVING THE PERFORMANCE OF BIGBLUEBUTTON FOR TEACHING ONLINE COURSES

Christian Uhl and Bernd Freisleben
Department of Mathematics and Computer Science, University of Marburg, Germany

ABSTRACT

BigBlueButton (BBB) is a web conferencing system designed for online learning. It consists of a set of pre-configured open-source software tools to realize video conferencing functionality primarily for teaching purposes. Due to the COVID-19 pandemic, our university decided to roll out BBB for the university's educational activities in the first nationwide lock-down in early 2020. Based on our experiences in deploying, operating, and using BBB at our university in the last 12 months, we present suggestions on how the services provided by BBB can be improved to meet the technical demands identified during online lecturing at our university. Our suggestions include the introduction of simulcast, improvements of encoding and muxing video feeds, and the 'Last-N' algorithm for video feed pagination. To demonstrate the benefits of the presented improvements, we experimentally evaluated most of them based on our own prototypical implementations.

KEYWORDS

BigBlueButton, Web Conferencing, Online Teaching

1. INTRODUCTION

Due to the currently prevailing COVID-19 pandemic and the disease control measures that have been put in place, many people are forced to abandon their accustomed behaviors and avoid human contact. For this reason, telepresence is increasingly used in workplaces, but also in teaching at schools and universities. This has led to an increased demand for web conference platforms to support distance teaching (de Campos). Due to a nationwide lockdown, our university had to provide a tailor-made web conference platform for teaching to all lecturers and students within less than a month, so that teaching activities could continue online as soon as possible.

The requirements within a university are quite diverse, depending on the particular teaching concept. For example, traditional top-down teaching based on lectures focuses on a single lecturer, with students taking a primarily passive stance. Such forms of teaching are also designed for large numbers of participants. In contrast, the number of participants (per group) is significantly lower in empowerment and participatory teaching. The focus here is on direct communication between participants, who often wish to see each other at all times. Thus, the following requirements have to be considered for distance teaching at a university:

- There are online lectures with more than 100 participants, in which at least one person uses a camera and a slide presentation.
- There are video conferences with over 30 active participants, in which each person shows a video of himself or herself.
- Some participants might use aged hardware or mobile devices with limited resources.
- There should be as little data traffic as possible.

In most cases, the hardware used by the participants is privately owned, which means that dedicated support for participants with weaker client hardware must be provided. Furthermore, the typical Internet connections of many home networks often have low bandwidths and/or low data volumes. This is especially relevant when a participant is connected via a mobile carrier. Currently, web conferencing providers such as Microsoft, Zoom, and Cisco are trying to expand their reach in teaching using proprietary tools. In the field of open-source software, popular projects are Jitsi (Jitsi Developer Community) and BigBlueButton (BBB) (BigBlueButton Developer Community). Both are based on the WebRTC (Web Real-Time Communication) protocol (Jansen, Goodwin und Gupta), (Zhang, Zhang and Qi), (Xue and Zhang). Unfortunately, none of these systems meet all of our requirements without restrictions. Nevertheless, our university decided to rollout BBB for the university's educational activities in the first nationwide lock-down in early 2020. To ensure fail-safety and thus undisputed teaching, our university decided to make WebEx from Cisco available to the lecturers in addition to BBB, but the university management recommends BBB as the primary system for distance learning.

Based on our experiences in deploying, operating, and using BBB at our university in the last 12 months, we present suggestions on how the services provided by BBB can be improved to meet the technical demands identified during online lecturing at our university. Our suggestions include the introduction of simulcast, improvements of encoding and muxing video feeds, and the 'Last-N' algorithm for video feed pagination. In addition, we discuss some proposals from the community that are promising to improve the performance of BBB with relatively little effort. To demonstrate the benefits of the presented improvements, we experimentally evaluate most of them based on our own prototypical implementations.

The paper is organized as follows. Section 2 reviews related work. Section 3 briefly describes BBB. In Section 4, we present usage statistics. Section 5 discusses our proposed client- and server-side improvements of BBB and evaluates their performance properties. Section 6 concludes the paper and outlines areas for future work.

2. RELATED WORK

There are several publications that evaluate functional aspects and performance issues of web conferencing systems, in particular BBB. For example, (Vasconcelos, de Araújo Freitas and Marques) use KVM and OpenVZ as virtualization platforms to deploy conference systems using BBB. The authors explore BBB's virtual performance under a real-world workload and a set of benchmarks that stress different aspects such as computing power, latency and memory, I/O, and network bandwidth. (Cižmešija and Bubas) present an approach to evaluate the use of BBB in e-learning. The authors combine established information system success criteria with models of usability and user experience in software use. (Lu, Zhao and Kuipers) evaluate four representative video conferencing applications with respect to various aspects, including traffic load control and load balancing algorithms, traffic shaping policies, and adaptively re-encoding streams in real time to limit the overall traffic. (Byrne, Furuyabu und Moore) analyze performance issues of Google Hangouts and Jitsi Meet when simultaneously using several video conferencing tools. (Petrangeli, Pauwels and van der Hooft) show that forwarding selective streams and dynamically adjusting bit rates on the fly leads to performance improvements of up to 15%.

Furthermore, several reports on developing and using web conferencing tools in online learning and teaching have been published in the literature. For example, (Sandars, Correia und Dankbaar) present a compendium of key principles and practical recommendations that allow educators to rapidly migrate to online learning during the COVID-19 pandemic. (Voegeli, Clark and Pullen) use web technologies to build the MIST/C open-source multimedia Internet client to support teaching in the classroom and online simultaneously. (J. M. Pullen) describes his experiences in synchronous online teaching and learning based on his own open-source software system called NetworkEducationWare. (Pullen and Clark) combine synchronous and asynchronous approaches to distance education, using Moodle and MIST/C, and report their experiences in supporting M.Sc. programs in computer science. None of these publications present approaches to improve the performance of BBB with respect to client and server improvements based on experiences of using BBB for teaching online courses.

3. BIG BLUE BUTTON

BBB (BigBlueButton Developer Community) is a collection of open-source software tools that implement services to provide a web conferencing platform as a local and/or on-premise web service. In particular, BBB relies on FreeSwitch (SignalWire) to provide basic phone integration, Kurento (Kurento) as a media server, LibreOffice (LibreOffice Foundation) for presentations, and Etherpad (Etherpad Foundation) for collaborative text editing. BBB itself is transmitted to the user as a web application via a web browser. The web browser connects to the physical audio and video devices via common communication interfaces and transmits the information to a media sharing server, which then passes it on to all other participants without conversion via an integrated media server. The underlying standard for service delivery has been defined by the W3C under the name WebRTC (Jansen, Goodwin und Gupta), (Xue and Zhang), (Zhang, Zhang and Qi).

A main strength of BBB is that a conference participant is not forced to install any software on his or her local machine. This strength is also BBB's biggest weakness, because web browsers can only communicate with the available hardware via supplied interfaces and usually require more local resources than a native application. Native applications can be optimized for the underlying hardware to improve the overall experience and implement features that are impossible to recreate inside a browser window. Furthermore, not every browser offers the same subset of functions and displayable formats. The general limiting factors of BBB (and generally all other video conferencing systems) belong to three major categories:

- *Traffic / maximum data throughput.* In conferences where each participant shares his or her own camera or media device, the amount of data to be transmitted increases quadratically with the number of total participants. Due to the fact that the data streams from the underlying media server (here a multi-point conferencing unit, MCU) are only distributed but not transformed, a large amount of traffic can be generated.
- *Client load.* The underlying technology of the web browser requires that each video is rendered in a separate subtask. This increases the required load on the end user devices proportionally to the number of participants and their quality settings. Even modern computers with considerable computing power quickly reach their performance limits.
- *Server load.* The administration, preparation, and delivery of video streams require sufficient computing power on the server. BBB is optimized by default to keep the server load as low as possible.

4. USAGE STATISTICS

To quantify the adoption of web conferencing systems for online teaching in our university, we collected usage data for BBB and WebEx. We set up a BBB installation consisting of up to 15 worker nodes and two load balancers. We started with BBB Version 2.2.3 and currently use BBB Version 2.3.3. The BBB instances were monitored using Prometheus and analyzed using Grafana. WebEx stores all necessary usage data by itself, eliminating the need for using external software for collecting data. The corresponding data has been exported via the WebEx admin panel and analyzed using Microsoft Excel. Since we apply a strict data minimization policy, only completely anonymized data is recorded. This prevents information about the organizer or participant from being collected. Therefore, we cannot distinguish the purpose for which a web conference has been opened. Thus, we primarily look at the number of concurrent web conferences, the number of web conference sessions in total, and the utilization of physical hardware.

4.1 Data

Currently, our university consists of 4,576 paid employees and 24,394 active students. These are combined as "staff". We recorded data during the period from 08/01/2020 to 01/25/2021. To interpret the data, it is important to know that the regular operation at our university took place from 10/12/2020 to 02/12/2021. Furthermore, there is an activity free period from 12/18/2020 to 01/08/2021.

4.2 Adoption

Over the course of the monitored period, a total of 75,071 web conferences with 611,585 participants were held using BBB and WebEx. It should be noted that these are not unique participants, since, as an example, reconnecting or participating in two web conferences at the same time cannot be attributed to a single person due to the need for data sparsity. The number of web conferences conducted with BBB during the entire time period was significantly higher than the number of WebEx conferences. There are 3.27 BBB attendees for every WebEx attendee, and for every web conference held in WebEx, there are 4.36 BBB conferences. The number of participants in the regular, lecture-free, and weekend periods together with the percentage of staff per day is shown in Table 1. The average conference duration was 59.01 minutes. This includes test connections to the web conferencing system. Assuming that all web conferences under 5 minutes or with less than two participants are tests and removing them from the data set, the average conference duration increases to 73.98 minutes. The maximum values of our BBB cluster per day are shown in Table 2. Here, a distinction is made between the number of meetings and participants, the active webcams, voice participants, and listeners.

Table 1. Participant data

	regular	lecture-free	weekend
Sum of participants	558,874	13,709	39,002
% of staff per day	17.44%	2.24%	6.38%

Table 2. Maximum values in BBB (per day)

Description	Numb	Description	Number
meetings	1,233	active came	1,352
participants	18,748	active audio	5,233
concurrent meetings	202	listener	11,741
concurrent participan	2,697		

4.3 Server Load

To evaluate the server load, only the values of BBB are considered. We cannot assess WebEx's server utilization because the underlying hardware infrastructure is not under our control and the usage information is not open to the public. We used 10 servers with Ryzen 7 3700X (8-core) and 64 GB RAM as our BBB test cluster. The web meetings were load-balanced between these servers using the software Scalelite. The CPU load was recorded with Netdata and normalized based on the available cores. The data visualized in Figure 1 shows a roughly linear slope of the required CPU load with increasing numbers of concurrent meetings / participants. This makes it very easy to estimate the resources required, even for large clusters.

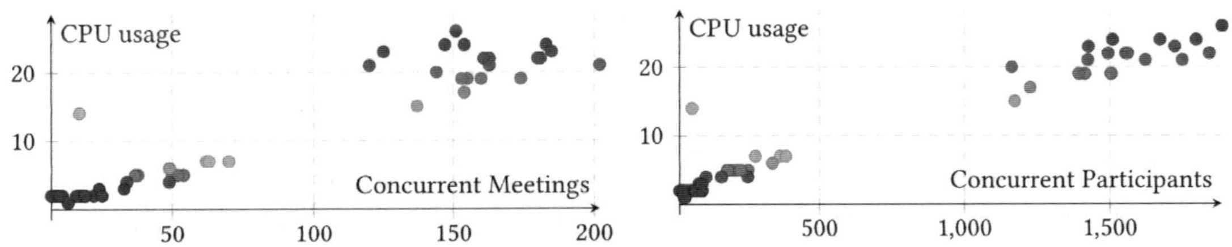

Figure 1. Performance of BBB in terms of CPU usage

5. IMPROVING THE PERFORMANCE OF BBB

We now present suggestions on how the services provided by BBB can be improved. To demonstrate the benefits of the presented improvements, we experimentally evaluated most of them using our own prototypical implementations. In our experimental evaluation, we used the following client and server devices:

Server Intel Xeon E2246G 64 GB RAM, Debian Buster
Client Macbook Pro 13" [2020] Core i5-1038NG7, 16 GB RAM, MacOS 10.15
Client Ryzen9 3900X, 64 GB RAM AMD RX5700XT, Ubuntu 20.04
Client Ryzen7 4750G, 32 GB RAM NVIDIA GTX1070, Windows 10
Client iPhone 11 Pro, iOS 14
Client Sony Xperia Z3C, Android 10

5.1 Client Performance Improvements

5.1.1 Pagination of Video Feeds

To improve the performance of a client, we can specify that never more than *N* videos should be displayed at once. If more video streams exist, pagination occurs and the user needs to scroll through them. This can be adjusted at the client and reduces both the load on the client and the number of data streams on both the client and the server.

Implementation. A simplified version of this feature was introduced in BBB in version 2.2.23 on August 26, 2020. It has fixed values and cannot be customized from within the client (BigBlueButton Developer Community). Based on this implementation, we rolled out a customized variant with N=8+1 video feeds per page in our live system.

Results. Due to the fact that only in rare cases more than 8 video feeds are used for teaching online courses at our university, no difference could be observed in the overall performance of the university wide cluster. In an individual test, the maximum data rate was capped at 1,081 kb/s and the CPU load reached a maximum at 63%, due to the upper limit of simultaneously displayed video feeds. A disadvantage of pagination with a static upper limit is a massive reduction of the comfort of use. The user must manually instruct the client which videos he or she wants to actively view by selecting the corresponding page. Therefore, the feature is not practicable as a single performance improvement. In combination with further improvements, such as a Last-N algorithm for calculating the most active or recent video feeds (as discussed later), the loss of comfort can be significantly reduced.

Summary. Our implementation demonstrates that pagination of video feeds can significantly reduce the load on the client and at the same time can reduce traffic. The BBB developer team should improve their simplified implementation of pagination of video feeds introduced in BBB version 2.2.23.

5.1.2 Simulcast and Scalable Video Coding

Simulcast (Bouras, Kioumourtzis and Gkamas) relies on the fact that each client makes its video available to the media server in various formats
and/or resolutions. The server decides individually which client gets which stream. In this way, the data transfer rate and the computational effort on the receiving clients can be greatly reduced. As an alternative to simulcast, a single video data stream can be divided into several layers via Scalable Video Coding (SVC) (Schwarz, Marpe und Wiegand). These layers depend on each other and are used to improve the quality of the video stream (W3).

Implementation. We developed a standalone implementation of simulcast using mediasoup (Mediasoup Developers) that uses similar technologies as BBB. This prototype was fed with three prerendered video feeds from the same video source (4K video pre-down-scaled to 1080p at 60 FPS (Peach Open Video Project) served through a virtual webcam driver from OBS (OBS)) to 720p30 FPS, 480p25 FPS, and 160p10 FPS. The clients were set up to submit a fixed performance score to pick the most appropriate feed. In our evaluation of SVC, we used the most widely supported implementation based on the H.264 codec. We modified the spatial (resolution) and temporal (frame rate) parameters of the codec on the fly. The quality for decoding was set to auto.

Results. Figure 2 shows the performance of using BBB on a MacBook Pro (2020) (a) without simulcast, (b) with simulcast on CPU and VA-API (Intel), and (c) using SVC. The x-axis shows the number of streams; the y-axis shows the MacOS system load. Since most conferences in our university have less than 10 active camera feeds, the effort for simulcast did not pay off in our measurements. Using the CPU to reencode the video feeds individually from the same source resulted in very high system loads. We were unable to finish the tests due to a reoccurring computer freeze whenever we exceeded 32 streams. Simulcast only became practical when hardware acceleration with the VA-API interface of the integrated graphics card was used and more than 20 video feeds were served. This is the break-even point of this setup. The outsourcing of the computations to the server caused a strong reduction of the maximum number of simultaneous users of our test system from about 200 to approximately 20 users. However, reencoding the videos can shift the load from the client to the server. This is beneficial if the clients are mobile devices with limited resources. In our tests, using SVC had a positive effect on performance. The disadvantages of computing a multi-stream were nearly eliminated, while the advantages are still present.

Summary. Our implementation demonstrates that the introduction of simulcast and SVC shifts some of the load from the receiver to the sender or the server. With many simultaneous participants, a significant reduction in traffic and client load can be achieved. To introduce simulcast and SVC in BBB, parts of the BBB server code have to be rewritten.

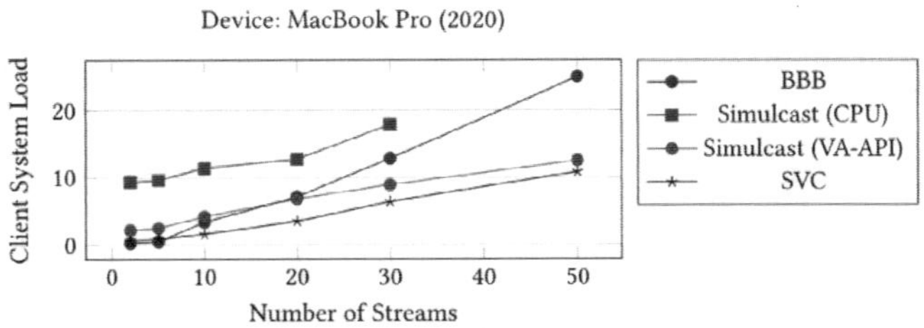

Figure 2. Performance of BBB (a) without simulcast and SVC, (b) with simulcast, (c) with SVC

5.1.3 MCU / Multiplexing

Using appropriate multiplexing (muxing) (Mekuria, Fennema and Griffioen) servers, it is possible to merge several video streams into one. For this purpose, the video streams are arranged into a grid model and then a new (high-quality) video stream is calculated from it. Instead of distributing the original video data, the new stream is distributed to the clients. This leads to a significant reduction of the load on the end devices. A further advantage is that such a data stream can be distributed via various media servers or content delivery networks. If placed within a local area network, it can be used to distribute the content within this network and reduce the overall network load on the wide area network interface. The Kurento media server used in BBB can be switched from the current SFU (Selective Forwarding Unit) mode to MCU (Multipoint Conferencing Unit) mode required for muxing.

Implementation. We developed a standalone MCU implementation using mediasoup (Mediasoup Developers) that uses similar technologies as BBB. In this implementation, we forwarded the source material using RTP to FFmpeg (FFmpeg), which merges and reencodes the received feeds to a newly mixed, grid-oriented video. This video is then reinjected into mediasoup as the primary video feed.

Results. The recomputation of a video is a resource hungry process for the media server. This approach suffered from similar performance issues as the reencoding required in simulcast described above and is only practicable when hardware acceleration is available. This approach is not practical for conference systems with multiple concurrent conferences, since even hardware accelerated systems can only run a limited number of concurrent de-/encoding tasks. Since several data streams are combined at the same time, the load on the server is lower than in the multi-stream approach described in the previous subsection, because only one reencoding and multiple decoding processes are required per conference, resulting in roughly 12 concurrent conferences. In our tests, the latency increases noticeably. Even under optimized conditions, an additional average offset of 522 ms was obtained. Since only a single video had to be displayed regardless of the number of participants, the load on the client decreased considerably. We only performed a limited number of measurements, since this approach is not feasible for our cluster. The additional latency as well as the elevated requirements on the server hardware were not acceptable.

Summary. Our implementation demonstrates that MCU increases the load on the server, but noticeably reduces traffic and client load. To introduce MCU in BBB, parts of the BBB server code have to be rewritten.

5.1.4 Dynamic Profiles

When entering a video conference in BBB, users are asked in which quality the video signal should be made available to the other participants. The profiles include general conditions such as resolution, frame rate, and data rate. One possibility to ensure stable operation of the service even at higher workloads is to dynamically adapt these parameters. For example, the quality of low-quality video signals can be reduced even further when the server is under a higher load. As a trigger for an adjustment, the load values of the server can be included. Examples include the statistical evaluation of lost data packets, client load, processor load, and network load.

Implementation. A simplified implementation, which is exclusively based on the number of concurrent video streams on the server, was introduced in BBB in version 2.2.22 on August 11, 2020 after a suggestion by us in the official BBB bug tracker (BigBlueButton Developer Community).

Results. The current implementation is designed to keep the server up and running and reduces quality if the server load exceeds the maximum limit. We measured a noticeable reduction in peak loads on the university's live system. Previously, a node was fully utilized about once a month. Using our implementation, the load of a node on the live cluster leveled off at 90% maximum.

Summary. Dynamically adjusting the broadcast profiles has a significant effect on reducing traffic but causes a noticeably inferior video quality. The current implementation available in BBB has too few triggers. To implement more triggers as suggested by us in the official BBB bug tracker, larger parts of the BBB source code must be modified.

5.1.5 Last-N Algorithm

The available computing capacity on both the client and server can be improved by displaying only the last *N* users (Grozev, Marinov and Singh). BBB already contains an indicator that highlights the last speaking persons. This function can therefore be chosen as a starting point for further improvements. Some examples are:

- *Throttling.* If the user has not communicated in the conference for a long time, the user's client can independently throttle its own bit rate by switching to a lower transmission profile. In this case, it is recommended to reduce the number of frames per second of the user's own video stream continuously down to a fixed minimum. The bit rate itself can also be reduced steadily.
- *Quality of service.* Based on this information, the priority of the data streams can be increased on the server side for active participants and reduced for inactive participants. This ensures that available resources do not have to be kept available for inactive participants and that a lack of free resources will not lead to noticeable failures.
- *Pagination.* In combination with pagination, less relevant video streams can be removed from the other participants' active field of view. This could also reduce the computational load of the clients.

Implementation. We manipulated the official BBB pagination using Javascript and the browser extension GreaseMonkey (Greasemonkey). Based on the activity indicator of the voice activation in BBB, we filled an array that subsequently replaced the displayed video feeds with the eight most active speakers of the last 5 minutes. The Last-N algorithm was officially introduced in BBB version 2.3.

Results. Our tests showed that the combination of a Last-N algorithm with pagination has a significant impact on the performance and stability of the overall system. Despite constant changes of the displayed video streams, the additional load on the client has only increased slightly (<10%) compared to a static upper limit of simultaneous video streams due to pagination. We assume that the load increased due to the use of an external browser extension. No measurable additional load could be identified when using the feature already implemented in BBB version 2.3. In combination with SVC, an even more significant increase in performance can be expected.

Summary. The use of the Last-N algorithm has a significant impact on the usability of the pagination function and renders it more acceptable by users. From a technical point of view, there is no reason to not activate this feature.

5.1.6 Efficient Video Codecs

At present, the VP8 codec (Bienik, Uhrina and Kuba) is used for WebRTC in BBB to encode video signals. Since January 2016, its successor VP9 (Mukherjee, Han and Bankoski) is supported in WebRTC by Google Chrome (version 48+) and since 2017 in Firefox (version 46+) (Alphabet), (Mozilla). Compared to VP8, VP9 offers higher visual quality at the same data rate.VP9 requires more effort in encoding/decoding the video streams than VP8. VP9 is also not supported by some hardware accelerators. To make it even more difficult, VP9 is not natively supported on Apple platforms and needs to be rendered in software. This leads to a doubling of the CPU load on systems with MacOS. Therefore, a change to VP9 is not (yet) recommended.

5.1.7 Switching the Default View from Grid View to Speaker View

Grid view, also known as gallery view, is currently the predominant form of presentation for web conferences. In grid view, all participants are displayed in the same size and aligned on a rectangular grid. With this type of presentation, the participants have the expectation that all participants are available in full quality at all times. In combination with other suggested improvements, especially dynamic profiles, the view can be changed to a speaker centered view. In this view, the currently dominant speaker is given most of the screen space, while the other participants are only shown as thumbnails. In speaker view, the visual quality is dynamically adjusted based on the position on the screen, which reduces the load on the client.

Implementation. We used the same implementation as in our Last-N algorithm described above based on GreaseMonkey, but replaced the default presentation inside the BBB conference window with the video feed of the most frequent user to mimic a different layout. Since this test was conducted within BBB, we were unable to modify the quality settings of the video feeds on the fly.

Results. We conducted a series of tests with several test persons. These tests were completed in the presence of a psychologist and included the presentation of a handwritten note, an active discussion between four people, and a short teaching session on a chalkboard. Although no differences in video quality were present, the test persons assumed that the video feed of the primary speaker had better video quality than the other video feeds. In the test with the handwritten note, some of the test persons explicitly asked the person presenting the note to create some noise or talk to get him or her into the main view instead of zooming on the existing feed. It should also be mentioned that the speaker view was perceived as choppy by some of our test persons and was generally less desirable than the normal grid view.

Summary. Our implementation and our experiments show that speaker view encourages the choice of lower quality video codecs, and in combination with dynamic profiles can lead to a reduction of client load as well as network traffic. To introduce speaker view in BBB, only few adjustments of the BBB source code are necessary.

5.2 Server Performance Improvements

5.2.1 IP Multicast

To reduce data transfer from the server, it is possible to use IP multicast (Ratnasamy, Sylvia; Ermolinskiy, Andrey; Shenker, Scott). For this purpose, the video streams are not transmitted individually to each client, but are made available to all participants at the same time. The underlying network infrastructure takes care of the distribution of the data stream to the recipients. IP multicast has no influence on the load or the size of the data stream at the clients. Only the server benefits from the fact that data packets do not have to be addressed and transmitted individually foreach client. IP multicast also requires a special configuration of the network, since most routers in the Internet do not forward multicast packets. The use of multicast also makes other optimization options (such as simulcast) more difficult and is therefore not recommended.

5.2.2 Low-latency Kernel on the Server

Operating system kernels optimized for low-latency (Belay, Prekas und Primorac) are often used for audio/video services. Ubuntu, the operating system used for BBB, offers its own precompiled kernel for low-latency tasks in the audio/video area (Canonical). The use of a low-latency kernel is therefore easy to implement by using a single command.

Implementation. We installed different kernels (regular, low-latency and real-time optimized) from the official Ubuntu back-port repository inside a virtual machine and conducted some automated tests using Selenium (Selenium) on 20 identical client machines in a computer laboratory of our university. We opened a WebRTC audio/video connection with a dummy webcam to the server and measured the latency at idle, 50%, and 100% utilization of the CPU and the network interface of the server. We also started BBB and performed a load test by increasing the load by slowly adding more clients to a single conference.

Results. We measured slightly lower latencies in audio streams (about 2 ms). However, the slight reduction of the latencies leads to a slight increase in the general server load compared to an unmodified kernel. Since the adjustments of the low-latency kernel are quite extensive and the effects on the various services are unknown, more precise measurements were not carried out.

Summary. Our implementation demonstrates that even though only minimal effort is required to install a low-latency kernel on the server, the disadvantages outweigh the advantages in our measurements.

5.2.3 Switching to IPv6

Considering that a significant part of the Internet is natively connected via IPv6, we can try to optimize WebRTC using IPv6 (Barik, Welzl and Elmokashfi). However, in the existing Internet infrastructure, there are many connections that are only connected via Dual-Stack Lite and therefore only have a shared IPv4 address or have to tunnel the IPv4 traffic via IPv6 (Chuangchunsong, Kamolphiwong and Kamolphiwong). This often leads to problems with the maximum transmission unit (MTU), since the address metadata must be appended to the data packets. This results in a higher packet loss rate. Furthermore, ping suffers. Also, users have often reported asynchrony between video and audio signals. Since BBB version 2.3, the availability of IPv6 is set as a minimum server requirement (Inc.).

Implementation. Although most of the legacy academic infrastructure at our university only supports IPv4, we rolled out IPv6 in our university BBB production system.

Results. After our IPv6 rollout, we measured significantly improved latencies on the live BBB cluster of the university, and the overall subjective quality of video conferencing increased. Our evaluations showed that the average latency of all users on the cluster over a period of one month dropped by 6 ms compared to the previous month. Outliers with over 500 ms latency have become much rarer.

Summary. Since BBB version 2.3, IPv6 is enabled as the default protocol. While BBB can still be used with only IPv4, this is not recommended in a production environment. IPv6 has shown only advantages in our tests and should be enabled at any time.

5.3 Discussion

Several of the proposed improvements applied to BBB are already available in competing commercial products such as Zoom, Microsoft Teams, and Google Hangouts. Some of them are supported by the underlying open-source components (including the Kurento Media Server) of BBB. Furthermore, some implementations are already available in other open source projects, such as Jitsi Meet. We have submitted some of our suggestions for improvement to the developers of BBB in the official bug tracker over the last year. Some of our proposals have already been implemented by the BBB developers, although not to the full extent we suggest in this paper.

To summarize, BBB has a lot of room for improvement. Not all of our proposals are useful in every situation. For example, the presented possibilities for improvement are only designed for regular web conferences and lead to unforeseen problems with handicapped conference participants. Conferences conducted in sign language in particular are made more difficult or even get impossible by some of our improvements. Therefore, the practicability of each suggested improvement must be evaluated individually for each application scenario.

6. CONCLUSION

Based on our experiences in deploying, operating, and using BBB at our university in the last 12 months, we presented suggestions on how the services provided by BBB can be improved to meet the technical demands identified during online lecturing at our university. Our suggestions include the introduction of simulcast, improvements of encoding and muxing video feeds, and the 'Last-N' algorithm for video feed pagination. To demonstrate the benefits of the presented improvements, we experimentally evaluated most of them based on our own prototypical implementations. There are several areas for future work. For example, the impacts of our improvements should be determined in tests with a significantly larger number of test devices and/or test constellations. Furthermore, most of our tests are based on prototypical implementations, which may perform differently if implemented inside BBB. Finally, the feasibility of further improvements inspired by the functionality of other web conferencing systems should be investigated in the context of BBB.

ACKNOWLEDGEMENT

We would like to thank our university computer center and especially Andreas Gabriel for the ongoing support in approving the implementation and evaluation of the presented suggestions for improving BBB.

REFERENCES

Alphabet, (accessed January 15, 2021), "Google Chrome Patchnotes VP9." *Google Chrome Patchnotes VP9.* <https://developers.google.com/web/updates/2016/01/vp9-webrtc>

Barik, R., et al, 2018, "Can WebRTC QoS Work? A DSCP Measurement Study." *2018 30th International Teletraffic Congress (ITC 30).* Vol. 01.. 167-175.

Belay, Adam, et al, 2016, "The IX Operating System: Combining Low Latency, High Throughput, and Efficiency in a Protected Dataplane." *ACM Trans. Comput. Syst.* 34 <https://doi.org/10.1145/2997641>.

Bienik, J., et al., 2016, "Performance of H.264, H.265, VP8 and VP9 Compression Standards for High Resolutions." *2016 19th International Conference on Network-Based Information Systems (NBiS)*.. 246-252.

BigBlueButton Developer Community, (accessed January 15, 2021), "BigBlueButton.". <https://bigbluebutton.org>

Tag 2.2.22 <https://github.com/bigbluebutton/bigbluebutton/releases/tag/v2.2.22>

Tag 2.2.23 <https://github.com/bigbluebutton/bigbluebutton/releases/tag/v2.2.23>

Bouras, C., G. Kioumourtzis and A. Gkamas, 2009, "Simulcast Transmission for Video Applications: Performance Evaluation with an Integrated Simulation Environment." *2009 International Symposium on Performance Evaluation of Computer Telecommunication Systems*. Vol. 41. 339-346.

Byrne, Jason, et al, 2020, "The Unexpected Problem of Classroom Video Conferencing: An Analysis and Solution for Google Hangouts and Jitsi Meet." *Journal of Foreign Language Education and Technology* 5 (.

Canonical, (accessed January 15, 2021), "Ubuntu Low Latency Kernel." *Ubuntu Low Latency Kernel.* <https://help.ubuntu.com/community/UbuntuStudio/RealTimeKernel>

Chuangchunsong, N., et al, 2014, "Performance Evaluation of IPv4/IPv6 Transition Mechanisms: IPv4-in-IPv6 Tunneling Techniques." *The International Conference on Information Networking 2014 (ICOIN2014)*. 238-243.

Cižmešija, Antonela and Goran Bubas, 2020, "An Instrument for Evaluation of the Use of the Web Conferencing System BigBlueButton in E-learning." *Central European Conference on Information and Intelligent Systems (CECIIS)*.. 1-9.

de Campos, Geraldo Lino, 1999, "Minimum Requirements for Effective Distance Teaching Systems." *Proceedings of the 4th Annual SIGCSE/SIGCUE ITiCSE Conference on Innovation and Technology in Computer Science Education*. New York, NY, USA: Association for Computing Machinery, 182. <https://doi.org/10.1145/305786.305926>.

Etherpad Foundation, .(accessed January 15, 2021), "Etherpad." *Etherpad.* <https://etherpad.org>

FFmpeg, (accessed January 15, 2021), "FFmpeg." *FFmpeg.* <https://ffmpeg.org>

Greasemonkey, (accessed January 15, 2021), "Greasemonkey Extension for Firefox Webbrowser." *Greasemonkey Extension for Firefox Webbrowser* <https://github.com/greasemonkey/greasemonkey>

Grozev, Boris, et al, 2015, "Last N: Relevance-Based Selectivity for Forwarding Video in Multimedia Conferences." *Proceedings of the 25th ACM Workshop on Network and Operating Systems Support for Digital Audio and Video*. New York, NY, USA: Association for Computing Machinery, 19–24. <https://doi.org/10.1145/2736084.2736094>.

Inc., BigBlueButton, (accessed June 13, 2021), "BBB 2.3 Installation" <https://docs.bigbluebutton.org/2.3/install.html>.

Intel, (accessed January 15, 2021), "VA-API." *VA-API.* <https://github.com/intel/libva>

Jansen, Bart, et al, 2018, "Performance Evaluation of WebRTC-Based Video Conferencing." *SIGMETRICS Perform. Eval. Rev.* 45 (: 56–68. <https://doi.org/10.1145/3199524.3199534>.

Jitsi Developer Community, (accessed January 15, 2021),"Jitsi." *Jitsi.* <https://jitsi.org>

Kurento, (accessed January 15, 2021), "Kurento." *Kurento* <https://www.kurento.org>

LibreOffice Foundation, (accessed January 15, 2021), "LibreOffice." *LibreOffice* <https://libreoffice.org>

Lu, Yue, et al, 2010, "Measurement Study of Multi-party Video Conferencing." *NETWORKING 2010*. Ed. Mark Crovella, et al. Berlin: Springer, 96–108.

Mediasoup Developers, (accessed January 15, 2021), "Mediasoup." *Mediasoup* <https://mediasoup.org>

Mekuria, Rufael, Jelte Fennema and Dirk Griffioen, 2016, "Multi-Protocol Video Delivery with Late Trans-Muxing." *Proceedings of the 24th ACM International Conference on Multimedia*. New York, NY, USA: Association for Computing Machinery 92–96. <https://doi.org/10.1145/2964284.2967189>.

Mozilla, (accessed January 15, 2021), "Mozilla Firefox Release Notes V46." *Mozilla Firefox Release Notes V46.* < https://wiki.mozilla.org/Media/WebRTC/ReleaseNotes/46>

Mukherjee, D., et al, 2013, "A Technical Overview of VP9 – The Latest Open-Source Video Codec." *SMPTE 2013 Annual Technical Conference Exhibition*. 1-17.

OBS, (accessed January 15, 2021), "Open Broadcast Studio." *Open Broadcast Studio*.<https://obsproject.com>

Peach Open Video Project, (accessed January 15, 2021), "Big Buck Bunny." *Big Buck Bunny*.<https://peach.blender.org>

Petrangeli, Stefano, et al, 2018, "Improving Quality and Scalability of WebRTC Video Collaboration Applications." *MMSys '18: Proceedings of the 9th ACM Multimedia Systems Conference*. Amsterdam Netherlands: ACM 533-536.

Pullen, J. Mark, 2006, "Scaling up a Distance Education Program in Computer Science." *Proceedings of the 11th Annual SIGCSE Conference on Innovation and Technology in Computer Science Education*. New York, NY, USA: Association for Computing Machinery, 33–37. <https://doi.org/10.1145/1140124.1140136>.

Pullen, John Mark and Nicholas K. Clark, 2011, "Moodle-Integrated Open Source Synchronous Teaching." *Proceedings of the 16th Annual Joint Conference on Innovation and Technology in Computer Science Education*. New York, NY, USA: Association for Computing Machinery, 353. <https://doi.org/10.1145/1999747.1999867>.

Ratnasamy, Sylvia; Ermolinskiy, Andrey; Shenker, Scott, 2006, "Revisiting IP Multicast." *SIGCOMM Comput. Commun. Rev.* 36: 15–26. <https://doi.org/10.1145/1151659.1159917>.

Sandars, John, et al, 2020, "Twelve Tips for Rapidly Migrating to Online Learning During the COVID-19 Pandemic." *MedEdPublish* 9.

Schwarz, H., D. Marpe and T. Wiegand, 2007, "Overview of the Scalable Video Coding Extension of the H.264/AVC Standard." *IEEE Transactions on Circuits and Systems for Video Technology* 17 : 1103-1120.

Selenium, (accessed January 15, 2021), "Selenium." *Selenium*.<https://www.selenium.dev>

SignalWire, (accessed January 15, 2021), "Freeswitch." *Freeswitch*.<https://freeswitch.com>

Vasconcelos, P. R. Magalhães, G. A. de Araújo Freitas and T. G. Marques, 2016, "Virtualization Technologies in Web Conferencing Systems: A Performance Overview." *2016 11th International Conference for Internet Technology and Secured Transactions (ICITST)*. 376-383.

Voegeli, Dorian, Nicholas K. Clark and John Mark Pullen, 2016, "Better Online Teaching Support Using Open-Source Web Applications." *Proceedings of the 2016 ACM Conference on Innovation and Technology in Computer Science Education*. New York, NY, USA: Association for Computing Machinery, 365. <https://doi.org/10.1145/2899415.2925489>.

W3, (accessed January 15, 2021), "W3 WebRTC and SVC." *W3 WebRTC and SVC*.<https://www.w3.org/TR/webrtc-svc>

Xue, Huaying and Yuan Zhang, 2016, "A WebRTC-based Video Conferencing System with Screen Sharing." *2016 2nd IEEE International Conference on Computer and Communications (ICCC)*. 485-489.

Zhang, Jie, et al, 2019, "A WebRTC e-Learning System Based on Kurento Media Server." *E-Learning and Games*. Ed. Abdennour El Rhalibi, et al. Cham: Springer International Publishing, 331–335.

SELECTIVE PRIVACY IN IOT SMART-FARMS FOR BATTERY-POWERED DEVICE LONGEVITY

Steph Rudd and Hamish Cunningham[1]
[1]*Prof.*
Department of Computer Science, University of Sheffield
211 Portobello, Sheffield S1 4DP, United Kingdom

ABSTRACT

This paper presents a payload security model to maintain the standards of TLS whilst removing obstacles associated with constrained devices and IoT network protocols. The domain of aquaponics as a smart-farming environment was used to test the novelty with ESP32 edge devices. The impact of privacy on message content illustrated the most appropriate security attribute configurations, followed by time and power analysis to calculate energy consumptions of each scenario. It was concluded that using this tailored payload security model rather than TLS was capable of extending the battery life of constrained devices by up to 81%, whilst maintaining TLS security standards, and applicable to various protocols.

KEYWORDS

IoT, Smart-Farms, Security, Privacy, Sensor Networks, Environment-Friendly Constructions

1. INTRODUCTION

With multiple threats to food systems including climate change, population increase, increase of transport costs and so forth, the demand for food production will increase by 70% by the year 2050 (Demestichas, Peppes and Alexakis, 2020). In response to this emerging threat, agriculture is transforming; IoT-powered smart-farms enable autonomous and self-sufficient food production systems to operate remotely (Vermani, 2019). Amongst the multitude of smart-farm solutions available (Navarro, Costa and Pereira, 2020), aquaponics represents a symbiotic relationship between plants and fish - fish produce ammonia from which bacteria then creates nitrates. These nitrates are then pumped around the planted beds as a natural fertiliser, several times an hour, with monitored temperature, PH level, and other variables necessary for plant-specific farming. Such an environment exemplifies a Wireless Sensor Network (WSN), or a series of spatially dispersed and dedicated IoT devices (Czelusniak *et al.*, 2019). This paper presents mechanisms for reducing energy usage for securing IoT control and monitoring devices in an aquaponics-based smart farming application.

Food production is now a critical issue, and attacks towards smart-farms add to the myriad of existing IoT-oriented information attacks such as CCTV (Doshi, Apthorpe and Feamster, 2018), or even children's toys (Keymolen and Van der Hof, 2019). Specifically regarding food, smart city attacks have witnessed sabotage of restaurant freezers and food poisoning (Rashid *et al.*, 2020). With a general indication of attacker interest in IoT, and a future where the population is high and food supply low, threats towards food supplies may be imminent. With such traction in both information attack vectors and the rise of IoT-powered sustainability, security is a basic requirement.

The issues pertaining to security are that of a 'balancing act' (Kane *et al.*, 2020), where integration is unattractive for two main reasons. Firstly, the value of security is not perceived until loss (Gan and Heartfield, 2016), and so if the domain is considered to be of little value to attackers in general, or beyond the chances of being targeted because they are considered 'low impact', then security can be seen as adding costs without benefits. Secondly, the predefined ciphersuites available to replicate the de facto security standard Transport Layer Security (TLS), are tremendously draining on constrained devices. For this reason security is considered a challenge (Del-Valle-Soto *et al.*, 2019), as TLS needs infrastructure, energy and processing - three things that contradict the nature of constrained IoT devices and networks.

In addition to the tension between TLS and IoT, the HTTP protocol is not ideal for IoT applications. Lighter protocols such as MQTT, LoRaWAN and BLE have their own security designs - usually based on TLS, and accompanied by the same problems. Perhaps if a decentralised TLS security model existed to secure payloads rather than protocols with considerably less burden on battery life, then the notion of including security as a fundamental requirement would not be so intimidating.

This paper presents an experiment in selective privacy for low energy and scalability:

Privacy assessment: to ascertain where security functions can be removed safely. We informed our design by the use of a Data Protection Impact Assessment (DPIA), typical of General Data Protection Regulation (GDPR) auditing.

Time analysis: of attributes for securing payloads using hardware acceleration. Timing security attributes as separate entities demonstrated the consumption differences with privacy on and off.

Power analysis: of the same security attributes to discover the lightest use of energy. Payload security with selective privacy demonstrated an energy saving of up to 81% compared with the same TLS implementation.

The ESP32 microcontroller was used to demonstrate the energy consumption of the design, acting as the edge device, while a Raspberry Pi posed as a gateway controller to the cloud.

The rest of this paper features the background problem as discussed in part II, related works of distributed and lightweight security are discussed in part III, the design in part IV, part V is testing, and the research is concluded with considerations of further work in part VI.

2. PROBLEM BACKGROUND

This section discusses the problems with integrating TLS into IoT networks, specifically the smart-farm aquaponics domain. The problem is divided into three areas; false perception of threat, unnecessary privacy, and inappropriate ciphers.

2.1 False Perception of Threat

Perhaps the biggest challenge of widespread security integration is overcoming the notion that a small, lightweight, IoT-enabled network such as one powered by BLE, is subject to threat. In addition to the 'unlikeliness' that a smart-farm will be subject to attack, the centralised nature of TLS requirements is demanding for an edge device such as the ESP32. TLS configuration is complex in structure, high in energy consumption, and promotes unnecessarily stringent protection levels. Certificate Authorities (CA's), Registration Authorities (RA's), and Verification Authorities (VA's), typical of an independent network security infrastructure present vulnerabilities and implementation challenges for IoT (Höglund *et al.*, 2020). Without such an infrastructure, employing a third-party for the same centralised functions presents a different set of challenges, such as trust, downtime, and the requirement of the internet whereas edge devices could otherwise operate on lighter protocols such as BLE alone.

With fewer restrictions and structural requirements than TLS, security in general would be a more realistic consideration. Attacks on protocols such as BLE, LoRaWAN and MQTT are emerging - and security is maturing slower than our dependence on them (Anand *et al.*, 2020). Absence of security provisions has not gone unnoticed either, with attacks under development towards BLE (Pallavi and Narayanan, 2019), LoRaWAN (Ingham, Marchang and Bhowmik, 2020), and MQTT (Firdous *et al.*, 2017).

2.2 Unnecessary Privacy

HTTP Security (HTTPS) employs TLS. This is a predefined set of rules including Confidentiality (privacy), Integrity, and Authentication (CIA), functions. Client and server devices traditionally employ TLS to negotiate a ciphersuite from a list, proceeding to exercise the full CIA protection on each message. Such enforcement is not good for constrained devices; the protection is largely overkill (Pérez Goya, 2015), and for many of the messages within smart-farm activity, content is sensor readings - predictable in nature. Traditionally, the general consensus of an adequate security design includes the CIA (Yin *et al.*, 2020), (Noor and Hassan, 2019). This triad demonstrates a construct that TLS has thrived on. Confidentiality as privacy of message content, so that only the recipient can view it. Integrity is the guaranteed non-tampering, so that it has not changed in transit. Availability is so that the content is complete, and from the alleged party sending it. Where the use of the CIA triad has provided a strong application in traditional TLS, the requirements for a full CIA composite could now be to the detriment of energy-conscious IoT solutions such as smart-farming.

2.3 Inappropriate Ciphers

Security attributes available for the ESP32 are not limited to TLS completely, since the functions are used for CertificateLess Signature (CLS), schemes such as using Digital Signature Algorithms (DSA), Blockchain and Advanced Threshold Systems (ATS) which use SHA. Thus, the board hosts hardware acceleration and a correlating library which alludes to TLS implementation, but not contracted to it.

Therefore, the functions RSA (asymmetric encryption), AES (symmetric encryption), SHA (compression functions), and RNG (Random Number Generation), provide standards recognised by NIST and FIPS, and that might be used as the basis of a novel, IoT-oriented security model.

The challenge is to discover the appropriate, or least-consumptive cipher configurations in terms of energy to maximise the battery life of the edge devices. Whilst doing so, a good standard of security can be achieved comparable to TLS, but abiding by the same regulations.

3. RELATED WORK

Below we break down the challenges into increasing battery life, security attributes, and topology.

3.1 Increasing Battery Life

(Weghorn, 2013) previously discussed the use of BLE and ANT+ in personal sports devices as a much lighter alternative to Bluetooth Classic (Weghorn, 2015). Shortly after, such devices were proven to have the ability of energy harvesting for power storage within superconductors (Weghorn, 2017). Energy harvesting by other means, such as solar, have also been used in conjunction with the storage capacity of superconductors (Elahi *et al.*, 2020).

In climates with long daylight hours and intense sunlight, solar harvesting would be viable for self-perpetuating BLE-powered networks - as would vehicular applications where devices are in regular motion. However, the smart-farm is a static model, and not guaranteed to survive limited sunlight provisions such as in the UK.

Other methods for enhancing the longevity of devices include using lighter protocols and applying security to them (Aloufi and Alhazmi, 2020), reducing clock speed (Suárez-Albela *et al.*, 2018), and lightweight hash functions (Dhanda, Singh and Jindal, 2020), and ciphers such as SIMON (Alassaf *et al.*, 2019).

3.2 Security Attributes

Perhaps exclusively to IoT smart-farming, the opportunity to differentiate between security and privacy could be of enormous contribution to the longevity of all protocols such as BLE (Zhang *et al.*, 2020).

Integrity and availability (or authenticity), are paramount for every message sent - but perhaps not so much for privacy. For IoT applications, the requirement for message protection may present a paradigm shift for the traditional CIA attributes, where there is an absence of private data (Pivoto *et al.*, 2018). Traditional security applications between HTTP-connected devices protected banking and shopping transactions, where most, if not all data featured highly sensitive exchanges. Such information has demonstrated enormous consequences in the absence of rigorous privacy, ie, fraud. However, in a typical smart-farm domain such as aquaponics or hydroponics, most of the messages from the client to the server are benign, predictable, and useless to all but the operator (Ruengittinun, Phongsamsuan and Sureeratanakorn, 2017). It is important that the value of such temperature and pH-level reading remain unaltered during transition (integrity), and that the origin of the data is verified (authentication). Beyond those two requirements, confidentiality for sensor readings is largely unnecessary.

The General Data Protection Regulation (GDPR), was an EU directive that came into force in May 2018. The GDPR proposed a series of subject rights and regulations to control the processing of personal data, introducing privacy as a separate topic to security, but with shared connotations and some overlap. Whereas security included the traditional CIA attributes, privacy was introduced as data protection under anonymisation, tokenisation, or pseudonymisation - data could be viewed by anyone, but only be of use to those who could interpret it. The difference between interpretation and encryption is a key; security models require keys to decrypt ciphertext into plaintext, and data under privacy protection does not.

Anonymisation, for anonymous data sharing, has demonstrated optimisation whilst retaining privacy (Sun *et al.*, 2011). Tokenisation has demonstrated lightweight solutions for authentication in IoT networks (Dammak *et al.*, 2019), and towards decentralisation to accommodate scalability (Naveed Aman *et al.*, 2019), but lack coverage in message security specifically. In the context of a smart-farm application domain, authenticating devices and sending messages between them are two separate studies; this paper discusses the latter. Finally, pseudonymisation has been successfully demonstrated in medical applications (Darwish, Nouretdinov and Wolthusen, 2018), incorporating query-based privacy models on distributed storage.

Amongst the recommendations and corresponding actions for GDPR compliance (Brodin, 2019), the Data Protection Impact Assessment (DPIA), is a framework for ascertaining the risks associated with data leakage. The nature of an application has a significant influence on how privacy should be modelled (Elliot *et al.*, 2018); confidentiality requirements can be addressed herewith.

3.3 Security Topologies

Centralised models are those in which a server, or possibly a server and a third-party hold accountability for some or all the network's security authorities, such as TLS. Decentralised models such as Blockchain exist without a central authority to govern them - but rather distributed trust and reputation systems. Distributed systems in general are considered preferable to centralised models for scalability, such as the IoT (Marquez et al, 2015).

Blockchain has demonstrated privacy through anonymisation (de Haro-Olmo, Varela-Vaca and Álvarez-Bermejo, 2020), and the same privacy capacity of voting systems centuries old (Tarasov and Tewari, 2017). Blockchain has a broad range of applications, notably crypto currency (Ben Sasson *et al.*, 2014), and IoT data sharing applications using distributed ledgers, such as Iota (Silvano and Marcelino, 2020).

As an example of a Distributed Ledger Technology (DTL), Iota provides data exchange via a ‘Tangle’; a reputation system by which transactions are authorised by validating two pre-existing ones. Therefore, the reputation, and enabling of data transfer, is validated as part of the network by another user. Each additional IoT device relies on the verification of pre-existing ones, providing scalability, access management, authentication and integrity in a continuously developing network (Novo, 2019), (Xu *et al.*, 2018).

Characteristically, Blockchain lends itself to the chaotic and large scale nature of IoT (Righi et al. 2018), but with a security caveat of trusting all connected devices (Kim *et al.*, 2019). Additionally, Blockchain introduces a storage and processing challenge for constrained devices - accumulative hashes, and the expectations of a reputation system to process them, known as a ‘hashrate’ in crypto currency mining.

In summary, maintaining battery life using energy harvesting is not practical for static environments with unreliable solar, and so other means of reducing energy consumption can be exercised by changing the configuration and topology of the security model. Firstly, the confidentiality aspect can be reduced where possible, and secondly, the central model of employing a server (or third-party), for the three authorities CA VA and RA can be removed. By removing the TLS requirement of a server and ciphersuites, protocols such as BLE, LoRaWAN and MQTT can be protected using less energy-consumptive attributes available through hardware acceleration.

4. DESIGN

Proposed are three design concepts to resolve the problems outlined in section II, including distributed infrastructure, selective privacy, and IoT-appropriate ciphers.

4.1 Distributed Infrastructure

The design does not propose use of a TLS channel, but on-board TLS functions using hardware acceleration to protect every message at source. The keys used are presumed to have already been shared during authentication (not part of this study).

Messages are secured as part of the procedure opening the protocol(s), so that any protocol used to communicate the message (BLE, LoRaWAN etc), can do so without a predefined ciphersuite, and thus without HTTPS. This 'plug-and-play' payload security design enables portability, and removes the stringent requirements of the TLS regulations to function.

A distributed infrastructure is proposed, where the central server is not required for security functions, but can, as any other device is able to, decrypt all messages for data handling. The removal of a central infrastructure aims to resolve the vulnerability and responsibility of a single entity undertaking all security processing - particularly as the network scales. In addition, enabling the ESP32 microcontrollers to undertake their own security processing makes the security model portable, and inclusive of any protocol used to send messages.

In addition, with simple implementation of only a short code to utilise the model, the design should promote the appeal of security and lessen user reluctance to integrate it. This would contribute towards the threat perception issue, and safeguard smart-farms in preparation for future vulnerability.

4.2 Selective Privacy

Without adhering to the stringent requirements of employing a TLS channel, it is also possible to remove the privacy condition, or the encryption algorithm which costs IoT networks so much energy. Although not advisable in every message, as some will contain session keys or proprietary code, the majority of messages will be sensor readings. Perhaps 99% of messages will not need encryption, saving on a lot of energy that would have otherwise been wasted.

TLS enforces the full CIA triad of security attributes within each message as part of its ciphersuite conditions. As TLS develops, the number of ciphersuites becomes fewer and more protective, and as a result, less energy-efficient. Newer ciphersuites include an all-in-one-function - the Authenticated Encryption with Associated Data (AEAD). This function incorporates a cipher for encryption, a compression, or hash, function for integrity - and a Hash-keyed Message Authentication Code (HMAC), to prove where it came from. TLS is encouraging the use of Galois Counter Mode (GCM), an AEAD function containing a very sophisticated and very IoT-averse algorithm. GCM uses around three times the energy that most other ciphers do - even with manually attached AEAD functions.

The proposal for reducing the burden of unnecessary encryption whilst still fulfilling the AEAD suggestions of TLS is to combine an available cipher with a hash function and an authentication function. If this is done manually, encryption for readings from the client to the server can simply not be included. For the majority of readings from the board to the Pi, this will be the case; every sensor reading will use a hash function and an authentication key, but no encryption. The rare exception to this rule is session reset. When the device generates a new key, every week, or month, or even year, it will require encryption. Keys will be made for each board by its own board as part of the decentralised infrastructure mentioned earlier. However, because the smart-farm contains a series of fixed, static systems, the key resets will be infrequent.

4.3 IoT-Appropriate Ciphers

Finally, the design makes use of the lightest 'safe' cipher available for the ESP32 hardware acceleration. By using a cipher without the built-in AEAD function, the full range of available ciphers can be tested for the lightest energy consumption.

The ESP32 has access to a native TLS library ported for embedded devices. The mbedtls library offers the expensive AEAD function, GCM, as well as four other standalone ciphers that can be assembled into AEAD by including a hash and HMAC. By using the lightest standalone cipher available in the mbedtls library, encryption could be left out for sensor readings from the edge devices to the gateway, but included when sending keys.

Structurally, ciphers require different implementations such as data tags, Initialisation Vectors (IV), and counter offsets. Any cipher will use a symmetric encryption key accelerated by the AES hardware accelerator, and this has always been shared at the session negotiation stage before sending a message can commence. In addition, the HMAC key responsible for ascertaining the authentic origin of the sender device, will assume a new, additional session key. In TLS, the HMAC key is encrypted as part of the message, and decrypted at the recipient end to justify authenticity of the message. However, where encryption will be mostly absent, it will act as a secret key in its own right, and should be treated with the same secrecy as a regular AES encryption key where encryption is absent.

5. IMPLEMENTATION TESTING

Testing was performed in three parts; privacy assessment, timing analysis and power analysis.

5.1 Privacy Assessment

We first performed a Data Protection Impact Assessment (DPIA), which considered each possible message between the gateway and the ESP32 edge device. The structure of a DPIA varies between templates, but the purpose is to calculate the risk severity of each type of data within a system, and use that risk score to address security measures (Ando, et al 2018). Complex systems holding a lot of user data in various forms, such as healthcare, require gradients of privacy measures including pseudonymisation and anonymisation. The smart-farm is simple in comparison, because there is a clear difference between the content of the systems, and that of living subjects. Security attributes for this application could be determined in a binary way; the messages were either private, and required encryption, or they were public, and they did not. This type of risk assessment is typically used by GDPR Practitioners as part of an ISO27001 audit (*ISO/IEC 27001:2013*, 2019).

Table 1. Privacy requirements of messages

Sender	Recipient	Message content	Sensitivity	Vulnerability	Impact	Score	Risk
Pi	ESP32	Farm control	2 Professional	1 Exceptional	2 Reputation	1.7	High
ESP32	Pi	Session keys	3 Private	1 Exceptional	3 Closure	2.3	Critical
ESP32	Pi	Temperature	0 Public	0 None	0 None	0.0	None
ESP32	Pi	Humidity	0 Public	0 None	0 None	0.0	None
ESP32	Pi	Nitrate	0 Public	0 None	0 None	0.0	None

Risks of a high or critical score required encryption, and risks returning low or zero scores did not. Fortunately, most of the readings from the ESP32 to the Pi did not require encryption.

5.2 Timing Analysis

Real-time data delivery for agricultural systems and reducing latency enables good practice (Lopes and Vaz, 2019). With the lowest energy consumption possible, a good security application should also reduce latency. Timing of each attribute was assessed by including the Arduino micros() command as a component of the ESP-IDF (*IoT Development Framework I Espressif Systems*, no date). Micros() was used to measure the processing time only of the attribute, excluding variables, parameters, and all printing to the serial monitor. Each attribute was repeated in iterations of 10, 20, 30 and 40 thousand to calculate an average time for a single iteration, across various results.

The board was prepared for fair testing by ensuring that the WatchDog Timer (WDT) was disabled, as this can cause interruptions and distort readings, and that all hardware accelerations were enabled under mbedtls (ARM Limited, no date b)options. These configurations were undertaken using the menuconfig option, part of the ESP-IDF.

A single character was defined as a byte, and text input volumes of two lengths were processed for each test. An input of 64 characters was used to demonstrate the energy required for securing a reading or other small string, and that of 512 bytes reflected a very strong key (4096 bits). A strong key length was chosen because of the intention to reset keys very infrequently, perhaps once a year.

Firstly, integrity and authentication functions where an HMAC-SHA of sufficient strength was tested for the shortest processing time. These were SHA lengths of 224 and above. It was important to assess HMAC-SHA independently of encryption modes to demonstrate how much more energy efficient messages could be without using a cipher.

Table 2. Integrity function time analysis measured in microseconds (μS)

Hash-keyed MAC function	64 bytes input	512 bytes input
HMAC-SHA224	150	403
HMAC-SHA256	91	163
HMAC-SHA384	102	165
HMAC-SHA512	105	167

Secondly, a time assessment of the cipher modes available in mbedtls on the ESP32 (ARM Limited, no date a); GCM, CBC, CTR, CBF8 and CFB128 was undertaken. Each cipher was coupled with the same HMAC-SHA function showing the shortest processing time in results set one.

Table 3. AEAD function time analysis measured in microseconds (μS)

AEAD function	64 bytes input	512 bytes input
AES128-GCM	178	856
AES128-CBC-HMAC-SHA256	124	276
AES128-CTR-HMAC-SHA256	123	352
AES128-CFB8-HMAC-SHA256	303	1782
AES128-CFB128-HMAC-SHA256	121	350

In full AEAD function using the lightest integrity and authentication, CFB8 proved to be the heaviest cipher, followed by GCM. The overall lightest mode was CBC, since CTR proved to increase significantly for larger messages. Although the two ciphers could be used simultaneously in practice, the structural requirements for CBC and CTR vary, and so the use of CBC alone would simplify implementation whilst remaining the lowest consistent encryption mode.

In summary, where privacy is not required, the lightest function was HMAC-SHA256, and where privacy is required, CBC mode was a low time consumer and most consistently low.

5.3 Power Analysis

Measurements were made at the necessary micro to milli levels for such protocols as BLE (Kamath and Lindh, 2010) using an oscilloscope for sampling (Zwerg *et al.*, 2011). Power in milliwatts (mW), was calculated by multiplying current in milliamps (mA), by voltage in millivolts (mV), with a known resistance in Ohms (Ω). The oscilloscope took the readings of the board using the digitalWrite() Arduino command to communicate the sketch over General Pin Input Output (GPIO), 21, and connecting from the ground pin to complete the circuit. As with timing analysis, integrity and availability power consumptions were assessed first, followed by the AES cipher in various modes, fulfilling the AEAD requirements with the least power-intense HMAC-SHA.

Table 4. Integrity function power analysis measured in milliwatts (mW)

Hash-keyed MAC function	64 bytes input	512 bytes input
HMAC-SHA224	156	157
HMAC-SHA256	155	155
HMAC-SHA384	156	157
HMAC-SHA512	154	154

Table 5. AEAD function power analysis measured in milliwatts (mW)

AEAD function	64 bytes input	512 bytes input
AES128-GCM	158	158
AES128-CBC-HMAC-SHA256	155	155
AES128-CTR-HMAC-SHA256	155	155
AES128-CFB8-HMAC-SHA256	155	155
AES128-CFB128-HMAC-SHA256	156	156

Finally, we summarise the energy consumptions of each attribute by multiplying time (μS) by power (mW) to conclude energy in seconds, Joules (J).

Table 6. Integrity function energy consumption measured in Joules (J)

Hash-keyed MAC function	64 bytes input	512 bytes input
HMAC-SHA224	23.4	63.271
HMAC-SHA256	14.105	25.265
HMAC-SHA384	15.912	25.905
HMAC-SHA512	16.17	25.718

Table 7. AEAD function energy consumption measured in Joules (J)

AEAD function	64 bytes input	512 bytes input
AES128-GCM	28.124	135.248
AES128-CBC-HMAC-SHA256	19.22	42.78
AES128-CTR-HMAC-SHA256	19.065	54.56
AES128-CFB8-HMAC-SHA256	46.965	121.21
AES128-CFB128-HMAC-SHA256	18.876	54.6

CBC in full AEAD mode demonstrated the best potential for battery longevity.

Where readings do not require privacy, the energy consumption is as low as 14 Joules, and if exchanging an instruction set for farm control without sensitive data, 25 Joules per second. Compared with the TLS recommendations of GCM at 28 and 135 Joules per second respectively, the energy saving without privacy can be between 50% for a small reading, and over 81% for a large exchange of 512 bytes.

If that data did require encryption and the full AEAD capacity such as a key, the difference between GCM and CBC in AEAD mode in this comparison is over 32% for smaller exchanges such as readings, and 68% lighter for key exchanges or sensitive instruction sets.

6. CONCLUSION

The contributions and further work of this research are concluded below.

Distributed infrastructure. Our security model uses microcontroller hardware as a source of security from dedicated board functions, and without supervision of a central server. This decentralised, distributed payload security model allows multiple protocols without protocol protection.

Selective privacy. By not requiring a TLS channel, the design proposed that messages are considered on individual merit with regards to confidentiality. Where the majority are composed of readings, benign and useless to all but the gateway, privacy can be forsaken for an energy saving of around 81%. Of course, integrity and authentication functions are provided for all messages.

IoT-appropriate ciphers. The design proposed full AEAD functionality for all ciphers and not just the predefined GCM recommended as part of the de facto TLS standard. Encouraged for content confirmed as high or critical risk, the alternative use of the CBC cipher still proved to be 68% more energy efficient in larger exchanges where full AEAD would be suitable - keys and instruction sets.

These savings are considerable, and could help overcome the perceived challenge of security applied to IoT-oriented smart-farm applications such as aquaponics. In addition, further work could include healthcare or smart city monitoring where anonymous data can be gathered from machines and living subjects separately.

REFERENCES

Alassaf, N. *et al.* (2019) 'Enhancing speed of SIMON: A light-weight-cryptographic algorithm for IoT applications', *Multimedia tools and applications*, 78(23), pp. 32633–32657.

Aloufi, K. S. and Alhazmi, O. H. (2020) 'Performance Analysis of the Hybrid IoT Security Model of MQTT and UMA', *arXiv [cs.NI]*. Available at: http://arxiv.org/abs/2005.06595.

Anand, P. *et al.* (2020) 'IoVT: Internet of Vulnerable Things? Threat Architecture, Attack Surfaces, and Vulnerabilities in Internet of Things and Its Applications towards Smart Grids', *Energies*, 13(18), p. 4813.

ARM Limited (no date a) *Encryption/decryption module - API Documentation - mbed TLS (Previously PolarSSL)*. Available at: https://tls.mbed.org/api/group__encdec__module.html (Accessed: 28 April 2021).

ARM Limited (no date b) *SSL Library mbed TLS / PolarSSL*. Available at: https://tls.mbed.org/ (Accessed: 28 April 2021).

Ben Sasson, E. *et al.* (2014) 'Zerocash: Decentralized Anonymous Payments from Bitcoin', in *2014 IEEE Symposium on Security and Privacy*, pp. 459–474.

Brodin, M. (2019) 'A Framework for GDPR Compliance for Small- and Medium-Sized Enterprises', *European Journal for Security Research*, pp. 243–264. doi: 10.1007/s41125-019-00042-z.

Czelusniak, M. N. *et al.* (2019) 'Wireless Sensor Networks in Agriculture: A revision', *Proceedings of the 16th International Conference on Applied Computing 2019*. doi: 10.33965/ac2019_201912r040.

Dammak, M. *et al.* (2019) 'Token-Based Lightweight Authentication to Secure IoT Networks', in *2019 16th IEEE Annual Consumer Communications Networking Conference (CCNC)*, pp. 1–4.

Darwish, S., Nouretdinov, I. and Wolthusen, S. (2018) 'A Dynamic Distributed Architecture for Preserving Privacy of Medical IoT Monitoring Measurements', in *Smart Homes and Health Telematics, Designing a Better Future: Urban Assisted Living*. Springer International Publishing, pp. 146–157.

Del-Valle-Soto, C. *et al.* (2019) 'Smart Campus: An Experimental Performance Comparison of Collaborative and Cooperative Schemes for Wireless Sensor Network', *Energies*, 12(16), p. 3135.

Demestichas, K., Peppes, N. and Alexakis, T. (2020) 'Survey on Security Threats in Agricultural IoT and Smart Farming', *Sensors* , 20(22). doi: 10.3390/s20226458.

Dhanda, S. S., Singh, B. and Jindal, P. (2020) 'Lightweight Cryptography: A Solution to Secure IoT', *Wireless Personal Communications*, 112(3), pp. 1947–1980.

Doshi, R., Apthorpe, N. and Feamster, N. (2018) 'Machine Learning DDoS Detection for Consumer Internet of Things Devices', in *2018 IEEE Security and Privacy Workshops (SPW)*, pp. 29–35.

Elahi, H. *et al.* (2020) 'Energy Harvesting towards Self-Powered IoT Devices', *Energies*, 13(21), p. 5528.

Elliot, M. *et al.* (2018) 'Functional anonymisation: Personal data and the data environment', *Computer Law & Security Review*, 34(2), pp. 204–221.

Firdous, S. N. *et al.* (2017) 'Modelling and Evaluation of Malicious Attacks against the IoT MQTT Protocol', *2017 IEEE International Conference on Internet of Things (iThings) and IEEE Green Computing and Communications (GreenCom) and IEEE Cyber, Physical and Social Computing (CPSCom) and IEEE Smart Data (SmartData)*. doi: 10.1109/ithings-greencom-cpscom-smartdata.2017.115.

Gan, D. and Heartfield, R. (2016) 'Social engineering in the internet of everything', *Cutter IT Journal*, 29(7), pp. 20–29.

de Haro-Olmo, F. J., Varela-Vaca, Á. J. and Álvarez-Bermejo, J. A. (2020) 'Blockchain from the Perspective of Privacy and Anonymisation: A Systematic Literature Review', *Sensors* , 20(24). doi: 10.3390/s20247171.

Höglund, J. *et al.* (2020) 'PKI4IoT: Towards public key infrastructure for the Internet of Things', *Computers & Security*, 89, p. 101658.

Ingham, M., Marchang, J. and Bhowmik, D. (2020) 'IoT security vulnerabilities and predictive signal jamming attack analysis in LoRaWAN', *IET Information Security*, 14(4), pp. 368–379.

IoT Development Framework I Espressif Systems (no date). Available at: https://www.espressif.com/en/products/sdks/esp-idf (Accessed: 28 April 2021).

ISO/IEC 27001:2013 (2019). Available at: https://www.iso.org/standard/54534.html (Accessed: 28 April 2021).

Kamath, S. and Lindh, J. (2010) 'Measuring bluetooth low energy power consumption', *Texas instruments application note AN092, Dallas*. Available at: https://discourse-production.oss-cn-shanghai.aliyuncs.com/original/3X/7/c/7c84d1dc683e86d61f4db95f90223453fc25861f.pdf.

Kane, L. E. *et al.* (2020) 'Security and Performance in IoT: A Balancing Act', *IEEE Access*, 8, pp. 121969–121986.

Keymolen, E. and Van der Hof, S. (2019) 'Can I still trust you, my dear doll? A philosophical and legal exploration of smart toys and trust', *Journal of Cyber Policy*, 4(2), pp. 143–159.

Kim, S. *et al.* (2019) 'PubChem 2019 update: improved access to chemical data', *Nucleic acids research*, 47(D1), pp. D1102–D1109.

Lopes, L. A. and Vaz, M. S. G. (2019) 'Specification of an Internet Architecture of Things for a Grain Traceability Framework', *Proceedings of the 16th International Conference on Applied Computing 2019*. doi: 10.33965/ac2019_201912r039.

Navarro, E., Costa, N. and Pereira, A. (2020) 'A Systematic Review of IoT Solutions for Smart Farming', *Sensors*, p. 4231. doi: 10.3390/s20154231.

Naveed Aman, M. *et al.* (2019) 'Token-Based Security for the Internet of Things With Dynamic Energy-Quality Tradeoff', *IEEE Internet of Things Journal*, 6(2), pp. 2843–2859.

Noor, M. B. M. and Hassan, W. H. (2019) 'Current research on Internet of Things (IoT) security: A survey', *Computer Networks*, pp. 283–294. doi: 10.1016/j.comnet.2018.11.025.

[No title] (no date). Available at: https://www.researchgate.net/profile/Mohammad_Al-Shorman/publication/332539387_Toward_Energy_Efficient_Microcontrollers_and_IoT_Systems/links/5cbadf7c92851c8d22f7b76d/Toward-Energy-Efficient-Microcontrollers-and-IoT-Systems.pdf (Accessed: 14 April 2021).

Novo, O. (2019) 'Scalable Access Management in IoT Using Blockchain: A Performance Evaluation', *IEEE Internet of Things Journal*, 6(3), pp. 4694–4701.

Pallavi, S. and Narayanan, V. A. (2019) 'An Overview of Practical Attacks on BLE Based IOT Devices and Their Security', in *2019 5th International Conference on Advanced Computing Communication Systems (ICACCS)*, pp. 694–698.

Pérez Goya, U. (2015) *Security in community sensor networks*. Universitat Politècnica de Catalunya. Available at: https://upcommons.upc.edu/handle/2099.1/25513 (Accessed: 14 April 2021).

Pivoto, D. *et al.* (2018) 'Scientific development of smart farming technologies and their application in Brazil', *Information Processing in Agriculture*, 5(1), pp. 21–32.

Rashid, M. M. *et al.* (2020) 'Cyberattacks Detection in IoT-Based Smart City Applications Using Machine Learning Techniques', *International journal of environmental research and public health*, 17(24). doi: 10.3390/ijerph17249347.

Ruengittinun, S., Phongsamsuan, S. and Sureeratanakorn, P. (2017) 'Applied internet of thing for smart hydroponic farming ecosystem (HFE)', in *2017 10th International Conference on Ubi-media Computing and Workshops (Ubi-Media)*, pp. 1–4.

Silvano, W. F. and Marcelino, R. (2020) 'Iota Tangle: A cryptocurrency to communicate Internet-of-Things data', *Future generations computer systems: FGCS*, 112, pp. 307–319.

Suárez-Albela, M. *et al.* (2018) 'Clock Frequency Impact on the Performance of High-Security Cryptographic Cipher Suites for Energy-Efficient Resource-Constrained IoT Devices', *Sensors* , 19(1). doi: 10.3390/s19010015.

Sun, X. *et al.* (2011) 'Injecting purpose and trust into data anonymisation', *Computers & Security*, 30(5), pp. 332–345.

Tarasov, P. and Tewari, H. (2017) 'Internet voting using zcash', *IACR Cryptol. ePrint Arch.*, 2017, p. 585.

Vermani, S. (2019) 'Farm to Fork: IOT for Food Supply Chain', *International Journal of Innovative Technology and Exploring Engineering*, 8(12), pp. 4915–4919.

Weghorn, H. (2013) 'Applying mobile phone technology for making health and rehabilitation monitoring more affordable', in *2013 ISSNIP Biosignals and Biorobotics Conference: Biosignals and Robotics for Better and Safer Living (BRC)*, pp. 1–5.

Weghorn, H. (2015) 'Efforts in developing android smartphone sports and healthcare apps based on bluetooth low energy and ANT+ communication standards', in *2015 15th International Conference on Innovations for Community Services (I4CS)*, pp. 1–7.

Weghorn, H. (2017) 'Supercapacitors Serving as Power Supply in Tiny Sport Sensors - Field Testing Through Heart Rate Monitoring in Endurance Trail Runs', *Proceedings of the 5th International Congress on Sport Sciences Research and Technology Support*. doi: 10.5220/0006515100560065.

Xu, R. *et al.* (2018) 'BlendCAC: A BLockchain-Enabled Decentralized Capability-Based Access Control for IoTs', in *2018 IEEE International Conference on Internet of Things (iThings) and IEEE Green Computing and Communications (GreenCom) and IEEE Cyber, Physical and Social Computing (CPSCom) and IEEE Smart Data (SmartData)*, pp. 1027–1034.

Yin, L. *et al.* (2020) 'Hierarchically defining Internet of Things security: From CIA to CACA', *International Journal of Distributed Sensor Networks*, 16(1), p. 1550147719899374.

Zhang, Y. *et al.* (2020) 'Bluetooth Low Energy (BLE) Security and Privacy', *Encyclopedia of Wireless Networks*, pp. 123–134. doi: 10.1007/978-3-319-78262-1_298.

Zwerg, M. *et al.* (2011) 'An 82µA/MHz microcontroller with embedded FeRAM for energy-harvesting applications', in *2011 IEEE International Solid-State Circuits Conference*, pp. 334–336.

EXPLORING SQL INJECTION VULNERABILITIES USING ARTIFICIAL BEE COLONY

Kevin Baptista, Anabela Bernardino and Eugénia Bernardino
Computer Science and Communication Research Center (CIIC)
School of Technology and Management, Polytechnic of Leiria, Portugal

ABSTRACT

Over the last couple of decades, there has been an enormous growth in technologies and services available on the internet. This growth must take security into account, although due to the increase in complexity of systems this is not an easy task. Nowadays, hardly any organization may say with certainty that their system is secure. The Open Web Application Security listed "Injection" as the most security risk for web applications in 2020. There are many automated tools to assist professionals in the field, in order to identify this vulnerability. However, keeping these tools up to date has proven to be a challenge. Therefore, there has been some interest in applying Artificial Intelligence (AI) in this field. In this paper, we propose an approach to detect SQL injection vulnerabilities in the source code, using Artificial Bee Colony (ABC). To test this approach empirically we used web applications purposefully vulnerable as Bricks, bWAPP, and Twitterlike. Simulation results verify the effectiveness of the ABC algorithm.

KEYWORDS

Artificial Bee Colony, SQL Injection, Vulnerabilities in Web Applications

1. INTRODUCTION

The growth and usage of the Internet worldwide (Barros and Dumas, 2006), has lead to attacks on information systems that are becoming every year more sophisticated and catastrophic, resulting many times in loss of personal data and, in extreme cases, human lives.

The Open Web Application Security (OWASP) listed the top 10 web application security risks for 2020 as injection, broken authentication, sensitive data exposure, XML external entities, broken access control, security misconfiguration, cross-site scripting, insecure deserialization, using components with known vulnerabilities and insufficient logging and monitoring (Stock et al., n.d.).

The focus in this paper is on injection, more precisely, SQL Injection. OWASP defines SQL Injection as a vulnerability that occurs when untrusted data is sent to the system as part of a query. The main goal for the attacker is to trick the interpreter into executing unintended queries in order to execute unauthorized actions like obtained unauthorized data.

Artificial Intelligence (AI) techniques have been successfully applied in many areas of software engineering (Columbus, 2008). In order to detect vulnerabilities of SQL Injection, we developed an automated tool, based on the application of an Artificial Bee Colony (ABC) algorithm. ABC is a simple and effective global optimization algorithm that has been successfully applied to several optimization problems of various fields (Karaboga et al., 2014). The main purpose of this tool is to be used in a white box scenario, having access to the code base. Thus, it could help developers to find potential vulnerabilities in their codebase.

To empirically evaluate our presented approach, we used several open-source projects that are known to have certain vulnerabilities, such as Bricks, bWAPP, and Twitterlike.

The rest of the paper is organized as follows. Section 2 presents some related work. Section 3 describes the identified problem. In Section 4, it is described how the problem was modelled in order to be used as an optimization problem. Section 5 describes the proposed ABC algorithm. Section 6 discussed the various experiments conducted to empirically validate the approach taken as well as the specifications used to conduct the analysis and the results obtained. Section 7 concludes this paper.

2. RELATED WORK

Mckinnel et al. (2019), make a comparative study of several artificial intelligence algorithms in exploiting vulnerabilities. In their study, the authors compiled several works in the area, in order to compare several algorithms, including unsupervised algorithms, Reinforcement Learning, Genetic Algorithms (GAs), among others. The authors conclude that the GAs performs better over time due to the evolutionary nature of generations. They suggest that its applicability needs to take into account a good definition of the fitness function in order to obtain better results. They recommend solutions designed for specific systems, instead of generic solutions since these more generic solutions only exploit shallower and simpler vulnerabilities.

Manual penetration tests, although effective, can hardly meet all security requirements that are constantly changing and evolving (Niculae, 2018). Furthermore, they require specialized knowledge which, in addition to presenting a high cost, is typically slower. The alternative is automated tools that, although faster, often do not adapt to the context and uniqueness of each application. In (Niculae, 2018), the author developed a reinforcement learning strategy capable of compromising a system faster than a brute force and random approach. This concluded that it is possible to build an agent capable of learning and evolving over time so that it can penetrate a network. Its effectiveness was equal to that of human capacity. Finally, he concludes that although the initial objective was long, there are still several directions to be explored. From the use of different algorithms for both an offensive (red team) and a defensive (blue team) security perspective. It suggests the application of game theory concepts (Nguyen et al., 2016), especially treating a problem like a Stackelber Security Game. These techniques have been successfully applied in various security domains such as finding the optimal allocation for airport security given the attackers' knowledge.

Alenezi and Javed (2016) analyzed several open-source projects in order to identify vulnerabilities. They concluded that most of these errors are due to negligence on the part of the people who developed the applications as well as the use of bad practices. To solve this problem, the authors suggest the development of a framework that encourages programmers to follow good practices and detect possible flaws in the code.

In Tripathi et al. (2018), the authors propose a solution to detect XSS (cross-site scripting) vulnerabilities based on the use of GAs as well as a proposal to remove the vulnerabilities found during the detection phase. The aim was to find as many vulnerabilities as possible with as few tests as possible. The results obtained were compared with other static analysis tools. As future work, they suggest the application of this technique in applications from other areas as well as to three types of XSS: persistent, reflected and based on DOM.

3. PROBLEM DEFINITION

Security vulnerabilities are flaws in web applications that allow attackers to execute actions that should not be allowed. SQL Injection is a vulnerability that happens when the attacker is able to execute SQL commands that should not be possible by sending very specific values to the server. The primary reason for this vulnerability to happen is the lack of input validation employed in the applications.

Most web applications have some sort of forms to be filled by the user, either to authenticate, to register, or to search. In consequence, the server receives the input sent by the client and executes some business rules to it. Commonly, the server communicates with a database (SQL or NoSQL) to save the data. During this process, the developer must have some attention to save the data in a safe manner, otherwise, it can be exploited by an attacker.

Let us consider the authentication in a web application. In this scenario, the user would be presented with a form with two input fields: one for the username and the other for the password. For the sake of simplicity, let us ignore other authentication methods available nowadays. On the server, it would be expected to see a query similar as follows:

```
SELECT * FROM users
WHERE username = '$username' AND password=md5('$password');
```

MD5 is a cryptographic algorithm, often used to store passwords in a database. Even though, this algorithm is no longer safe, due to be easily cracked by brute force and having dictionary tables for it (Zheng and Jin, 2012). Nevertheless, this is not an issue for the current problem. Any algorithm with salt could be used to represent this problem, however, this one was used due to its simplicity.

The users fill the form with username “John” and password “example”, then we would have the following execution:

```
SELECT * FROM users
WHERE username = 'John' AND password=md5('example');
```

This query searches for a user that has the username "John" and the hash of the password "example". If the result of the search is not empty, then it would authenticate the user.

The problem comes when an attacker sends a value that would trick the system. Consider that the attacker fills username as "any" and password as "x') OR 1=1; --". Then the query would look like the following:

```
SELECT * FROM users
WHERE username = 'any' AND password=md5('x') OR 1=1; --';
```

Simplified we would find three conditions: *username='any'* which is false; *password=md5('x')* which is also false; but then *1=1* is true. In other words, we would have:

```
false AND false OR true
false OR true
true
```

So, it does not matter what the client sends as username or password, if they were able to manipulate the query to execute a third condition with "OR true". The consequence would be that a user can be able to login into the system without valid credentials. In general, a successful SQL injection attack attempts different techniques, such as the one demonstrated above in order to carry out a successful attack.

SQL injection could have catastrophic consequences and is the number one vulnerability risk according to OWASP (Stock et al., n.d.). However, there are a couple of measures that can be implemented in order to prevent this injection. The preferred option is to use a safe API, which avoids the use of an interpreter entirely or provides a parameterized interface, or even migrates to an Object Relational Mapping tool (ORM).

4. PROBLEM REPRESENTATION

In order to use an ABC as an optimization algorithm to find SQL Injection, the process was divided into two steps: (1) identification of all SQL queries (Figure 1); (2) use of ABC to generate attack vectors to be injected in the queries (Figure 2).

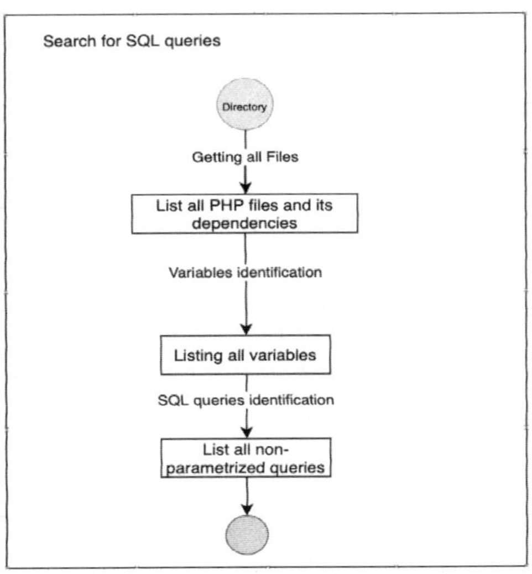

Figure 1. First step in the process: Searching for Queries

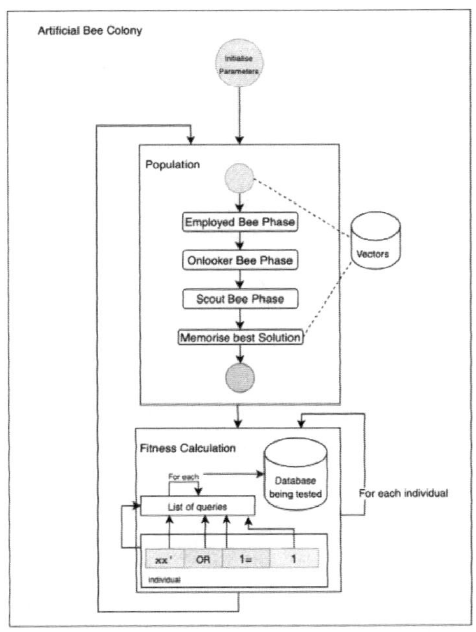

Figure 2. Second step in the process: Finding Best Solution

4.1 Search for SQL Queries & Find Best Solution

In Figure 1, we can see an overview of the process of searching for SQL queries, where the main goal is to obtain all non-parametrized queries. In order to obtain this goal, first, it is necessary to perform a search to list all PHP files recursively in a given folder. Afterwards, all variables in the code are indexed and their history is kept. This step is crucial to capture SQL queries that are parametrized, but still vulnerable because the vulnerabilities occurred before in the code. These queries and all non-parametrized queries are kept in a list to be used in the second phase by the Artificial Bee Colony algorithm.

The next step occurs in the ABC domain as we can observe in Figure 2. The main goal of this step is to find a vector that could compromise one of the queries listed in the previous step. So, the algorithm starts by initializing all the needed parameters, creates a population, and executes all steps in the ABC.

In order to inject vectors in the queries, which are selected by the algorithm, a dataset is provided beforehand and stored in a database. This dataset was built based on Friedl (2017) and Mishra (n.d.).

4.2 Individual Representation

In our representation, individuals are derived from SQL injection database which was constructed based on different resources (Friedl, 2017; Mishra, n.d.). Each individual is made up of a set of four genes. Each gene is a String. In Figure 3, there is a possible representation for the individual. Each gene could be either a logic operator (for example OR, AND, NOT, etc.) or a value (for example: "xx'", "1", "1=", " -- "). The key point of encoding an individual as a list of strings is that, when we calculate the fitness of an individual, we will use this string as multiple attack vectors.

xx'	OR	1=	1

Figure 3. Example of an individual

4.3 Fitness

As represented in Figure 2, each gene in the individual is going to be tested as an attack vector, and also all of them as one attack. To illustrate this idea, let us consider again the individual in Figure 3 and the code presented in Figure 4.

```
<?php
        $uagent = $_SERVER['HTTP_USER_AGENT'];
        $sql= "SELECT * FROM users WHERE ua='$uagent' ";
?>
```

Figure 4. Example of PHP code

The queries executed for this scenario are illustrated in Table 1 and as we can observe, an individual which has 4 genes executes 5 queries. For this example, only one of them is valid and vulnerable.

Table 1. Executed queries

Query	Valid / Invalid / vulnerable	Success
SELECT * FROM users WHERE ua='xx''	Invalid Query. Not vulnerable.	No
SELECT * FROM users WHERE ua='OR'	Valid Query. Not vulnerable.	No
SELECT * FROM users WHERE ua='1='	Valid Query. Not vulnerable.	No
SELECT * FROM users WHERE ua='1'	Valid Query. Not vulnerable.	No
SELECT * FROM users WHERE ua='xx' OR 1=1	Valid Query. Vulnerable.	Yes

The fitness function used for this problem is as follows (Eq. 1):

$$fitness(i) = \frac{U_{vul} * 5 + G_{vul} * 2}{totalGenes} \quad (1)$$

where i is the individual being tested, $totalGenes$ is the total number of genes in an individual, U_{vul} is the number of unique vulnerabilities detected by the individual. G_{vul} is the number of genes that detected at least one vulnerability.

Fitness is used to evaluate the performance of an individual for a given problem. An individual with bigger fitness means that has better performance, or in other words, was able to crack successfully more queries.

Applying this fitness function to the example described above means we would get the fitness:

$$fitness = \frac{1 * 5 + 1 * 2}{4}$$

We have only analysed one query, thus at best the U_{vul} is one, which is the case. As can be seen, every gene tested individually did not get any success. On the other hand, when tested grouped it got one success, thus $G_{vul} = 1$. It is important to remember, that this example is very simple when we are testing only one SQL query. In empirical tests, there are several queries, so the success might be different.

5. ARTIFICIAL BEE COLONY

ABC was proposed by Karaboga (2005) to optimise numerical problems. ABC simulates the intelligent behaviour of a bee colony (Karaboga and Basturk, 2007a,b; Karaboga and Akay, 2009a,b). The minimal model of swarm-intelligent forage selection in a honey bee colony, that ABC algorithm adopts, is based on three kinds of bees: employed bees, onlooker bees, and scout bees (Karaboga and Akay, 2009a,b). To our knowledge, this work presents the first application of ABC to solve the problem presented in this paper.

5.1 ABC Steps

In order to apply ABC to a problem, some steps should be performed. Each iteration of the search consists of four steps (Karaboga and Akay, 2009a,b):

1) Sending the employed bees onto their food sources and evaluating their nectar amounts;
2) After sharing the nectar information of food sources, selecting food source regions by the onlookers and evaluating the nectar amount of these food sources;
3) Determining the scout bees and then sending them randomly onto possible new food sources;
4) Memorising the best food source.

These four steps are repeated through a predetermined number of iterations defined by the user. In a robust search process, the exploration and exploitation processes must be carried out together. In the ABC algorithm, while onlookers and employed bees carry out the exploitation process in the search space, the scouts control the exploration process. The main steps of the ABC algorithm are described in the next sections.

5.1.1 Initialisation of Parameters

The following parameters must be defined by the user: number of employed bees (*ne*), number of onlooker bees (*no*>=*ne*), number of modifications (*nm*), and maximum number of iterations (*mi*).

5.1.2 Food Source Position Initialisation

At the first step, ABC generates randomly an initial bee population.

5.1.3 Employed Bees Phase

Employed bees are responsible for: (1) exploiting the nectar sources explored before and (2) giving information to the other waiting bees (onlooker bees) in the hive about the quality of the food source site which they are exploiting. In this phase, each employed bee produces a new food source in its food source site and exploits the best source. In our implementation, the position of a food source represents a possible solution to the problem and the nectar amount of a food source corresponds to the associated solution quality (fitness – Eq. 1). The number of employed bees is exactly the number of initial solutions. The employed bees share the information related to the nectar of the food sources and their position with the onlooker bees. An artificial onlooker bee chooses a food source, depending on the probability value associated with that food source, pr_i. The probabilities are calculated using Eq 2.

$$totalFitness = \sum_{n=1}^{ne} fit_n \qquad pr_i = \frac{fit_i}{totalFitness} \qquad (2)$$

5.1.4 Onlooker Bees Phase

Onlooker bees wait in the hive and decide which food source to exploit according to the information shared by the employed bees. In this phase, each onlooker bee selects a source depending on the quality (fitness value) of its solution, produces a new food source in the selected food source site and exploits the best source (the source with the best fitness value).

An onlooker bee evaluates the nectar information taken from all employed bees and chooses a food source with a probability related to its nectar amount. Our algorithm computes the number of onlooker bees, which will be sent to food sources of employed bees (Eq. 3), according to the previously determined probabilities:

$$no_i = pr_i * no \qquad no_i\text{ =number of onlooker bees sent to food source } i. \tag{3}$$

A neighbour is obtained by performing multiple attempts to improve the solution, which length is specified as *nm* (number of modifications). The algorithm performs *nm* modifications to find a new position for the onlooker bee. A modification consists of changing the value of a position of the individual to another random value (a string, as represented in Figure 3). The algorithm repeats this process until at least one exchange with improvement is made or until the *nm* is reached. If the nectar amount of the solution is higher than the nectar amount of the previous one, the bee memorises the new position and forgets the old one.

5.1.5 Scout Bees Phase

Scouts randomly search the environment in order to find a new food source depending on an internal motivation, possible external clues or randomly. In this phase, the food source of which the nectar is abandoned by the bees is replaced with a new food source by the scouts. In our implementation, this is simulated by producing new solutions and replacing the worst employed bees. This means that the food sources with lower nectar amounts are abandoned.

The worst employed bees as many, as the number of scout bees in the population, are respectively compared with the scout solutions. If a scout bee is better than an employed bee, the employed bee is replaced with the scout bee. Otherwise, the employed bee is transferred to the next cycle without changes. In our implementation, we consider the number of scout bees equal to 10 % of the number of employed bees (see Eq. 4).

$$ns = 0.1 * ne \tag{4}$$

5.1.6 Best Solution Memorization

In this step the algorithm memorises the best solution achieved so far.

6. EXPERIMENTAL RESULTS

All experiments were performed on a Raspberry PI 4 Model B, 8GB of RAM, quad-core 64-bits of 1.5Ghz.

The results produced by ABC are compared with manual analysis and with another tool, Web Application Protection (WAP) - http://awap.sourceforge.net/- that uses a static analysis approach to detect vulnerabilities in web applications written in PHP.

As mentioned previously, we have first identified SQL Injection vulnerabilities manually. We consider our manual analysis as the true value. Table 2 shows the results from this manual analysis.

In order to obtain the best combination of parameters, several smoke tests were performed. Figure 5 shows the effect that the number of modifications has on the quality of a solution. On the y-axis we have the total number of vulnerabilities detected. In the Bricks and Twitterlike projects, there are no effect with the number of modifications studied. On the other hand, there is a slight improvement with 2 modifications on the bWAPP project. This is probably due to the overall size of the project. Both Bricks and Twitterlike are relatively small when compared with bWAPP.

The relation between population size and execution time could not be measured and compared accurately. One improvement done during the testing phase was to cache queries that were already known as vulnerable or as not vulnerable. This had a huge impact in the performance point of view of the research. Taking as an example a population of 100 individuals, for 100 generations, for 30 different seeds, in the bricks projects (which has 11 queries identified) and each individual, 4 genes, that would translate in 100*100*30*11*(4+1) = 16 500 000 queries done in the database for one set of parameters.

Table 2. Results from the manual analysis

Web Application	Total SQL injection
Bricks	12
bWAPP	56
Twitterlike	17

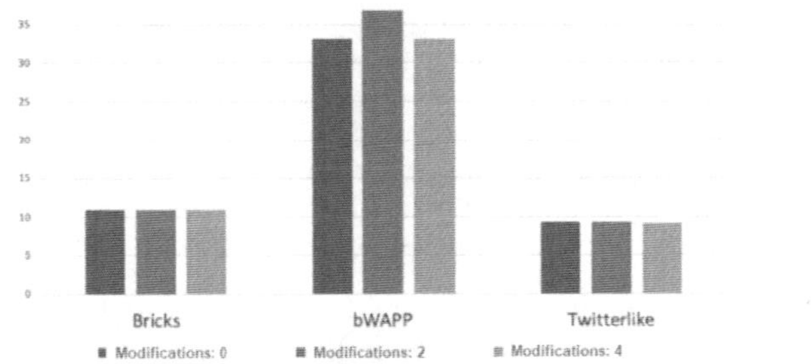

Figure 5. Impact of number of number of modifications on number vulnerabilities detected

The execution time that a query takes in a local database, depends on many factors, from the specifications of the machine to the complexity of the query. After some empirical tests, we conclude that our machine was taking around 130ms to return the result, which means that for the use case described before it would take almost 25 days to execute. Using a caching strategy, which stores the success or unsuccess of a query in memory, and using the same machine, a million access to one element of a map is taking around 80ms, which means that in average each access is taking $8 * e^{-5}ms$.

Taking into account the number of queries mentioned before, we reduce the time to 1320ms which is ~1.3seconds. As shown, this improvement was extremely efficient. Although now, parameters of the artificial bee colony have basically no impact on the execution time. When a query hits the cache it is extremely faster, which means the first sets of parameters to be explored will eventually be slower, because the cache is empty or almost empty. So, depending on the order we execute tests we can have situations where a bigger population is faster than a smaller one, due to the number of hits in the cache.

Table 3 illustrates the ABC parameters settings used that obtained the best values in all projects tested. Table 4 shows the results in terms of the vulnerabilities found with the ABC. Table 5 presents some examples of attack vectors found by this approach, that could be used in order to take advantage of SQL injection and corresponding examples of queries used with success. Table 6 shows the results when using WAP.

Table 3. Parameters that obtained best results

Parameter	Value
Max iterations	50
Number Employed bees	20
Number Onlooker bees	50
Number of modifications	2

Table 4. Results from Artificial Bee Colony

Web Application	Total SQL Injection Found
Bricks	11
bWAPP	47
Twitterlike	10

Table 5. Example of successfully vectors and query examples

Vector	Query executed
x'='x' --	`SELECT * FROM users WHERE email = 'x'='x' --';`
x'='x	`SELECT * FROM heroes WHERE login = 'x'='x';`

Table 6. Results using WAP

Web Application	Total SQL injection
Bricks	11
bWAPP	15
Twitterlike	5

As can be seen, with our approach most vulnerabilities are detected. For the case of bWAPP, only 50% of the vulnerabilities were detected with these parameters. This is probably due to the fact that an individual has a fixed genome in terms of size, which sometimes leads to invalid queries. An approach with a dynamic genome size could potentially bring better results in terms of total SQL injection vulnerabilities found.

When comparing with WAP tool, the ABC was able to identify more vulnerabilities. Only for the bricks use case, we got the same results when comparing to the same tool.

7. CONCLUSION

SQL injection is a current problem in web applications and can have serious implications and consequences. In order to detect those vulnerabilities, we presented an approach to detect these vulnerabilities in the code base, using a white-box approach. The problem was addressed using Artificial Bee Colony as a way to optimize the search of potential vulnerabilities in the code. Dividing the process into two steps, starting with a searching phase for queries, then followed by an optimization search to find the best vectors, it was possible to obtain good results. As we could observe in Section 6, there was a slight improvement in results using the ABC when compared with static analysis.

The tool has been developed in Java, with support to analyse PHP applications, since PHP is one of the most used languages for web applications (Mishra, 2014), although, as other languages are gaining more presence online, the tool should be expanded to support multiple languages.

Another point that has a direct impact on the results obtained is the initial dataset given to the ABC. Having it in mind, it is crucial to expand this dataset in order to obtain better results and as mentioned previously, testing an individual with a dynamic genome could also bring some interesting results to the problem.

The scope of this article was constrained to SQL injection, but there are other injection problems and even other vulnerabilities that could potentially benefit from this approach.

ACKNOWLEDGEMENTS

This work was supported by national funds through the Portuguese Foundation for Science and Technology (FCT) under the project UIDB/04524/2020.

REFERENCES

Alenezi, M. and Javed, Y., 2016. Open source web application security: A static analysis approach. *Proceedings of the 2016 International Conference on Engineering and MIS.*

Barros, A.P. and Dumas, M., 2006. The Rise of Web Service Ecosystems. *In IT Professional*, 8 (5), pp. 31-37.

Columbus, L., 2018, January 12. 10 charts that will change your perspective on artificial intelligence's growth. *Forbes*.

Friedl, S., 2017, March 6. *SQL Injection Attacks by Example*. Retrieved Feb. 28, 2021, from http://www.unixwiz.net/techtips/sql-injection.html.

Karaboga, D. 2005. *An idea based on honey bee swarm for numerical optimization*, Technical report TR06. Erciyes University, Engineering Faculty, Computer Engineering Department.

Karaboga, D. and Akay, B., 2009a. Artificial Bee Colony (ABC), Harmony Search and Bees Algorithms on Numerical Optimization. *IPROMS 2009 Innovative Production Machines and Systems Virtual Conference*, Cardiff, UK.

Karaboga, D. and Akay, B., 2009b. A comparative study of Artificial Bee Colony algorithm. *In Applied Mathematics and Computation*, 214:108–32.

Karaboga, D. and Basturk, B., 2007a. Artificial Bee Colony (ABC) Optimization Algorithm for Solving Constrained Optimization Problems. *Proceedings of the 12th International Fuzzy Systems Association World Congress on Foundations of Fuzzy Logic and Soft Computing*. Berlin Heidelberg, Springer-Verlag, pp. 789–798.

Karaboga, D. and Basturk, B., 2007b. A powerful and efficient algorithm for numerical function optimization: artificial bee colony (abc) algorithm. *In Journal of Global Optimization,* 39(3), pp. 459–71.

Karaboga, D. et al, 2014. A comprehensive survey: artificial bee colony (ABC) algorithm and applications. *In Artificial Intelligence Review*, 42, pp. 21–57.

McKinnel, D.R. et al, 2019. A systematic literature review and meta-analysis on artificial intelligence in penetration testing and vulnerability assessment. *In: Computers & Electrical Engineering*, 75, pp. 175-188.

Mishra, A., 2014. Critical Comparison of PHP And ASP.NET For Web Development - ASP.NET & PHP. *In International Journal of scientific & Technology Research*, 3(7), pp. 331-333.

Mishra, D., n.d. SQL Injection Bypassing WAF. *OWASP*. Retrieved Feb. 28, 2021, from https://www.owasp.org/index.php/SQL_Injection_Bypassing_WAF.

Nguyen, T.H. et al, 2016. Towards a Science of Security Games. *In: Toni B. (eds) Mathematical Sciences with Multidisciplinary Applications*. Springer Proceedings in Mathematics & Statistics, 157. Springer, Cham.

Niculae, S., 2018. *Applying Reinforcement Learning and Genetic Algorithms in Game-Theoretic Cyber-Security*. Master Thesis.

Stock, A. et al, n.d. OWASP Top Ten. *OWASP*. Retrieved Feb. 28, 2021, from https://owasp.org/www-project-top-ten/.

Tripathi, J., Gautam, B. and Singh, S., 2018. Detection and Removal of XSS Vulnerabilities with the Help of Genetic Algorithm. *In International Journal of Applied Engineering Research*, 13(11), pp. 9835-9842.

Zheng, X. and Jin, J., 2012. Research for the application and safety of MD5 algorithm in password authentication. *9th International Conference on Fuzzy Systems and Knowledge Discovery*, pp. 2216-2219.

ESTIMATING CONTAMINATION RISK USING ARTIFICIAL INTELLIGENCE MODELS A CASE OF THE PATIÑO AQUIFER, PARAGUAY

Eliane H. Fernández[1], Liz Báez[1], Miguel Garcia-Torres[2], Juan Pablo Nogués[3] and Cynthia Villalba[1]

Facultad Politécnica, Universidad Nacional de Asunción, San Lorenzo, Paraguay[1]

División de Ciencias de la Computación, Universidad Pablo de Olavide, Sevilla ES-41013, España [2]

Facultad de Ciencias de la Ingeniería, Universidad Paraguayo Alemana, San Lorenzo, Paraguay [3]

ABSTRACT

Studying the risk of contamination is essential for the protection of aquifers. In Paraguay, one of the major drinking water supplies is the Patiño Aquifer. A previous study, using a deterministic model, identified that 42% of the aquifer have a high risk of contamination. This work uses artificial intelligence (AI) models, with regression and classification approaches, to estimate the contamination risk of the urban zone of the Patiño aquifer by Total Nitrogen (TN). The Supervised Committee Machine with Artificial Intelligence (SCMAI) model is applied as a regression model, which combines the Artificial Neural Network (ANN), Mamdani Fuzzy Logic (MFL), Sugeno Fuzzy Logic (SFL) and Neuro Fuzzy (NF) models. Root Mean Square Error (RMSE), Mean Absolute Error (MAE) and the correlation of estimated risk with TN concentration are used for the evaluation. The Decision Trees (DT), Bayesian Network (BN) and K-Nearest Neighbor (KNN) models are used for the low and not low risk classification approach. These models were evaluated based on the precision, recall and accuracy indicators. The SCMAI model improved the performance and correlation of the ANN, MFL and SFL models, with RMSE, MAE and correlation values of 2.33, 1.38 and 0.86 respectively. The J48 and PART algorithms, applied to the DT model, and the KNN model obtained an accuracy of 99%, and the BN model obtained an accuracy of 98%. Precision and recall values showed that the DT algorithms failed less, by 10%, and that it is able to identify 81% of the cases of the not low risk levels. It was observed that both approaches give a competent picture of the state of the Patiño aquifer in relation to the risk of contamination.

KEYWORDS

Artificial Intelligence, Regression, Classification, Machine Learning, Contamination risk, Patiño Aquifer

1. INTRODUCTION

The intrinsic characteristics of the aquifer determine the vulnerability of contamination. These characteristics, anthropogenic pressure, and the existence of pollutants, determine the risk of contamination (Saidi, 2011). A well-known model for estimating the contamination vulnerability is the DRASTIC model (Aller, 1985). This model performs a linear combination of weights and scores of seven hydrogeologic parameters. The calibration of the model requires the modifications of these weights and scores. Some techniques such as Analytic Hierarchy Process (AHP), Genetic Algorithm (GA) and fuzzy logic are used to do this calibration (Sahoo et al, 2016; Jafari et al, 2016; Souleymane et al, 2017, Neshat et al, 2015). Another way to optimize/calibrate the DRASTIC model is by the incorporation of extra parameters. These extra parameters are usually chosen because they add anthropogenic information.

The Artificial Intelligence (AI) models can replace the DRASTIC model for estimating contamination risk. Machine learning (ML) models such as Artificial Neural Network (ANN), Boosted Regression Trees (BRT), Multivariate Discriminant Analysis (MDA) and Support Vector Machine (SVM) (Baghapour et al, 2016; Sajedi et al, 2018) are some of them. Fijani et al (2013) and Barzegar et al (2013) applied the ANN, Mamdani Fuzzy Logic (MFL), Sugeno Fuzzy Logic (SFL) and Neuro Fuzzy (NF) models for estimating the contamination risk. From the results of those independent models, they performed a nonlinear combination through the application of an ANN model as a combiner, this established the Supervised Committee Machine with Artificial Intelligence (SCMAI) model, which constitutes a committee of AI models and allows taking the advantages of each independent model (Fijani et al, 2013). In many cases, ML models are applied by considering the problem of estimating the contamination risk as a regression problem. However, it can also be considered as a classification problem.

In Paraguay, the Patiño aquifer supplies about 38% of the national population. Due to its location, easy and uncontrolled access, contamination risk is a latent threat (Cardozo, 2006). In a previous study (Baez et al, 2019), total nitrogen (TN) contamination risk maps of the Patiño aquifer were calculated using the modified DRASTIC statistical method (Panagopoulos et al, 2006). The results indicated that 42% of the aquifer have a high risk of contamination. In the present work, artificial intelligence (AI) models with regression and classification approaches are applied to estimate the risk of Total Nitrogen (TN) contamination in the urban area of the Patiño aquifer. Therefore, the following objectives were defined: a) Discuss the solution of the contamination risk estimation problem as a regression and classification problem. b) Apply the SCMAI as a regression model, to estimate the contamination risk of the urban zone of the Patiño aquifer. c) Apply the Decision Trees (DT), Bayesian Network (BN) and K Nearest Neighbour (KNN) models, due to the simplicity of the risk estimation rules, to estimate the contamination risk levels of the urban zone of the Patiño aquifer. d) Evaluate the performance of the regression models using different input parameters. e) Compare the risks estimated by the regression models with the TN concentrations. f) Evaluate the classification models with defined levels of risks.

The paper is structured as follows. Section 2 presents the description of the study area. Section 3 presents the materials, models used, and experiments performed for the development of this work. Section 4 presents the results and discussions. Section 5 presents the conclusions of the work.

2. STUDY AREA

The Patiño Aquifer is located beneath the surface of the city of Asunción, the capital of Paraguay, and 21 other surrounding cities (Figure 1). It is an unconfined aquifer with a total extension of 1173 km^2 (T.N.O., 2001). The area is bordered on the northwest and west by the Paraguay river. The aquifer is approximated a triangular basin, 300 m deep, 65 km long and 30 km wide. The recharge is mainly by precipitation and through leaks of the water distribution system. Rivers and streams are the natural sinks for the discharge. Anthropogenic sinks are attributed to private and public cesspools.

The waters of the aquifer supply a population of around 2,000,000 inhabitants (DGEEC, 2015), in the largest and most densely populated urban area of the country, where an important part of the commercial, industrial and agricultural sector is also concentrated. This leads to many potential sources of contamination and runs the risk of constant contamination from discharges into the water table and poor sewage coverage.

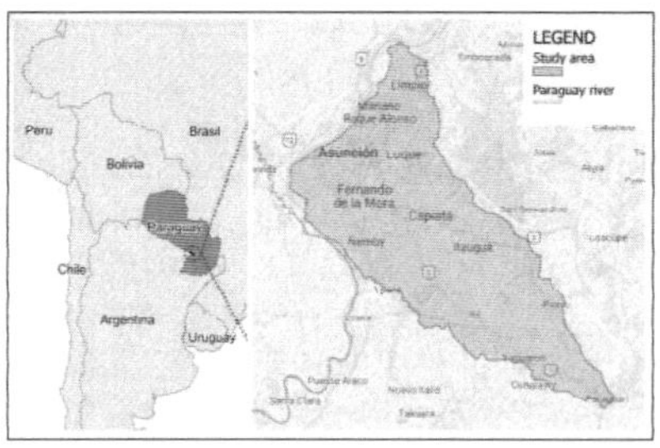

Figure 1. Location map of the study area, the Patiño Aquifer

3. MATERIALS AND METHODS

This section presents the description of the models applied, the source and preparation of the data, the details of the experiments performed, the evaluation model and the process followed to generate the risk maps.

In order to estimate the contamination risk of the urban zone of the Patiño aquifer, the SCMAI model was applied through different experiments. The model and the results were evaluated and validated, and then contamination risk maps were generated. In addition, the DT, KNN and BN models were applied, and the estimated risk levels were evaluated.

3.1 SCMAI Model

The SCMAI model consists of applying the ANN model as a supervised combinator of independent AI models, as proposed by Fijani et al (2013). The structure of the SCMAI model is shown in Figure 2. First, the risks were estimated with each of the independent SFL, MFL, NF and ANN models. Next, the ANN model was applied to estimate the risk from the risks obtained by the ANN, SFL, MFL and NF models. The input layer of the SCMAI model consists of one neuron for each risk obtained by the SFL, MFL, NF and ANN (Fijani et al, 2013).

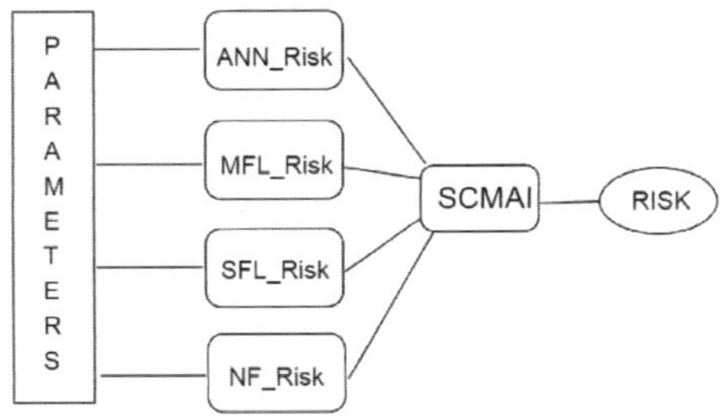

Figure 2. Structure of the SCMAI model

The ANN model consists of units called neurons that are organized in layers. The multilayer perceptron is a type of artificial neural network consisting of an input layer, one or more hidden layers and an output layer. The MFL and SFL models are two types of fuzzy models that differ on the inference systems. The NF model combines the advantages of neural networks and fuzzy logic. The network uses five layers for performing the inference steps (Fijani, 2013).

3.2 Classification Models

The DT model consists of a root node, intermediate nodes and leaf nodes. Each node of the tree consists of one decision. Two algorithms were applied to the construction of the decision tree: J48 (optimized C4.5 (Ross, 1993)) and PART (Eibe et al, 1998). The BN models the data by means of an acyclic directed graph where nodes and arcs represent the set of random variables, conditional variables and the conditional dependencies between them. The KNN model requires the calculation of distances and the assignment of weights to the nearest neighbors. The label of a new instance is classified based on the major labels of the K nearest neighbors. This is done by assigning a high weighting to the nearest neighbors (Dudani, 1976).

3.3 Data Preparation

This work uses the same parameters (hydrogeological and anthropogenic) that were used in (Baez et al, 2019). Each parameter is defined over a 689x615 spatial grid.

The Water Depth (D) was determined from the static level values (NE) of 35 parameters from 2007 (CKC-JNS, 2007). These were interpolated with the Co-kriging method to get values over the entire grid.

The Recharge (R) was calculated combining the precipitation recharge, artificial recharge and land use, proposed by Nobre et al (2007). Artificial recharge was obtained from the difference of distribution and billing of drinking water in 2011. Precipitation data were obtained from the Climate Research Unit (CRU) database (Harris et al, 2014; Jarvis et al, 2013). Further details of the calculation are given in (Baez et al, 2019).

The Aquifer Lithology (A) values were obtained from scanned images of well profiles from Consorcio CKC-JNS (CKC-JNS, 2007).

The Soil Type (S) data were obtained from the soil reconnaissance map of the Eastern Region of Paraguay (Lopez et al, 1995).

The Topography (T) for the study area was obtained from the Digital Elevation Model (DEM) that was downloaded in a raster format from the International Research Centre website (Jarvis et al, 2013).

Hydraulic Conductivity (C) values were obtained by the interpolation of 61 Geo-referenced values from 2007, collected in the studies (CKC-JNS, 2007; Wehrle et al, 2007). The values were interpolated with the Co-kriging method.

The Land use (LU) was obtained from the Paraguayan land use coverage map, recompiled from the Facultad de Ciencias Agrarias de la Universidad Nacional de Asunción (FCA-UNA) and the Forestry and Forest Products Research Institute (FFPRI) in 2013 (Forestry, 2011).

Density of cesspool (DC) values were obtained from thematic maps included in the study database (Wehrle, 2007).

Transport Routes (TR) data correspond to the main paved routes (CKC-JNS, 2007), these influence the location of contamination sources such as dwellings, factories, service stations, commercial areas.

TN concentrations were obtained from interpolating 72 wells distributed in the urban area. The TN concentrations of these wells were extracted from a campaign carried out in 2018 (Báez et al, 2021).

3.4 Experiments Carried out through Regression Models

Two experiments were conducted for estimating the contamination risk. Experiment I (EXP I) had the objective of estimating risk using the hydrological parameters (actual values of D, R, T, C and assigned grades of A, S). Experiment II (EXP II) had the purpose of estimating the contamination risk using the hydrological and anthropogenic parameters (real values of DC, TR and grades assigned to LU), because they are indicators of possible sources of contamination.

The output parameter of the models was the risk; through this, the models were calibrated with TN concentrations. The risk was calculated following the proposal in (Fijani et al, 2013), using the following equation:

$$Risk_i = \frac{(Vul_i * TN_i)}{Vul_{max}} * 100 \qquad (1)$$

where Vul_i is the vulnerability calculated through DRASTIC, Vul_{max} is the maximum vulnerability calculated, TN_i is the TN concentration at point i, $Risk_i$ is the risk at point i.

In the DRASTIC equation, considering the hydrological parameters, the weights and ratings proposed by Aller (1985) were used, and for the anthropogenic parameters, those proposed by (Baez et al, 2019) were used.

For the experiments, 101914 data grids were used. These data grids were selected randomly and with a uniform distribution around the urban areas of the aquifer. Thirty percent of the data were used for validation and the rest for training. Cross-validation was performed to ensure that the results were independent of partitioning.

The Root Mean Square Error (RMSE) and Mean Absolute Error (MAE) were used to evaluate the performance of the ANN, MFL, SFL, NF and SCMAI models. In addition, the risks estimated by the models were validated with TN concentrations by calculating the Spearman's correlation coefficient (ρ).

The Matlab Fuzzy Logic Toolbox was used for applying the MFL, SFL and NF models, and TensorFlow with Python for applying the ANN and SCMAI model. The configurations of the models in the experiments are detailed below.

For the SFL model, the Subtractive Clustering (SC) algorithm was used for the clustering of inputs and outputs. The cluster radius is a parameter that determines the number of clusters and inference rules. The value of the cluster radius is in the range [0, 1]. Clustering was performed several times, by increasing the cluster radius from 0 to 1. For the NF model, the same configurations of the SFL model were applied. For the MFL model, the Fuzzy C-Means (FCM) algorithm was used for the clustering of inputs and outputs. Gaussian functions were applied as membership functions. Runs were performed using different defuzzification methods and varying the number of clusters. For the ANN model, a single hidden layer was used. By considering that the number of hidden layers should include at least two or three times the number of input nodes, multiple runs were made to find the optimal number. Furthermore, one neuron was counted for the output layer. The LINEAR activation function was applied to the output layer. Besides, runs were made varying the type of activation function in the hidden layer. The Backward Propagation (BP) algorithm was employed for training.

Contamination risk maps were generated using Geographic Information System (GIS). In order to cover the urban area of the Patiño Aquifer, the results were interpolated. To help the comparison between maps, a min-max normalization of the predicted risks on a scale of 1 to 100 was performed.

3.5 Experiments carried out Through Classification Models

The experiment was aimed at estimating the risk of contamination at two risk levels: Low, Not Low.

The input parameters of the models were the hydrogeological and anthropogenic parameters. The output parameter was the risk in two categories, extracted from (Afshar et al, 2007): Low (risk from 0 to 47), Not Low (risk from 48 to 100). For that, the risk calculated from equation (1) was normalized and divided into these categories.

A cross-validation was performed with 10 iterations for a total of 101914 wells. The confusion matrix was used to evaluate the model performance. The performance indicator considered was the accuracy, precision, and recall. Waikato Environment for Knowledge Analysis (Weka) were used, and the configurations are detailed below.

In the J48 and PART algorithm, the minimum number of instances per rule was 2, the number of data to reduce the pruning error was set to 3, and the confidence threshold for pruning was set to 0.25. In the KNN model, the number of neighbors was set to 1. The linear search was applied using the Euclidean function. In the case of the BN, the simple estimator was used for the estimation of the conditional probability tables.

4. RESULTS AND DISCUSSIONS

In this section, the results obtained from the regression and classification models are shown. Besides, the contamination risk maps obtained through the SCMAI model are shown.

Equation (1) produced risk values varying from 0 to 54 (experiment I and II). These risk values were used as output parameters in the training step. The risks estimated by the SCMAI model varied from 0 to 22.7 (experiment I) and from 0 to 30.08 (experiment II). In the testing step, the RMSE, MAE and the ρ correlations were calculated. Table 1 summarizes these values, obtained with the ANN, MFL, SFL, NF, SCMAI models, in the different experiments. The columns show the values of RMSE, MAE and ρ per experiment.

Table 1. Regression model results

	EXP I			EXP II		
Model	RMSE	MAE	ρ	RMSE	MAE	ρ
ANN	3.32	2.26	0.68	2.76	1.82	0.75
MFL	4.83	3.02	0.52	4.63	3.05	0.49
SFL	2.51	1.51	0.84	2.39	1.41	0.86
NF	2.48	1.49	0.85	2.34	1.38	0.86
SCMAI	**2.48**	**1.49**	**0.85**	**2.33**	**1.38**	**0.86**

The SCMAI model was established with 12 neurons in the hidden layer in all experiments. With 100 epochs of training, the better RMSE, MAE and ρ values were obtained in the experiment II. However, similar values were obtained with the NF model. The incorporation of the anthropogenic parameters in experiment II altered the results slightly.

Considering the independent models, the NF model improved the correlation values of the SFL model with a clustering radius of 0.2. The ANN model obtained the results after 100 epochs of training with the RELU activation function, and 25 and 28 neurons in experiment I and II respectively. The RMSE and MAE values improved those obtained by the MFL model. The MFL model showed a low correlation and performance compared to the others. For defuzzification, the bisector method was established with 55 clusters. Figure 3 shows the maps with the estimated normalized risk values. The areas with the highest risk are in the northwestern region of the Patiño aquifer. The percentages of not low risks (risk from 48 to 100) were 6% and 5% in experiment I and II respectively.

The performance of the classifier models was evaluated by means of the precision, recall and accuracy indicators. Table 2 summarizes these values. The best accuracies were 99.9% and 99.8% obtained with the J48, PART and KNN algorithms. The precision values showed that these models failed classifying Not Low risk levels by 12%, 11%, and 24% respectively. The BN algorithm failed by 78%, however, as seen with the recall values, of the cases that it should have classified as Not Low risk level, it was able to identify the largest number. Based on the confusion matrix of the models, shown in Table 3, there is a balanced amount of correctly predicted risk levels. According to the performance indicators measured, the algorithms were good classifiers. On the other hand, based on the characteristics of each algorithm, the DT algorithms present an advantage for the contamination risk estimation problem. They produce interpretable results that would help to understand the problem.

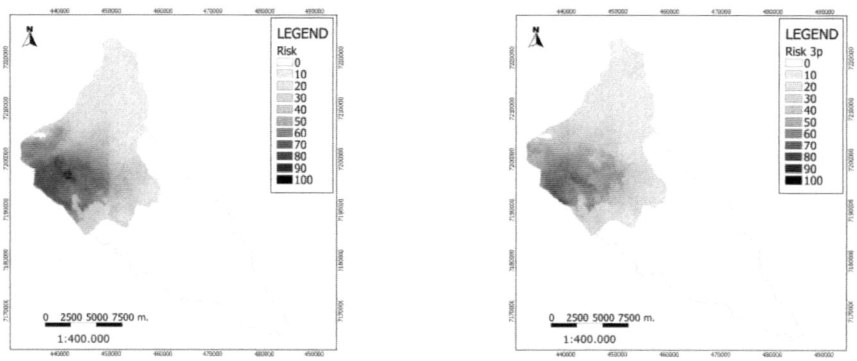

Figure 3. Risk map generated by the SCMAI model in the experiments I and II respectively

Table 2. Accuracy, precision and recall values of the classifier models

J48 (Accuracy = 99.9%)		PART (Accuracy= 99.8%)		KNN (Accuracy=99.8%)		BN (Accuracy=98.8%)		
Precision	Recall	Precision	Recall	Precision	Recall	Precision	Recall	
0.99	1.00	0.99	1.00	0.99	0.99	1.00	0.99	a = Low
0.88	0.81	0.89	0.81	0.76	0.73	0.22	0.97	b = Not Low

Table 3. Confusion matrix of the classifier models

J48			PART			KNN			BN		
a	b	classified as	a	b	classified as	A	b	classified as	a	b	classified as
101549	36	a = Low	101552	33	a = Low	101511	74	a = Low	101470	1115	a = Low
63	267	b = Not Low	60	270	b = Not Low	90	240	b = Not Low	9	321	b = Not Low

The classification models were able to obtain accuracy values greater than 98%, i.e. the number of correctly classified cases was high. However, when looking at the regression models, it was observed that the RMSE values did not fall below 1.37. Thus, the application of the regression models and the subsequent visualization of the risk maps provide a complete picture of the state of the aquifer. On the other hand, with the application of the classification models, a greater accuracy in the results and a concise view of the risk levels is obtained.

5. CONCLUSION

Regression and classification models were applied to estimate the contamination risk of the Patiño aquifer in Paraguay. On one side, the SCMAI model was applied, which involves the results of four independent models ANN, MFL, SFL, NF. On the other side, the DT, BN and KNN models were applied.

The regression models were calibrated with TN concentrations, used as representative indicators of groundwater quality degradation. The SCMAI model obtained values of RMSE= (2.48, 2.33), MAE= (1.49, 1.37) and ρ= (0.84, 0.86) in the experiments. The results indicated that the independent models are also applicable for risk estimation. Despite including the anthropogenic parameters (experiment II), no better correlations were seen in most of the independent models. The calibration of models, defined by the output parameter, allowed the fit of the models despite the input data. The results indicated that the areas with a not low risk of contamination were those located in the northwestern part of the aquifer, which corresponds to an area with a high population density in the capital of the country.

The accuracy, recall and precision indicators, and the balance in the estimated risk levels indicated that the classifiers models can be used for contamination risk estimation. The algorithms showed an accuracy of at least 98%. When classifying the Not Low risk levels, because of their minority of cases, the classifiers made more mistakes. However, DT algorithms obtained precision and recall values of approximately 0.88 and 0.81 respectively. For this reason and because they produce interpretable results, DT algorithms are suggested for application to the risk estimation problem.

Thus, this work confirms the suitability of the regression and classifier models to estimate contamination risks. The models can be successfully used as an effective tool by researchers, stakeholders and decision-makers towards the protection of aquifers.

As future work, it is proposed to apply time series networks to obtain the risk index of the Patiño aquifer. Thus, to verify the degree of contamination and its progress over the years. In addition, it would be interesting to apply the SCMAI model to estimate the contamination risk of other aquifers.

REFERENCES

Afshar, A. et al, 2007. Rule-based fuzzy system for assessing groundwater vulnerability. *Journal of Environmental Engineering*, Vol. 133, No. 5, pp. 532-540.

Aller, L., 1985. *DRASTIC: a standardized system for evaluating groundwater pollution potential using hydrogeologic settings*. Robert S. Kerr Environmental Research Laboratory, US Environmental Protection Agency.

Antonakos, A. K. et al, 2007. Development and testing of three hybrid methods for the assessment of aquifer vulnerability to nitrates, based on the drastic model, an example from NE Korinthia, Greece. *Journal of Hydrology*, Vol. 333, No. 2-4, pp. 288-304.

Báez, L. et al, 2019: Comparison of contaminant-specific risk maps for an urban aquifer: Patiño aquifer case. *Environmental Earth Sciences*, Vol. 78, No. 5, pp. 137.

Báez, L. et al, 2021. Designing and validating a groundwater sampling campaign in an unmonitored aquifer: Patiño aquifer case. *Environmental Earth Sciences,* Vol. 80, No. 11, pp. 1-16.

Baghapour, M. A. et al, 2016. Optimization of DRASTIC method by artificial neural network, nitrate vulnerability index, and composite DRASTIC models to assess groundwater vulnerability for unconfined aquifers of Shiraz Plain, Iran. *Journal of Environmental Health Science and Engineering*, Vol. 14, No. 1, pp. 1-16.

Barzegar, R. et al, 2016. A supervised committee machine artificial intelligent for improving DRASTIC method to assess groundwater contamination risk: a case study from Tabriz plain aquifer, Iran. *Stochastic environmental research and risk assessment*, Vol. 30, No. 3, pp. 883-899.

Barzegar, R. et al, 2018 Mapping groundwater contamination risk of multiple aquifers using multi-model ensemble of machine learning algorithms. *Science of the total environment*, Vol. 621, pp. 697-712.

Cardozo L.S. et al, 2006. Estudio de la Contaminación del Acuífero Patiño, Trabajo Final de Grado. Universidad Nacional de Asunción, Paraguay.

CKC-JNS, 2007. Estudio de Políticas y Manejo Ambiental de Aguas Subterráneas en el Área Metropolitana de Asunción-Acuífero Patiño. In: S. E. N. A. S. A. Servicio Nacional de Saneamiento Ambiental (ed) Informe técnico 1.1: Resumen Ejecutivo, Asunción.

Dirección General de Estadísticas Encuestas y Censos, D. G. E. E. C, 2015. Encuesta Permanente de Hogares, Asunción.

Dudani, S. A., 1976. The Distance-Weighted k-Nearest-Neighbor Rule, *in IEEE Transactions on Systems, Man, and Cybernetics*, Vol. SMC-6, No. 4, pp. 325-327.

Frank E. et al, 1998. Generating Accurate Rule Sets Without Global Optimization". *Proceedings of the Fifteenth International Conference on Machine Learning*, Madison, US, pp. 144-151.

Fijani, E. et al, 2013. Optimization of DRASTIC method by supervised committee machine artificial intelligence to assess groundwater vulnerability for Maragheh-Bonab plain aquifer, Iran. *Journal of hydrology*, Vol. 503, pp. 89-100.

Forestry and Forest Products Research Institute, F. F. P. R. I., and Facultad de Ciencias Agrarias UNA, F. C. A, 2016. Cobertura de la Tierra Paraguay, San Lorenzo.

Foster S et al, 2003. Protección de la calidad del agua subterránea. Banco Mundial.

Harris, I. P. D. J et al, 2014. Updated high resolution grids of monthly climatic observations—the CRU TS3. 10 Dataset. *International Journal of Climatology*, Vol. 34, No. 3, pp. 623–642.

Instituto Holandés de Geociencias Aplicadas, T. N. O., 2001. Estudio del Acuífero Patiño. Fortalecimiento de los Estudios Hidrogeológicos del SENASA (FEHS). In: S. E. N. A. S. A. Servicio Nacional de Saneamiento Ambiental (ed) Asunción.

Inclam-Hqa (2017). Diagnóstico del Acuífero Patiño, Proyecto BID PR-T 1207 *Estudio de Recursos Hídricos y Vulnerabilidad Climática del Acuífero Patiño*. Available at: http://www.mades.gov.py/wp-content/uploads/2019/09/PR-T1207-Diagnostico.pdf (Accessed: 5 March 2021).

Jafari, S. M. et al, 2016. Groundwater risk assessment based on optimization framework using DRASTIC method. *Arabian Journal of Geosciences*, Vol. 9, No. 20, pp. 1-14.

Jarvis A, Reuter HI, Nelson A, Guevara E (2013). *Hole-filled SRTM for the Globe Version 4.1 CGIAR-CSI SRTM 90 m Database 2008*. Available at: http://srtm.csi.cgiar. org. (Accessed: 5 March 2021).

López O, González E, et al, 1995. Proyecto de Racionalización del Uso de la Tierra. In: M. A. G. Ministerio de Agricultura y Ganadería, S. E. R. N. M. A. Subsecretaria de Estado de Recursos Naturales y Medio Ambiente, Banco BM, Mundial (eds) Estudio de Reconocimiento de Suelos, Capacidad de Uso de la Tierra y Propuesta de Ordenamiento Territorial Preliminar de la Región Oriental del Paraguay, vol I, Asunción.

Mades Website. (2016). *SEAM presenta informe de los monitoreos realizados en el Acuífero Patiño.* Available at: http://mades.gov.py/content/seam-presenta-informe-de-los-monitoreos-realizados-en-el-acuífero-patiño (Accessed 5 March, 2021).

Mogaji, Kehinde Anthony et al, 2014. Modeling groundwater vulnerability to pollution using Optimized DRASTIC model". *In IOP Conference Series: Earth and Environmental Science*. IOP Publishing, p. 012002.

Neshat, A. et al, 2015. An integrated DRASTIC model using frequency ratio and two new hybrid methods for groundwater vulnerability assessment. *Natural Hazards*, Vol. 76, No. 1, pp. 543-563.

Neshat, A. et al, 2015. Risk assessment of groundwater pollution with a new methodological framework: application of Dempster–Shafer theory and GIS. *Natural Hazards*, Vol. 78, No. 3, pp. 1565-1585.

Neshat, A. et al, 2014. Groundwater vulnerability assessment using an improved DRASTIC method in GIS. *Resources, Conservation and Recycling*, Vol. 86, pp. 74-86.

Nobre R. C. M. et al, 2007. Groundwater vulnerability and risk mapping using GIS, modeling and a fuzzy logic tool. *Journal of Contaminant Hydrology*, Vol. 94, No. 3-4, pp. 277-292.

Pathak, D. R. et al, 2011. An integrated GIS based fuzzy pattern recognition model to compute groundwater vulnerability index for decision making. *Journal of Hydro-environment Research*, Vol. 5, No. 1, pp. 63-77.

Panagopoulos GP et al, 2006. Optimization of the DRASTIC method for groundwater vulnerability assessment via the use of simple statistical methods and GIS. *Hydrogeoly Journal,* Vol. 14, No. 6, pp. 894–911.

Ross Quinlan, 1993. C4.5: Programs for Machine Learning. Morgan Kaufmann Publishers, San Mateo, CA.

Sahoo, S. et al, 2016. Index-based groundwater vulnerability mapping using quantitative parameters. *Environmental Earth Sciences*, Vol. 75, No. 6, pp. 522.

Saidi, S., et al, 2011. Assessment of groundwater risk using intrinsic vulnerability and hazard mapping: application to Souassi aquifer, Tunisian Sahel. *Agricultural Water Management*, Vol. 98, No. 10, pp. 1671-1682.

Sajedi-Hosseini et al, 2018. A novel machine learning-based approach for the risk assessment of nitrate groundwater contamination. *Science of the total environment*, Vol. 644, pp. 954-962.

Souleymane, K. et al, 2017. A novel method of sensitivity analysis testing by applying the DRASTIC and fuzzy optimization methods to assess groundwater vulnerability to pollution: the case of the Senegal River basin in Mali".w *Natural Hazards and Earth System Sciences*, Vol. 17, No. 8, pp. 1375-1392.

Wehrle A, Sekita K, 2007. Informe técnico 2.8: Ensayos de Bombeo. In: CKC-JNS (eds) Estudio de Políticas y Manejo Ambiental de Aguas Subterráneas en el Área Metropolitana de Asunción—Acuífero Patiño, Asunción.

Wehrle A, 2007. Informe técnico 2.9: “Inventario de Fuentes Potenciales de Contaminación". In: CKC-JNS (ed) Estudio de Políticas y Manejo Ambiental de Aguas Subterráneas en el Área Metropolitana de Asunción—Acuífero Patiño, Asunción.

AN AUTOMATED PARALLEL COMPATIBILITY TESTING FRAMEWORK FOR WEB-BASED SYSTEMS

Yeisson Chicas and Stephane Maag
Télécom SudParis, Samovar, Institut Polytechnique de Paris, France

ABSTRACT

With the growth and wide use of web-based applications in many domains, it is crucial to check their conformance with regards to their requirements. Among the important set of testing types, compatibility testing is of high importance. Indeed, ubiquity is required and the way of interacting with these applications can be performed in many manners. Compatibility testing aims at determining if the web application is proficient enough to run in different browsers, database, hardware, operating system, mobile devices, networks, etc. In this context, one challenge for compatibility testing is how to execute multiple tests cases, in a correct and efficient way, that may cover several environments and functionalities of the tested applications, while reducing the consumed resources and time. In our work, we propose a methodology to efficiently perform compatibility tests through several environments with different versions of operating systems (OS) and browsers. We emphasize on resource consumption improvement by using parallel testing and containerization.

KEYWORDS

Compatibility Testing, Automation Testing, Selenium Grid, Docker, Web-Based Systems

1. INTRODUCTION

Web-based applications are part of our daily lives. According to (WebsiteSetup Editorial, 2021) it is estimated that around 1.7 billion web pages currently exist used by 4.5 billions people all over the world.

With the growth and use of all these web-based applications in many domains (e.g., industry, financial, academia, security, etc.), they need to be safe, conform to their requirements in order to provide the expected functionalities. It is therefore necessary to test them. There exist several research works, approaches, methods and tools to test such webRTC applications (Al-Ahmad and Al Debei, 2020). Among the important set of testing types, compatibility testing becomes more and more important. Indeed, ubiquity is needed and the way of interacting with these applications can be performed in many manners.

Compatibility testing has diverse definitions. The one we will use here is the process to determine whether the web application is proficient enough to run in different browsers, database, hardware, operating system, mobile devices, networks, etc[1].

In this context, one challenge for compatibility testing is how to execute multiple tests cases, in a correct and efficient way, that may cover several environments and functionalities of the tested applications. Another important aspect to consider is the maintenance of testing processes when a web-based application is modified. Indeed, this can cause the whole process to become poor, slow, consuming too many resources. In our work, we propose a methodology to efficiently and correctly perform compatibility tests through several environments and contexts with different versions of operating systems (OS) and browsers. Furthermore, we emphasize on resource consumption improvement by using parallel testing and containerization. Finally, we summarize our main contributions.

- we propose a framework based on containerization and test parallelization for compatibility testing with resources and time reduction.
- we demonstrate that our approach improves the time processing when testing compared to traditional and sequential testing.
- thanks to our methodology, we show that, although not commonly used in the Internet, some browsers behave very well and pass many of our tests cases.

[1] https://www.softwaretestinghelp.com/software-compatibility-testing/

2. RELATED WORKS

WebRTC automation testing is studied for some years now (Garcia et al., 2017) and there exist several re- search papers dedicated to compatibility testing in many areas such as vulnerability detection (Hayek et al., 2019), GUI (Ki et al., 2019) or cross-browsers domains (Liu et al., 2019). However, there are few if we consider compatibility testing of web-based systems such as web applications. We cite in the following the related works we get inspired of.

A very first work on functional testing was proposed by Garcia et al in (Garcia et al., 2016). The authors present a framework based on Selenium for functional test cases and the assessment of quality of experience (QoE) while using web services. Although this work is not determined to compatibility testing, the metrics they use for the assessment of the quality of WebRTC applications are relevant.

Recently, Al-Ahamad et al provided an up-to-date survey on the testing methods for web applications (Al-Ahmad and Al Debei, 2020). Compatibility testing approaches are reviewed and compared. Giving detailed definitions, viewpoints, architectures and interesting challenges especially in terms of test cases execution. The authors highlight the main challenges and issues the tackle in this area.

In his Master's thesis (Heinonen, 2020), J. Heinonen shows the importance of parallelizing the testing process while performing compatibility testing through multiple browsers. Configurations and testbed setup is of high importance as mentioned into that paper. The author raised the difficulty to orchestrate docker and to distribute the test cases as well as the required resources. This is what we manage in our work by using Selenium Grid and Docker.

Another very recent and relevant work is (Bertolino et al., 2020). It deals with the distribution of test cases through the parallelization of the executions. They use a platform prototype, ElasTest, for evaluating the QoE of WebRTC applications. Their work is innovative and demonstrates the needs and efficiency of virtualization and parallel executions for testing. However, their approach is not dedicated to compatibility testing, the resources are not evaluated and real experiments are not deeply studied.

Besides, Tanaka provides formal definitions and ways for designing test suites in (Tanaka, 2019). The approach is dedicated to visual compatibility testing using selenium. However, the parallelization and containerization are not performed. This is the same in (Yu, 2019) in which relevant approaches for compatibility testing are presented demonstrating the importance of combinatorial tests of various settings, aspects considered in our work and eased by our methodology.

We also study the work of Villanes et al. (Villanes et al., 2020) devoted to test cases exploration and in particular, the ways to decide which use cases could be useful in terms of compatibility testing scenarios. This is somehow what we try to experience in our paper by providing our testing verdicts.

In our paper, we get inspiration of all these related works and present a novel approach based on containerization and parallelization of multiple test suites execution for web applications compatibility testing.

3. BACKGROUND

3.1 Selenium

Selenium[2] is an automated testing framework, open-source, based on JavaScript, used for web application testing. It allows to run tests directly with different browsers: popular browsers like Firefox, Google Chrome, Safari, enabling interactions with the desired websites. It reduces repetitive manual testing that consumes time and effort. Selenium is quite popular in the industry[3] and recent studies make mention that it is one of the best frameworks (Garcia et al., 2020).

[2] https://www.selenium.dev
[3] https://enlyft.com/tech/products/selenium

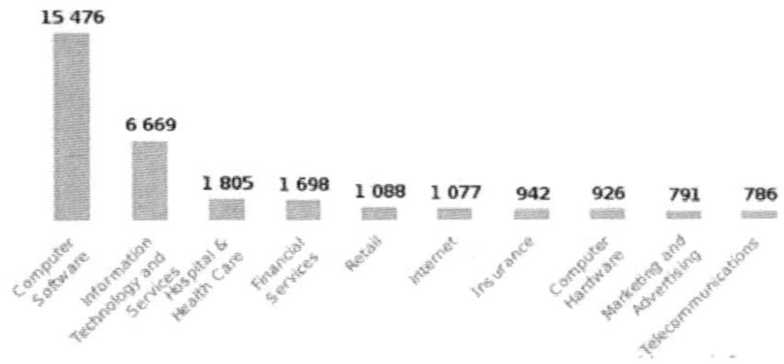

Figure 1. Distribution of companies using Selenium by Industry

Selenium has advantage of allowing testers to write their own tests by providing some templates and standards, as well as a lot of flexibility and portability across multiple operating systems such as Windows, Linux and Mac OS. Selenium can be controlled from various programming languages including Java, Python, PHP, C# and others. It also allows integration with other tools.

Selenium WebDriver It is a tool used to automate the testing of web applications and handling a browser in a native way. It handles the browser as a real user. Basically, WebDriver provides an interface to create and execute test scripts in an automated way, it communicates through an API which sends commands to control the different browsers.

Selenium Grid This tool enables to run tests in parallel across multiple machines at the same time, making a considerable reduction of time. It is an ideal tool for our approach that deals with parallel tests executions in different environments with different versions of browsers and OS. Selenium Grid gives the possibility to control and manage in a simpler way. It provides a hub that acts as a central point where Selenium sends commands to each node connected to it.

3.2 Docker

Docker is a platform[4] designed to create, deploy, distribute, and run applications using containers. Containers are kept running in isolation on top of the OS kernel. They allow developers to package an application with all its necessary parts, such as libraries and other dependencies and deploy them in a single package. It is an open-source platform in which many people contribute and keep updated so that they can add more features. Although Docker is widely used in many areas (e.g., cloud computing), this is not common for compatibility testing of web-based systems.

4. OUR METHODOLOGY

As above mentioned, and as studied in the cited related works, compatibility testing methods herein aim at evaluating web applications through diverse environments (OS, resources, scale, users, etc.). In order to assess the proper functioning of these applications, the testers need these environments reflecting the real contexts and users utilizing the web applications every day. Traditionally, this involves the use of browsers and devices to present and test all possible scenarios. It may lead to an increase of consumption and cost, factors that researchers and companies are constantly trying to reduce. Besides, they work on decreasing time processes to implement and complete the entire testing process from the generation of scripts, the creation of the necessary contexts and the execution of test cases. Basically, obtaining and processing such environments is often costly in terms of resources and time.

The methodology used in this work is based on the combination of different components and tools that lead to the execution of the compatibility tests as illustrated in Figure 2.

[4] https://www.docker.com

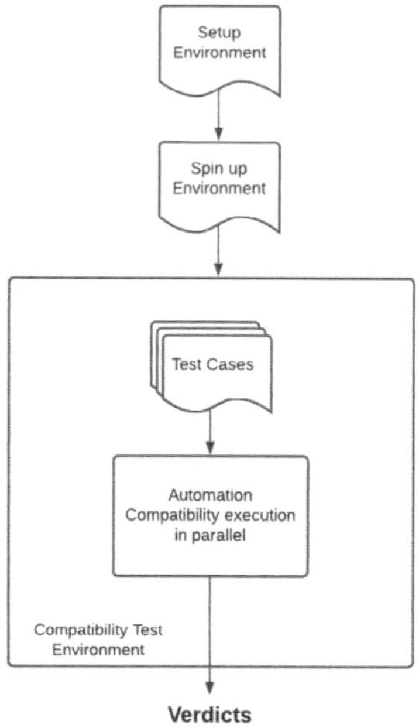

Figure 2. Our framework methodology

- **Setup environment** This component aims at defining all initial configuration parameters by targeting in particular on the behaviors of our desired framework features. It allows to define the wished OS, environments, browsers, memory, space, number of entities/instances, users, etc. This component plays an important role on how the whole operations will behave and evolve.
- **Spin up environment** This component defines the deployment of our entire framework, using the previous setup configurations. It is responsible for executing the necessary commands so that we can deploy the entire environment from the main device to the different nodes. This obtained architecture will be utilized for the distribution and execution of the test cases.
- **Compatibility test environment** This is the main component where everything is put in place. The test generation element contains all the test cases to be evaluated. It is worth noting that any test case we need to evaluate within the framework can go here at runtime; they can be modified, extended, updated, removed. This element generates the test scripts that will be executed in parallel using Selenium Grid throughout the framework environment. Then, the automated parallel execution element executes each of the test scripts and verify its functionalities on the different deployed Docker nodes.

Note that the whole process of methodology ends up issuing verdicts which are defined on the basis of what is evaluated. In general, according to our testing purpose, obtained verdicts are PASS, FAIL or ERROR. They are depicted in the following sections.

5. EXPERIMENTAL STUDIES

5.1 Framework

Our framework is intended to meet the requirements of providing environments in which various web-based applications can be tested. Based on the above, the components that are part of the experimental framework are the following:

- *Host Device* one of the advantages of this framework is that it can be used on a variety of computers that meet the following minimum requirements:
    - 64bit processor
    - Hardware virtualization support
    - 4Gb system RAM

In our case, host device (computer) was used with the specification given in the Table 1.

Table 1. Framework host device specification

Operating system	MacOS version 11.2
Processor	2.5GHz Quad-Core Intel Core i7
Memory	16GB 1600 MHz
SSD	512GB

- *Docker* it enables to have different operating systems inside containers, called nodes, as well as to decide which browsers to install, in which nodes and what tests to deploy and where.
- *Browser versions* The Table 2 shows the different versions of browsers used in the implementation of our framework. These browsers were installed in the different nodes. Browser images with the latest version 5 were used, but it is possible to install earlier versions and other images.

Table 2. Web Browsers versions

Firefox	85.0.2
Google Chrome	88.0.4324.150
Opera	74.0.3911.107
Safari	14.1
Brave	88.0.43

- *Docker container images* the docker images that were used as nodes in our framework container the following specifications as show in Table 3.

Table 3. Docker images specifications

Architecture	Amd64
OS	Linux
Size	940829711
Node Port	5555

- *Selenium Grid* (v3.141.59) is the tool used in our framework to distribute our tests through the nodes. By using one of the main features of Selenium Grid, which is its client-server model, it is possible to connect within a Docker container to the hub and the other nodes that are also in containers. As above mentioned, our setup file generates in an automated way our test architectures. Once the architecture is built, it is necessary to use Selenium WebDriver to detect which browser is utilized and consequently to provide the required driver for communication and coordination. The Figure 3 shows the interactions between scripts, WebDrivers and browsers.

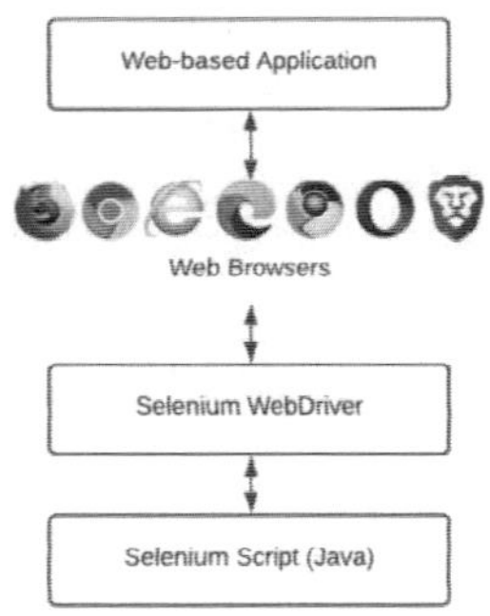

Figure 3. Selenium WebDriver

One of our testing architecture is illustrated in Figure 4. Besides, our framework enables the creation of any amount of nodes instances and install browsers as we require in our experimental studies.

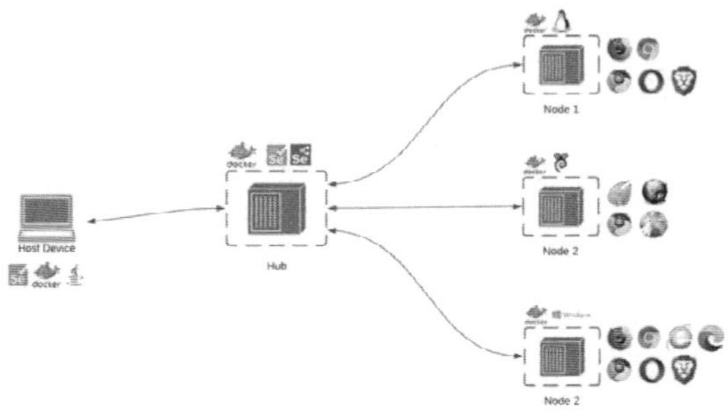

Figure 4. One of our testing architectures

5.2 Experiments

This section is organized as it follows. First, we introduce the scenarios and test cases considered. This is followed by the framework requirements of the host device. Finally, we present the tuned testbed that runs the different scenarios.

5.2.1 Experimented Scenarios and Test Cases

In our experiments, we propose four different assessed usage scenarios as shown in the Table 4. In these scenarios, we execute the two test cases defined as in the next section.

Table 4. Experimental scenarios

Scenarios	**Description**
Scenario 1	This scenario has 2 nodes, 1 node with Google Chrome browser, and 1 node Firefox browser.
Scenario 2	This scenario has 10 nodes, 2 nodes for each browser (Google Chrome, Firefox, Opera, Safari, and Brave).
Scenario 3	This scenario has 20 nodes, 4 nodes for each browser (Google Chrome, Firefox, Opera, Safari, and Brave).
Scenario 4	This scenario has 30 nodes, 6 nodes for each browser (Google Chrome, Firefox, Opera, Safari, and Brave).

5.2.2 Our Test Cases

- *Login Test* this Login test is executed when a user wants to log in to a web-based application as shown in Figure 5. We aim at testing the ability to enter information in the requested fields and thus evaluating the way the layout is displayed, verifying that it is the same in different browsers and operating systems, following policies that are not affected by the default settings that browsers bring and consequently, not show different behaviors noticeable from the requests/responses. Steps to perform for the test:
    - Obtain IP address and por of the node,
    - Identify the browser used on the node,
    - Request the WebDriver specified for this browser,
    - Identify the login fields within the application structure,
    - Enter the default values for each field,
    - Wait for a response from the application.

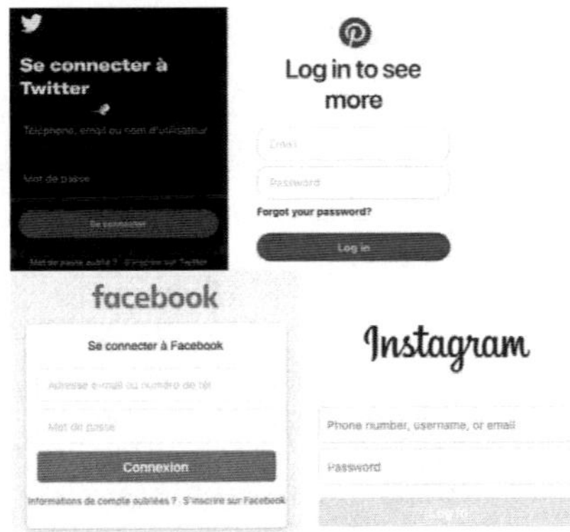

Figure 5. Login Test

- *Broken links test* the test case named Broken links checks the operations of the internal links that the web-based application may contain as shown in Figure 6. It verifies that there are no broken links or links that cannot be reached, a malfunction of which may affect the overall experience and operation of the application. We can check what kind of error we get when we test a link. Note that we can use the HTTP status code to determine where the problem might be, for example, we get a status code 200 because it is a valid and working link, if we get a status code 400 because the error is on the client side (in the browser or in the operating system where the browser is running) or we get a status code of 500 because the error corresponds to the server providing the application. This is tested in different environments with different configurations to observe the behavior and get results. Steps to perform for the test:
  - Obtain IP address and port of the node,
  - Identify the browser used on the node,
  - Request the WebDriver specified for this browser,
  - Analyze and obtain all the anchor elements of the application,
  - Verify the HTTP response code of each link.

Figure 6. Broken Links Test

5.3 Framework Requirements

To implement and use the framework in our working environment, we did integrate:

- Docker
- Docker Compose
- Docker images
- Java SDK
- Eclipse
- TestNG library
- Selenium Grid

5.3.1 Framework Tuning

While using the various elements of our framework, it is necessary to make a special adjustment where the difference is made and we achieve our goal. Therefore, we present below some of the important configurations in order to execute the proposed scenarios.

The entire architecture runs on Docker containers that gives the advantage to process a single configuration file to automate the deployment and nodes configuration, as well as the main node that will contain the Selenium Grid Hub. Next, we present the configuration of the main node, where we can set various variables, for example:

- Services - List of all images and configurations,
- image - Defines which image we will use for the container,
- ports - Ports used in this special format host:container,
- GRID MAX SESSION - This declares how many browsers can run in parallel at time.

```
services:
   hub:
       image: selenium/hubports:
           - "4444:4444"
       environment:
           GRID_MAX_SESSION: 100
           GRID_BROWSER_TIMEOUT: 3000
           GRID_TIMEOUT: 3000
```

In the same file named docker-compose.yml, we insert the nodes configurations with different OS, architectures and browsers. In this configuration, we set values for the Docker image to use if the deployment of our node depends on another, in these cases, all nodes depend on the central/main node (hub), as well as port configurations and how many browsers we want to have in each node. The following is the basic configuration of a node with google chrome browser.

- *container name* - Name to identify the container
- *depends on* - Is the required dependency previous to deploy the node, for example each framework node depends on the hub node
- *NODE MAX SESSIONS* - How many instances of a browser can run over the node
- *NODE MAX INSTANCES* - How many instances of different browsers can run in parallel in the same node

```
environment-chrome:
   image: selenium/node-chrome container_name: web_environment_chrome
   depends_on:
       - hub environment:
       HUB_PORT_4444_TCP_ADDR: hubHUB_PORT_444_TCP_PORT: 4444
       NODE_MAX_SESSIONS: 1
       NODE_MAX_INSTANCES: 1
   volumes:

       - dev/shm:/dev/shmports:
       - "9001:5900"
   links:
       - hub
```

5.3.2 Framework Tuning

The Login Test: The script generated for its execution looks like the one illustrated in the Figure 7, where we have code blocks to identify the type of browser used, as well as the main method of testing the process of logging into a web-based application.

```
@Parameters("browser")
pubic void setup(String browser) throws Exception{
    //Check if browser is Firefox
    if(browser.equalsIgnoreCase('firefox')){
        //Create firefox instance
        System.setProperty('webdriver.gecko.driver', path_of_firefox_driver);
        driver = new FirefoxDriver();
    }
    //Check if browser is Chrome
    else if(browser.equalsIgnoreCase('chrome')){
        //Create chrome instance
        System.setProperty('webdriver.chrome.driver', path_of_chrome_driver);
        driver = new ChromeDriver();
    }
    //Check if browser is Opera
    else if(browser.equalsIgnoreCase('opera')){
        //Create opera instance
        System.setProperty('webdriver.opera.driver', path_of_opera_driver);
        driver = new OperaDriver();
    }
    //Check if browser is Safari
    else if(browser.equalsIgnoreCase('safari')){
        //Create safari instance
        System.setProperty('webdriver.safari.driver', path_of_safari_driver);
        driver = new SafariDriver();
    }
    //Check if browser is Edge
    else if(browser.equalsIgnoreCase('edge')){
        //Create edge instance
        System.setProperty('webdriver.edge.driver', path_of_edge_driver);
        driver = new EdgeDriver();
    }
    else {
        throw new Exception('Browser is not correct');
    }

}
```

```
public class LoginTest {

    @Test public void loginTest() {
        driver.get(website);

        webElement username=driver.findElement(By.id('username'));
        webElement password=driver.findElement(By.id('password'));
        webElement login=driver.findElement(By.xpath("//button[text()='Log in']"));

        username.sendKeys('username-example@gmail.com');
        password.sendKeys('password');
        login.click();
        String actualUrl = 'https://twitter.com/login';

        String expectedUrl = driver.getCurrentUrl();
        Assert.assertEquals(expectedUrl, actualUrl);
    }
}
```

Figure 7. Login scenario Java script

The Broken Links Test: To determine if a web-based application has broken links, we need to follow the steps below:

- Collect the links that are present in the web-based application, these links can be found within the HTML structure with the < a > element, in this element there is the href attribute where we can find the URL that the link redirects to,
- Send a HTTP request to each link,
- Check the HTTP response codes,
- Evaluate the codes and determine whether it works or not.

```
//Obtain all the a elements
List<WebElement> links = driver.findElements(By.tagName("a"));
Iterator<WebElement> iterator = links.iterator();
url = iterator.next().getAttribute("href");
link = (HttpURLConnection)(new URL(url).openConnection());link.connect();

httpResponse = link.getResponseCode();if(httpResponse >= 400){
    System.out.println(url
    + " is a broken link");
} else{
    System.out.println(url
    + " is a valid link");
}
```

5.4 Results and Discussions

5.4.1 Framework Runtime Improvement

In order to assess the runtime improvement of our methodology and framework by running tests sequentially and in parallel, we illustrate in the Figure 8 the results obtained after implementing the four scenarios proposed above. In the Figure 8a, we have the results of executing the login tests in the scenarios and we notice a linear behavior where the more nodes we add, the more time it takes to execute each test and complete the tasks. In Figure 8b, we observe the behavior and results that prove our improvement after running the same tests in parallel.

Below we show a more detailed analysis between each scenario run sequentially and in parallel, in which we observe the different slopes of each graph as well as the speedup factor analysis for each scenario. The speedup factor refers to the improvement of the execution speed of a task in two ways, by executing the same tests sequentially and in parallel.

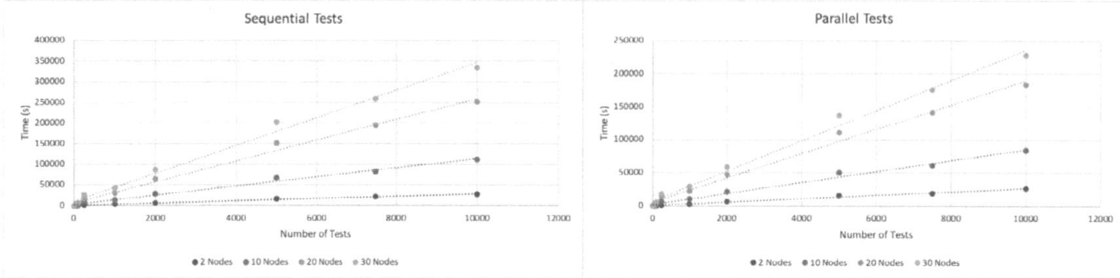

(a) Sequential Tests (b) Parallel Tests

Figure 8. Execution time Sequential vs Parallel

The speedup factor is the ratio between the linear regressions for sequential tests and linear regression for parallel tests. It is defined by the equation $speedup = \frac{sequential}{parallel}$

The linear regressions are computed as it follows. Let be X our data points obtained, it is important to mention that in our case, X is a matrix of values and the variable Y is the vector of times. As a result, we get the different coefficients in θ, if we do all these analyses, we get the equation of linear regression in the following way $\theta = (X'X)^{-1}X'Y$ (X ′ being the transpose of the X matrix).

Below, the execution time of 10 to 10,000 tests in sequential and parallel execution are shown:

- **Scenario 1 – Sequential and parallel**
  - 10 tests execution time sequential: 52s
  - 10,000 test execution time sequential: 27,980s
  - 10 tests execution time parallel: 51s
  - 10,000 tests execution time parallel: 26,600s
  - Speedup factor = 1.067811
- **Scenario 2 – Sequential and parallel in Figure 9**
  - 10 tests execution time sequential: 208s
  - 10,000 tests execution time sequential: 111,920s
  - 10 tests execution time parallel: 156s
  - 10,000 tests execution time parallel: 83,940s
  - Speedup factor = 1.333333
- **Scenario 3 – Sequential and parallel in Figure 10**
  - 10 tests execution time sequential: 468s
  - 10,000 tests execution time sequential: 251,820s
  - 10 tests execution time parallel: 341.64s
  - 10,000 tests execution time parallel: 183,828.6s
  - Speedup factor = 1.369863
- **Scenario 4 – Sequential and parallel**
  - 10 tests execution time sequential: 624s
  - 10,000 tests exec. Time seq.: 335,760s (~4 days)
  - 10 tests execution time parallel (etp): 424.32s
  - 10,000 tests etp: 228,316.8s (~2.5 days)
  - Speedup Factor = 1.470588

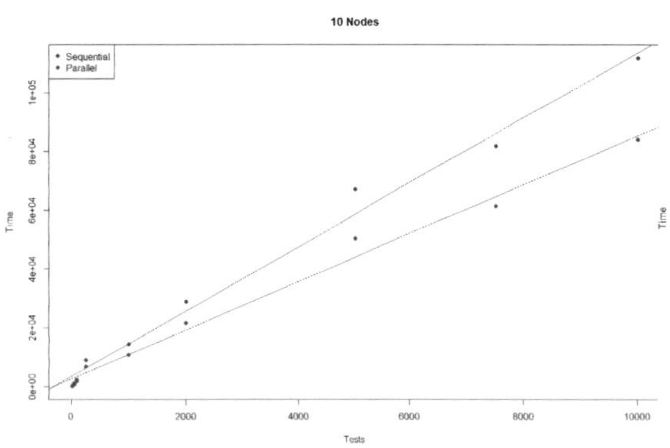

Figure 9. Scenario 2

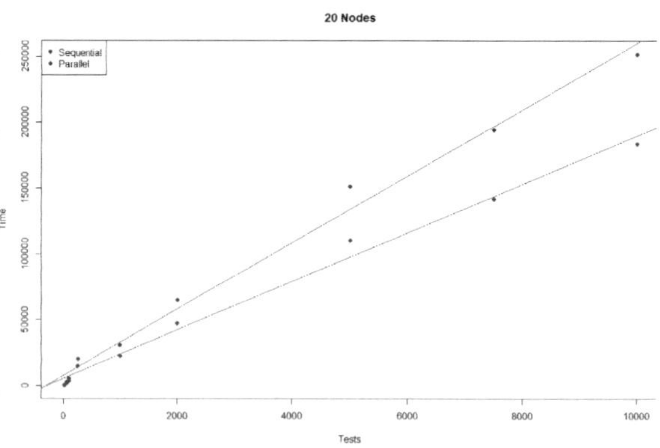

Figure 10. Scenario 3

5.4.2 Compatibility testing automation

In order to test these scenarios, we define criteria for processing the final tests verdicts on test case 2 (Broken Links) as it follows:

- *PASS* is processed if the test manages to find the correct answer to all the links covered.
- *FAIL* is processed if one of the analyzed links returns an HTTP 400 code as response, it means that it is a broken link.
- We process an *ERROR* if the web page does not contain a link, if a null value is returned in our "links" variable after all elements have been captured, or if it is not possible to access the web app.

These are the results we obtained under the tests in our framework. By running Broken link tests, we get automation for compatibility testing that extends the coverage of our tests and is able to deploy them in multiple environments in parallel. It validates the performance of web-based applications across multiple operating systems, architectures, and browsers.

After deploying our different environments and having prepared the tests to be evaluated, in Table 5 we can observe the global market share of each of the browsers used in this test according to Kinsta[5] and the tests results obtained.

Table 5. Compatibility test against 20 websites

Browser	**Market Share**	**Pass**	**Fail**	**Error**
Chrome	77.0%	84%	15%	1%
Safari	8.87%	72%	16%	9%
Firefox	7.69%	85%	12%	3%
Opera	2.43%	63%	19%	18%
Brave	0.05%	79%	15%	6%

Note that the websites for this test case were randomly selected from the database of top websites that Alexa[6] provides, and all had properties optimized for most browsers. As part of the results, we can notice that Opera gets low results compared to the rest. Within the popularity of browsers, the most popular are Google Chrome and Firefox, though in terms of usage Safari makes the list, which is why it was added to these tests.

We also took into account the Brave browser, which is an open-source browser that is gaining popularity and offering improvements in security issues among other things. An important detail about Brave is that it is based on Chromium allowing to perform tests using the same Selenium WebDriver used by Google Chrome.

In the results, we notice that Opera is the one with the highest percentage of errors, this can be either because the webDriver did not get all the links on the page or because the web page could not be loaded correctly, remember that Opera is not one of the most used browsers, so there can be compatibility issues.

In Figure 12, we can observe that we have better results with the Firefox browser, with which we obtained a higher percentage in tests with PASS verdicts, followed by Google Chrome. The behavior of Brave is pretty good, let us take into consideration how it was mentioned before Brave uses the same engine as Chrome, so we can conclude that this is the reason why it has a good coverage. Nevertheless, the overall results of this browser were surprising being the browser with the lowest usage percentage, its results were quite good compared to other competitors like Safari and Opera, which are more popular. In third place we have Safari, this browser has good coverage as well, which is interesting because it is the most used browser by Apple users, therefore, it makes sense that many web-based applications try to be optimized for this browser. Lastly, we have Opera, which impresses us with its performance as it is not that far behind the other browsers.

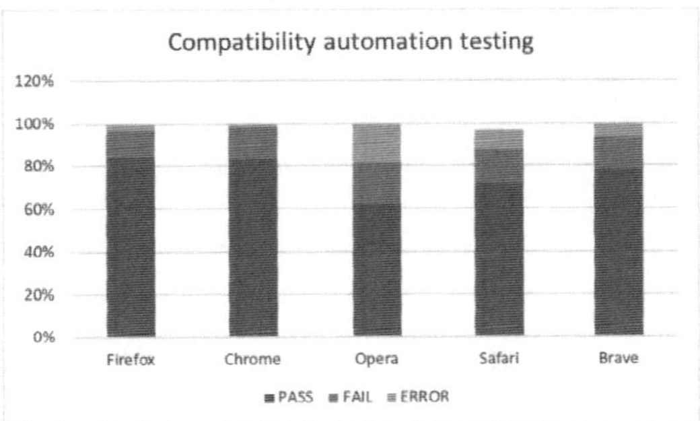

Figure 12. Compatibility Automation Testing results

[5] https://kinsta.com/browser-market-share/
[6] https://www.alexa.com/topsites

At the end of the tests conducted over 20 different applications, the most popular browsers such as Firefox and Google Chrome perform best, both in PASS and ERROR verdicts. It is interesting to note Brave's results has a lower ERROR rate than Safari, as it is a relatively unused browser. What we also found in these tests is that many browsers have issues with pages that are entirely JavaScript based and how to handle that. But even with that, Safari is not that far away from good performance, as is Opera.

6. CONCLUSION AND PERSPECTIVES

In this paper, we have presented a novel framework for testing the compatibility of web-based applications in parallel. Containers have been processed with Docker to enable the design of a scalable testing architecture.

Thousands of test cases have been executed demonstrating the efficiency of our methodology in the running time improvement and the feasibility. Furthermore, these experiments have highlighted that the compatibility of under-used browser can be very good. Finally, these tests have also shown that applications containing most of its code in JavaScript could provide bad compatibility testing results and then issues.

As perspectives, we tackle a highest number of tested web applications, nodes, OS, browsers versions and test scenarios. Increasing these parameters will assess the scalability of our compatibility testing approach as well as raise existing issues within some web applications.

We also plan to perform a machine learning approach that we already applied in a previous work. We guess that such a technique could guide the testers in the execution of the test cases (providing priorities to specific nodes or test scenarios), in defining new test purposes (based on the obtained observations), and in refining the testing verdicts results (in terms of detailing the results of the obtained FAIL and ERROR).

ACKNOWLEDGEMENT

This research was partially supported by Labex DigiCosme (project ANR-11-LABEX-0045- DIGICOSME) operated by French ANR as part of the program "Investissement d'Avenir" Idex Paris-Saclay (ANR-11-IDEX-0003-02).

REFERENCES

Al-Ahmad, B. and Al Debei, K. (2020). Survey of testing methods for web applications. *IJST*, pp 9(12):1–22.

Bertolino, A., Calabró, A., De Angelis, G., Gortázar, F., Lonetti, F., Maes, M., and Tuñón, G. (2020). Quality- of-experience driven configuration of webrtc services through automated testing. In 2020 IEEE *20th International Conference on Software Quality, Reliability and Security (QRS)*, pp 152–159. IEEE.

García, B., Gallego, M., Gortázar, F., and Jiménez, E. (2017). Webrtc testing: State of the art. In *ICSOFT*

García, B., Gallego, M., Gortázar, F., and Munoz-Organero, M. (2020). A survey of the selenium ecosystem. *Electronics*, 9(7):1067.

García, B., López-Fernández, L., Gallego, M., and Gortázar, F. (2016). Testing framework for webrtc services. In Proceedings of the 9th *EAI International Conference on Mobile Multimedia Communications*, pp 40–47.

Hayek, M., Farhat, P., Yamout, Y., Ghorra, C., and Haraty, R. A. (2019). Web 2.0 testing tools: A compendium. In 2019 *International Conference on Innovation and Intelligence for Informatics, Computing, and Technologies (3ICT)*, IEEE.

Heinonen, J. (2020). Design and implementation of au- tomated visual regression testing in a large software product.

Ki, T., Park, C. M., Dantu, K., Ko, S. Y., and Ziarek, L. (2019). Mimic: Ui compatibility testing system for android apps. In 2019 *IEEE/ACM 41st International Conference on Software Engineering (ICSE)*, pp 246–256. IEEE.

Liu, Y., Zhang, T., and Cheng, J. (2019). Survey on crowdbased mobile app testing. In Proceedings of the 2019 *11th International Conference on Machine Learning and Computing*, pp 521–527.

Tanaka, H. (2019). X-brot: Prototyping of compatibility testing tool for web application based on document analysis technology. In *2019 International Conference on Document Analysis and Recognition Workshops*, vol. 7, IEEE.

Villanes, I. K., Endo, A. T., and Dias-Neto, A. C. (2020). Using app attributes to improve mobile device selection for compatibility testing. In *Proceedings of the 5th Brazilian Symposium on Systematic and Automated Software Testing*

WebsiteSetup Editorial (2021). How many websites are there in 2021 websitesetup. https://websitesetup.org/news/how-many-websites-are-there/. Accessed: 2021-02-03.

Yu, J. (2019). Exploration on web testing of website. In *Journal of Physics: Conference Series*, vol 1176, IOP Publishing.

PERSONAL GREENHOUSE MONITORING WITH THE AID OF THE INTERNET OF THINGS ACROSS CONTINENTS

Richard A. Teunen and Henri E. van Rensburg
North-West University, Potchefstroom, South Africa

ABSTRACT

Greenhouses have been a staple of many countries for hundreds of years and personal greenhouses have grown in popularity since the introduction of the Internet of Things (IoT). IoT have allowed users to control a variety of devices over the internet, including the ability to monitor and control personal greenhouses. Affordable technologies such as Raspberry Pi's have been introduced that have the capabilities to control various devices and sensors placed within greenhouses to monitor and evaluate their conditions. The goal of this study was to create an affordable system that is capable of remotely monitoring the conditions within personal greenhouses by utilizing IoT technologies. The completed artefact made use of a Raspberry Pi, along with a GrovePi and various sensors to monitor the conditions within a greenhouse. Furthermore, WhatsApp communication messages were utilized to inform the user of any undesirable changes within their greenhouses. The final artefact proved to be cost-effective and displayed the capabilities of utilizing the IoT architecture to not only monitor personal greenhouses, but to be able to automate certain tasks such as controlling water pumps and light conditions, and provided the users with all of the necessary features through a user friendly interface.

KEYWORDS

Greenhouse Monitoring, System, Internet of Things

1. INTRODUCTION

The Internet of Things (IoT) have made it possible to control a variety of devices over the internet. This technology has been implemented by an increasing number of large-scale organizations to increase their overall efficiency in a multitude of areas such as customer service, decision making, process- and supply chain management, and many more. However, few systems have been developed to assist with monitoring personal greenhouses. Therefore this study aims to determine how IoT technology can be utilized to assist users with monitoring their greenhouses by developing an integrated system to remotely monitor personal greenhouses.

In the next section some background is provided on agricultural IoT systems followed by contextualizing the motivation for the proposed IoT solution to personal greenhouse monitoring and control.

2. BACKGROUND AND LITERATURE

Automation and management systems have been used to manage industrial-sized greenhouses for many years to improve their efficiency and sustainability. These systems are capable of not only monitoring various conditions such as temperature and humidity, but are also capable of automatically performing basic tasks within a greenhouse without the need for any manual labor (Phillips, 2019). In a survey completed in 2018 by the US-based magazine, Greenhouse Grover technology determined that more than 50% of the surveyed farmers were interested in investigating these types of systems especially the machines that would reduce their dependency on labor and that would increase their profit margins (Phillips, 2019).

The IoT architecture is a system of interrelated computing devices or objects capable of connecting to the internet that can transfer data across a network without the need for human-to-human or human-to-computer interaction (Rouse, 2016). These devices can range from heartbeat sensors to GPS chips found within automobiles to track the delivery of goods. IoT technologies have various applications in both industrial and consumer-based fields such as home automation and traffic control. A survey done by IoT Analytics in 2018 investigated over 1600 implemented IoT projects and classified these projects according to their industry sector (Scully, 2018). Although many farmers are interested, only 4% of current IoT projects were aimed at assisting the agricultural sector (Scully, 2018). The Asian and Pacific regions hold the majority of the smart agriculture IoT projects and have seen massive growth in the overall performances of their agricultural institutions, especially those focusing on greenhouses (Scully, 2018).

There have been many agricultural IoT systems that have been successfully implemented to assist farmers with data collection of temperature, humidity, rainfall, and many other key indicators that they can use to effectively determine the needs of their crops. These systems are extremely effective but can also be extremely expensive to implement. Greenhouses are not only being used by large agricultural organizations but are also implemented on a small-scale for personal use. There are currently very few systems out there that can be implemented to monitor these small-scale personal greenhouses efficiently and cost-effectively.

Several conditions have to be carefully monitored within these personal greenhouses to ensure that the plants within them have the best possible chance of blooming. These factors include the greenhouse temperature, humidity, soil pH, water levels, ventilation as well as the amount of sunlight within the greenhouse in order to keep the plants in a healthy state. The optimal values for these conditions will vary depending on the specific plants grown within the greenhouse and will therefore have to be continuously monitored. In order to do this, various available sensors can be attached to computing devices such as Raspberry Pi's or Arduino in order to collect the required data for these conditions. Automation of tasks within a greenhouse could prove difficult depending on the type of instruments within the user's greenhouse. Some personal greenhouses have smart devices such as sprinklers and lights that can be easily controlled remotely but the majority of personal greenhouses will not be equipped with these advanced devices and thus the proposed system will only focus on automating very basic tasks such as turning on the greenhouse light at certain times of the day.

Therefore, the goal of this study is to create a fully functional system based on IoT technology that is capable of both monitoring a greenhouse remotely as well as automating tasks within a greenhouse environment.

2.1 Greenhouses

The idea of growing plants and vegetables within an area where the environment could be monitored and adjusted has been around since Roman times as humans seek to find new ways to improve the amount of produce that their crops could provide (Van den Muijzenberg, 1980). This lead to the creation of greenhouses in the early 1800s that have evolved over the centuries and allow certain crops such as wheat and barley to grow throughout the year instead of only within a certain season.

The very first documented use of artificial methods and structures to grow plants and vegetables throughout the entire year was during Roman times. The Roman gardeners would make use of oiled cloths or white sheets of selenite to cover their structures in the hopes of maintaining the optimal conditions for growing fruits and vegetables especially cucumbers as the Roman Emperors seemed to be quite fond of these fruits (Van den Muijzenberg, 1980). The very first heated greenhouse was reportedly developed in South Korea during the Joseon Dynasty and was said to be mainly used to store and cultivate vegetables during the cold winter seasons.

Both the Netherlands and England experimented with various ways of constructing their greenhouses, however, these greenhouses had trouble with regulating and controlling both the heat and humidity within these greenhouses. A French botanist by the name of Charles Lucien Bonaparte is often credited with the creation of the very first modern-day greenhouse that could be used in a practical way (Dutta & Sen, 2013). Charles Bonaparte originally used the structure to grow medicinal plants that could originally only be found in tropical areas, however many others soon realized the potential of these structures and the greenhouses quickly spread to the estates of the wealthy (Dutta & Sen, 2013). Modern-day greenhouses are described as any structure with walls and a roof made of a transparent material, such as glass, that was capable of housing plants that required controlled environments to be able to grow (Webster, 2019).

The field of botany caused the greenhouse concept to move to the universities and this led universities to compete amongst one another to see who could build the largest and most efficient structures possible (Van den Muijzenberg, 1980). Greenhouses have come a long way in both sophistication and affordability and construction techniques for managing the conditions within the greenhouses have been developed and refined since then.

2.1.1 Conditions to Monitor within Greenhouses

Several conditions have to be carefully monitored within these personal greenhouses to ensure that the plants within them have the best possible chance of blooming. These factors include the greenhouse temperature, humidity as well as the amount of sunlight within the greenhouse. The pH- and water levels of the soil within the greenhouse also plays a major role in keeping the plants in a healthy state.

Temperature - greenhouses must be able to maintain their designated temperature as many crops will only prosper under specific conditions and could die if the inner conditions of the greenhouse were to change drastically. The biggest problem with heating greenhouses is the inability of the coverings of the greenhouses to trap the heat inside the greenhouse as the coverings were specifically designed to allow light to filter into the structure which greatly decreased their ability to insulate the structure efficiently (Kurpaska, 2014).

Humidity - every different crop has its own unique optimal VPD (Vapor-pressure deficit) range and these can even vary depending on the current growth stage of the crops. If the humidity in a greenhouse is to low it often stresses plants by accelerating the transpiration properties of the plants to a level that the roots are incapable of handling or translocating (Peterson, 2018). Ensuring that there is a constant circulation of air through the greenhouse is an extremely cost-effective manner of managing the humidity levels within greenhouses.

Soil pH and Water levels - water is supplied to the plants through various means (through either automated or manual means) and this water contains various dissolved mineral elements that are crucial in providing the crops with the required nutrients required to grow (Pennisi & Thomas, 2009).

Light intensity - these artificial light sources are especially useful in the winter months where any natural light hours are limited or in climates where drastic weather changes occur regularly. Different crops often require different types of light such as partial shade, full sun, or any other similar light condition so the greenhouse must be monitored to ensure that the crops receive the correct of light to allow them to grow as efficiently as possible.

Ventilation - the main goal of ventilation is to ensure that both the temperature and humidity within the greenhouse are regulated and remain at a stable level as well as ensuring the continuous movement of air within the greenhouse (Parra et al., 2004). Many pathogens that can cause harm to crops are only capable of surviving in still air conditions so by continuously providing the greenhouse with air movement ventilation can protect the crops from many of these harmful diseases (Parra et al., 2004).

2.2 The Internet of Things

The IoT architecture is a system of interrelated computing devices or objects capable of connecting to the internet that can transfer data across a network without the need for human-to-human or human-to-computer interaction (Rouse, 2016). These devices can range from heartbeat sensors to GPS chips found within automobiles to track the delivery of goods. These devices can vary, however, they have some necessary components in common.

2.2.1 Components of the Internet of Things

There are four major components required to create a fully functioning IoT system namely; sensors and actuators, connectivity, data processing and a user interface.

Sensors and actuators - sensors are any device that is used to collect any minute details from the surrounding environment and can range from incredibly complex devices such as live video feeds or can be simple devices such as an electronic thermostat (García et al., 2017). Actuators are any devices that are capable of accepting a set of instructions and then cause either the contacted device or any connected devices to perform a certain task (García et al., 2017). Devices can consist of multiple sensors and actuators that work together to complete their tasks. The greenhouse monitoring system will have various sensors such as temperature and humidity sensors that will capture the conditions within the greenhouse and will make use of relays to power and control any of the devices within the greenhouse such as lights or heating devices.

Connectivity - once the sensors have collected all of the data regarding their environments they need to process this data to be able to make assumptions regarding the environment and can then decide if any actions need to be taken. This data, however, needs a transport medium to be able to transfer data from the device to a cloud processing infrastructure. These devices can be connected to the cloud structures using various means such as Bluetooth, WiFi, Wide area networks, and many more (Zaidan et al., 2018).

Data processing - once the data has been collected and transported to the cloud processing location the software needs to quickly and efficiently process the acquired data to forward or make sense of the data.

Various data analysis methods such as deep machine learning have greatly increased the ability of these processing infrastructures and have expanded the applications for the Internet of Things (Pramanik et al., 2018).

User Interface - the Internet of Things system has now obtained data, sent and through for processing, and has done all the necessary processing to retrieve valuable information from the retrieved data. After this, the system needs to be able to share information and should also provide the ability to perform any required actions through the actuators connected to the IoT system.

3. GREENHOUSE MONITORING SYSTEM

The resulting system that was developed to monitor personal greenhouses will be discussed along with the necessary components required to monitor and display the greenhouse information to the user.

The greenhouse monitoring system consists of seven main components shown in Figure 1. These seven components will be discussed in the sections below along with the role and functioning of each component contributing to the success of the system as whole.

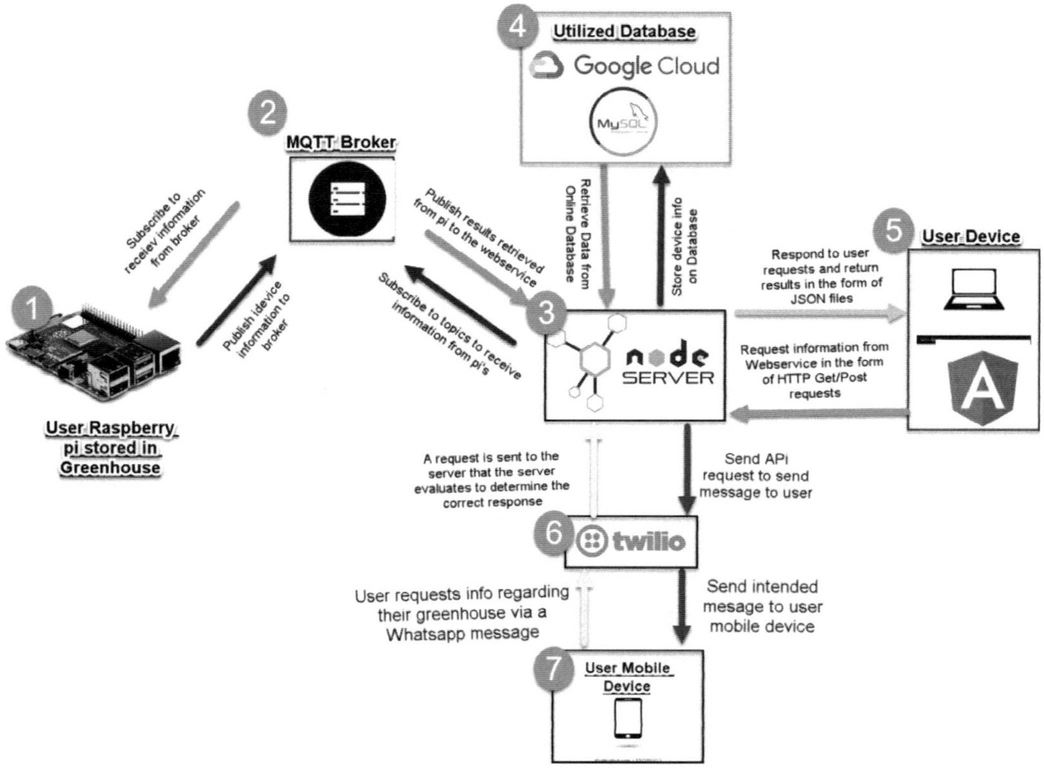

Figure 1. Greenhouse monitoring system

3.1 Raspberry Pi (Physical Monitoring Device)

The device used to monitor the greenhouses of the users was a Raspberry Pi 3 that also has a GrovePi hat (add-on board) attached that provides additional digital and analog ports that the GrovePi sensors can easily attach to without the need for any additional setup and configuration. Figure 2 displays the full functioning prototype of the created system and each of the connected components (A to J) will be discussed below.

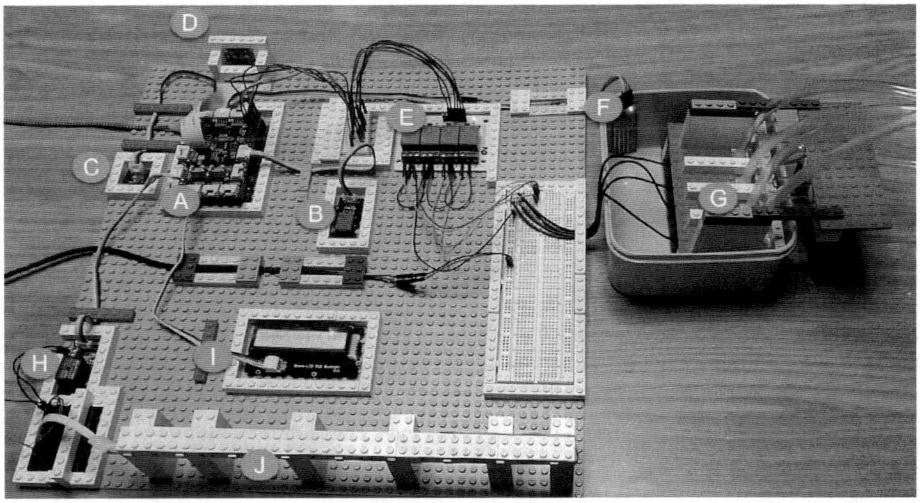

Figure 2. Raspberry Pi and components

A. The main component of the developed prototype is the Raspberry Pi along with the GrovePi hat is used to capture all of the greenhouse conditions from the attached sensors and makes use of the MQTT protocol to transfer information between the greenhouse and the global Web service.

B. This component is a temperature and humidity sensor that was connected in order to measure the temperature in degrees Celsius and the humidity as a percentage.

C. A light sensor, Light Dependent Resistor (LDR), was attached that could measure the amount of light within the greenhouse and the returned light intensity measured in Lux. This light sensor was used in conjunction with a LED strip (Component J) that would automatically turn on when low light levels was detected or the inverse and could also be manually controlled by the user. The sensor was also set up in such a manner that the light emitted from Component J would not affect any of its readings.

D. A camera module was attached to periodically take photos of the greenhouse, storing them on the Raspberry Pi and having the ability to send these images to the main server.

E. An addition of 4 relays that were capable of powering four water pumps that could automatically provide water to any of the plants stored within the Greenhouse. These can be turned on by the user using the designed Web app or through the use of WhatsApp commands that is discussed in the next sections.

F. A water level sensor has been connected and placed within the water reserve that will be used by the water pumps (Component G). This sensor will alert the user if the water reserves of the greenhouse are running low and will also prevent the pumps from running if the reserve is low.

G. As mentioned above there are four water pumps with hoses attached to them and they are able to transfer water from the reserve into any of the plants stored within the greenhouse. These pumps were powered using a 5V power source separate from the Raspberry Pi power source.

H. An additional relay has been connected to the GrovePi to power the LED strip that works in conjunction with the light sensor (Component C).

I. For display purposes, an LCD was connected that is used to provide key information directly to the user. This could be used to show the current conditions within the greenhouse or could turn red when the water reserve is running low.

J. The final attached component is an LED strip that is controlled by Component H and receives power from a 12V power source separate from the Raspberry Pi power source. The user can set these lights to go on and off depending on the amount of light measured by Component C or could be manually turned on using WhatsApp or the web application.

In addition to the connected components, the Raspberry Pi has some useful features and services that could be set up that assisted with the development and overall success of the project. These features and services include; Ethernet and WiFi connections, FTP server, VNC Viewer and the Paho MQTT python library. The Raspberry Pi is able to connect to a network or the internet using the equipped Ethernet Port or the built in WiFi adapter, where the latter was used to connect to the user's home network. The Dexter Industries operating system that was used on the Raspberry Pi which comes with File Transfer Protocol (FTP) software that makes it easy to transfer files between to and from the Raspberry Pi. Another useful tool, provided by the Raspberry Pi is the ability to connect to VNC Viewer that is a screen sharing application that allows the user to remotely control the Raspberry Pi. This means that users can use their personal computers to monitor their Raspberry Pi instead of connecting an additional monitor, mouse and, keyboard to the system within the greenhouse. Additional GPIO (General Purpose Input Output) pins are available on the Raspberry Pi that can be used to connect any additional components required by any specific application. Paho MQTT is an open-source python library that allowed the Raspberry Pi to connect to a MQTT broker enabling the application to send and receive messages from the global web service as long as a valid internet connection is maintained. All of the information captured in the greenhouse is stored locally on the Raspberry Pi and is periodically sent to the web service where the online database is synced.

3.2 MQTT and MQTT Brokers

In order to facilitate communication between the Raspberry Pi and the developed web service, the system made use of an IoT protocol known as MQTT (Message Queuing Telemetry Transport). The protocol is described as a lightweight IoT protocol that makes use of the publish-subscribe network to transfer messages between devices. The protocol allows devices to subscribe to certain topics and also allows the device to publish messages to certain topics.

By subscribing to a topic the device will immediately be notified if a different device posts a message on the subscribed topic and this is an excellent way to quickly share information between our Raspberry Pi and the hosted web service. In the developed system the Raspberry Pi subscribes to certain user-defined commands such as TurnOnLights or TurnOnPumps and then the web service can use these topics to control aspects of the greenhouse. Similarly, the this, the greenhouse can then publish or post all of the information has been collected and can then be processed by the web service.

3.3 Node Web Service

The Node web service is one of the most important components in this project as it is responsible for facilitating communication between all of the other main components.

The web service will receive streams of information from all of the registered greenhouse monitoring systems and will process and transform the data into a format that can be entered into the database. On average the web service will receive 6-10 readings from the greenhouse per minute, however the device will calculate the average per minute which is stored within the online database. The web service is responsible for evaluating all of the values that are received from the greenhouse monitoring systems and must be able to alert users if the conditions within the greenhouse exceed the predetermined limits. The Twilio messenger application (discussed in section 3.6) will be used to send WhatsApp messages to communicate any irregular conditions. The web service will also integrate with the developed web application to provide the user with a visual representation of the greenhouse conditions and provide the website with the latest available information stored within the online database. The created web service will be the only component that is able to interact directly with the global application and thus the service must ensure that the integrity of the database is maintained whilst also ensuring that all of the other applications have access to all of the information required to perform their tasks.

The final responsibility of the web service is to handle any commands that are received from the greenhouse owners via WhatsApp messages. The Twilio API will receive the WhatsApp messages from the user and will pass the received message to the web service. It is the responsibility of the web service to interpret the message and it must ensure that the correct actions are performed based on the message received.

3.4 Online MySQL Database

For the Online database, the project utilizes the Google SQL online platform to host a MySQL database on one of their servers meaning that the database will always be online and be available to the web service without the need to host the database locally. For the development phase, the web service makes use of a cloud SQL proxy to be allowed to connect to the database and the main website of the web service, which has been whitelisted on the Google Cloud SQL platform meaning that the database is protected from outside interference whilst still providing the web service with the appropriate rights to access and change the database.

3.5 Angular Web Application (User Device)

The Angular web application is the primary way for users use to gain access to greenhouse information and is hosted online so that it is available to all users at any given time and has been optimized for browsers on personal computers or laptops. The web application allow users to create an account that will be linked to their greenhouse monitoring device. The accounts will ensure that users only have access to their own greenhouse data with extra security measures put in place and enabled on the web application.

The website displays a list of all of the available devices that the user has linked to their account and will allow them to retrieve the latest information received from their greenhouse using the web service and global database. The website will also display key information such as the last time the device was updated as well as the current status of all of their devices.

3.6 Twilio Messenger API

The Twilio messenger API is a commercial API that specializes in creating automatic messenger applications and has an additional feature that allows users to create a WhatsApp sandbox that is capable of receiving messages and can also redirect incoming messages to an alternative URL where they can be interpreted. The node web service is able to integrate with the Twilio messenger API and is therefore able to receive-, and send messages to any number that is registered or activated on the WhatsApp sandbox. Any incoming messages will be redirected to the node web service where additional instructions have been coded on how to handle the incoming messages.

3.7 User Mobile Device

At this stage the system does not include a standalone mobile application, however, the user will be able to request their greenhouse information from the web service and will also be able to send simple commands to their greenhouse device using WhatsApp on any number that was registered to their account.

4. RESULTS

The Raspberry Pi (physical monitoring device) as illustrated in Figure 2, represents the implementation of an IoT greenhouse monitoring device and was powered using an external power bank capable of powering the GrovePi and all the sensors along with an additional power supply for the water pumps and the led strip.

The resulting IoT greenhouse monitoring system was set up with monitoring devices in two locations across different continents, with one device being set up in South Africa and the other device being set up in Belgium. This was done to prove that the device is fully capable of being placed anywhere around the globe and will still be able to function correctly. The web service was hosted locally (in South Africa at that time) and each device was given a unique ID that could be used to connect to the MQTT broker and the developed web service. The devices were both kept online for 3 days and data was continuously collected from both these devices at the same time, showcasing the ability of the web service to handle incoming data from both devices at physically different locations at the same time as shown in Figure 3.

The greenhouse monitoring system proved to be able to store the information captured by the two greenhouses without any unforeseen problems. Various conditions were tested to simulate a change in the greenhouse environment in order to test whether the web service would notify the user of these changes. Every time the greenhouse environment changes, the user would get a WhatsApp message notifying them of the changes that were encountered in the greenhouse.

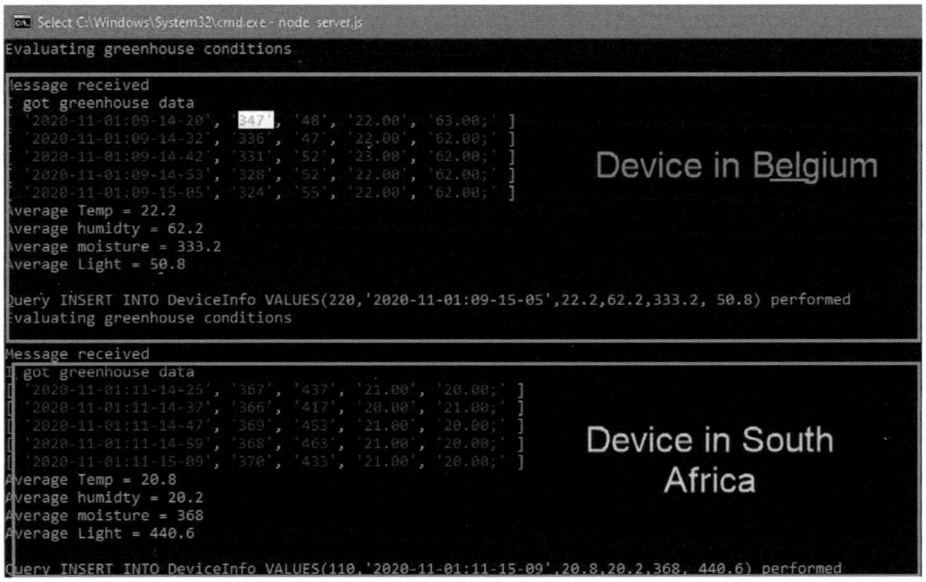

Figure 3. Greenhouse data from different continents

An example of these WhatsApp notifications is shown in Figure 4. These messages illustrate the notifications received when abnormal greenhouse conditions is detected such as when water in the reservoir was running low. Figure 4 furthermore illustrates the results of the backwards communication to the monitoring device to perform a specific action based on a command or to obtain sensory data of current greenhouse conditions. The “Get info” command provides the user with a brief summary of all of their devices and their connected sensors within the greenhouse.

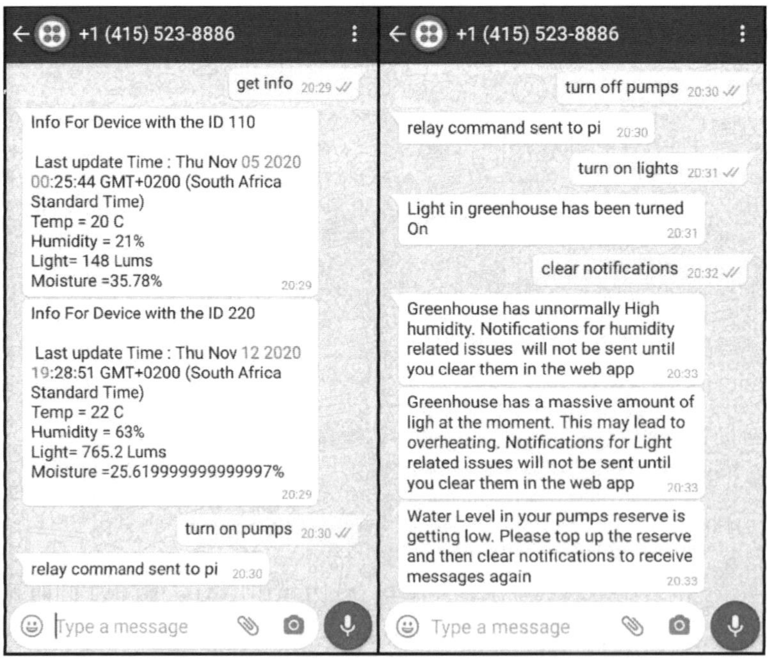

Figure 4. Greenhouse WhatsApp notifications

In addition, there were various other WhatsApp commands to control certain components within the greenhouse. "Turn on Pumps" and "Turn off Pumps" will turn all of the Pumps that are connected to your device on or off. Similarly with "Turn on light" and "Turn off light" to control to lighting in the greenhouse and override the automatic switching of lights. The "Clear Notifications" command can be used to clear all of the notifications that the user has received and will allow the system to send notification messages again.

In addition to the functional results achieved by the greenhouse monitoring system, the cost of the resulting system is of interest as this is one of the concerning factors that prevent the adoption and implementation of small-scale greenhouse monitoring systems. The ZAR (South African Rand) to USD (United States Dollar) exchange rate during the creation of the artefact was $1 = R15,40 which was used for calculating the price of all of the components which resulted in the entire monitoring system costing only R2700 ($175). Hosting the online database cost no additional funds and was completely free with a Google account and the web service hosted by the Google App Engine at no additional cost.

5. SUMMARY AND CONCLUSION

This study highlighted the fact that there is a need for technological solutions to personal greenhouse monitoring however few commercial system are available to suit the needs of small-scale implementations in a cost-effective way. Affordable technologies such as Raspberry Pi's have been introduced that have the capabilities to control various devices and sensors placed within greenhouses to monitor and evaluate their conditions. By investigating the required conditions to monitor within greenhouses and the capabilities of the IoT architecture, key components was identified to guide the development of a comprehensive system capable of remotely monitoring the conditions within personal greenhouses.

The resulting personal greenhouse monitoring system proved to be cost-effective solution that displayed the capabilities of the IoT architecture to not only monitor personal greenhouses, but to be able to automate certain tasks remotely through a fully functioning IoT system.

REFERENCES

Dutta, I. & Sen, V. 2013. Greenhouse farming in gujarat: A march towards sustainable agriculture. *OIDA International Journal of Sustainable Development*, Vol. 6, No. 8, pp 63-68.

García, C.G. et al. 2017. A review about smart objects, sensors, and actuators. *International Journal of Interactive Multimedia & Artificial Intelligence*, Vol. 4, No. 3, pp 7–10.

Kurpaska, S., 2014. Energy effects during using the glass with different properties in a heated greenhouse. *Technical Sciences/University of Warmia and Mazury in Olsztyn*, Vol. 17, No. 4, pp 351-360.

Parra, J.P. et al. 2004. Natural ventilation of parral greenhouses. *Biosystems Engineering*, Vol. 87, No. 3, pp 355–366.

Pennisi, S.V. & Thomas, P.A. 2009. Essential pH management in greenhouse crops-part 1: PH and plant nutrition. Athens: University of Georgia. https://secure.caes.uga.edu/extension/publications/files/ Date of Access: 12 June 2020.

Peterson, D. 2018. Managing humidity in the greenhouse. Sparta: Greenhouse Product News. https://gpnmag.com/article/managing-humidity-in-the-greenhouse/ Date of access: 12 June 2020.

Phillips, L. 2019. Latest trends in greenhouse technology. Sutton: Farmer's weekly. https://www.farmersweekly.co.za/agri-technology/farming-for-tomorrow/latest-trends-in-greenhouse-technology/ Date of access: 25 March 2020.

Pramanik, P. K. D. et al. 2018. *IoT data processing: The different archetypes and their security & privacy assessments.* 3rd ed. Copenhagen: River Publishers.

Rouse, M. 2016. *Internet of Things (IoT).* IoT Agenda. http://internetofthingsagenda.techtarget.com/definition/Internet-of-Things-IoT Date of access: 26 June 2020.

Scully, P. 2018. *The top 10 IoT segments in 2018.* Hamburg: Iot Analytics. https://iot-analytics.com/top-10-iot-segments-2018-real-iot-projects/ Date of access: 16 March 2020.

Van den Muijzenberg, E. W. 1980. *A history of greenhouses.* 1st ed. London: Oxford University Press.

Webster, M. 2019. *Greenhouse definition.* https://www.merriam-webster.com/dictionary/greenhouse Date of access: 10 April 2020.

Zaidan, A.A. et al. 2018. A survey on communication components for IoT-based technologies in smart homes. *Telecommunication Systems*, Vol. 69, No. 1, pp 1-25.

PRESERVING INDIGENOUS KNOWLEDGE THROUGH E-LEARNING: A CONCEPTUAL THEORETICAL MODEL

Katazo N. Amunkete[1], Corne J. van Staden[2] and Marthie A. Schoeman[2]
[1]Namibia University of Science and Technology, Faculty of Computing and Informatics
13 Jackson Kaujeua Street, Windhoek, Namibia
[2]University of South Africa, School of Computing
28 Pioneer Ave, Florida Park, Roodepoort, 1709, South Africa

ABSTRACT

Indigenous knowledge can advance sustainable development, and its preservation is of the utmost importance. Indigenous knowledge is mostly present within older generations, and without preservation, it will die with its custodians. African communities rely heavily on indigenous knowledge, which is dynamic and is constantly evolving. A digital tool that can preserve practices relating the knowledge can highlight its dynamic nature. This paper presents a conceptual theoretical model to guide the design of an e-learning system aimed at facilitating the preservation of indigenous knowledge. Data was collected utilizing a literature review. The conceptual theoretical model shows that preserving indigenous knowledge through e-learning would require, among other things, engagement with the relevant knowledge custodians and compliance with necessary legal requirements.

KEYWORDS

Digital Preservation, E-learning, Indigenous Knowledge, Indigenous Knowledge Models, Indigenous Knowledge Preservation

1. INTRODUCTION

There is a lack of information technology tools aimed at preserving and disseminating indigenous knowledge (Dlamini & Ocholla, 2018). Indigenous knowledge is not static and is constantly changing. E-learning was investigated as a technological tool to preserve and present the knowledge in a way that can allow for its dynamic nature.

E-learning refers to digital learning technologies that enable learning to take place. E-learning is viewed as an internet technology that allows one to learn from anywhere as long as the person has a computing device and access to the internet (Potcovaru, 2018). E-learning enables implicit knowledge to be internalized by the individuals that work through the content presented on it (Liebowitz & Frank, 2011).

A major technology being used in digital learning technologies is the Learning Management System (LMS) (Al-Busaidi, 2013). An LMS provides course management capabilities and administrative tools, such as the development, documentation, and delivery of e-learning content (Al-Busaidi, 2013). LMS are used because of their advantages, such as "convenience, flexibility, accessibility, and cost-effectiveness" (Al-Shboul and Alsmadi, 2010, pp. 4-5). The internet allows for indigenous knowledge to be made available globally (Dlamini & Ocholla, 2018) and has raised interest in indigenous knowledge (Dlamini, 2017).

The study contributes to indigenous knowledge preservation efforts by developing a conceptual theoretical model to guide the design of an e-learning system aimed at facilitating the digital preservation of indigenous knowledge.

The e-learning system is envisioned to facilitate the preservation and transformation of explicit indigenous knowledge by converting it to tacit knowledge and internalizing it within people that will make use of the e-learning system.

An implementation of the model will be beneficial to researchers and other people interested in learning about indigenous knowledge. The preservation of the knowledge is expected to be two-fold: knowledge preserved in the repository of the e-learning system, as well as knowledge preserved internally within the individuals working through the content on the system.

The rest of the paper is structured as follows, in Section 2 the methodology used in the study is provided, Section 3 is on the literature review, in Section 4 the conceptual theoretical model developed in the study is discussed and the paper ends with a conclusion in Section 5.

2. METHODOLOGY

A qualitative research approach was followed. Data was collected using a literature review. The literature review focused on existing indigenous knowledge models and frameworks, and these assisted in identifying possible requirements for a conceptual theoretical model for preserving indigenous knowledge. A search on models and frameworks used in preserving indigenous knowledge revealed five models and frameworks.

3. LITERATURE REVIEW

Literature searches were carried out on the following databases: Science Direct, JSTOR, Emerald Insight, ACM Digital Library, ProQuest Science and Technology, Taylor and Francis; IEEExplore, and Google Scholar.

This section is divided into two sections. In Section 3.1, indigenous knowledge is discussed, while existing models and frameworks that are used for the digital preservation of indigenous knowledge are discussed in Section 3.2. Requirements used to develop a conceptual theoretical model for preserving indigenous knowledge are also provided in Section 3.2. This conceptual theoretical model is discussed in Section 4.

3.1 Indigenous Knowledge

Plockey defines indigenous knowledge as "people or things originating from a particular place and native to the place" (2015, p. 33). Indigenous knowledge is mostly present in the minds of its custodians and is primarily transferred through an oral tradition, i.e. spoken communication and demonstrations that are not easily transferred (Sraku-Lartey et al., 2017). When a custodian dies without sharing their indigenous knowledge, the knowledge dies with them and is lost forever (Moahi, 2012). The oral tradition of exchanging indigenous knowledge from generation to generation is also ineffective, as there can be miscommunication within the transmission. It is thus important to document indigenous knowledge for preservation (Agyepong, 2017).

3.2 Models and Frameworks used in the Digital Preservation of Indigenous Knowledge

The models and frameworks for digitally preserving indigenous knowledge found in literature are:

- The Tripartite Digitization Model (TDM) in Figure , used to digitize indigenous knowledge (Rodil & Winschiers-Theophilus, 2018).

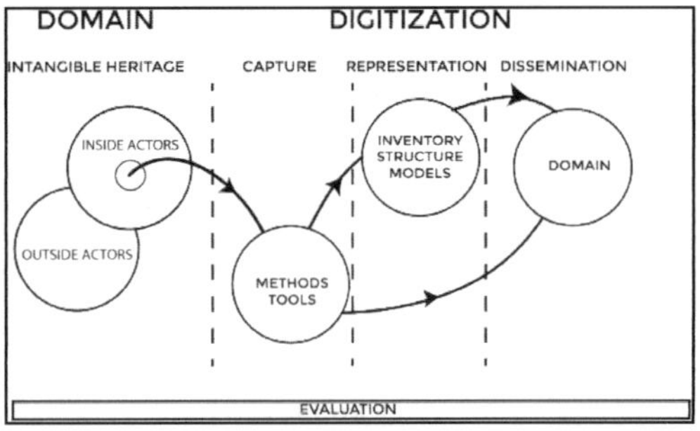

Figure 1. The Tripartite Digitization Model (TDM)

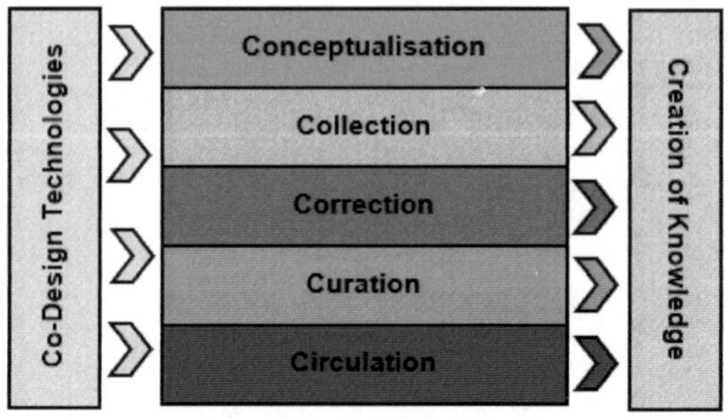

Figure 2. The 7C Model

- The Digital Indigenous Knowledge Preservation Framework (The 7C Model) in Figure 2, designed to guide the process of preserving indigenous knowledge with the use of information technologies (Maasz et al., 2018).
- The Traditional Wood Carvers Database Framework (TWCDF) in Figure 3, developed to preserve indigenous knowledge on the word sculpting skill of carving (Coleman, 2016).

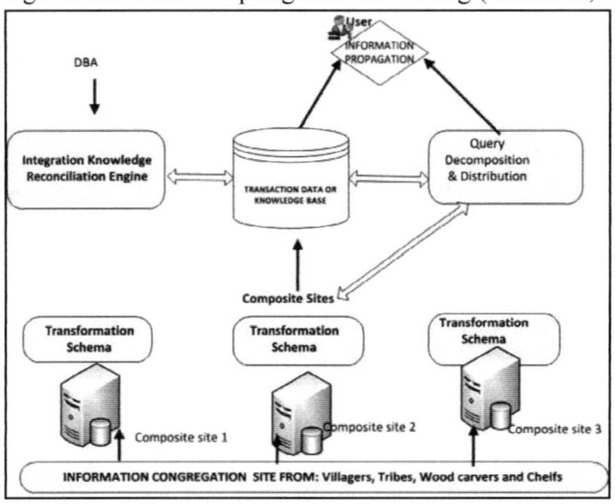

Figure 3. Traditional Wood Carvers Database Framework

- The National IK Management System (NIKMAS) Software Architecture Framework in Figure 4, developed to preserve South African indigenous knowledge (Fogwill et al., 2011).
- The E-cultural Heritage and Natural History (ECHNH) in Figure 5, used to store, disseminate, and preserve indigenous knowledge on cultural heritage and natural history in a digital format (Kurniawan et al., 2011).

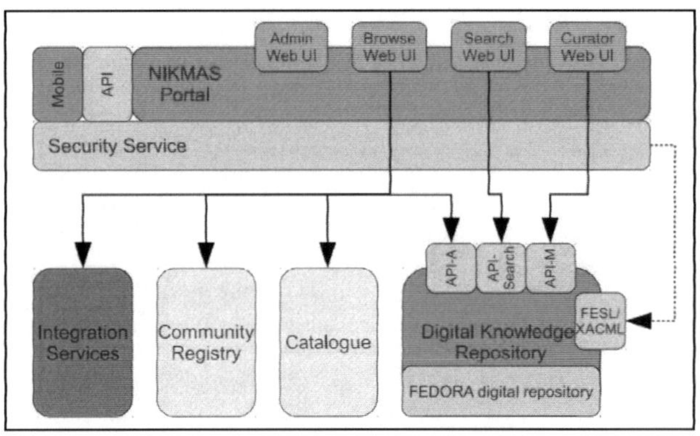

Figure 4. NIKMAS Software Architecture Framework

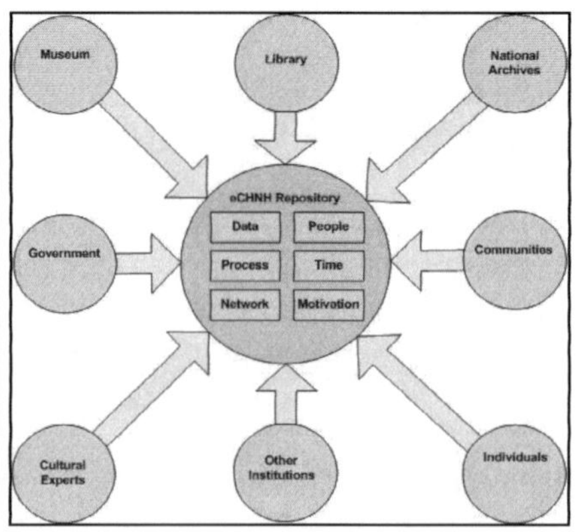

Figure 5. ECHNH Framework

Nine requirements identified from the five models and frameworks were used to develop a conceptual theoretical model for the preservation of indigenous knowledge. Table 1 displays these requirements and the type of knowledge and knowledge transformation that they represent. The requirements, Data recovery mechanisms; Access control and authentication mechanisms; Identification of stakeholders, and Legal requirements do not involve knowledge transformation. The first seven requirements were abstracted from the existing models and frameworks, while the last two emerged from other literature on indigenous knowledge preservation.

Table 1. Requirements from the literature

Requirement to include	**References**	**Type of knowledge**	**Knowledge transformation process**
Methods and tools to capture indigenous knowledge	(Rodil & Rehm, 2015); (Maasz et al., 2018)	Tacit knowledge	- Socialization - Externalization - Combination
Tools to disseminate the data	(Rodil & Rehm, 2015); (Maasz et al., 2018)	Explicit knowledge	- Externalization
Co-designing with and validation by indigenous communities	(Rodil & Rehm, 2015); (Maasz et al., 2018); (Rodil & Winschiers-Theophilus, 2018)	Tacit knowledge	- Socialization - Externalization
Community of practice	(Kok, 2005)	Explicit knowledge	- Externalization
Digital knowledge repository (database)	(Fogwill et al., 2011)	Explicit knowledge	- Externalization - Combination
Data recovery mechanisms	(Coleman, 2016); (Nurhudatiana et al., 2018)		
Access control and authentication mechanisms	(Fogwill et al., 2011)		
Identification of stakeholders	(Kurniawan et al., 2011)		
Legal requirements	(Shizha, 2017); (Gallert et al., 2018)		

3.2.1 Requirements Abstracted from Current Models and Frameworks

The following requirements were identified from the existing models and frameworks:

- The TDM and 7C models identified capturing data and disseminating it to its intended audience as important in a model for indigenous knowledge preservation. Other important requirements were co-designing with indigenous communities, selecting the media to be used to represent the data and the technology to be used to disseminate it. Methods for capturing the indigenous knowledge data should be determined and the LMS to be used for dissemination identified. The co-design principle highlights the need for indigenous knowledge holders to evaluate the knowledge captured and presented on a technological tool to ensure its accuracy before dissemination.
- The TWCDF highlights the importance of ensuring data recovery in case of system failures. An e-learning system comprises a database to store the content presented on the system (Nurhudatiana et al., 2018). In-built functionalities are present on e-learning platforms that safeguard against the loss of valuable data (Bouchrika et al., 2018).
- The NIKMAS includes a Data Knowledge Repository that emphasizes the importance of having a repository to store indigenous knowledge which users of a system can query. The database on e-learning systems acts as a knowledge repository for queries on data (Tessier & Dalkir, 2016).
- The NIKMAS also shows that authentication and authorization processes are paramount to a system. Most e-learning systems employ basic authentication procedures using a username and password. However, stronger authentication measures such as biometric procedures are explored (Fenu et al., 2018).

- The ECHNH highlights the importance of identifying stakeholders to ensure the success of a digital preservation endeavor. Different stakeholders are needed to determine their roles and responsibilities in the preservation endeavor (Ravenwood et al., 2015).

3.2.2 Additional Requirements from the literature

The requirements obtained from other literature are:

The protection of indigenous knowledge is of paramount importance to its preservation and thus a legal requirements factor was added to the model to be developed (Gallert et al., 2018; Mazonde & Thomas, 2007). Codifying indigenous knowledge into explicit formats and rendering it for public consumption is a controversial issue and intellectual property rights need to be taken into consideration when disseminating it, therefore policies and procedures are required to ensure a valid portrayal of the indigenous knowledge according to set procedures (Shizha, 2017). The use of information technology in the preservation of indigenous knowledge should not infringe on copyright issues (Mazonde & Thomas, 2007).

To effectively preserve indigenous knowledge, the knowledge should be managed innovatively and creatively; a community of practice consisting of three important stakeholders: the community, outsiders, and facilitators, should be formed to facilitate the transfer of knowledge (Kok, 2005). The community possesses the knowledge and can contribute to the knowledge base. Outsiders are people who have knowledge that can be used by the community. Facilitators have the responsibility of managing the knowledge base.

4. A CONCEPTUAL THEORETICAL MODEL FOR THE DIGITAL PRESERVATION OF INDIGENOUS KNOWLEDGE

The requirements were incorporated into a conceptual theoretical model for the digital preservation of indigenous knowledge. The model is displayed in Figure 6.

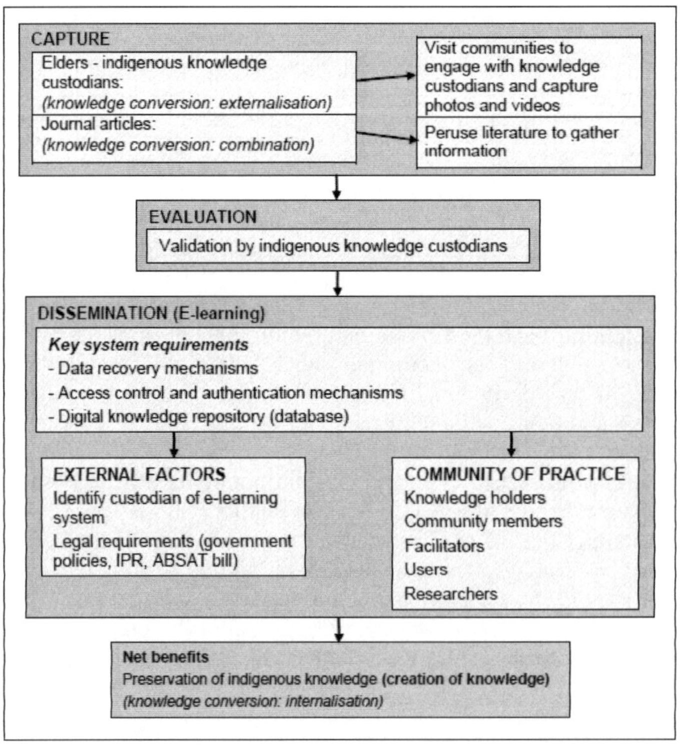

Figure 6. A conceptual theoretical model for the preservation of indigenous knowledge

The model comprises five components:

- Capture – the methods by which the knowledge to be presented on the e-learning system is captured. In the conceptual theoretical model, indigenous knowledge is captured from journal articles and indigenous knowledge holders. Media used to capture knowledge from indigenous knowledge holders include inter alia photos and videos. Journal articles were included, as the authors used information from journal articles to develop the content presented on the prototype e-learning system. Transforming knowledge from a tacit format into an explicit format is referred to as externalization while transforming explicit knowledge into another form of explicit knowledge is referred to as combination (P. N. Dlamini, 2017; Mangare & Li, 2018; Nonaka, 1994). The tacit indigenous knowledge from elders will be externalized into an explicit format for presentation on the e-learning system. The knowledge from the journal articles will be transformed into another format of explicit knowledge that can be presented on the e-learning system.
- Evaluation – the validation of the information on the e-learning system by the knowledge custodians. Indigenous knowledge holders will be required to validate the information presented on the e-learning system.
- Dissemination – the e-learning platform is the disseminating tool, and key requirements to preserve indigenous knowledge are included under the dissemination component:
    - Data recovery mechanisms to ensure the recovery of the indigenous knowledge data preserved on the system in the event of a disaster that results in the loss of the data.
    - Access control and authentication mechanisms to ensure that users are assigned different roles.
    - A data repository to ensure the storage of the indigenous knowledge data and enable users to query the repository.
- External factors – factors outside the e-learning system, including identifying the custodian of the e-learning system and adhering to legal requirements such as government policies when designing and presenting information on the e-learning system. External requirements will impact the information that can be presented on the e-learning system. A custodian of the e-learning system who will be responsible for making the system available to the public needs to be identified. Possible custodians include a public library or a government or private institution that deals with the preservation of indigenous knowledge. The custodian should have a direct interest in preserving indigenous knowledge.
- A community of practice – identifying the stakeholders of the system and their roles and responsibilities. The stakeholders should be identified to determine who will add knowledge to the system and who the intended audience is. The intended audience may include "urbanized" indigenous people as well as researchers who want to learn more about indigenous knowledge. The community of practice including community members, facilitators, or outsiders such as authors, can contribute knowledge.

The community of practice and external factors play an important role in dissemination. The net benefit to be derived from using the e-learning system is the internalization of tacit knowledge by its users from the explicit indigenous knowledge presented on the system. This internalization will result in the preservation of the knowledge. Indigenous knowledge is unique to a community or group of people (Tharakan, 2015) and thus technology tools being developed for its preservation should be unique to the community in which the indigenous knowledge is located (Agber, 2017).

The authors acknowledge that the model may not be adequate for rural areas where there is a lack of technological infrastructure such as electricity and access to the internet. It is most suitable for an environment with adequate infrastructure to support e-learning.

5. CONCLUSION

This study contributes to the theoretical body of knowledge on e-learning and the digital preservation of indigenous knowledge through the development of a conceptual theoretical model for digitally preserving indigenous knowledge via an e-learning platform. There is a need to digitally preserve indigenous knowledge because most of the elders who are the custodians of the indigenous knowledge of their communities are advancing in age and dying. At the time of this study, the authors did not come across any literature on e-learning being used in preserving indigenous knowledge. Only literature written in the English language was consulted.

There is a need to validate the developed model in a prototype, e.g., to present knowledge about indigenous plants used for medicinal purposes and extend it. Other types of data collection tools, such as interviews, could be explored to obtain additional data. Possible hindrances to implementing the model, such as legal requirements, should be investigated. Models aimed at ensuring that information technology tools are not used to exploit the knowledge of indigenous communities could be explored. The preservation of indigenous knowledge should not be confined to e-learning alone, but other digital platforms such as serious games can be investigated for their suitability for preserving the knowledge.

A study with e-learning expert evaluators and designers to determine what might be lacking from the conceptual theoretical model and what other requirements need to be taken into consideration could also be useful.

Future development of the model could include true e-learning strategies, such as assessments and incorporating the use of Artificial Intelligence into the model.

REFERENCES

Agber, T. C. (2017). Factors Militating Against the Development of Tiv Indigenous Knowledge. In P. Ngulube (Ed.), *Handbook of Research on Theoretical Perspectives on Indigenous Knowledge Systems in Developing Countries* (pp. 422–443). Hershey, PA: IGI Global. https://doi.org/10.4018/978-1-5225-0833-5.ch020

Agyepong, A. O. (2017). Indigenous Communication : A Narrative of Selected Indigenous Practices of the Akan Group of Ghana. In P. Ngulube (Ed.), *Handbook of Research on Theoretical Perspectives on Indigenous Knowledge Systems in Developing Countries* (pp. 411–421). Hershey, PA: IGI Global. https://doi.org/10.4018/978-1-5225-0833-5.ch019

Al-Busaidi, K. A. (2013). An empirical investigation linking learners' adoption of blended learning to their intention of full e-learning. *Behaviour & Information Technology*, *32*(11), 1168–1176. https://doi.org/10.1080/0144929X.2013.774047

Al-Shboul, M., & Alsmadi, I. (2010). Challenges of utilizing e-learning systems in public universities in Jordan. *International Journal of Emerging Technologies in Learning*, *5*(2), 4–10. https://online-journals.org/index.php/i-jet/article/view/1147

Bouchrika, I., Harrati, N., Mahfouf, Z., & Gasmallah, N. (2018). Evaluating the Acceptance of e-learning Systems via Subjective and Objective Data Analysis. In S. Caballé & J. Conesa (Eds.), *Software Data Engineering for Network eLearning Environments* (Vol. 11, Issue Lecture Notes on Data Engineering and Communications Technologies (LNDECT), pp. 199–219). Springer, Cham. https://doi.org/10.1007/978-3-319-68318-8_10

Coleman, A. (2016). Preservation of indigenous wood carving knowledge of African traditional people through the use traditional wood carvers database framework (Twcdf). *Indian Journal of Traditional Knowledge*, *15*(3), 370–377. http://nopr.niscair.res.in/handle/123456789/34272

Dlamini, P. N. (2017). Use of Information and Communication Technologies Tools to Capture, Store, and Disseminate Indigenous Knowledge: A Literature Review. In P. Ngulube (Ed.), *Handbook of Research on Theoretical Perspectives on Indigenous Knowledge Systems in Developing Countries* (pp. 225–247). Hershey, PA: IGI Global. https://doi.org/10.4018/978-1-5225-0833-5.ch010

Dlamini, P., & Ocholla, D. N. (2018). Information and Communication Technology Tools for Managing Indigenous Knowledge in KwaZulu-Natal Province, South Africa. *African Journal of Library, Archives and Information Science*, *28*(2), 137–153. https://www.questia.com/library/journal/1G1-598461204/information-and-communication-technology-tools-for

Fenu, G., Marras, M., & Boratto, L. (2018). A multi-biometric system for continuous student authentication in e-learning platforms. *Pattern Recognition Letters*, *113*, 83–92. https://doi.org/10.1016/j.patrec.2017.03.027

Fogwill, T., Viviers, I., Engelbrecht, L., Krause, C., & Alberts, R. (2011). A software architecture for an indigenous knowledge management system. *Indigenous Knowledge Technology Conference 2011: Embracing Indigenous Knowledge Systems in a New Technology Design Paradigm*. http://researchspace.csir.co.za/dspace/bitstream/handle/10204/5525/Fogwill_2011.pdf?sequence=1

Gallert, P., Stanley, C., & Rodil, K. (2018). Perspectives on Safeguarding Indigenous Knowledge and Intangible Cultural Heritage. *Proceedings of the Second African Conference for Human Computer Interaction: Thriving Communities (AfriCHI '18), Windhoek, Namibia*, 1–4. https://doi.org/10.1145/3283458.3283520

Kok, J. A. (2005). Can models for knowledge management be successfully implemented to manage the diversity of indigenous knowledge?. *South African Journal of Information Management*, *7*(4). https://doi.org/10.4102/sajim.v7i4.286

Kurniawan, H., Salim, A., Suhartanto, H., & Hasibuan, Z. A. (2011). E-cultural heritage and natural history framework: An integrated approach to digital preservation. *Proceedings of the 2011 International Conference on Telecommunication Technology and Applications (CSIT), Singapore*, *5*, 177–182.

Liebowitz, J., & Frank, M. (Eds.). (2011). *Knowledge Management and E-Learning*. New York: Auerbach Publications. https://doi.org/10.1201/b10347

Maasz, D., Winschiers-Theophilus, H., Stanley, C., Rodil, K., & Mbinge, U. (2018). A Digital Indigenous Knowledge Preservation Framework: The 7C Model - Repositioning IK Holders in the Digitization of IK. In D. S. Jat, J. Sieck, H. N. Muyingi, H. Winschiers-Theophilus, A. Peters, & S. Nggada (Eds.), *Digitisation of Culture: Namibian and International Perspectives* (pp. 29–47). Singapore: Springer. https://doi.org/10.1007/978-981-10-7697-8_3

Mangare, C. F., & Li, J. (2018). A Survey on Indigenous Knowledge Systems Databases for African Traditional Medicines. *Proceedings of the 2018 7th International Conference on Bioinformatics and Biomedical Science (ICBBS '18), Shenzhen, China*, 9–15. https://doi.org/10.1145/3239264.3239266

Mazonde, I. N., & Thomas, P. (Eds.). (2007). *Indigenous Knowledge System and Intellectual Property Rights in the Twenty-First Century: Perspectives from Southern Africa*. Oxford: African Books Collective. https://muse.jhu.edu/book/16900

Moahi, K. H. (2012). Promoting African indigenous knowledge in the knowledge economy: Exploring the role of higher education and libraries. *Aslib Proceedings: New Information Perspectives*, *64*(5), 540–554. https://doi.org/10.1108/00012531211263157

Nonaka, I. (1994). A Dynamic Theory of Organizational Knowledge Creation. *Organization Science*, *5*(1), 14–37. https://doi.org/10.1287/orsc.5.1.14

Nurhudatiana, A., Hiu, A. N., & Ce, W. (2018). Should I Use Laptop or Smartphone? a Usability Study on an Online Learning Application. *2018 International Conference on Information Management and Technology (ICIMTech), Jakarta, Indonesia*, 565–570. https://doi.org/10.1109/ICIMTech.2018.8528134

Plockey, F. D. (2015). Indigenous Knowledge Production, Digital Media and Academic Libraries in Ghana. *The Journal of Pan African Studies*, *8*(4), 32–44.

Potcovaru, A. (2018). Using the Methods of e-Learning in Educational System. *ELearning & Software for Education*, *4*, 208–215. https://doi.org/10.12753/2066-026X-18-244

Ravenwood, C., Muir, A., & Matthews, G. (2015). Stakeholders in the Selection of Digital Material for Preservation: Relationships, Responsibilities, and Influence. *Collection Management*, *40*(2), 83–110. https://doi.org/10.1080/01462679.2015.1011816

Rodil, K., & Rehm, M. (2015). A Decade Later: Looking at the Past while Sketching the Future of ICH through the Tripartite Digitisation Model. *International Journal of Intangible Heritage*, *10*, 47–60.

Rodil, K., & Winschiers-Theophilus, H. (2018). Why is she naked? An Iterative Refinement of the Digitisation of ICH with the OvaHimba Tribe in Namibia. *International Journal of Intangible Heritage*, *13*, 143–154.

Shizha, E. (2017). Indigenous Knowledges and Knowledge Codification in the Knowledge Economy. In P. Ngulube (Ed.), *Handbook of Research on Theoretical Perspectives on Indigenous Knowledge Systems in Developing Countries* (pp. 267–288). Hershey, PA: IGI Global. https://doi.org/10.4018/978-1-5225-0833-5.ch012

Sraku-Lartey, M., Acquah, S. B., Samar, S. B., & Djagbletey, G. D. (2017). Digitization of indigenous knowledge on forest foods and medicines. *IFLA Journal*, *43*(2), 187–197. https://doi.org/10.1177/0340035216681326

Tessier, D., & Dalkir, K. (2016). Implementing Moodle for e-learning for a successful knowledge management strategy. *Knowledge Management & E-Learning*, *8*(3), 414–429. https://search.proquest.com/docview/1955087654?

Tharakan, J. (2015). Integrating indigenous knowledge into appropriate technology development and implementation. *African Journal of Science, Technology, Innovation and Development*, *7*(5), 364–370. https://doi.org/10.1080/20421338.2015.1085176

Gap in pagination due to formatting issues.

Pages 192-194

ASSESSING THE INCONSISTENCY IN ONLINE NEWS

Honour Chika Nwagwu, Guy Pascal Kibuh, Hyacinth Agozie Eneh and Stanley Abhadiomhen
Computer Science Department, University of Nigeria, Nsukka, Nigeria

ABSTRACT

The information on the web can be inconsistent across different web pages. News articles are examples of information on the web that are inconsistent and this paper proposes an approach that enables the visual analysis of inconsistencies in online news. It presents an approach which will enable the visual identification of inconsistencies associated to a news headline of interest. It uses a visual assessment approach that relies on two techniques, namely Fault Tolerance and Co-occurrence techniques. The Fault Tolerance technique is used in extracting related news headlines on the internet while the Co-occurrence technique is used for grouping and scaling related news headlines on the web. Also the bar-chart is used to plot charts that summaries the inconsistencies from which news readers can visually assess related news headlines of particular context.

KEYWORDS

Inconsistency, News, Fault Tolerance, Colour Coding, Charts, Co-Occurrence

1. INTRODUCTION

A new reader must have a holistic understanding of his news of interest to be able to filter the noise associated with the news. Evidently, existing approaches for searching and viewing online news articles require much effort, concentration, attention to detail and time to identify related news to the context of interest of the news reader. This is because the news reader must go through different web pages of different websites while reading and assessing the validity of information related to his news of interest to properly assess any associated inconsistency (diverse opinions of editors). News readers are likely not to have a holistic understanding of a news context published where they cannot assess the different dimensionalities to the news. For example, a real-life evaluation about "Trump's Facebook ban" using Google news search on the 9th of June 2021 reveals the information depicted in Table 1. The Table shows different news headlines from different sources about Trump's Facebook ban.

Certainly, different news articles about the same context often offer a variety of perspectives (Liu et al., 2019). Also, there are possibilities of bias when forming news title and these biases can be related to political affiliation, misinformation, and systematic errors among others. For example, Journalists can express their ideological view of news by misrepresenting the essence of the story (Gangula et al., 2019). Consequently, a news reader who reads about "Trump's Facebook ban" for example, should be interested in reading about most of the different dimensionalities associated to Trump's Facebook ban as evident in Table 1.

Unfortunately, the existing approaches for identifying related news articles require much effort, concentration, attention to detail and time to identify the different news relating to the context of interest. Existing approaches to dealing with the inconsistencies in news do not empower news readers or the data analysts with the ability to easily visualise, the multidimensionality associated to news of a particular context. For example, a traditional approach to reading news implies that the news reader has to search for news of interest, get a list of corresponding news headlines and repeatedly click on associated headlines to read the content of the news. This is very tedious as there are hundreds of related news articles with similar headlines on different web pages on the internet. Even news websites that display related news such as BBC and CNN, which provide the functionality for news reader to see related news headlines at the bottom of each news article, do not reveal the inconsistencies across the web unlike the approach proposed in this work. Also, these commercial news websites do not allow the news reader to determine the relatedness of the displayed headlines to the headline of interest which our approach allows.

Table 1. Examples of Inconsistencies in news where "Trump's Facebook ban" is a search string in Google News Search Engine

S/No	Headline	News Media	Web Source
1.	What Happened When Trump Was Banned on Facebook and Twitter	The New York Times	https://www.nytimes.com/interactive/2021/06/07/technology/trump-social-media-ban.html
2.	Poll: 51 percent of Americans support Trump's 2-year Facebook ban	Politico	https://www.politico.com/news/2021/06/07/poll-trump-facebook-suspension-492046
3.	Facebook suspends Trump accounts for two years	BBC	https://www.bbc.com/news/world-us-canada-57365628
4.	Trump is suspended from Facebook for 2 years and can't return until 'risk to public safety is receded'	The Washington Post	https://www.washingtonpost.com/technology/2021/06/03/trump-facebook-oversight-board/
5.	Facebook to suspend Trump's account for two years	The Guardian	https://www.theguardian.com/us-news/2021/jun/04/facebook-donald-trump-oversight-board-instagram
6.	Facebook's Trump Ban Will Last at Least 2 Years	The New York Times	https://www.nytimes.com/2021/06/04/technology/facebook-trump-ban.html
....	.....	......	.....

The review process of the existing approaches showed a categorization of the existing approaches to dealing with the inconsistencies in news to include among others, those of the traditional approaches, the artificial intelligence approaches, and the sentiment approaches. These are discussed in section 2. A novel approach to enhancing the assessment of the inconsistencies among similar online news, which combines Fault Tolerance and Co-occurrence approaches is proposed in section 3. The results from implementing the approaches are discussed in section 4. Finally, a conclusion and future work are outlined in section 5.

2. EXISTING APPROACHES TO DEALING WITH THE INCONSISTENCIES IN NEWS

2.1 Traditional Web Search Approaches

An online news reader manually assesses news on the internet. This necessitates the news reader to search for news of interest, get the web links of corresponding news headlines and click on each web link to read the news contents. The news readers read through all of the articles to be able to mentally mine the contradictions, missingness or reason with any inconsistencies associated to the news. However, there are thousands of news articles on the internet and it is important that a news reader identifies the related news. The traditional approach takes so much time for an online news reader to find and read all the news articles relating to his article of interest.

Also, the traditional approach does not enable the news reader to easily identify false or misleading news. Examples of this approach as proposed by different authors to assessing news include; coding or theoretical frameworks such as discourse analysis and content analysis as outlined in (Gangula et al., 2019; Chen et al., 2018; Armstrong et al. 2018). The appropriateness of news headline to its content was manually analysed and presented in (Gangula et al., 2019). An approach for bias flipping news headlines is presented in (Chen et al., 2018). The authors in (Chen et al., 2018) manually annotated news headlines and automatically used Rouge Score in evaluating the headlines to identify opposite biased articles. The traditional approach also applies advanced deep learning model to flip the bias of news headlines. Also, several datasets that present bias or enable the analysis of news and news headline are curated from different sources and discussed in (Horne et al., 2018; Piotrkowicz et al., 2017).

The manual approaches to analysing the inconsistencies in news do not enable the evaluation of bias or fake news in real-time. They do not provide the online news analyst a platform to evaluate the news about his topic of interest. Also, the approach requires a lot of effort, concentration, attention to detail and time. This is because the news reader must go through different web pages of different websites while reading and assessing or curating the information of interest to properly assess inconsistencies in news.

2.2 Artificial Intelligence Approaches

The artificial intelligence approaches (MLA) include machine learning and natural language processing approaches. MLA involves algorithms that can learn and build mathematical models to make predictions and decisions. There are numerous MLA currently in use in assessing inconsistencies in news. A curation of crime-related information from multi-sources which are digitally published news articles were collected over a period of five years and analysed using deep convolution recurrent neural network model to extract different crime related entities and events is documented in (Dasgupta et al., 2018). The application of deep convolution recurrent neural network model enables the detection of crimes from the database. Even so, it does not enable the analysis of the inconsistencies associated to the news articles.

Also, it is explained in (Liu et al., 2019), how the frame detection approach is used to automatically detect frames of news headlines related to gun violence. This approach enables large-scale analysis of framing trends surrounding the gun violence issue in the United States. A hierarchical architecture that models a complex textual representation of news articles, and measures the incongruity between news headlines and body text approach is proposed in (Yoon et al., 2019). An approach to detect incongruity between a news headline and body text of a news article using a graph-based hierarchical dual encoder (GHDE) is the work of (Yoon et al., 2021). A deep hierarchical attention network that trained to extract hidden patterns in fake news using the concatenation of news headlines and their corresponding body text as input data-set is proposed in (Meel and Vishwakarma, 2021). Also, Natural Language Processing (NPL) network based detection approaches include the headline attention network as discussed in (Gangula et al., 2019) where it is used to automatically detect bias in newspaper articles.

2.3 Sentiment Analysis Approach

Sentiment analysis approaches are applied in analysing inconsistencies in news. They provide techniques through which the polarities of opinions are classified and analysed. A news can be positive, negative, republican, and democrat among others. Social emotion lexicons have been generated through calculation of the probabilities of the emotions as evident in (Lei et al., 2014). Similarly, a lexicon based sentiment analysis approach that investigates the emotion (positive, negative, neutral) in news articles is explained in (Taj and Meghji, 2019). The lexicon based sentiment analysis approach uses some predefined lists of words which are associated to specific sentiment to define the document based sentiment level of the investigated article through the use of the Rapid Miner tool. The authors applied the lexicon based sentiment analysis approach in investigating 2225 British Broadcasting Cooperation (BBC) news articles. It was observed that a majority of the investigated articles fell into the negative or positive categories with a minor percentage of articles having neutral sentiments. However, the sentiment based approaches does not present an efficient approach for evaluating the inconsistencies in massive news articles.

3. PROPOSED METHODOLOGY

The vast amount of news articles, disseminated about a news context, highlight the need for visual analytic systems where the information user can visually investigate news of interest. Such visual analytic systems will enable the web user to understand the trend in news relating to his interest and will enhance his experience when exploring the related news articles. Mining and visualization approaches provide human driven approaches to dealing with inconsistencies in news. It enables news readers to explore the interrelationships among data rather than reading mere numbers and text. There are many visualisation techniques for dealing with online information as presented in (Chen et al., 2018), and they include scrolling, pagination, distortion, and suppression. This proposed approach limits its techniques to the use of Fault Tolerance and Co-occurrence in mining and scaling news headlines.

This proposed approach is based on the principle that news headlines are more likely to convey the context of a story by providing the reader with insights about the context of the news. A news headline provides summarization of the major content of the news. Consequently, news readers are likely to have a holistic understanding about a news context which is published where he assesses the different dimensionalities (headlines) to the particular context of interest. Here, a web based platform that iterates through news websites, by using open source news aggregators to identify related news to a news headline of interest, is developed as ViewNews[1]. News aggregators are portals which aggregate current news from different news sources with their associated web links. The proposed approach combines Fault Tolerance and Co-occurrence techniques in order to enable news readers to visually identify any inconsistency in a news headline.

A news headline is evaluated for instance(s) of inconsistencies by exploring associated headlines. An online reader selects a news headline of interest and the system tokenizes it, thereby enabling the news reader to select some of the keywords as mandatory tokens based on his interest. The percentage of the mandatory tokens (fault tolerance) is calculated by using the formula:

$$FT = 100 - \left(\frac{size(m)}{size(t)}\right) * 100;$$

Where FT = Fault Tolerance, size (m) = the number of tokens in the array of mandatory data, and size (t) = the number of tokens in the array of the news headline.

The identified headlines are depicted as inconsistencies in bars of a bar chart, where each bar is plotted against its Fault Tolerance value. Also, a View Links section is designed to enable a news analyst to view web links of all the depicted headlines enabling him to read the content of the news.

The co-occurrence technique enables the news analyst to select headlines with equal tolerance levels, depicted with the same colour in a bar chart and equal number of words. As a result, similar news headlines can be viewed by selecting particular co-occurring levels. This enables the news reader to view news that is biased towards a particular context. The use of Co-occurrence helps the news analyst to assess the level of popularity of a news headline. For example, when the level of co-occurrences is many, it means that the headlines are observed among many publication houses.

The use of ViewNews app is simple. The news reader or news analyst types the web link of ViewNews (https://view-news.herokuapp.com/#) into his browser to access the app. The news headline of interest is selected from the 'select headline' section. Also, mandatory keywords are selected from the select mandatory keyword(s) section. The mandatory keywords are words that make up the initially selected headline. It should be noted that the more the selection of words from the headline, the less tolerance level to be used by the system. A click on search reveals the inconsistencies associated to the news headline of interest. The co-occurrence is consequently selected to view the co-occurrences of keywords which are peculiar. More than one instance of the co-occurrences can be selected and viewed in a bar chart to enhance understanding of the investigated news headline. Examples of the use of Fault Tolerance and Co-occurrence techniques to visually analyse a news headline of interest for associated noise is as evident in section 4.0

4. RESULTS

ViewNews enables a news analyst to evaluate a news headline for instances of inconsistency by crawling the web through its news aggregators and displaying associated headlines. For example, the headline "Amazon To Open African Headquarters in South Africa" was assessed for issues of inconsistency across the web. Obviously, a look at the headline will imply that Amazon has agreed to open its headquarters in South Africa. However, when this headline is searched for, through the ViewNews platform at 75% tolerance where Amazon and Headquarters are selected as the mandatory keywords, more than 70 other headlines are identified (see Figure 1). Each bar in Figure 1 is associated to a headline that contains the selected keywords. It becomes obvious to the news analyst that the issue of a headquarters for Amazon is a controversial one. Consequently, the app user can click the 'View Links' button on the platform to view all the displayed news headlines and read his news of interest by clicking the associated web link.

[1] https://view-news.herokuapp.com/

Also, inconsistencies in the news headlines "Amazon To Open African Headquarters in South Africa" was investigated by selecting co-occurring levels 2 as evident in Figure 2. This enabled us to identify other headlines of related articles. For example, the headline as depicted in Figure 2 "Amazon may have just dropped a clue about the home of its new headquarters-…" is written by Hayley Peterson at Dec 15, 2017, the second headline "Amazon may have just dropped a clue about the home of its new headquarters" is written by Leanna Garfield at Dec 18, 2017 while the headline that we are examining (100% tolerance) was written by SaharaReporters, New York at April 21, 2021. These headlines and their context are discussing about a different headquarters for Amazon in different years. The inconsistencies in the news were easy to identify through investigating the bar chart and clicking on the associated web links of the headlines while using ViewNews app.

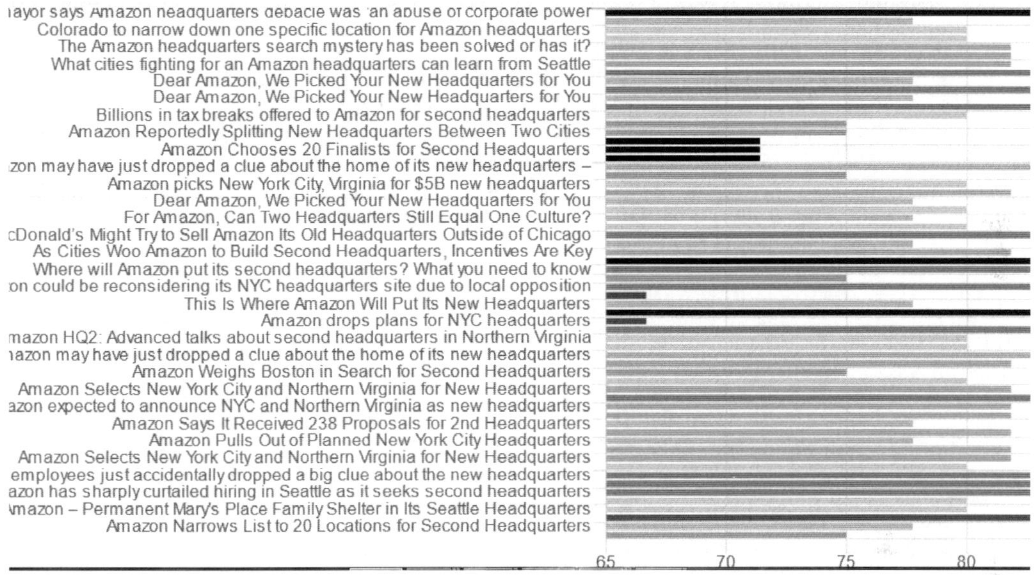

Figure 1. ViewNew exploration of "Amazon to Open African Headquarters in South Africa" news headline using the fault tolerance technique

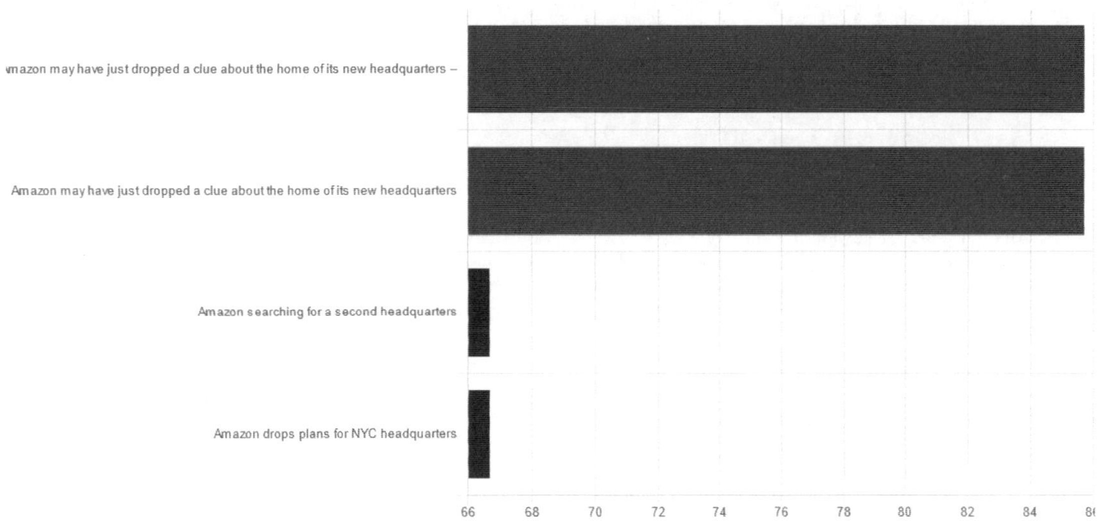

Figure 2. ViewNew exploration of "Amazon to Open African Headquarters in South Africa" news headline using co-occurrence technique for Co-occurrence 2

5. CONCLUSION AND FUTURE WORK

This paper describes the Fault Tolerance and Co-occurrence techniques. The Fault Tolerance technique is used for varying the associated news headlines according to their common tokens. It enables the extraction of related news headlines on the internet. The Co-occurrence technique is used for grouping and scaling related news headlines. Results from Fault Tolerance and Co-occurrence techniques are used to plot a bar chart. Interestingly, most news websites provide the functionalities of enabling their news reader to see related news headlines at the bottom of each news article. However, such related news headline is selected within the news website and do not reveal the inconsistencies across the web. Unlike the use of Fault Tolerance in ViewNews, they do not allow the news reader to determine the relatedness of the displayed headlines to the headline of interest. The approach adopted in this work empowers news analysts and news readers to investigate news of interest for instances of inconsistencies across the web. It enhances the experience of the news analyst when exploring the web. It enables them to identify possible instances of fake news, popular news, and biased news among others. Nevertheless, this work falls short of efficiency issues in ViewNews algorithms and quantitative evaluation of ViewNews app. Consequently, further research is ongoing in visual analysis and assessment of online news. The Fault Tolerance and Co-occurrence algorithms of ViewNews, efficiency issues of implementing the algorithms and the application of ViewNews to analyze instances of incompleteness in news are being investigated. In addition, consideration is given towards possible collaboration with other researchers for the purposes of presenting novel approaches to dealing with the issues of inconsistency in online news.

REFERENCES

Liu, S., Guo, L., Mays, K., Betke, M. and Wijaya, D.T., 2019, January. Detecting frames in news headlines and its application to analyzing news framing trends surrounding US gun violence. In *Proceedings of the 23rd Conference on Computational Natural Language Learning (CoNLL)*. Hong Kong, China, pp 504–514.

Gangula, R.R.R., Duggenpudi, S.R. and Mamidi, R., 2019, August. Detecting political bias in news articles using headline attention. In *Proceedings of the 2019 ACL Workshop BlackboxNLP: Analyzing and Interpreting Neural Networks for NLP*. Florence, Italy, pp. 77-84.

Chen, W.F., Wachsmuth, H., Al Khatib, K. and Stein, B., 2018, November. Learning to flip the bias of news headlines. In *Proceedings of the 11th International conference on natural language generation.* Tilburg, The Netherlands, pp. 79-88.

Armstrong, G., Vijayakumar, L., Niederkrotenthaler, T., Jayaseelan, M., Kannan, R., Pirkis, J., and Jorm, A. F. (2018). Assessing the quality of media reporting of suicide news in India against World Health Organization guidelines: A content analysis study of nine major newspapers in Tamil Nadu. *Australian & New Zealand Journal of Psychiatry*, Vol. *52*, No. 9, pp 856-863.

Horne, B.D., Khedr, S. and Adali, S., 2018, June. Sampling the news producers: A large news and feature data set for the study of the complex media landscape. In *Twelfth International AAAI Conference on Web and Social Media*. Vol. 12, No. 1.

Piotrkowicz, A., Dimitrova, V., Otterbacher, J. and Markert, K., 2017, May. Headlines matter: Using headlines to predict the popularity of news articles on twitter and facebook. In *Proceedings of the International AAAI Conference on Web and Social Media* Vol. 11, No. 1.

Dasgupta, T., Dey, L., Saha, R. and Naskar, A., 2018, August. Automatic Curation and Visualization of Crime Related Information from Incrementally Crawled Multi-source News Reports. In *Proceedings of the 27th International Conference on Computational Linguistics: System Demonstrations*. New Mexico, USA, pp. 103-107

Yoon, S., Park, K., Shin, J., Lim, H., Won, S., Cha, M. and Jung, K., 2019, July. Detecting incongruity between news headline and body text via a deep hierarchical encoder. In *Proceedings of the AAAI conference on artificial intelligence.* Vol. 33, No. 1, pp. 791-800.

Yoon, S., Park, K., Lee, M., Kim, T., Cha, M. and Jung, K., 2021. Learning to Detect Incongruence in News Headline and Body Text via a Graph Neural Network. *IEEE Access*, Vol. *9*, pp.36195-36206.

Meel, P. and Vishwakarma, D.K., 2021. HAN, image captioning, and forensics ensemble multimodal fake news detection. *Information Sciences*, *567*, pp.23-41.

Lei, J., Rao, Y., Li, Q., Quan, X. and Wenyin, L., 2014. Towards building a social emotion detection system for online news. *Future Generation Computer Systems*, Vol. *37*, pp.438-448.

Taj, S., Shaikh, B.B. and Meghji, A.F., 2019, January. Sentiment analysis of news articles: A lexicon based approach. In *2019 2nd International Conference on Computing, Mathematics and Engineering Technologies (iCoMET)* (pp. 1-5). IEEE.

DIALOGBOOK2: AN IMPROVEMENT OF E-PORTFOLIO SYSTEM FOR INTERNATIONAL COMMUNICATION LEARNING

Jun Iio[1], Shigenori Wakabayashi[2] and Junji Sakurai[3]
[1]*Faculty of Global-Informatics, Chuo University, 1-18 Ichigaya-Tamachi, Shinjuku-ku, Tokyo, 162-8478, Japan*
[2]*Faculty of Letters, Chuo University, 742-1 Higashinakano, Hachioji-shi, Tokyo, 192-0393, Japan*
[3]*Sekisaibo LLC, 3-7-1 Akebono, Kashiwa-shi, Chiba, 277-0841, Japan*

ABSTRACT

In recent years, an educational revolution has been progressing toward the globalization of Japanese society by teaching English in elementary academic courses. However, traditional English education overweighs reading and writing and tends to disregard fostering skills in hearing and speaking, which are required to have smooth English conversations. Real globalization is one in which a globalized person can participate in borderless communications in any context. Essential aspects are to understand different cultures and achieve more in-depth communication while respecting others. Therefore, to improve the global sense of high-school students, we started the Students Meet Internationally through Language Education (SMILE) project during the fiscal year of 2020. The characteristics of the project include giving the participants with opportunities to communicate with international students and providing systematic procedures as a general educational program package. Furthermore, we support the efficient learning of students by offering a simple and easy-to-use e-portfolio system called Dialogbook. This paper presents an overview of the first SMILE project, problems, and requirements acquired from the use of the first version of Dialogbook. The article then outlines a novel redesigned system.

KEYWORDS

Online Meeting Tools, Dialogbook, E-Portfolio System, Intercultural Education, SMILE Project

1. INTRODUCTION

Online meeting tools, such as Zoom, Webex, Google Meet, and Microsoft Teams, allow users to hold online meetings instantly (Keshlaf et al., 2021). The online sessions supported by these tools are not only domestic but also forms of international communication. From 2020, the COVID-19 pandemic has prevented us from easily traveling abroad. However, such online meeting tools enable international communication through the Internet. Almost all academic meetings have also moved online, and their activities have been maintained by holding international conferences in a virtual environment (Kashiwazaki et al., 2021).

The workshop initiative for language learning (WILL) prepared the Students Meet Internationally through Language Education (SMILE) project, which has provided intercultural education courses for Japanese and foreign high schools. A pilot project was carried out during the last quarter of 2020 (Wakabayashi et al., 2021). Two pairs of high schools from Japan and Taiwan, Hinode High School and Fucheng High School, and Ichihara Chuo High School and Donggang High School, respectively, participated in the project. Both pairs of schools held three interactive classes during the project period. Students from Japan and Taiwan communicated using online meeting software (one team used Zoom and the other used Webex).

The SMILE project also provides a system implemented for a project called Dialogbook (Iio and Wakabayashi, 2020), where students can record their learning activities. Dialogbook is designed as a simple e-portfolio system or an easy-to-use learning management system (LMS). The system has a characteristic function that enables students to self-evaluate by providing rubrics items and memos for learning records.

Figure 1 shows an overview of the SMILE project. The students participating in the project communicated to the students from the counterpart school using an online communication tool and recorded their activities in Dialogbook and on cloud storage. The teachers encouraged the students to have smooth conversations and interact with each other. Furthermore, the staff from WILL assisted the students and teachers by offering them technical support, templates on the course materials, and some help in preparing interactive classes between the two schools.

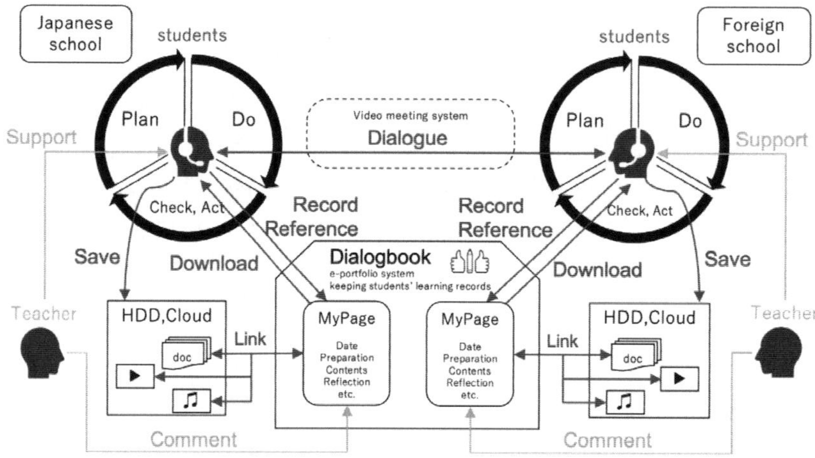

Figure 1. Overview of the SMILE project. The major players are students from Japanese and Foreign high schools. Teachers support student learning activities. In addition, the staff of WILL helps them by coordinating interactive classes, offering learning materials, and providing technical support

Based on the experience of the first project, we recognized several problems and requirements to improve the Dialogbook. Therefore, we redesigned a new system for the next project, which will be conducted in this year. This paper presents an overview of the project, problems, and improvement points of the system.

2. FIRST SMILE PROJECT

WILL carried out the first project during the last quarter of 2020. The preparation for the project started in August 2020, and online interactive classes were held from October to December (see Table 1).

Table 1. Schedule of online communication classes

	Hinode and Fucheng	Ichihara and Donggang
First interaction	October 29, 2020	November 11, 2020
Second interaction	November 12, 2020	November 18, 2020
Third interaction	December 10, 2020	December 9, 2020

A total of 20 to 30 first- and second-grade high school students from each school participated in the project. During the online interactive classes, students were placed into groups of two or three students, and the online meeting tools connected the groups from Japan and the counterpart country, allowing them to communicate interculturally. When preparing the communication classes, teachers scheduled approximately 50 min in their school timetables. For each class, 20 min sessions were conducted twice.

There is a significant need to conduct real-time communications. Hence, the SMILE project expects schools in countries near Japan with no broader time difference to be used as counterparts. During the first project, all interactive classes were conducted in Japanese and Taiwanese time throughout the morning.

Figure 2. Students participating in the interactive class connected using the online meeting tool. The left photograph shows the students at Hinode high school (Japan), and the right shows students at Fucheng high school (Taiwan)

The photograph on the left of Figure 2 shows the class at Hinode high school using laptop computers, and the right side of Figure 2 shows Taiwanese students communicating with Japanese students using their smartphones. The students utilized not only personal computers but also various devices to achieve online interactions during the project.

Through this practice, WILL offered the Dialogbook system to Hinode, Ichihara, and Donggang high schools. Three applications were independently deployed to Heroku and allowed the teachers and students in each school to access the system. Only Fucheng high school did not use Dialogbook. The data on the learning activities and reflections at that school were collected offline using worksheets printed on paper.

3. PROBLEMS AND IMPROVEMENTS

From the experiences of the three high schools, we obtained several problems and requirements regarding the first implementation of Dialogbook.

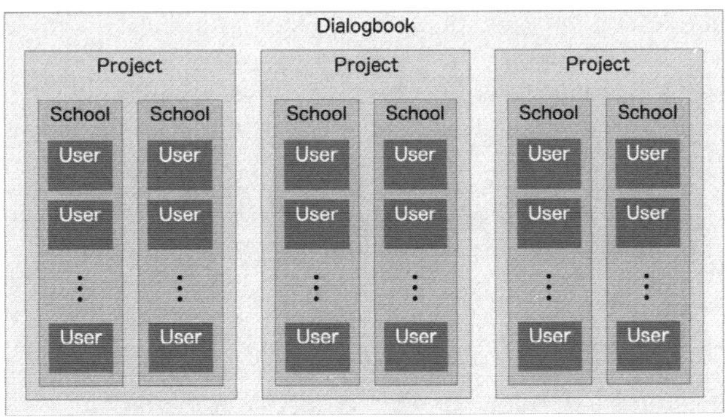

Figure 3. The data structure containing multiple projects in one application

The first problem is a management issue, which is troublesome, particularly for our administrative procedure. As mentioned previously, we deployed the three applications separately for use on the Heroku platform. Therefore, the simultaneous administration of the three applications was slightly complicated. They should be integrated into one application that has multiple schools (see Figure 3). The new architecture makes administration simpler than the previous operation and can increase the magnitude of the project.

The second problem is a lack of meeting management functions. Throughout the previous project, we encountered some problems related to misconnections. Students are often unfamiliar with using online meeting tools, much fewer hosting meetings. Students frequently missed the meeting invites and thus were unable to connect as scheduled. Hence, we need a function for managing the meeting link information, i.e., when the next meeting will be held and where we should connect.

The last requirements are convenient functions that assist teachers. The improved system (see Figure 4) implemented a teacher's dashboard that includes lesson (rubrics) management, meeting management, user account management, student comments, and a data download function.

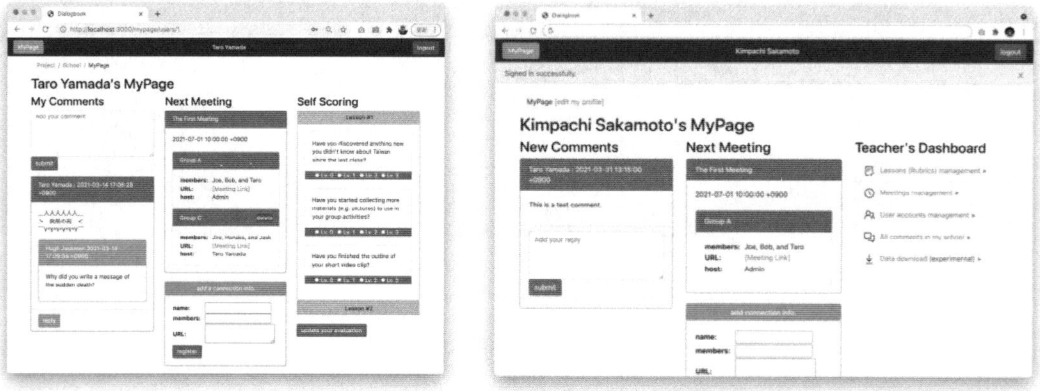

Figure 4. Screenshots of new Dialogbook. The left image is a student's MyPage and the right one is a teacher's MyPage

As with the previous implementation, the new system (Dialogbook2) is currently implemented over Ruby on Rails (version 6.1.3.2) and deployed on the Heroku platform.

4. CONCLUSIONS

WILL conducted the first SMILE project during the last quarter of 2020. The four schools, two high schools from Japan, and two high schools from Taiwan, participated in the project. They were connected using online meeting tools to create intercultural education classes.

During the project, WILL provided support to the students and teachers, such as the scheduling of interactive classes, templates for the educational materials, and a simple e-portfolio system called Dialogbook. Throughout the execution of the project, we experienced several problems and obtained some requirements to improve the Dialogbook system. A novel version of Dialogbook was designed and re-implemented. We are currently planning to evaluate a new system for the next project scheduled for this year.

REFERENCES

Keshlaf, A. A., Alahresh, A. A. and Aswad, M. K., 2021. Factors influencing the use of on-line meeting tools. *IEEE 1st International Maghreb Meeting of the Conference on Sciences and Techniques of Automatic Control and Computer Engineering MI-STA*, pp. 908–912, doi: 10.1109/MI-STA52233.2021.9464370.

Kashiwazaki, H., Ozaki, T., Shimada, H., Komiya, Y., Sakane, E., Mishima, K., Sakashita, S., Yamai, N., Kitaguchi, Y. and Miyashita, K., 2021. Japanese activities to bring online academic meetings against COVID-19: How we learned to stop worrying and love the online meetings. *In* Association for Computing Machinery, New York, NY, USA *ACM SIGUCCS Annual Conference (SIGUCCS '21)*, pp. 54–59. doi:https://doi.org/10.1145/3419944.3441174.

Wakabayashi, S., Iio, J., & Sakurai, J. (2021) Practice of IT4C in Asian International Collaboration Courses for Language Learning: Students Meet Internationally through Language Education (SMILE Project) by Workshop Initiatives for Language Learning (WILL), Invited Speaker, The Virtual Language and Communication Postgraduate International Seminar (VLCPIS), online. (2021.8.23).

Iio, J. and Wakabayashi, S., 2020. Dialogbook: A proposal for simple e-portfolio system for international communication learning. *International Journal of Web Information Systems,* Vol. 16, No. 5, pp. 611–622.

COST REDUCTION ESTIMATION METHOD OF A SOFTWARE VULNERABILITY MANAGEMENT TOOL

Satoshi Yashiro[1,2], Pranay Verma[3], Norihisa Komoda[4] and Takenao Ohkawa[5]
[1]*Graduate School of System Informatics, Kobe University, 1-1 Rokkodai-cho, Nada-ku, Kobe 657-8501, Japan*
[2]*Research & Development Group, Hitachi, Ltd., 292, Yoshida-cho, Totsuka-ku, Yokohama 244-0817, Japan*
[3]*R&D Centre, Hitachi India, Pvt.*
World Trade Center, #S 704, 7th floor, Brigade Gateway Campus, No.26/1, Dr. Rajkumar Road, Malleswaram-Rajajinagar, Bengaluru 560-055, India
[4]*Code Solutions Co., Ltd., 1-2-11-9F, Edobori, Nishi-ku, Osaka 550-0002, Japan*
[5]*Graduate School of System Informatics, Kobe University, 1-1 Rokkodai-cho, Nada-ku, Kobe 657-8501, Japan*

ABSTRACT

Software vulnerability identification is necessary work to have IT assets secure in organizations. There can be so many vulnerabilities found as usual, and the severities of the vulnerabilities are various. Attack path analysis is known as helpful to clarify the severities, and a vulnerability management tool with attack path analysis will reduce vulnerability management cost. However, the amount of cost reduction by applying the tool is not clear in each case. Also, it is difficult to estimate the amount of the cost reduction. In this paper, we introduce an efficient approach to estimate the cost benefit of implementing a vulnerability management tool with attack path analysis into actual vulnerability management process by integrating qualitative analysis with quantitative analysis.

KEYWORDS

Vulnerability Management, Attack Path Analysis, CBA: Cost Benefit Analysis, Cost Factor Tree

1. INTRODUCTION

In these days, cyber security risks are getting severer. Attackers are trying to intrude to business systems by using malware or penetration tools. Those malware or tools typically use software vulnerability of servers or devices, so it is important to identify software vulnerabilities regularly and fix them immediately.

On the other hand, organizations tend to pay less efforts to vulnerability scanning and fixing activity because such activities typically spend much cost. Some security tools provide aids to reduce such costs, and one of the known tools is vulnerability management tool with attack path analysis. When we use the tool, we can detect vulnerabilities in enterprise network systems with less efforts and identify how attackers will intrude each server or device by attacking the vulnerabilities step by step. Even though some servers or devices have severer vulnerabilities, actual severity is not so high when the servers or devices are far from the attack path. This means that attack path analysis may contribute to prioritize vulnerabilities to be fixed and reduce costs by focusing on really severe vulnerabilities. This tool typically automates vulnerability scanning procedure, so cost reduction by implementing the tool into security monitoring process will also affect vulnerability scanning procedure.

Qualitatively, we can understand the tool will bring a certain amount of cost reduction in security monitoring process, but it is not easy to identify how much the cost will be reduced quantitatively.

In this paper, we introduce a method on cost reduction analysis of software vulnerability management process with a tool which supports attack path analysis. We also show the method needs less efforts to estimate the reduction. The method based on a CBA (Cost Benefit Analysis) that is originally invented for cost reduction analysis of production process in plants is expanded to software intensive management process.

2. VULNERABILITY SCANNING AND UPDATE PROCESS

2.1 Typical Procedure of Vulnerability Scanning and Update

In an enterprise network system, there are many instances of software running on servers or devices. Those instances unfortunately have vulnerabilities in some time. Security organizations such as NIST (National Institute of Standards and Technology) announce existence of such vulnerabilities regularly, and vendors of the software or OSS (Open-Source Software) community disclose patches to the vulnerable version of software. IT asset management teams in organization scan the assets and survey the vulnerability disclosure. Once they find vulnerabilities which may affect to their IT assets, they try to fix the vulnerabilities to avoid cyber security attacks.

Software vulnerability scanning and update procedure typically follows the manner described in figure 1.

Figure 1. Typical procedure of software vulnerability scanning and update

Figure 2 shows a concept of attack path analysis and vulnerability prioritizing procedure that is covered by the vulnerability management tool with attack path analysis. The tool initially collects IT assets information into the asset repository, then executes vulnerability scan regularly. Once vulnerabilities are found, the tool conducts an attack path analysis. Based on the result of the analysis, the tool calculates priorities of the vulnerabilities to be fixed. Sometimes the priorities are different from severities of the vulnerability itself. For example, a vulnerability with higher severity in a server placed in a secluded area has less priority to a vulnerability with middle severity in a web server opened to the Internet. In the case of figure 2, there are five vulnerabilities found in the network, where *v1* has the highest severity and *v5* has the lowest severity. However, once the attack path is found as *v1*, *v2*, and *v5*, then the priority of *v5* becomes higher than *v3*. In this case, not to fix *v3* and *v4* immediately can be an option. When the option is chosen, the team can save the costs on vulnerability fixing process. From the other viewpoint, to minimize vulnerabilities to be fixed immediately could contribute to avoid opportunity losses that are brought by server down during the patching.

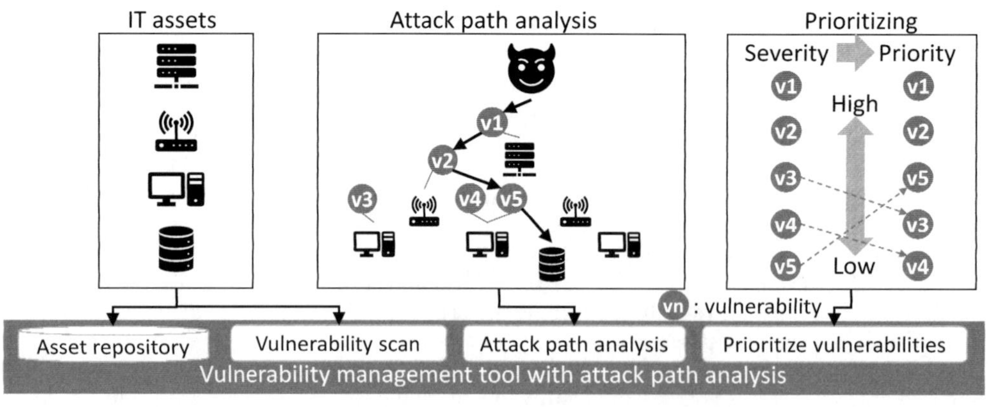

Figure 2. Concept of vulnerability scanning and prioritizing process with attack path analysis

2.2 Difficulty of Cost Reduction Estimation

Vulnerability scanning and update process is a process that is needed to execute often and regularly, and workload of the process would be large when an organization has large numbers of severs or devices. The process typically becomes costly work. Also, downtime of servers or devices during patching will bring loss cost such as sales loss or production loss. Qualitatively, it is easier to understand the vulnerability management tool will contribute to reduce such costs, but quantitatively, it is not easy to understand the investment of the tool will pay for the amount of cost reduction or not. If the investment will not pay for the amount of the cost reduction, not using the tool might be a reasonable option.

The cost reduction estimation is typically difficult work, because there can be a lot of cost factors to be considered. Some factors will contribute to cost reduction directly, but some other factors will affect indirectly. Also, to quantify each cost factors or contribution ratio is difficult work. That is why quantitative effect estimation has not usually been conducted before we make a decision that the software vulnerability management tool should be introduced to the actual software vulnerability management process or not.

3. PROCEDURE OF COST REDUCTION ANALYSYS

3.1 Basic Idea of the Proposed Method

In this paper, we propose a CBA based effect estimation method. In the CBA approach, secondary effect or thirdly effect can be considered, but we focused on only primary effect to avoid over estimation. In vulnerability management case, primary effect means reduction of work time, rework time, or unit human cost of skilled persons to conduct vulnerability management process. When the vulnerability management tool is implemented into the management process, work process would be changed, so we can estimate the changes of work cost by focusing on only changed work items. To identify work process and affected work items, we introduce "stakeholder table" which makes identifying process easier. Stakeholder table is a table which lists stakeholders of vulnerability management process, their concerns, and their happy and unhappy situation about the concerns. This table contributes to list all work items related to the stakeholders and identify which work items will be affected by the vulnerability management tool.

Once all stakeholders are listed, work activities of the stakeholders would be depicted. The vulnerability management tool will affect some activities, and the activities may change as automated, less manual work, or less professional skills. Such changes of activities are drilled down to the cost drivers, and we can finally estimate the cost difference by giving assumed parameters to the cost drivers.

To identify the stakeholders, their concerns, their activity changes, cost drivers and cost parameters, series of workshops are conducted. Basically, the workshops are held at three or four times as illustrated in figure 3. Software vulnerability management process is common process in any organizations even when they have IT assets, so the structures of the cost factor trees are expected as almost the same. Only cost parameters are expected as different in the organizations. Therefore, once a cost factor tree is produced through the workshops, it is expected to reuse the tree to estimate the amount of cost reduction in other organization case by just arranging cost parameters.

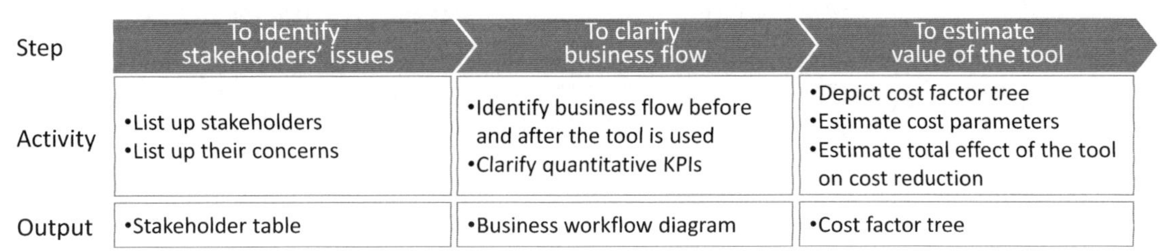

Figure 3. Outline of cost reduction estimation workshops

Table 1. Identified stakeholder's concern, happy and unhappy situation by applying Stakeholder table

Stakeholder	Concerns	Happy	Unhappy
CSO: Chief Security Officer	• Decision making • Correctness of decision • Performance of security operations	• Speedy • Right • Easy to monitor	• Slow • Wrong • Difficult to monitor
Security Analysis and Planning Team	• Audit process • Compliance level • Mitigation plan • Remaining high vulnerabilities • Vulnerability detection • Report to CSO • Patch effectiveness	• Less manual work • Meets standards • Speedy and accurate • Least • Full coverage • Easy loss estimation • Less side effects	• Much manual work • Doesn't meet standards • Slow and less accurate • Many • Low coverage • Difficulty to access loss • Much side effects
...	...	...	...

3.2 Identification of Stakeholders and their Concerns

The first step of the analysis is to identify stakeholders of software vulnerability management process and their concerns. In this step, all stakeholders should be captured, and their concerns, happy and unhappy situation about the concerns should be identified. Table 1 is an example of the stakeholder table.

3.3 Identification of Procedure Changes by Applying the Tool

The second step is to clarify stakeholders' work items using "Ex-table (Experience table)" diagram. Ex-table is a table formed diagram which lists stakeholders in the row direction and work phases in the column direction and illustrates each stakeholders' work items as a swim-lane. Figure 4 is an example of Ex-table. It is supposed that the vulnerability management tool will contribute to automated vulnerability detection. Automation of vulnerability detection will bring fewer remaining vulnerabilities than those in manual work. Such state change is also captured using a comment box in the Ex-table.

3.4 Identification of Cost Drivers

The final step is to estimate cost before and after vulnerability management tool is implemented. To conduct this analysis, cost factor tree is used. Figure 5 is an example of cost factor tree. First level is total cost, second level is total cost of a work phase that is same as a column in the Ex-table, and third level is cost of an activity that is same as a work item in the Ex-table. Fourth and deeper levels are cost drivers or elements to calculate cost drivers.

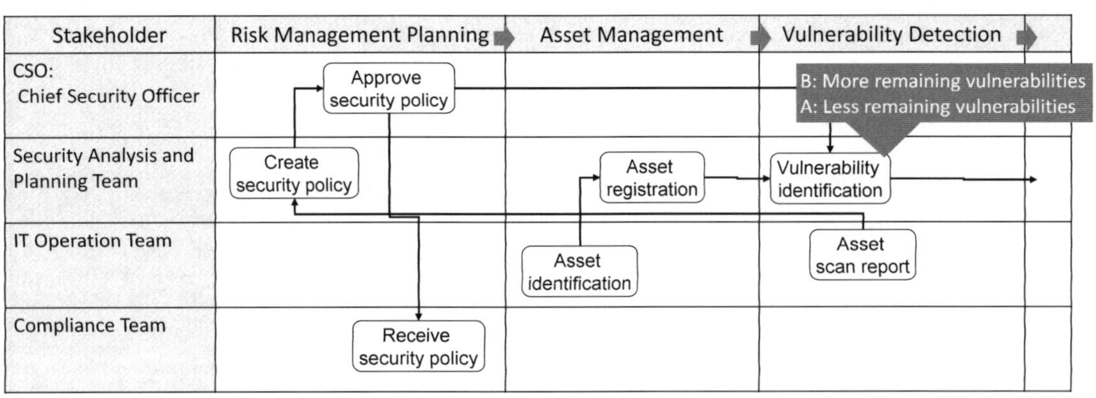

Figure 4. Process swim lane by applying Ex-table

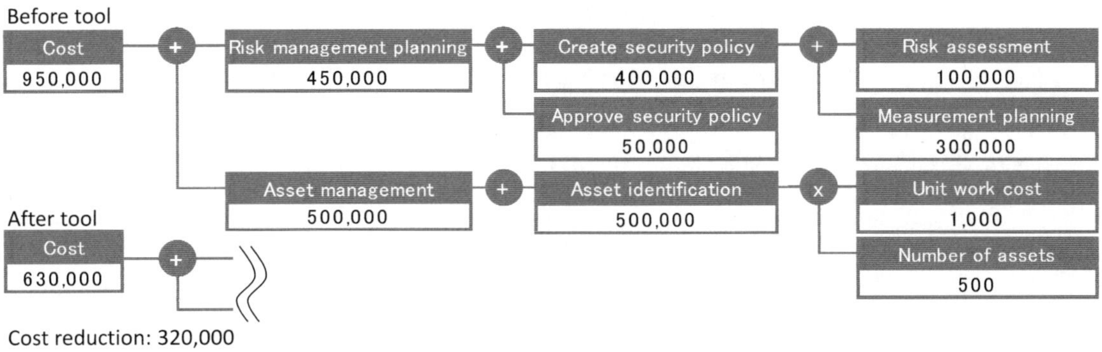

Figure 5. Example of cost reduction analysis by cost factor tree

4. RESULTS AND EVALUATION OF COST REDUCTION BY APPLYING VULNERABILITY MANAGEMENT TOOL

4.1 Conditions of Cost Reduction Estimation

We conducted an estimation of cost reduction on vulnerability management process by applying the method explained in chapter 3. To conduct the estimation, we assumed some cost parameters which are typical case in enterprise organization in India. One of them is unit human cost per day shown in table 2(a), where INR is the currency unit in India. There are five persons in different roles listed, and they have different unit costs. Another parameter is average quantities of assumed enterprise network shown in Table 3(b). There are four cost parameters listed, number of servers, number of security reports per year, number of vulnerabilities per server, and number of audits per year. These parameters are estimated by security researchers who joined the workshops, based on their experiences on working with security management team in India.

Table 2. (a)Unit human cost, and (b)Quantities of cost parameters

(a)

Assumed assigned person	Cost (INR/day)
CSO (Chief Security Officer)	10,000
Senior security team member	5,000
Junior security team member	2,500
IT operator	1,000
Compliance team member	3,500

(b)

Cost parameter	Quantity
Average number of servers per network	500
Average number of security reports per year	52
Average number of vulnerabilities per server	20
Average number of audits per year	2

4.2 Results of Each Step

Through the first step, we derived five stakeholders such as CSO (Chief Security Officer) or IT operation team, and nineteen concerns of them. Security planning and analysis team has the most concerns, and it suggests that the team might be the main target of the vulnerability management tool.

Through the second step, we derived ten work phases and thirty-one activities. Four out of the thirty-one activities are suggested to change by applying the vulnerability management tool.

Finally, we estimated cost change before and after the tool applied by using cost factor tree. In the third step, it is found that only four activities are changed by applying the tool, but the estimation was required to almost all activities. Because once quantity change of high severity vulnerability happens, the change affects later activities.

4.3 Total Amount of Cost Reduction Estimation

Total amount of cost reduction is estimated as in table 3. In table 3, where only amount changed activities are listed. Two activities, vulnerability identification and report vulnerability are totally automated, and its work-related costs become zero. Activity of identify severity becomes much cost down thanks to the tool's support. Other activities become cost down because some of high severity vulnerabilities become lower priority based on attack path analysis and need of immediate patching is lower.

As the result of applying the method to cost reduction analysis of software vulnerability management tool, we successfully identified the estimated quantity of the cost reduction. Necessary and sufficient cost drivers are captured by depicting Ex-table diagram, and the cost drivers are divided into cost parameters through cost factor analysis.

The analysis was conducted by six or eight members through three days workshop. Three out of the eight members have knowledge on the vulnerability management process and the vulnerability management tool with attack path analysis, and other two out of the eight members have experiences to conduct this kind of workshop. During the workshops, the members are required to do some pre-assignments, but only six hours are spent in actual workshop discussion. This result shows the proposed method gives supports to conduct efficient quantitative effect analysis of software vulnerability management tool. Also, we can reproduce another estimation in assuming different organizations or different countries by altering assumed cost parameters described in table 2.

Table 3. Result of cost reduction analysis

Phase	Activity	Cost before the tool (M-INR/year)	Cost after the tool (M-INR/year)	Cost difference (M-INR/year)
Vulnerability detection	Vulnerability Identification	5.0	0	-5.0
Vulnerability analysis	Report vulnerabilities	3.86	0	-3.86
	Identify severity	4.24	0.618	-3.622
	Decide action to high-risk vulnerabilities	0.13	0.0325	-0.0975
Patch testing	Patch approval	0.13	0.065	-0.065
Patch execution	Patch execution	0.22	0.20	-0.02
Compliance check	Check compliance	6.26	5.69	-0.57
Security monitoring	Risk analysis and report	125	25	-100
Total		144.84	31.61	-113.23

5. CONCLUSION

In this paper, we introduced a method to estimate cost reduction of software vulnerability management process with a software vulnerability management tool which supports attack path analysis. Through a six hours workshop with eight persons based on the introduced method, we found that the tool will qualitatively contribute to some cost reduction especially in security monitoring related activities. Also, it is clarified that the amount of expected cost reduction was 113.23 M-INR/year in typical situation. The introduced method can efficiently estimate the reduction cost and can reproduce another estimation in different organizations or different countries by altering some assumed cost parameters.

REFERENCES

R. L. Minz, et al., 2018. Cyber Security Using Bayesian Attack Path Analysis. in Proc. on *CYBER 2018 – The Third International Conference on Cyber-Technologies and Cyber-Systems*, pp.15-22.

S. Yashiro, et al., 2020. Proposal of Estimation Method on Cost Reduction by Applying Manufacturing Execution System to Pharmaceutical Process. *IEEJ Transactions on Electronics, Information and Systems.* Vol.140 No.10 pp.1147-1155 (written in Japanese).

W. Peng, S. Yao and J. Chen, 2009. Recognizing Intrusive Intention and Assessing Threat Based on Attack Path Analysis. in Proc. on *2009 International Conference on Multimedia Information Networking and Security*, pp. 450-453.

OPTIMISING THE PERFORMANCE OF TELECOMMUNICATION BULK EXPORT USING A MACHINE LEARNING CLOSED LOOP SYSTEM BASED ON HISTORIC PERFORMANCE

Barbara Conway, John Francis and Enda Fallon
Athlone Institute of Technology, Co. Westmeath, Ireland

ABSTRACT

Failures in telecommunication systems are typically resolved by the application of software patches or updates. These solutions tend to be specific to the failure type. Such bespoke system alterations are time consuming and financially expensive to implement. This paper proposes and evaluates a machine learning closed loop system to optimize the performance of the bulk configuration management data export. An evaluation file export service is developed and managed based on the industry standard JSR352 specification. The service produces failures reducing its overall performance. Rather than providing a specific solution for individual system failures, an adaptive and extensible machine learning closed loop system is introduced. The framework enables the file export service to learn from historic performance and to predict imminent failures. This type of closed loop system is optimized by providing the capability to re-learn based on new training data. This capability brings a dynamic approach to providing solutions. Solutions are reactive rather than static. Failures in software behavior can depend on environmental conditions like high load on a persistence layer, high volumes of traffic, insufficient hardware dimensioning. When failures occur due to factors like these, a dynamic redirection of the software to another flow stabilizes and improves the systems overall performance.

KEYWORDS

Machine Learning, File Parsing, System Optimization, Failure Prediction

1. INTRODUCTION

1.1 Introduction

This work evaluates the performance of a telecommunications network bulk export system which historically experiences system failure in 10% of scenarios. This work proposes and evaluates a machine learning closed loop system to optimize the performance of the bulk export system. An evaluation file export service is developed and managed based on the industry standard JSR352 specification. The export job is partially successful due to some failing exports. Rather than providing a specific solution for the failures, a framework, comprising of a machine learning closed loop system is implemented and evaluated. The Framework provides an adaptable interface to allow the file export service to train data generated by the service. The Framework accepts test data to predict failures based on the file export services past results. Training and test data produced and derived from the export service is in csv form. The export service uses the prediction to adapt the export to avoid the future failure. The Framework includes a feedback loop, so that it can be optimized by re-learning based on new data. The models developed within the machine learning closed loop system are based on supervised and unsupervised learning.

The system provides an extensible approach in which specific machine learning strategies can be transparently introduced. In this evaluation, an analysis of Bayes theorem, SMO/Support Vector/Sequential Minimal Optimization, and the Simple KMeans clustering-based algorithms were carried out. Results illustrate that supervised learning achieved 95% processing success with fewer recorded failures. The machine learning enabled approach to the export data system has removed the need for time consuming and costly manual intervention in the system process. It has shown an improved efficiency and flexibility of the entire end to end bulk export management process and the concept can be adapted at industrial scale.

This paper is organized as follows, relevant literature is discussed in Section 2, system design is outlined in Section 3, conclusions are documented in Section 4.

2. LITERATURE REVIEW

According to (E. Elahi, et al. 2021) early identification of faulty modules improves the software quality and thus the software produced will be of higher quality and cost effective. (W. Huanhuan, et al. 2021), proposed a network structure algorithm based on machine learning. The algorithm learnt and was trained according to the output function parameters of the circuit, in order to accurately determine the cause of the circuit fault and locate the fault through quantitative analysis, demonstrates the benefits of a failure prediction systems like the one outlined here. Machine learning can be used in identifying failures or predicting failures. It's widely used in medical research, like in (J. Ma, 2020) where it used six classical machine learning models, including logistic regression, support vector machine, decision tree, random forest, boosting and neural network, to make a prediction model for diabetes diagnosis. (K. Al Mayahi & M. Al-Bahri, 2020) created a machine-based learning model to predict a student's educational performance. The developed model relied on the student's previous data and performance in the last stage of the school. Machine Learning can be used to develop an application software for visualization of fault data recorded on OSS, (Y. Tamura, et al. 2016). It can be used to detect failures in hardware also, like a Machine Learning (ML) based algorithm for arc fault detection and an experimental testbed for validation. The ML algorithm is trained with experimental arc fault data. The chosen ML algorithm resulted in a high accuracy performance within a relatively low delay time compared to conventional detection methods. (V. Le & X. Yao, 2019) (V. Mhetre & M. Nagar, 2017) focuses on identifying slow, average and fast learners among students and displaying it by predictive data mining model using classification-based algorithms. Student Details have been referred from Sardar Patel Institute of Technology College MCA Department and prediction of learners is done by applying Naïve Bayes, J48, ZeroR and Random Tree using WEKA as an Open Source Tool, as suggested in this thesis.

To implement a machine learning service, there are steps involved in creating a machine learning model, reference (IBM, 2021). The training data needs to be properly prepared and checked for imbalances or biases that could impact the training. It should also be divided into two subsets: the training subset, which will be used to train the application, and the evaluation subset, used to test and refine it. An algorithm is chosen to run on the training data set. The type of algorithm depends on the type (labeled or unlabeled) and the amount of data in the training data set and on the type of problem to be solved.

Training the algorithm is an iterative process–it involves running variables through the algorithm, comparing the output with the results it should have produced, adjusting weights and biases within the algorithm that might yield a more accurate result, and running the variables again until the algorithm returns the correct result most of the time. The resulting trained, accurate algorithm is the machine learning model.

The final step is to use the model with new data and, in the best case, for it to improve in accuracy and effectiveness over time. Where the new data comes from will depend on the problem being solved. Machine Learning can be categorized into supervised and unsupervised based on the approach. Supervised learning works with a set of data that contains both the inputs and the desired output — for instance, a data set containing various characteristics of a property and the expected rental income. Supervised learning is further divided into two broad sub-categories called classification and regression: classification algorithms are related to categorical output, like whether a property is occupied or not, regression algorithms are related to a continuous output range, like the value of a property. Unsupervised learning, on the other hand, works with a set of data which only have input values. It works by trying to identify the inherent structure in the input data. For instance, finding different types of consumers through a data set of their consumption behavior.

3. SYSTEM DESIGN

Introducing a machine learning closed loop system within a distributed system is outlined in this chapter. The file export system is a service used by a Client to parse large log files in search of key words or phrases. The parsing of these files can lead to failures. This would normally result in a software fix which would apply to all file parsing. Instead, this project demonstrates that a machine learning closed loop system can predict a failure and the software solution is a re-direction in the software flow.

3.1 System Architecture

The architecture of the file export service is based on JSR 352, reference (JSR, 2021). The reason for choosing Batch JSR 352 is the ability to batch the jobs with flexibility of threading, retry mechanism, custom implementations on Reader/Processor/Writers. Key decision points can be made at various parts within the architecture. For example, based on a prediction, it can allow the service to retry a given file, it can change the number of parallel files to be read concurrently or it can be used to provide the ability for the service to provide different processing/writing mechanism.

The job is described by XML. It provides the order and description of main operating java classes and steps within the job from start to completion. There are three items related to the job step. ResourceReader implements ItemReader and retrieves data for the job step to operate on. An "item" of data is a file in this case. ResourceProcessor implements ItemProcessor and performs the business logic on the data item that was provided by the ItemReader. In this case, parsing and generating a new file containing all instances of the key word or phrase. ResourceWriter implements ItemWriter and is used to write the output of the ResourceProcessor. The overall job is recorded by writing job details to a database or file. This allows the client to show the performance of the file export system.

The following figure illustrates the architecture of the proposed closed loop adaptive framework for bulk data processing.

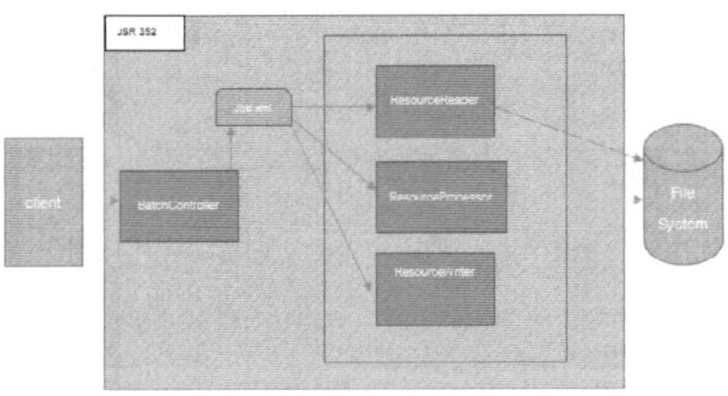

Figure 1. File Parsing Service is built on JSR 352, reference (JSR, 2021)

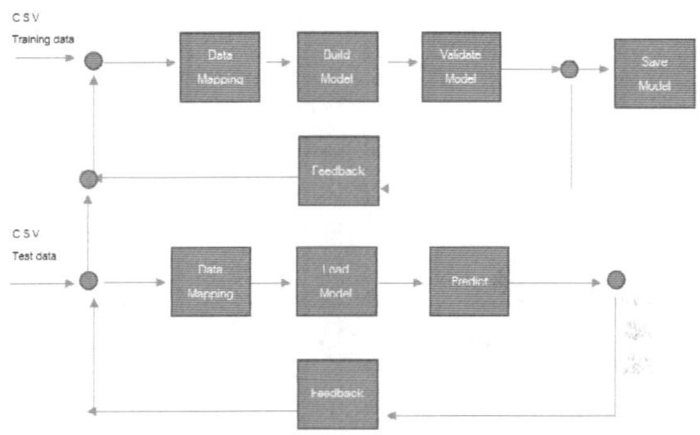

Figure 2. Machine Learning Closed Loop System

Training and test data are input in the form of comma separated features. The data sets are transformed to Attribute-Relation File Format. The build model component dynamically builds a series of models based on many algorithms. The validate model component chooses the model with the highest performing results. The model is saved for future re-use. The load model component loads the saved model and the predict component uses the test data to predict the outcome based on the trained model.

3.2 Algorithm Evaluation

190 samples of data were selected for training. There are 3 features, file size, file type and parsing status. The feature selected for classification is parsing status which can have results FAILED or SUCCESS. Out of the 190 samples, 19 are FAILED and 171 are SUCCESSFUL during normal operation showing a reduction in the file export service performance of 10%.

Several algorithms were considered and tested. These include the RepTree decision-tree based algorithm, IBK K-Nearest Neighbor, the SMO/Support Vector/Sequential Minimal Optimization algorithm, the Simple KMeans clustering based algorithm. The same training data was executed against different models. In all cases, a model is trained and then tested to predict an output. The expected output is described, and the corresponding result is recorded. The preferred algorithms for the system are Support Vector and Bayes Classifier. Figure 3 shows how Weka evaluates each algorithm.

Table 1. Algorithm Appraisal On evaluation of this data set, SMO values show greater results. This is for evaluation purposes only

Naive Bayes Evaluation summary	**SMO - John Platt's sequential minimal optimization algorithm** Evaluation summary
Correctly Classified Instances 183 96.3158 % Incorrectly Classified Instances 7 3.6842 % Kappa statistic 0.7682 Mean absolute error 0.0605 Root mean squared error 0.1583 Relative absolute error 32.9848 % Root relative squared error 52.7709 % Total Number of Instances 190	Correctly Classified Instances 187 98.4211 % Incorrectly Classified Instances 3 1.5789 % Kappa statistic 0.9102 Mean absolute error 0.0158 Root mean squared error 0.1257 Relative absolute error 8.6124 % Root relative squared error 41.8814 % Total Number of Instances 190
P(SUCCESS) = 170/190 P(File size = SUCCESS) = 171/190 P(File type = SUCCESS) = 173/190 171/190 * 173/190 = 0.819 P(FAILED) = 13/190 P(File size = FAILED) = 19/190 P(File type = FAILED) = 21/190 19/190 * 21/190 = 0.011 Since P(SUCCESS | File size) > P(FAILED | File size) Then a prediction of FAILURE can occur if the File size or File type don't comply with the values as follows: (mean values) SUCCESS FAILED File size 52327735.2062 91842033.9312 File type text/x-log (134 ok) text/plain (39 ok)	Weka normalised the data as follows. Classifier for classes: SUCCESS, FAILED BinarySMO 3.4299 * (normalized) FileSize + 1.9808 * (normalized) FileType=text/plain - 4.4054 Number of kernel evaluations: 826 (62.943% cached) There were 826 evaluations from the kernel with 62.943% already calculated.
13 are correctly classified as FAILED, 1 incorrectly classified as SUCCESS. 170 are correctly classified as SUCCESS and 6 incorrectly classified as FAILED	17 are correctly classified as FAILED, 1 incorrectly classified as SUCCESS. 170 are correctly classified as SUCCESS and 2 incorrectly classified as FAILED

4. FUTURE WORK

As this is an evaluation project, future work will include the integration of the machine loop closed system onto an actual bulk export system to train the actual bulk export data results. The results can be compared to the evaluation project to determine the actual effectiveness of the machine loop closed system in an industrial setting. This small scale evaluation can be extrapolated to an industrial scale. As the machine learning closed is independent of the service and the data provided to it, the closed system can be used by other services. The implementation of the machine learning closed loop system can be achieved using other frameworks like Python or Scala as opposed to Weka.

5. CONCLUSION

This work proposes a machine learning closed loop system to optimize the performance of bulk configuration export in a telecommunications environment. An evaluation file export service is developed and managed based on the industry standard JSR352 specification. Rather than providing a specific solution for individual failures, a new framework, comprising of a machine learning closed loop system is implemented and evaluated. The Framework provides an adaptable interface to allow the file export service to train data generated by the service and test new data to predict failures based on the file export services past results. Based on a specific file type the system learns and adapts how particular export files should be parsed to avoid system failure.

The evaluation investigates the benefit of using machine learning algorithms including Bayes theorem, SMO/Support Vector/Sequential Minimal Optimization, and the Simple KMeans clustering-based algorithm. The results from Naïve Bayes illustrated that 13 were correctly classified as failed, 1 incorrectly classified as success. The results from the SMO algorithm illustrated that 17 were correctly classified as failed, 2 had incorrectly classified as failed.

The results gathered from evaluating these algorithms suggests that the performance of the file export service increases due to the correct detection of 13 failed results using Naïve Bayes or 17 failed results using SMO. This proves that the introduction of the machine learning closed loop system can detect future failures based on past results and can improve the file export service performance.

The extensible and adaptive machine learning enabled approach to file export has removed the need for time consuming and costly manual intervention in the system process. It has improved the efficiency and flexibility of the entire end to end bulk export management process in an industry scale telecommunications environment.

REFERENCES

E. Elahi, A. Ayub and I. Hussain, "Two staged data preprocessing ensemble model for software fault prediction,"2021 International Bhurban Conference on Applied Sciences and Technologies (IBCAST), 2021, pp. 506-511, doi: 10.1109/IBCAST51254.2021.9393182.

Jbossas.jboss.org. 2021. JBoss Application Server - JBoss Community. [online] Available at: <http://jbossas.jboss.org/> [Accessed 19 May 2021].

Jcp.org. 2021. The Java Community Process(SM) Program - JSRs: Java Specification Requests - detail JSR# 314. [online] Available at: <https://www.jcp.org/en/jsr/detail?id=314> [Accessed 19 May 2021].

Oreilly.com. 2021. O'Reilly Media - Technology and Business Training. [online] Available at: <https://www.oreilly.com/> [Accessed 19 May 2021].

V. Le and X. Yao, "Ensemble Machine Learning Based Adaptive Arc Fault Detection for DC Distribution Systems," 2019 IEEE Applied Power Electronics Conference and Exposition (APEC), 2019, pp. 1984-1989, doi: 10.1109/APEC.2019.8721922.

V. Mhetre and M. Nagar, "Classification based data mining algorithms to predict slow, average and fast learners in educational system using WEKA," 2017 International Conference on Computing Methodologies and Communication (ICCMC), 2017, pp. 475-479, doi: 10.1109/ICCMC.2017.8282735.

W. Huanhuan, Z. Ming, X. Xin and R. Xiaoming, "Fault diagnosis and prediction of accelerometer servo circuit based on machine learning algorithm," 2021 7th International Symposium on Mechatronics and Industrial Informatics (ISMII), 2021, pp. 256-260, doi: 10.1109/ISMII52409.2021.00061.

wildfly.org. 2021. Redhat Wildfly. [online] Available at: <http://wildfly.org/ https://docs.wildfly.org/20/Getting_Started_Developing_Applications_Guide.html https://docs.wildfly.org/17/Getting_Started_Guide.html> [Accessed 19 May 2021].

Y. Tamura, S. Ashida and S. Yamada, "Fault Identification Tool Based on Deep Learning for Fault Big Data," 2016 International Conference on Information Science and Security (ICISS), 2016, pp. 1-4, doi: 10.1109/ICISSEC.2016.7885852

APPLICATION DEVELOPMENT FOR MUSIC RECOMMENDATION SYSTEM USING DEEP DETERMINISTIC POLICY GRADIENT

Rathin S. Kamble, Sujala D. Shetty and Aljo Jose
Department of Computer Science, Birla Institute of Technology & Science, Pilani, Dubai Campus
Academic City, Dubai, U.A.E

ABSTRACT

Recommendation Systems works as an information filtering system which helps to feed and recommend content personalized for the taste of the user. From the use in e-commerce to generic advertisement, recommender systems are proven to be highly effective and go-to solution for personalized content promotion. This project aims to develop and design a Machine Learning model which can be integrated into an Android application to help recommend music for the app user. For this purpose, a Deep Deterministic Policy Gradient model was used along with an underlying architecture for designing the android application which contains playlist of the user's songs and considering the likes and dislikes from the user, the app with the help of the ML model helps suggest user an additional array of songs.

KEYWORDS

Reinforcement Learning, DDPG, Recommendation System, TensorFlow, BigQuery, Firebase

1. INTRODUCTION

Most of the common recommendation systems model used are designed to maximize the short-term reward while overlooking the fact whether the suggestion would likely lead to a more profitable reward in the long run/long-term reward. This project was implemented using the Keras and TensorFlow libraries to develop and train a Deep Deterministic Policy Gradient (DDPG) model, which takes the recommendation system approach as a sequential interaction between the user and the model, thus leveraging the Reinforcement Learning (RL) methods to automatically learn and update the strategies until the system converges to an optimal policy. Using this approach ensures that the optimal strategy generated maximizes the expected long-term rewards. An android app was developed which holds the user's music playlist and the trained model was exported to the app using Firebase and BigQuery as a backend service for storing and aggregating the data and mediating the flow of data from the TensorFlow Colab Notebooks and Android application.

2. OVERVIEW OF REINFORCEMENT LEARNING

As the task at hand was for the recommender agent to provide recommendations, we can model this problem with the help of Markov Decision Process (MDP). In MDPs, we have an agent which is interacting with an environment. The agent takes actions, gets next state to proceed to and the reward (scalar value) associated with the action it took. Hence, formally an MDP consists of the tuple of attributes (S, A, P, R, γ).

- State Space (S): Defined as browsing history of the user which are the previous N items that a user browsed before time t.
- Action Space (A): An action At implies a list of items given to user at time t based on the current state St.
- Transition Probability (P): Probability p (St+1|St, At) defines the probability of state transition from St to St+1 when Recommender agent takes an action At

- Reward (R): Based on the current state St and the action taken At, i.e.- the agent recommending a list of items to user, the agent receives the immediate reward Rt
- Discount Factor (γ): The immediate reward is considered by a greater factor and the delayed rewards over time are reduced by a factor. This is used to solve the problem of infinite horizon where we must make use of discounted aggregation of rewards achieved over time. ($\gamma \in [0, 1]$)

3. RELATED WORK

This section briefly reviews the related work to this project. In (2016), Paul, C., Jay, A., Emre, S. published paper on how deep learning brought significant improvements to their system. Given that YouTube generates a large amount of data every single hour, they provided various insights on designing and maintaining such massive recommendation system. Rafael Glauber and Angelo Loula (2019) explains the differences and similarities between two main commonly used methods of recommendation systems that is Collaborative Filtering and Content-based Filtering. They proposed to conduct experiments for comparison between the two algorithms for different approaches. Wu et al. (2016) provided a session-based recommendation model using Recurrent Neural Network for real world e-commerce website. They integrated the RNN with Feedforward network which is used to represent the user-items correlation and thus increased accuracy dramatically. Nguyen et al. (2017) implemented a tag recommendation system which makes use of Convolutional Neural Networks (CNNs) for visual information and make use of user's preferences. Hybrid recommender systems implemented by Robin Burke (2002) are used to enhances the effectiveness of the recommendations ranked by the collaborative filtering method. Shani et al. (2005) implemented an MDP-based recommendation system and made use of an n-gram model which incites on Markov-chain model of user behavior. Peter et al. (2015) implemented a deep reinforcement learning model for Slate MDP for high-dimensional states and action spaces. They introduced a new type of MDP called the Slate MDP and applied deep Q-learning for feature representation of both the state and action space. Mahmood et al. (2009) made use of reinforcement learning strategies for implementing a conversational recommendation agent with the same goal of increasing the cumulative rewards. Taghipour et al. (2007, 2008) looked at the web page recommendation problem as a Q-learning problem and made recommendation based on the web page usage data as the actions and applies the reinforcement learning strategies to constantly learn and attain an optimal policy. X. Zhao, L. Zhang, L. Xia, Z. Ding, D. Yin, and J. Tang (2019) makes use of Deep reinforcement learning for List-wise recommendation strategy to recommend items to user. The model acts on a Markov Decision process and leverages the reinforcement learning methods to come up with a framework to work as an online user-agent interaction simulator giving a list-wise recommendation.

4. METHODOLGY AND IMPLEMENTATION

In this project, a Deep Deterministic Policy Gradient (DDPG) was used to model the sequential interaction between users and recommendation system. For a recommendation process, given a current state s_t the agent recommends a list of items a_t to provide the feedback. In our case, the feedback is captured by the user in the app clicking whether the song (item) is liked or disliked. The agent then receives the immediate reward r according to the user's feedback. Hence to simulate the mentioned process, we need to build a simulator to predict a reward based on the current state and action selected. The data/information from the playlist is processed and used by the model to generate a memory M = {m1, m2, ...} to store users' historical browsing history where m_i is a user agent interaction tuple.

The current state and the action recommended by the recommender agent are matched to the historical state action pair such that we can generate a simulated reward. In depth, if the initial state and the historical session are denoted as s0 = {s1, · · · , sN} and {a1, · · · , aL } then we can observe current state (s), current action (a) and reward list (r) and store the triple ((s,a) → r) in memory. For instance, the recommendation agent recommends a list of five songs denoting as {a1, · · · , a5} to the user, then if the user likes a3 and a4, then update the current state by removing the number of items liked from the top of the state resulting in s = {s3, · · · , sN , a3, a4}. We calculate the overall reward r_t of the whole recommended list as follows:

$$r_t = \sum_{k=1}^{K} \Gamma^{k-1} u_x^k \quad (1)$$

Here K is the length of the recommendation list, $\Gamma \in (0, 1]$ and u denotes the reward permutation list.

For each interaction of training the model, there are two stages. In the first stage, given the current state, the recommendation agent recommends a list of items a_t. The actor ($f_\theta\pi$) and critic network ($Q(s, a \mid \theta\ \mu)$) are initialized with random weight along with the target network f' and Q'. Similarly, the capacity of the replay memory D is initialized as well. The actor then generates a weight vector list using the following equation:

$$f_\theta \pi : s_t \rightarrow w_t \quad (2)$$

Here, $f_\theta \pi$ is a function parameterized by θ^π. Then for each weight the recommendation agent scores the items in the item space. The item with the highest score is selected and added to the recommendation list and the item is removed from the item space to prevent repetitive recommendation. Then the agent observes the reward from the simulator procedure mentioned above (1) and updates the state accordingly, storing the transitions (s_t, a_t, r_t, s_{t+1}) into the replay memory D. In the next stage, the recommender agent then samples mini-batch of these transitions from replay memory D and then updates the parameters of the actor and critic networks based on the standard procedures of DDPG which can be given as follows:-

1. Update Critic:-
   a. Minimizing RPE : $\delta_t = r_t + \gamma Q(s_t{+}1 , \pi(st{+}1) \mid \theta) - Q(s_t , a_t \mid \theta)$
   b. Computing the desired output: $Y_i = r_i + \gamma Q'(s_{i+1} , \pi(s_i{+}1) \mid \theta')$ and Update θ by minimizing the Loss function:
   c. $L = 1/N * \Sigma (Y_i - Q(s_i , a_i \mid \theta))^2$
2. Update Actor using the sampled policy gradient equation.
3. Update Critic and Actor target network:-
   a. Critic = $\theta^{\mu'} \leftarrow \tau\, \theta^{\mu} + (1 - \tau)\theta^{\mu'}$
   b. Actor = $\theta^{\pi'} \leftarrow \tau\, \theta^{\pi} + (1 - \tau)\theta^{\pi'}$

5. ANDROID APPLICATION, FIREBASE, AND BIGQUERY

While designing the android app, Android Studio is used which is an integrated development environment (IDE) for Google's android operating system since it is specifically designed for Android development. Apps can be developed using Java, C++, Kotlin which differs based on programmer's choice. For this project, Java was used as the preferred language to develop the app. Android Studio has features such as gradle-based build support, android specific refactoring, rich layout editors that allows drag and drop UI components with an option to preview layouts. More importantly, it has a built-in support for Google Cloud Platform, thus enabling integration with Firebase and Google App engine.

5.1 Android App Architecture

Since the project is based on pulling the recommendations provided by the model from TensorFlow which is in a remote data source, a need for using the proper architecture for the android app was essential. For this purpose, the MVVM (Model-View-View Model) architecture is suitable to structure the code such that the code can be more modular and have better separated components such that each part of the program has different responsibility and can be separately modified without affecting other component.

5.2 Firebase

For getting the recommendations, we must gather the data from the app. For this project, making use of Firebase mainly due to Android studio having built-in support for Google Cloud Platform, thus enabling integration with Firebase. Firebase is a useful platform for mobile and web applications. It can be a back end for many services such as user authentication, data storage, static hosting, real-time database etc. It provides a user-friendly platform for building mobile and web apps. This project enables the Google analytics through Firebase such that with Google Analytics we can obtain the user-behavior data (in this case which song the user likes in a sequential order). This can be done by sending an Analytics event each time the user likes or dislikes the song.

5.3 BigQuery

The Firebase and Google Analytics helps to get the user's likes and dislikes of song as Analytics events to Firebase. Hence, to store this data and aggregate it, make use of BigQuery. BigQuery is a Google Cloud product that allows you to examine and process large amounts of data. It is serverless, highly scalable multi-cloud data warehouse and it is a great integration with Firebase. The Firebase console for this project was connected with BigQuery so that the analytics data generated by the app is automatically exported to BigQuery into the intraday table and groups events in the events table. The dataset required for Recommendations System needs to be large enough to extract meaningful outputs. So, there is a need to import the sample dataset used into the BigQuery. We used the public One Million Song dataset for this case.

Next step was to create service account credential in the Google Cloud Console to access and load the BigQuery data from the Google Colab environment. This is for importing the BigQuery data, preprocess this data for training the recommendation model and exporting the model in TFLite format suitable for using in mobile app.

5.4 Connection between TensorFlow and Firebase-BigQuery

The analytics data from the BigQuery was imported into the Colab Notebook. For accessing the BigQuery data from the Colab notebook, upload the service account file.Then load the analytics data collected in the app with the Firebase analytics into the notebook using pandas pre-processing libraries to preprocess the data and extract the necessary information needed to feed it as input to the model. BigQuery provides several convenience IPython magics (commands) that will fetch data Finally, extract the information passed from the app into the Colab notebook.

Once the training of the DDPG model is finished, it was saved and then compressed to export the model into a TFLite file so that it can be used on the App to show the recommendations. The model was then deployed to the Firebase Console using Firebase ML. To do so the use of Firebase Admin SDK was needed.

6. CONCLUSION AND FUTURE SCOPE

The model was downloaded into the app and launched each time you wanted recommendations for the songs you liked. The list of the recommendation can be seen when the floating action button is clicked. The recommendation comes from the model which gives a list of songs from the dataset along with the song liked by the user. Since the model is based on the public One Million song dataset, comparing the mean average accuracy, model is seen to have more diverse selection of music (9.3% vs 7.6%) and better identifies the songs that are skipped by the users (49% vs 54%).

This project was designed to suggest recommendations for music songs while using a reinforcement learning approach. Deep Deterministic Policy Gradient model was developed for this purpose using TensorFlow libraries with the help of Firebase and BigQuery Google Cloud Services to store and aggregate the likes and dislikes of the user through the app. The use of DDPG model acts as a Markov Decision Process and takes advantage of Deep Reinforcement Learning to automatically learn the optimal policy for recommendation of items. Using this ensures that the cumulative rewards over the long run are maximized. There are several researching directions for this project, one of which can include applying the model for different applications. Further, addition with other model architectures like RNN, CNN to find better agent-user pattern and investigate how to model these additions mathematically for recommendations would also serve as some future researching prospects to look at.

REFERENCES

Burke, R., 2002. Hybrid Recommender Systems: Survey and Experiments User Modeling and User-Adapted Interaction, 12(4), pp.331-370.

Covington, P. et al, 2016. Deep Neural Networks for YouTube Recommendations. *Proceedings of the 10th ACM Conference on Recommender Systems.*

Kun Zhou, et al. 2020. S3-Rec: Self-Supervised Learning for Sequential Recommendation with Mutual Information Maximization. *In Proceedings of the 29th ACM International Conference on Information & Knowledge Management Association for Computing Machinery, New York, NY, USA*, 1893–1902. DOI: https://doi.org/10.1145/3340531.3411954

M. H. Mohamed, M. H. Khafagy and M. H. Ibrahim, "Recommender Systems Challenges and Solutions Survey," 2019 *International Conference on Innovative Trends in Computer Engineering (ITCE)*, 2019, pp. 149-155, doi: 10.1109/ITCE.2019.8646645.

Nguyen, H. et al, 2017. Personalized Deep Learning for Tag Recommendation. *Advances in Knowledge Discovery and Data Mining, pp.186-197.*

Nima Taghipour and Ahmad Kardan. 2008. A hybrid web recommender system based on q-learning. *In Proceedings of the 2008 ACM symposium on Applied computing. ACM, 1164–1168.*

Nima Taghipour, Ahmad Kardan, and Saeed Shiry Ghidary. 2007. Usage-based web recommendations: a reinforcement learning approach. *In Proceedings of the 2007 ACM conference on Recommender systems. ACM, 113–120.*

Rafael, G., Angelo, L., (2019): Collaborative Filtering vs. Content-Based Filtering: differences and similarities, *arXiv:1912.08932v1 [cs.IR]*

Shani, G. et al, 2002. An MDP-Based Recommender System | *The Journal of Machine Learning Research.*

Sunehag, Peter & Evans, et al. (2015). Deep Reinforcement Learning with Attention for Slate Markov Decision Processes with High-Dimensional States and Actions.

Tariq Mahmood and Francesco Ricci. 2009. Improving recommender systems with adaptive conversational strategies. *In Proceedings of the 20th ACM conference on Hypertext and hypermedia. ACM, 73–82.*

Wu, S. et al, 2016. Personal recommendation using deep recurrent neural networks in NetEase. *2016 IEEE 32nd International Conference on Data Engineering (ICDE).*

Xiangyu Zhao et al., 2019. Deep Reinforcement Learning for List-wise Recommendations.

Xiangyu Zhao, et al. 2018. Recommendations with Negative Feedback via Pairwise Deep Reinforcement Learning. *In Proceedings of the 24th ACM SIGKDD International Conference on Knowledge Discovery & Data Mining. ACM, 1040–1048.*

Xiangyu Zhao, et al. 2019. Model-Based Reinforcement Learning for Whole-Chain Recommendations.

IN OTHER WORDS: A NAIVE APPROACH TO TEXT SPINNING

Frederik S. Bäumer[1], Joschka Kersting[2], Sergej Denisov[1] and Michaela Geierhos[3]
[1]*Bielefeld University of Applied Sciences, Bielefeld, Germany*
[2]*Paderborn University, Paderborn, Germany*
[3]*Bundeswehr University Munich, Research Institute CODE, Munich, Germany*

ABSTRACT

Content is the new oil. Users consume billions of terabytes a day while surfing on news sites or blogs, posting on social media sites, and sending chat messages around the globe. While content is heterogeneous, the dominant form of web content is text. There are situations where more diversity needs to be introduced into text content, for example, to reuse it on websites or to allow a chatbot to base its models on the information conveyed rather than of the language used. In order to achieve this, paraphrasing techniques have been developed: One example is Text spinning, a technique that automatically paraphrases text while leaving the intent intact. This makes it easier to reuse content, or to change the language generated by the bot more human. One method for modifying texts is a combination of translation and back-translation. This paper presents NATTS, a naive approach that uses transformer-based translation models to create diversified text, combining translation steps in one model. An advantage of this approach is that it can be fine-tuned and handle technical language.

KEYWORDS

Paraphrasing, Text Spinning, Transformer, Sequence-to-Sequence

1. INTRODUCTION

After years of considerable progress in Natural Language Processing (NLP), there are still some areas of interest with unsolved challenges. These mainly concern the hand-crafted tasks that still have to be done to obtain better results (e.g., Kersting/Geierhos 2021). Examples include legal issues such as reviewing long contract documents, or domain-specific text generation, summarization, and paraphrasing. This paper deals with a subtopic of paraphrasing, called text spinning, in which the information of the text remains the same, while the words and grammar are changed (Prentice/Kinden 2018). So, this is not a matter of a classic style transfer here, but rather of finding the exact text and tone in different manifestations. This approach has many motivations, but is mainly used in online editorial systems and in dialog systems.

Here, we address two application areas to prove and discuss our approach at an early stage: search engine optimization (SEO) and chatbots. On the one hand, text spinning is commonly used in SEO to reuse content without degrading the search engine ranking of existing content. Rudimentary methods replace words with synonyms, while more sophisticated techniques also change sentence structure. Usually, spinning strategies distinguish between generation, summarization, and translation. In the case of generation, new texts are written based on existing texts, while in the case of summarization, only essential content is compiled. In translation, content is translated into one or more languages ("chained") before being re-translated to obtain a new text structure with the same intention. On the other hand, text spinning is also used for chatbots. These dialog systems are a form of artificial intelligence in which a program is developed to communicate with human users. That is, chatbots tend to have dedicated use cases in which they assist persons – a topic that is also applied in On-the-Fly (OTF) Computing (Karl et al. 2020: 467ff.), where apps are generated on-the-fly, based on the descriptions made by users. Studies have shown that it is beneficial to elaborate user queries with the help of a chatbot application (Bäumer et al. 2019: 7ff.). OTF Computing frees developers from building full-stack apps and allows them to build specialist services that can be composed *ad hoc* into fully functioning apps (Karl et al. 2020: 467f.). Here, however, it is promising to focus on the main functionality of the chatbot assistant instead of focusing on language. The wording used should not always be the same in order to communicate adequately with the user. Hence, a text spinning model can serve well to enable the division of labor. That is, developers can focus on developing and improving the main functions of the chatbot. At the same time, the text spinning model can modify the output of a chatbot before it is shown to the user. In an increasingly complex world, this approach facilitates specialization and efficiency.

Previous studies have dealt with this in different ways, i.e., most research deals with style transfer (Yang et al. 2018) and translation (Lewis et al. 2020: 7871ff.), as well as general paraphrasing (Androutsopoulos/Malakasiotis 2010: 135ff.), while text spinning is rather a marginal topic. Lancaster and Clarke (2009: 25ff.) present notable approaches to essay spinning, i.e., student's methods of plagiarizing. However, while these approaches are more traditional, we attempt to construct an up-to-date and naive method that rather simply makes use of large-scale, pre-trained transformer models.

2. NATTS – NAIVE APPROACH TO TEXT SPINNING

In traditional text spinning, as applied in SEO, the focus is on the richness of variants in order to achieve the greatest possible distance from the original text. There is no requirement to use one's own linguistic style or words, as is often the case with paraphrasing. The focus is entirely on the text distance while keeping the information. With NATTS, we try to improve existing techniques to achieve this goal. We call our approach naive because we knowingly misappropriate an existing NLP transformer model and still obtain convincing results. We benefit significantly from the flexibility of current NLP techniques.

2.1 Approach

Large-scale, pre-trained transformer models such as BERT (Devlin et al. 2019: 4171ff.) have taken NLP applications to a new level, especially in terms of robustness, adaptability, and flexibility. Transformers (Vaswani et al. 2017: 5998ff.) are deep neural network models that use attention mechanisms. These are usually pre-trained on large amounts of text data and later fine-tuned to downstream tasks. Significant progress has already been made in the field of machine translation. Models such as mBART50 (Tang et al. 2020), mT5 (Xue et al. 2021: 483ff.), and M2M-100 (Fan et al. 2020) can translate between up to 100 languages. The models differ in terms of methods, datasets, and the internal translation strategy (e.g., whether a transfer language such as English is used). We reinterpret the sentence translation task in the sense that we generate training data using translation services and then fine-tune the translation models to build our text spinning model.

Our approach is to fine-tune an existing translation model, defining the target language and the source language in German. Based on our own extensive dataset of paraphrased sentence pairs, we modify the model to translate "German to German". That is, it generates a variant of an input sentence. A well-known transformer-based model for translation is mBart50, which translates between 50 languages and uses English as the transfer language (Tang et al. 2020). Given the source and target languages, texts can be translated very efficiently and with high quality, although not all languages have been trained with the same amount of training data. The language pair "German to English" has been trained with a tremendous amount of data and is correspondingly robust and exhibits good translation quality. The model thus forms a solid basis for our project.

For the training, evaluation and test datasets, we made a split of 90 % / 5 % / 5 %. The machine for fine-tuning the pre-trained mBART50 model had two RTX 3090 GPUs, 256 GB RAM, and a Ryzen Threadripper 3960X CPU with 24 cores. The following parameters were used to fine-tune the model: 3 training epochs, a batch size of 20 per GPU, a learning rate of 5e-5, warmup ratio of 0.0625 and weight decay of 0.01. Using the DeepSpeed deep-learning optimization library (Rasley et al. 2020: 3505f.), we used much larger batch sizes, which significantly reduced the computation time by a factor of two.

2.2 Dataset: Acquisition and Preparation

The dataset is composed of two sources. The first part comes from CCAligned. We extracted the sentences with the highest similarity scores and translated the English variant of the German-English corpus back into German. In this way, we obtained German-German sentence pairs and discarded pairs that were too similar. Table 1 shows examples of resulting sentence pairs.

Table 1. Examples of training data (S: source sentence, T: target sentence, E: translation)

S: *Das Projekt hat eine Laufzeit von 2 Jahren* ***und endet am 15. Juli 2020.***
T: *Das Projekt hat eine Laufzeit von 2 Jahren* ***und soll am 15. Juli 2020 enden.***
E: The project has a term of 2 years and is scheduled to end on July 15, 2020.
S: *Füllen Sie das Formular* ***weiter unten*** *aus und wir* ***übermitteln*** *Ihnen* ***schnellstmöglich*** *unser Angebot.*
T: *Füllen Sie das Formular* ***unten*** *aus und wir werden* ***so schnell wie möglich*** *mit unserem Angebot* ***antworten.***
E: Fill in the form below and we will reply with our offer as soon as possible.

While CCAligned is a "a massive collection of cross-lingual web-document pairs", the second part of the dataset comes from software description texts crawled from the web describing the applications and their functionality. This dataset was available in English, so we translated it into German, then into Spanish, and back into German to obtain two German versions. After processing the records, we removed duplicates.

Table 2. Statistical information about the training dataset

Mean # Characters	Median # Characters	Mean # Tokens	Median # Tokens	Mean Cosine Similarity (DE-DE)	Mean BERT Score (DE-DE)	Number of Sentences
83	62	12	9	0.69	0.91	1,089,051

As can be seen in Table 2, the training sentences used are rather short, with an average of 83 characters, while the median is 62. We have on average only 12 tokens in each sentence, while the median is 9. However, the fact that we have short sentences from thousands of texts means that we can guarantee a variety of data, which is beneficial for large-scale deep learning models. The mean cosine similarity (Manning et al. 2009: 121) of the training sentences was 0.69, which means that we have quite different sentences in terms of word vectors. 1.0 would mean that the sentences are identical. Since we used translation to generate our sentences, they convey the same messages and information, but have different words that receive different vector representations. Word vectors are calculated based on the context in which words appear, and therefore do not fully represent synonyms. The specific context of words is distinctive. Moreover, if we read many sentences, we are sure to have satisfactory training data. In addition, the BERTScore (Zhang et al. 2020) of 0.91 has a high cosine similarity when the context is considered. That is, BERT computes embeddings based on context, and our high similarity score of over 0.9 shows that we have sentences with the same meaning. Of note is the difference between the standard mean cosine similarity (0.69) and the BERT variant (0.91).

3. EVALUATION AND DISCUSSION

The evaluation of spinning results is a challenging task, which is shown by following examples:

Table 3. Examples of paraphrased sentences (O: original, P: resulting paraphrase, E: translation)

O: *Apple iTunes für Windows: Update* ***bessert*** *mehrere Sicherheitslücken* ***aus***
P: *Apple iTunes für Windows:* ***Das*** *Update* ***behebt*** *mehrere Sicherheitslücken*
E: Apple iTunes for Windows: Update fixes several security holes
O: *Die GPU kann bei kompatiblen Systemen mit stabilen OpenCL-Treibern* ***optional hinzugezogen*** *werden.*
P: *Die GPU kann* ***optional auch auf kompatiblen*** *Systemen mit stabilen OpenCL-Treibern* ***hinzugefügt*** *werden.*
E: The GPU can optionally be used in compatible systems with stable OpenCL drivers.
O: *Als erstes Unternehmen der Welt* ***ist*** *der* ***Öl-Konzern*** *Shell* ***vom*** *Gericht zu schärferen Klimazielen verurteilt* ***worden.***
P: *Als erstes Unternehmen der Welt* ***wurde*** *Shell* ***von einem*** *Gericht zu schärferen Klimazielen verurteilt.*
E: The Shell oil company was the first company in the world to be sentenced to stricter climate targets by the court.
O: *Was* ***DAS*** *kostet, wenn* ***sie*** *mit Familie in den Urlaub fahren*
P: *Was kostet* ***es,*** *wenn* ***Sie*** *mit* ***der*** *Familie in den Urlaub fahren****?***
E: What THAT costs when you go on vacation with your family

On the one hand, values such as semantic similarity or the distance between characters help. However, a person still has to decide whether the content has not been corrupted by spinning. For this reason, we generated a subsample and evaluated the quality manually. As can be seen in Table 3, the sentences convey the same information while changing their wording and structure to some extent[1]. Our model keeps essential words such as technical names and changes the less important words to add variety to the language used. As the fourth example in Table 3 shows, the model also generates a question based on a statement. The model even uses the correct spelling of the word "*Sie*", a German formal pronoun (in the third person singular). Furthermore, changes in the sentence structure (see second and third example) and new phrasing stand out (see first and second example). Nevertheless, there are also cases where there are errors.

Table 4. Examples for paraphrased sentences with mistakes (O: original, P: resulting paraphrase, E: translation)

O: *Wie viel ist* ***drei*** *[3] plus* ***sieben*** *[7]?* P: *Wie viel ist* ***eins*** *[1] plus* ***sechs*** *[6]?* E: How much is three plus seven?
O: *Haben* ***Sie*** *Fragen? Kontaktieren Sie uns jetzt!* P: ***Du*** *hast Fragen? Kontaktiere uns jetzt!* E: You have questions? Contact us now!

As can be seen in Table 4, the model also produces errors. An illustrative example can be seen in the first row, where the original numbers for the target text are changed. For example, three becomes one in the generated sentence. The model does not consider the actual semantics of the numbers and transforms them. This derives from the traditional understanding of word vectors, where vectors pointing in the same direction or with a small distance in the n-dimensional space are considered to carry similar information. Another reason for this is that different numbers often appear in the sentence pairs in the training data. Therefore, the model learns to change numbers. The second example in Table 4 demonstrates a challenge of the German language that we addressed earlier in this section. In the example, the formal pronoun in the third person singular is changed, although this changes the information conveyed in our sentences. The message of the sentence changes quite significantly, for example, when customers are addressed in an informal way compared to the usual formal style. Hence, this is not desirable. In addition to the qualitative test, we also aim for a numerical evaluation. As far as we know, there are no suitable evaluation measures for this task. However, we have introduced the cosine similarity and the BERT Score in Section 2.2. We now present these scores again, but this time they are computed between input phrases from our training data on the one side and the generated output phrases on the other.

Table 5. Evaluative calculation of similarity scores (comparison scores in parentheses)

Mean Cosine Similarity (DE Generation)	Mean BERT Score (DE Generation)
0.77 (0.70)	0.92 (0.91)

We present our similarity values in Table 5. They differ from the values in Table 2 because they are calculated based on the newly generated data and the test set instead of all data (in parentheses). They are quite similar. The mean cosine similarity is 0.77 compared to 0.70 for the generated and test data. The BERT score, a type of cosine similarity based on the BERT vectors, is almost identical at 0.92 and 0.91. We consider this as a favorable result because our newly generated sentences differ from the input sentences in the same way as the test sentence pairs. That is, we have successfully trained a model that can perform text spinning. However, some cases are not handled correctly. We have shown such examples in Table 4. Especially when dealing with numbers, we need to take additional measures to catch possible incorrect text spinning results. But this can be accomplished with rule-based measures and does not affect the overall result of our research on NATTS. Apart from these cases, our naive approach is robust and therefore useful for text spinning.

4. CONCLUSION

In this short paper, we presented our early work on the text spinning approach NATTS, which uses a naive spinning approach that produces good results. The goal is to automatically generate text variants that keep the conveyed information of the input text but differ in wording and in grammatical structure. The presented

[1] The translation was added for a better understanding of this work.

method already achieves this goal, but still has some weaknesses. We think that we can eliminate these errors in the future by optimizing the parameterization and by using a new dataset. Our database is growing by thousands of sentence pairs every day, so we are confident that we will get a more and more robust model. As we continue to work on this issue, we are evaluating different translation models that we can use as a basis for the spinning process. An important topic for us is domain-specific spinning, which considers the specifics of a domain, for example in word choice. In this course, we are currently working on creating and training sub-corpora using topic modeling.

ACKNOWLEDGMENT

This work was partially supported by the German Research Foundation (DFG) within the Collaborative Research Centre On-The-Fly Computing (SFB 901).

REFERENCES

Androutsopoulos, I. and Malakasiotis, P., 2010. A Survey of Paraphrasing and Textual Entailment Methods. *Journal of Artificial Intelligence Research*, Vol. 38, pp. 135-187.

Bäumer, F. S., Kersting, J. and Geierhos, M., 2019. Natural Language Processing in OTF Computing: Challenges and the Need for Interactive Approaches. *Computers*, Vol. 8, No. 1.

Devlin, J., Chang, M.-W., Lee, K. and Toutanova, K., 2019. BERT: Pre-training of Deep Bidirectional Transformers for Language Understanding. *Proceedings of the 2019 Conference of the North American Chapter of the ACL: Human Language Technologies*, Minneapolis, MN, USA, pp. 4171-4186.

Fan, A., Bhosale, S., Schwenk, H., Ma, Z., El-Kishky, A., Goyal. S., Baines, M., Celebi, O., Wenzek, G., Chaudhary, V., Goyal. N., Birch. T., Liptchinsky, V., Edunov, S., Grave, E., Auli, M. and Joulin, A., 2020. Beyond English-Centric Multilingual Machine Translation. *Journal of Machine Learning Research.* Vol. 22, No. 107, pp. 1-48.

Karl, H., Kundisch, D., Meyer auf der Heide, F. and Wehrheim, H., 2020. A Case for a New IT Ecosystem: On-The-Fly Computing. *Business & Information Systems Engineering*, Vol. 62, No. 6, pp. 467-481.

Kersting, J. and Geierhos, M., 2021. Towards Aspect Extraction and Classification for Opinion Mining with Deep Sequence Networks. *Natural Language Processing in Artificial Intelligence.* Vol. 939. Cham, Switzerland, pp. 163-189.

Lancaster, T. and Clarke, R., 2009. Automated Essay Spinning - An Initial Investigation. *10th Annual Conference of the Subject Centre for Information and Computer Sciences*. Canterburry, UK, pp. 25-29.

Lewis, M., Liu, Y., Goyal, N., Ghazvininejad, M., Mohamed, A., Levy, O., Stoyanov, V., and Zettlemoyer, L., 2020. BART: Denoising Sequence-to-Sequence Pre-training for Natural Language Generation, Translation, and Comprehension. *Proceedings of the 58th Annual Meeting of the ACL*, Washington, USA, pp. 7871-7880.

Manning, C., Raghavan, P. and Schütze, H., An Introduction to Information Retrieval, Cambridge University Press. Cambridge, MA, USA: 2009. Available: https://nlp.stanford.edu/IR-book/pdf/irbookonlinereading.pdf [2021-07-05].

Prentice, F.M. and Kinden, C.E., 2018. Paraphrasing Tools, Language Translation Tools and Plagiarism: An Exploratory Study. *International Journal for Educational Integrity*, Vol. 14, No. 11, pp. 1833-2595.

Rasley, J., Rajbhandari, S., Ruwase, O., and He, Y., 2020. DeepSpeed: System Optimizations Enable Training Deep Learning Models with Over 100 Billion Parameters. *Proceedings of the 26th ACM SIGKDD International Conference on Knowledge Discovery & Data Mining*. New York, USA, pp. 3505-3506.

Tang, Y., Tran, C., Li, C., Chen, P.-J., Goyal, N., Chaudhary, V., Gu, J., and Fan A., 2020. Multilingual Translation with Extensible Multilingual Pretraining and Finetuning. *CoRR*. 2008.00401, cs.CL.

Vaswani, A., Shazeer, N., Parmar, N., Uszkoreit, J., Jones, L., Gomez, A.N., Kaiser, L. and Polosukhin, I., 2017, Attention is All You Need. *Advances in Neural Information Processing Systems,* Vol. 30. Long Beach, CA, USA, pp. 5998-6008.

Xue, L., Constant, N., Roberts, A., Kale, M., Al-Rfou, R., Siddhant, A. and Raffel, C., 2021. mT5: A Massively Multilingual Pre-trained Text-to-Text Transformer. *Proceedings of the 2021 Conference of the North American Chapter of the Association for Computational Linguistics: Human Language Technologies*. Online, pp. 483-498.

Yang, Z., Hu, Z., Dyer, C., Xing, E. P., and Berg-Kirkpatrick, T., 2018. Unsupervised text style transfer using language models as discriminators. *Adv. in Neural Information Processing Systems*, Vol. 31, Montréal, Canada, pp. 483-498.

Zhang, T., Kishore, V., Wu, F., Weinberger, K.Q., and Artzi, Y., 2020. BERTScore: Evaluating Text Generation with BERT. *International Conference on Learning Representations*. Online, pp. 1-43.

EVALUATION OF NAMED ENTITY RECOGNITION FOR THE GERMAN E-COMMERCE DOMAIN

Sergej Denisov and Frederik S. Bäumer
Bielefeld University of Applied Sciences, Bielefeld, Germany

ABSTRACT

Large online marketplaces offer search engines as an important navigation aid for their customers to navigate through the enormous number of different products and merchants. The quality of the search results depends to a large extent on the product information provided by the retailers. One way to improve search quality is to perform linguistic enhancement of the product data. For this, we use Named Entity Recognition to identify specific e-commerce entity types and give them higher weighting in the search. Typical entity types for the e-commerce domain are products, brands, and various product attributes. Recognition of e-commerce entity types for the German language remains a challenge due to the limited availability of existing resources and linguistic complexity. We address this challenge by acquiring data from two online e-commerce marketplaces to create six NER datasets based on German product titles and descriptions. Across these datasets, we evaluate the NER performance of the state-of-the-art models mBERT, GermanBERT, and XLM-RoBERTa. As a result, the XLM-RoBERTa model archived the best performance with an F1 score of 0.8611 averaged over all datasets.

KEYWORDS

Information Retrieval, Transformer, Named Entity Recognition, E-Commerce

1. INTRODUCTION

Modern artificial intelligence models based on the transformer architecture have proven to achieve state-of-the-art results in downstream NLP tasks (Lothritz et al. 2020). Furthermore, recently several multilingual models have been released that improve cross-lingual language understanding (Conneau et al. 2020) and can address research questions such as domain-specific Named Entity Recognition (NER) (Tjong Kim Sang and De Meulder 2003) or Named Entity Recognition in Query (NERQ) (Du et al. 2010) for different languages.

NER is a subtask of Information Extraction (IE) (Carstensen et al. 2009) and deals with the Identification and Classification of named entities in texts. While NER usually focuses on more extended texts, NERQ is primarily for web search applications and focuses on queries, which tend to be short. This work focuses on the e-commerce domain, where it is essential to extract named entities from the unstructured product information data and user search queries. As the products offered on online marketplaces come from different merchants, the quality of product descriptions varies significantly. While professional merchants usually provide detailed and structured descriptions of the products they offer, most sellers provide only unstructured descriptions (Joshi et al. 2015: 1). Because of this and the vast number of products on offer, marketplace vendors must ensure that customers get the best possible results for their search query. Our proposed approach can classify tokens from search queries, product titles, and descriptions into predefined e-commerce entities, e.g., brand and product. Enriching data with entities can improve understanding of users' search intentions and therefore provide better search results. As a result, a more pleasant shopping experience leads to higher customer loyalty.

Our research approach, which we briefly present in this short paper, consists of two separate tasks. For the first task, we acquire product titles and descriptions in the German language from online marketplaces. Following, we improve the data quality by applying various preprocessing steps to the HTML documents. Next, the preprocessed data is analyzed to verify the quality of the data and guarantee diversification within the categories. Finally, for the annotation with the Prodi.gy framework (Montani and Honnibal 2018), we take subsamples of data to create six German datasets for product titles and descriptions. The second task consists of evaluating models based on the transformer architecture, such as BERT (Devlin et al. 2018), and XLM-RoBERTa (Conneau et al. 2020). Finally, we use the created datasets to fine-tune the models and apply the Weights & Biases library (Biewald 2020) for hyperparameter search.

2. DATASETS AND TRAINING

Since there are no publicly available German e-commerce datasets, we had to collect data from various online marketplaces. Therefore, we acquired data from Amazon and Online-Shop to create our own datasets. This section provides insight into the data preprocessing and the distribution of entities. Furthermore, we describe our method for fine-tuning the transformer-based models with the six resulting German datasets.

2.1 Datasets

The Scrapy framework was used for the data acquisition. We collected a total of 1,871,200 product records for 74 different categories from Amazon and a total of 16,159 product records from the Online-Shop. Merchants on Amazon publish the content according to their quality standards, while the content in the Online-Shop is professionally maintained. Amazon data was collected between October and December 2019, and Online-Shop data in April 2020. We applied several heuristics to preprocess the captured data for the final annotation process. These include extracting text data from HTML, deduplicating text, removing unwanted characters, discarding product titles with less than one token, and product descriptions with less than two sentences. We were additionally filtering out product descriptions and titles that were not classified as German by the langdetect framework with a probability of more than 0.999. Finally, we use scikit-learn for calculating pairwise cosine similarity to find the most diverse product titles and descriptions. Then, we randomly select 1,000 documents for the different categories to create the datasets. In the annotation phase, we focused on the two different categories of computer and automotive. We selected the following e-commerce entities: “Brand”, “Product”, “Model”, “ItemNo”, “Quantity”, “Color”, “Size” and “Attribute”. In addition, we annotated some product attributes that do not belong to the selected categories. The intention is that the datasets can be extended with more entities, e.g., the new entity “State” for used products. The tag distribution over the eight entities for each product title and description dataset is shown in Figure 1.

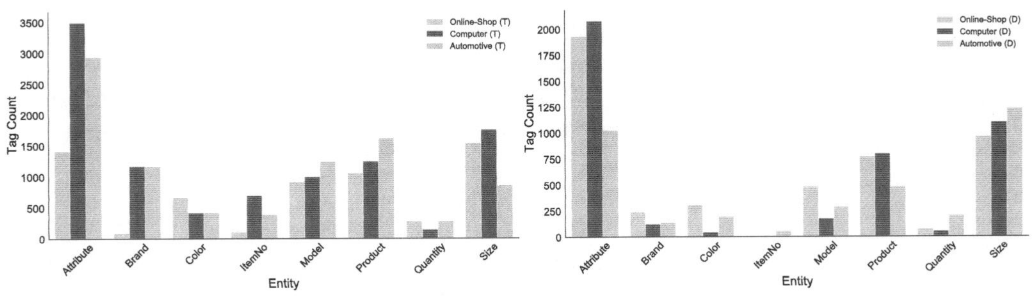

Figure 1. Tag distribution for the title (left) and description (right) datasets.
For a more precise overview, the **B**, **I**, **L** and **U** tags have been combined and the O tag removed

In Figure 1, it is shown that the distribution of entities is uneven. The title datasets have more entities than the description datasets. For the titles and description datasets, the most frequent entity is “Attribute”. Besides that, “Size”, “Product”, and “Model” appear frequent. The entities “Quantity”, “Color” and “ItemNo”, on the other hand, occur less frequently.

2.2 Training of the Models

Lately, many different pre-trained models based on the transformer architecture have been released. In this work, we used a CRF model (Lafferty et al. 2001), as our baseline approach and compared it with mBERT (Devlin et al. 2018), GermanBERT[1], and XLM-RoBERTa. The BERT architecture consists of 12 bidirectional transformer encoder blocks, 768 hidden layers, 110 million parameters (Devlin et al. 2018: 4173) and uses the Attention mechanism (Luong et al. 2015). The original BERT model was pre-trained based on two pre-training tasks. The first task is the "Masked Language Modeling" (MLM), and the second task is the "Next Sentence Prediction" (NSP) (Devlin et al. 2018: 4174). Within the MLM task, the model predicts 15 % of random masked words from a sentence. In the second task, the model gets pairs of sentences as input and predicts if the second sentence in the pair is the original document's subsequent sentence. XLM-RoBERTa model was trained with an MLM objective like BERT on monolingual data from 100 languages and therefore improved cross-lingual language understanding (XLU) and achieves state-of-the-art performance for various languages in different tasks (Conneau et al. 2020).

We used the CRFsuite implementation for the CRF model and did not specifically optimize the hyperparameters for the CRF model (Lafferty et. al 2001), as this model served as a baseline for all further experiments.

For fine-tuning the Transformers models, we worked with the Python library Simple Transformers (Rajapakse 2019). It has been observed that for Transformers models, large datasets (e.g., more than 100,000 labeled training examples) are much less sensitive to the choice of hyperparameters than small datasets (Devlin et al. 2018). Therefore, finding the best performing hyperparameters for our relatively small datasets is essential.

We applied the Weights & Biases Framework for hyperparameter search and experiment tracking. It supports running Sweeps for the model optimization. We conducted Bayes searches to determine optimized hyperparameters for the mBERT, GermanBERT, and XLM-RoBERTa models. After running the hyperparameter optimization on our datasets, we discovered that a batch size of 8, a learning rate of 5e-5, and 4 training epochs produced the highest F1 scores for the mBERT and GermanBERT model. For XLM-RoBERTa, the highest F1 score was achieved with the same batch size and learning rate but 10 training epochs.

3. EVALUATION AND DISCUSSION

The split for the datasets is 80/20 (training/evaluation). For measuring the performance, precision, recall, and F1 scores are used. Because of the imbalanced distribution of the entity types, we focus on the micro-averaged calculation of the scores. This calculation takes each entity type's frequency into the count. In Table 1, the results for the four models and all datasets are shown.

[1] Available at https://www.deepset.ai/german-bert, last accessed 2021-07-19.

Table 1. Micro-averaged precision, recall, and F1 score results of individual model for all datasets. Bold text indicates the highest F1 score for the dataset. **OS**, **A**, and **C** designate Online-Shop, Automotive, and Computer dataset. **T** and **D** indicate the title or description dataset, respectively

	OS-T	A-T	C-T	OS-D	A-D	C-D	Avg.
CRF							
Precision	0.8320	0.7082	0.7387	0.7572	0.7471	0.6901	0.7456
Recall	0.8354	0.7394	0.7394	0.7621	0.7050	0.6758	0.7360
F1-Score	0.8337	0.7182	0.7390	0.7596	0.7255	0.6828	0.7431
mBERT							
Precision	0.9106	0.8396	0.7682	0.8396	0.7923	0.7476	0.8164
Recall	0.9195	0.8625	0.8019	0.8697	0.8617	0.7635	0.8465
F1-Score	0.9150	0.8509	0.7847	0.8544	0.8544	0.7555	0.8310
GermanBERT							
Precision	0.9333	0.8282	0.7757	0.8227	0.7821	0.7463	0.8147
Recall	0.9390	0.8700	0.8111	0.8615	0.8686	0.7984	0.8581
F1-Score	0.9362	0.8486	0.7930	0.8416	0.8231	0.7715	0.8357
XLM-RoBERTa							
Precision	0.9468	0.8542	0.8340	0.8481	0.8201	0.7817	0.8475
Recall	0.9549	0.8733	0.8574	0.8729	0.8824	0.8120	0.8755
F1-Score	**0.9508**	**0.8637**	**0.8455**	**0.8603**	**0.8501**	**0.7965**	**0.8611**

As shown in Table 1, the three transformer-based models perform better than the CRF model. The transformer-based models achieve higher precision, recall, and F1 scores for each dataset than the CRF model. In particular, the results show that the XLM-RoBERTa model provides the highest F1 scores for each dataset. In addition, the transformer-based models achieve higher precision, recall, and F1 scores for each data set than the CRF model.

The conducted experiments have shown that the Online-Shop datasets achieve better results than the Amazon datasets. These results conclude that the quality of the data heavily influences the performance of the individual models. The Amazon data contains mostly unstructured and inaccurate titles and descriptions, while the Online-Shop data has a specific structure because the content is professionally maintained. Moreover, the Amazon product titles and descriptions contain several errors. The most critical ones are spelling and grammatical errors. Furthermore, there are products in the wrong category with incorrect information. Besides that, text formatting errors like missing spaces are present.

The analysis of the performance of the different entities showed that the distribution of entities within the dataset should be as balanced as possible for better results. Especially the entity types with a small number of entities performed poorly. Therefore, optimization towards more annotations for entity types with few examples is crucial. To determine if we annotated enough data and if larger datasets would perform better, we trained all models with a proportion of the Online-Shop (T) dataset. Therefore, we reduced the dataset size from 1,000 examples to 250, 500, and 750 examples. As a result, with only 250 examples of the Online-Shop title dataset, the CRF model achieves an F1 score of 0.7452, and the transformer-based models achieve an F1 score between 0.7759 and 0.8376. For 500 examples, the best result achieves XLM-RoBERTa with an F1 score of 0.9219. Moreover, using more than 500 examples of the datasets only leads to a slight increase in the F1 score.

4. CONCLUSION

In this work, we examined search optimization for online marketplaces by applying NER. This approach is essential if the search results of online marketplaces do not include any or only a few of the desired products for the search query. To address this research, we created six German e-commerce NER datasets consisting of product titles or descriptions. These datasets were essential to training the CRF model and fine-tuning the three transformer-based models. Moreover, our experiments reveal that the distribution of entities and data quality is crucial for the model results.

For the best possible NER results, the distribution of entities should be as even as possible. Therefore, the most rarely occurring entities must be supplemented with additional annotations. For our datasets, it is also possible to obtain additional entities from the "Property" entity. It would result in a more balanced distribution of entity types. Furthermore, the created datasets confirm that online marketplaces have different quality standards for publishing product titles and descriptions. Therefore, improvement of data quality should be achieved by further preprocessing.

In summary, our experiments show that the transformer-based models achieve excellent NER performance for the German language with a small amount of data. Furthermore, XLM-RoBERTa provides the best performance for all datasets with an average F1-score of 0.8611. Consequently, XLM-RoBERTa can be used for product search engine optimization for the German e-commerce domain.

REFERENCES

Biewald, L., 2020. Experiment Tracking with Weights and Biases. *Web Resource*: https://www.wandb.com/

Carstensen, K.U., et al, 2010. *Computerlinguistik und Sprachtechnologie: Eine Einführung*. Spektrum Akademischer Verlag, Heidelberg, Germany.

Conneau, A., et al, 2020. Unsupervised Cross-lingual Representation Learning at Scale. *Proceedings of the 58th Annual Meeting of the ACL*. pp. 8440–8451.

Devlin, J., et al, 2018. BERT: Pre-training of Deep Bidirectional Transformers for Language Understanding. *Proceedings of the 2019 Conference of the North American Chapter of the ACL: Human Language Technologies*, Volume 1 (Long and Short Papers), ACL: Minneapolis, MN, USA, 2019, 4171–4186.

Du, J., et al, 2010. Using Search Session Context for Named Entity Recognition in Query. *In Proceedings of the 33rd ACM SIGIR International Conference of Research and Development on Information Retrieval*. pp. 765–766.

Joshi, M., et al, 2015. Distributed Word Representations Improve NER for e-Commerce. *Proceedings of the 1st Workshop on Vector Space Modeling for Natural Language Processing*. pp. 160–167.

Lafferty, J. D., McCallum, and Pereira F. C. N., 2001. Conditional Random Fields: Probabilistic Models for Segmenting and Labeling Sequence Data. *Proceedings of the Eighteenth International Conference on Machine Learning*. pp. 282–289.

Liu, Y., et al, 2019. RoBERTa: A Robustly Optimized BERT Pretraining Approach. *CoRR*. 1907.11692, cs.CL.

Lothritz, C., et al, 2020. Evaluating Pretrained Transformer-based Models on the Task of Fine-Grained Named Entity Recognition. *Proceedings of the 28th International Conference on Computational Linguistics*. pp. 3750-3760.

Luong, T., Pham, H., and Manning, C. D., 2015. Effective Approaches to Attention-based Neural Machine Translation. *Proceedings of the 2015 Conference on Empirical Methods in Natural Language Processing*. pp 1412-1421.

Manning, C. D. and Schütze, H., 1999. Foundations of Statistical Natural Language Processing. The MIT Press, Massachusetts, USA.

McCallum, A., Freitag, D., and Pereira F. C. N., 2000. Maximum Entropy Markov Models for Information Extraction and Segmentation. *Proceedings of the 17th International Conference on Machine Learning*. pp. 591-598.

Montani, I. and Honnibal, M., 2018. Prodigy: A new annotation tool for radically efficient machine teaching. *Web Resource*: https://prodi.gy/

Rajapakse, T. C., 2019. Simpletransformers. *Web Resource*: https://github.com/ThilinaRajapakse/simpletransformers

Tjong Kim Sang, E.F. and De Meulder, F., 2003. Introduction to the CoNLL-2003 Shared Task: Language-Independent Named Entity Recognition. *Proceedings of the Seventh Conf. on Natural Language Learning at HLT-NAACL 2003*. pp. 142–147.

Wolf, T., et al, 2020. HuggingFace's Transformers: State-of-the-art Natural Language Processing. *CoRR*. 1910.03771, cs.CL

Zhu, Y., et al, 2015. Aligning Books and Movies: Towards Story-Like Visual Explanations by Watching Movies and Reading Books. *Proceedings of the 2015 IEEE International Conference on Computer Vision*. pp. 19-27.

Gap in pagination due to formatting issues.

Pages 231-232

GENOMIC DATA ANALYSIS: CONCEPTUAL FRAMEWORK FOR THE APPLICATION OF ARTIFICIAL INTELLIGENCE IN PERSONALIZED TREATMENT OF ONCOLOGY PATIENTS

Renata Kelemenic-Drazin and Ljerka Luic
University North
Trg dr. Zarka Dolinara 1,48000 Koprivnica, Croatia

ABSTRACT

Oncology is one of the most dynamic branches of medicine. As a result of numerous oncology studies, there has been a significant increase in scientific and clinical data that the human brain cannot store. Advances in artificial intelligence (AI) technology have led to its rapid clinical application. In this paper, we wanted to see the role of the use of artificial intelligence (AI) in oncology. We conducted an unsystematic search of databases (Pub Med, MEDLINE, and Google Scholar) using the keywords: artificial intelligence, deep learning, machine learning, oncology, personalized medicine. From a large number of articles available to us, we singled out review articles and clinical trial results according to their clarity and innovation regarding the use of artificial intelligence in oncology. Of particular importance to us was the ability to apply their results in everyday clinical work. The possibilities of using artificial intelligence in oncology are innumerable. Thus, AI can be used for diagnostic purposes (malignant screening, histopathology, and molecular diagnostics), therapeutic purposes (personalized treatment, prediction of treatment side effects and response to therapy, treatment decisions) as well as for prognostic purposes (risk stratification, 5-year survival, monitoring). The implementation of AI in clinical practice presents new challenges for clinicians. Namely, in the era of evidence-based and patient-centered medicine, they will have to master statistical as well as computer skills in addition to clinical ones. Therefore, it is necessary to start educating future doctors about the importance of AI in medicine as soon as possible.

KEYWORDS

Data Analytics, Artificial Intelligence, Oncology, Personalized Medicine

1. INTRODUCTION

Oncology, a field of medicine that deals with the prevention, diagnosis, and treatment of cancer, is one of the most dynamic branches of medicine (National Cancer Institute, 2021). In recent years we have witnessed a rapid increase in scientific and clinical data in oncology to better understand cancer and develop personalized and effective oncology care. But to effectively use the handful of available data, which an individual cannot absorb due to the amount of information, we need the help of artificial intelligence, not only in the field of oncology research but also in everyday clinical practice (Nagy et al., 2020). Artificial intelligence (AI) is defined as the ability of a machine to perform tasks typically associated with intelligent human behaviour. In the mid-20th century, Turing and McCarthy laid the foundations of artificial intelligence, which began to be studied more and more. But wider use required advances in technology (Turing, 1950; McCarthy, 2021). Machine learning (ML) is part of artificial intelligence that uses mathematical and statistical models to improve computer characteristics, and deep learning is part of machine learning (ML). It is based on the operation of complex interconnected artificial neural networks (ANNs) and processes information like neurons in the human brain.

There are different types of neural networks. Thus, convolutional neural networks (CNN) are intended for image processing, recurrent neural networks (RNN) are intended for handling sequential data (data from time series) and are used to exploit data from electronic health records while transformer networks are intended for processing textual data contained in medical records. Each neural network specializes in its specific data structure, and their combinations could interpret more complex phenomena. But in addition to neural networks, other methods are used, such as regression methods, tree algorithms, and other algorithms (Nagy et al., 2020).

The application of deep learning requires large data sets, but it is equally necessary that medical professionals have a basic knowledge of deep learning, including its application, but also potential shortcomings. The main disadvantage of AI is the possible violation of an individual's privacy due to potential access to personal data (Shimizu & Nakayama, 2020). On the other hand, in-depth learning can based on the use of radiological and pathological images, help us diagnose disease in a way that exceeds the clinician's performance (Teare et al., 2017; Ehteshami Bejnordi et al., 2017). The focus of our interest is to see where artificial intelligence can help us in oncology.

2. METHODS

We conducted an unsystematic search of databases (Pub Med, MEDLINE, and Google Scholar) using the desk research method and using the keywords: artificial intelligence, deep learning, machine learning, oncology, personalized medicine. From a large number of articles available to us, we singled out review articles and clinical trial results according to their clarity and innovation regarding the use of artificial intelligence in oncology. Of particular importance to us was the ability to apply their results in everyday clinical work.

3. RESULTS AND DISCUSSION

The possibilities of using artificial intelligence in oncology are innumerable. It can be used for diagnostic purposes (screening programs, histopathology, and molecular diagnostics), therapeutic purposes (personalized treatment, prediction of treatment side effects and response to therapy, treatment decisions), as well as for prognostic purposes (risk stratification, survival prediction, monitoring).

Thus, for example, the use of stored mammograms can help us identify breast cancer, while the use of stored digital pathology images can help us diagnose prostate cancer (determination of Gleason score) or breast cancer (determination of Her2 status or tumour-infiltrating lymphocytes (TIL)). AI is expected to be an important tool soon to significantly assist pathologists in their daily work (Niazi et al., 2019; Nagpal et al., 2019; Saltz et al., 2018; Vandenberghe et al., 2017; Chang et al., 2019). The application of AI has also found its place in dermatology where the recognition of skin lesions, such as melanoma, by analysis of stored dermoscopy images, is as effective as and the recognition of skin lesions by a dermatologist (Esteva et al., 2017). But for this, a large amount of imaging data is needed which still needs to be worked on. In general, we can say that AI is already used to perform various tasks in oncology at a level equal to or sometimes greater than the level of clinicians (Rodriguez-Ruiz et al., 2019; Litjens et al., 2016).

3.1 Personalized Treatment

The goal of modern oncology is personalized treatment. Given the large amount of data to which oncologists are exposed daily, if we want to personalize oncology, or choose the best treatment for each patient individually, we need the help of AI.

Namely, the precondition for personalized treatment is knowledge of the genomic data of the tumour, whether there are possible genomic mutations in the tumour as target points of oncology treatment. Hundreds of thousands of articles are published annually on genomic mutations and cancer. Therefore, databases are being created that aim to help clinicians. An example of a database linking genomic variation and disease is COSMIC. Thus, in 2019, COSMIC isolated almost 10 million genomic mutations related to cancer (Forbes, 2017). This database also helped to link genomic mutations to drug susceptibility, which can then be used in clinical practice (Lee et al., 2018).

ExPecto also works on this principle, using all publicly available genome-related studies to help find a link between genomic mutations, cancer, and drug sensitivity, and there are more and more such examples (Shimizu & Nakayama, 2020).

3.2 Analysis of Genomic Data

At the centre of oncology interest is the connection between genomic mutations and disease. This is supported by the fact that only in 2017. FDA approved several genomic tests in oncology (Oncotype Dx, Praxis Extended RAS Panel, MSK-IMPACT, and FoundationOne CDx) to personalize medicine (Shimizu & Nakayama, 2020).

Namely, currently, the diagnosis, as well as the classification of oncology disease, is based on histopathological examination and the expression of molecular markers of the tumour cell (biological information about the tumour).

If we use gene analysis we can predict the prognosis of cancer without other biological information about the tumour. By implementing tools that allow us to do this in clinical practice, such as the molecular prognostic result (mPS), we can avoid over-treatment of cancer patients (Shimizu & Nakayama, 2019).

The role of artificial intelligence in healthcare is growing and more and more artificial intelligence-based tools have been approved by the FDA, such as Arterys, an imaging platform that uses magnetic resonance and computed tomography to help physicians follow-up lung and liver cancer patients (2018) or the PAIGE.AI platform (Digital Pathology Platform) that uses AI for the diagnosis and prognosis of certain types of cancer (2019).

3.3 Conceptual Framework for the Application of Artificial Intelligence in Oncology

A prerequisite for the wider use of artificial intelligence in oncology is the creation of large databases, such as The Cancer Imaging Archive [http://www.cancerimagingarchive.net] and the Genomic Data Commons Data Portal [https: //portal.gdc. rak.gov].

It is also important to use AI when analysing the data obtained. Given the dynamics of AI development and the speed of AI implementation in medicine, and thus in oncology, soon we can certainly expect radical changes (Shimizu & Nakayama, 2020).

So although the application of AI in oncology seems very complex and still inaccessible to all oncology centres, given the required infrastructure and skills of clinicians, some segments of AI can already be used in everyday clinical practice. Thus, AI can help us make decisions about oncology treatment. Namely, decisions on oncology treatment are based on the assessment of the patient's clinical condition (PS = performance status). It is a subjective assessment made by the clinician by observing the patient's condition and based on data obtained in conversation with the patient (Pirl et al., 2015).

However, a prospective study by Gresham et al (2018) showed that monitoring patient activity (steps, distance, stairs) can help us not only to assess the clinical condition of patients with metastatic cancer but also to assess clinical outcomes (side effects, hospitalization, survival). A correlation was observed between the number of average daily steps and the clinical condition of the patient ($p < 0.01$) and possible adverse events (OR: 0.34, 95% CI 0.13, 0.94), hospitalization (OR: 0.21 95% CI 0.56, 0.79) and risk of death (HR: 0, 48 95% CI 0.28–0.83). All of this points to the feasibility of using activity monitor carriers to assess PS in patients with metastatic cancer and suggests their potential use for predicting clinical outcomes such as hospitalization and patient-reported outcomes. These findings should be confirmed in larger, randomized trials (Gresham et al., 2018).

The results of a study by Pirl et al. (2015) are on the same track. It included 41 patients with metastatic non-small cell lung cancer (NSCLC). The patient activity was measured using an actigraph (ACTIWATCH 2) over 72 hours and compared with the performance status (PS) determined by the oncologist. This study concludes that measuring patient activity using an actigraph may be useful in determining a patient's PS (Pirl et al., 2015).

4. CONCLUSION

Objective assessment of patients' clinical condition (PS = performance status) is difficult because patients spend most of their time outside the hospital. But objective real-time activity data that we can collect with physical activity monitoring devices, such as smartphones or smartwatches, can help. In this way, the subjectivity and bias associated with current assessments during the clinical examination itself can be avoided. The active introduction of AI technology is considered an inevitable trend in the future of medicine. The implementation of AI in clinical practice presents new challenges for clinicians. Namely, in the era of evidence-based and patient-centered medicine, they will have to master statistical as well as computer skills in addition to clinical ones. Therefore, it is necessary to start educating future doctors about the importance of AI in medicine as soon as possible.

ACKNOWLEDGEMENT

The publication of this paper was possible by the funds of the University of the North, intended to support scientific research of the development project "E-learning – digital curriculum for digital time", for which the authors of this paper are extremely grateful.

REFERENCES

Chang HY. et al, 2019. Artificial intelligence in pathology. *J Pathol Transl Med..*, 53: 1- 12.

Ehteshami Bejnordi B. et al, 2017. Diagnostic Assessment of Deep Learning Algorithms for Detection of Lymph Node Metastases in Women with Breast Cancer. *JAMA*, 318(22), p.2199.

Esteva A. et al, 2017. Dermatologist-level classification of skin cancer with deep neural networks. *Nature*, 542: 115- 118.

Forbes SA. et al, 2017. COSMIC: somatic cancer genetics at high-resolution. *Nucleic Acids Res.*, 45: D777- D783.

Gresham G. et al, 2018. Wearable activity monitors to assess performance status and predict clinical outcomes in advanced cancer patients. *npj Digital Medicine* 1, 27.

Lee JS. et al, 2018. Harnessing synthetic lethality to predict the response to cancer treatment. *Nat Commun,* 9: 2546.

Litjens G. et al, 2016. Deep learning as a tool for increased accuracy and efficiency of histopathological diagnosis. *Sci Rep.*, 6: 26286.

McCarthy J., 2021. *A Proposal for the Dartmouth Summer Research Project on Artificial Intelligence*. [online] Jmc.stanford.edu. Available at: <http://jmc.stanford.edu/articles/dartmouth.html> [Accessed 5 April 2021].

Nagpal K. et al, 2019. Development and validation of a deep learning algorithm for improving Gleason scoring of prostate cancer. *npj Digital Medicine*, 2(1).

Nagy M. et al, 2020. Machine Learning in Oncology: What Should Clinicians Know? *JCO Clinical Cancer Informatics*, (4), pp.799-810.

National Cancer Institute. 2021. *NCI Dictionary of Cancer Terms*. [online] Available at: <https://www.cancer.gov/publications/dictionaries/cancer-terms> [Accessed 2 January 2021].

Niazi M. et al, 2019. Digital pathology and artificial intelligence. *The Lancet Oncology*, 20(5), pp. e253-e261.

Pirl W. F. et al, 2015. Actigraphy as an objective measure of performance status in patients with advanced cancer. *J. Clin. Oncol.* Abstr. 33(Suppl. 62), 29.

Rodriguez-Ruiz A. et al, 2019. Stand-Alone Artificial Intelligence for Breast Cancer Detection in Mammography: Comparison With 101 Radiologists. *JNCI: Journal of the National Cancer Institute*, 111(9), pp.916-922.

Saltz J. et al, 2018. Spatial Organization and Molecular Correlation of Tumor-Infiltrating Lymphocytes Using Deep Learning on Pathology Images. *Cell Rep.*, 23: 181- 193.e187.

Shimizu H. and Nakayama K., 2020. Artificial intelligence in oncology. *Cancer Science*, 111(5), pp.1452-1460.

Shimizu H. and Nakayama KI., 2019. A 23 gene-based molecular prognostic score precisely predicts overall survival of breast cancer patients. *EBioMedicine,* 46: 150- 159.

Teare P. et al, 2017. Malignancy Detection on Mammography Using Dual Deep Convolutional Neural Networks and Genetically Discovered False Color Input Enhancement. *Journal of Digital Imaging*, 30(4), pp.499-505.

Turing A., 1950. Computing machinery and intelligence. *Mind,* 59:433-460.

Vandenberghe M. et al, 2017. Relevance of deep learning to facilitate the diagnosis of HER2 status in breast cancer. *Sci Rep.*, 7: 45938.

VALIDITY CHECKING OF PROVENANCE DATA FROM SOFTWARE DEVELOPMENT PROCESSES

Marcela Gomes Pinheiro and Gabriella Castro Barbosa Costa
Federal Center for Technological Education of Minas Gerais (CEFET-MG) - 36700-001 - Leopoldina - MG - Brazil

ABSTRACT

Provenance refers to the origin of data, in other words, a historical record of data. After capturing provenance, it is possible to perform interpretation and analysis of what occurred during the process of data creation and transformation and a diagnosis of the problems that may have occurred during these processes is provided. Among the problems related to the use of data provenance in software development processes there is a definition of how comprehensive the data should be captured and the procedure that should be used for this capture, including checking if the captured provenance data is valid. Considering the definition of the data that should be captured, some provenance models are proposed in literature. As examples, we can cite the PROV model, which can be used to enable the inter-operable interchange of provenance information in heterogeneous environments such as the Web, and PROV-SwProcess model, developed as an extension of the PROV model to capture provenance data from software development processes. This paper briefly details a work in progress about the procedure for capturing provenance data from the software development process, mostly regarding the validity checking of the captured data, using a tool called ProvValidator. In the end, an example composed of a set of data from a software development process is checked through the validation proposal presented in this work.

KEYWORDS

Provenance Data, Software Development Process, Provenance Data Validity

1. INTRODUCTION

In the development of high-quality software, it is necessary to combine two fundamental pillars, which are the good practices of software engineering with an efficient development process. The software development process (SDP) is aimed at creating safe and quality software, through methodologies and actions that will ensure that the basic criteria for creation are met, demonstrating successful software engineering (Pressman, 2019). During the SDP, some data can be captured to be analyzed in the evaluation phase of the process. The analysis of these data can be of two different types: deductive analysis and retrospective analysis (Wolf and Rosenblum, 1993). The last one has as goal by discovering patterns of anomalous behavior that can be eliminated in future enactments of the process. Besides that, and regarding the provenance data to be captured during the SDP, data provenance models can be used.

Provenance refers to the origin or provenance of data, that is, a record of their history, which enables the interpretation and analysis of what occurred during the processes of creation and transformation of data and even the diagnosis of problems that occurred during these processes (Lim *et al.*, 2010). Buneman *et al.* (2000) defines data provenance as a complementary documentation that contains the information of how, when, where and why certain data were obtained and who obtained them. Among the problems related to the use of data provenance in SDP there is the definition of how comprehensive the data should be captured, as well as the procedure to be adopted for this capture, including checking if the provenance data is valid. Related to the definition of how comprehensive data provenance should be captured, the use of provenance models is an alternative. PROV model (Moreau and Groth, 2013) allows the interoperable exchange of provenance information in heterogeneous environments, such as the web. In turn, the PROV-SwProcess model (Costa *et al.*, 2018), was developed as an extension of the PROV model specifically to capture provenance data from SDP. This model provides a framework of a more in-depth analysis which actually occurred during software process development (Costa *et al.*, 2018). After capturing the provenance data of SDP, validating whether they are in accordance with the adopted provenance model becomes crucial, in order to allow all the analysis and possible improvements to be made in the process in question. In this sense, one of the existing tools is ProvValidator (Moreau *et al.*, 2014), a tool that performs model validations that extend from the PROV model.

The main goal of this work is to detail the methodology for checking the validity of the captured data, which consists of the last step of the procedure for capturing data from SDP. Besides that, an example composed of a set of data from a SDP is checked through the validation proposal that will be presented. The remaining of this paper is organized as follows: Section 2 details our procedure for capturing provenance data from SDP; Section 3 presents the proposed methodology for checking the validity of provenance data from SDP and, finally, in Section 4 there is the conclusions followed by acknowledgments and references.

2. CAPTURING PROVENANCE DATA FROM SDP

The systematics presented in Figure 1 was defined considering the need of capturing data from SDP and/or adapting them to a provenance model that should be used. It was an improvement of the systematics proposed on the iSPuP approach (Costa *et al.*, 2018). Considering the activity ***Define the provenance data to be captured***, a set of SDP execution can be stored for each SDP, according to PROV-SwProcess: (i) Executed processes with their name and responsible; (ii) Performed activities of each process, with their name, start, and end time; (iii) Stakeholders associated with the performed activity (mandatory) and their specific role (optional); (iv) Artifacts changed, used, or generated by the performed activity; (v) Procedures adopted for the execution of the performed activity (optional); (vi) Hardware and / or Software resources used by the performed activity (optional); (vii) Responsibility among stakeholders (optional); (viii) Process standard model and process intended model definition (optional). Activities 2, 3, and 4 are automated tasks with additional toll support to the capture, transformation, and storage. Finally, activity 5 ***Check the validity of provenance data*** is the focus of this work and is presented in the following section.

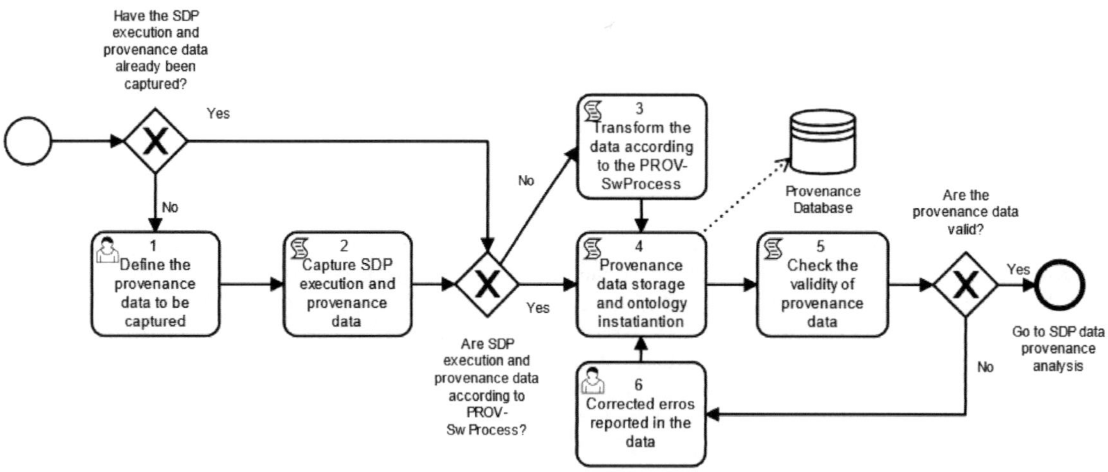

Figure 1. Systematics for SDP provenance data capture and storage

3. METHODOLOGY

In order to ***Check the validity of provenance data*** from some SDP (captured or transformed according to PROV-SwProcess) ProvValidator tool was used, according to the following step-by-step and the Figure 2:

1. Go to the site: https://openprovenance.org/services/view/validator
2. To perform validation using a file, simply save it in one of the acceptable formats (xml, ttl,rdf, provn, trig, json). Attach them to the indication [2] and right after clicking the "Validate" button indicated by [1].

3. If the validation to be performed is through URL, simply add in the indication [5] and click the "Validate" button indicated by [1].
4. There is also the option to perform validation through code fragments, just select the desired language in the indication [3], attach the code fragment to [4] and click the "Validate" button indicated by [1].
5. After proper validations, the system will display a screen indicating possible errors or showing the validation of the proposed entry.

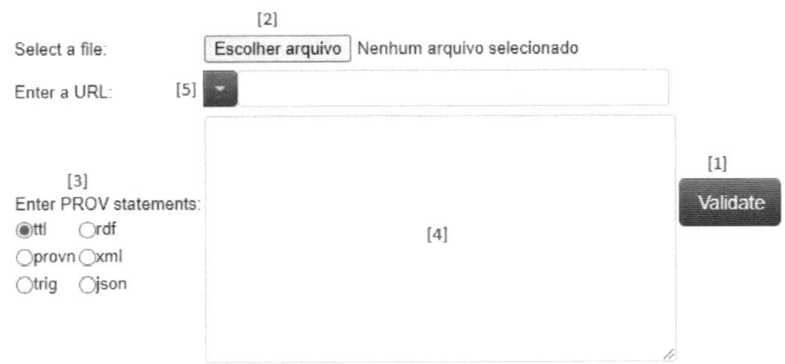

Figure 2. ProvValidator Interface

To illustrate the use of the ProvValidator tool the following example was used. It shows a *Software_Process* identified as *New_Resource_Development*. This *Software_Process* was composed by the activities *New_Resource_Specification*, *Codification*, *Test_Cases_Definition*, *Test*, and *Deploy* (line 10 of Figure 3), and was assigned to the Stakeholder *Anna*, using the relation *wasAttributedTo* (line 11 of Figure 3). In lines 13 and 14 of Figure 3, the prospective provenance of this *Software_Process* was stablished. It is composed by the same five activities listed on its retrospective provenance (*New_Resource_Specification*, *Codification*, *Test_Cases_Definition*, *Test*, and *Deploy*) and *Anna* stakeholder is the process responsible. In this example, there were no differences between what was planned and what was actually executed. Finally, Figure 4 shows the validation result performed on the tool.

```
1  @prefix rdfs:     <http://www.w3.org/2000/01/rdf-schema#> .
2  @prefix xsd:      <http://www.w3.org/2001/XMLSchema#> .
3  @prefix owl:      <http://www.w3.org/2002/07/owl#> .
4  @prefix prov:     <http://www.w3.org/ns/prov#> .
5  @prefix provswprocess:  <http://purl.org/provswprocess#> .
6  @prefix :         <http://example.com/> .
7
8          :New_Resource_Development
9                  a owl:NamedIndividual , provswprocess:Software_Process ;
10                 provswprocess:wasComposedBy :New_Resource_Specification , :Codification , :Test_Cases_Definition , :Test , :Deploy ;
11                 prov:wasAttributedTo :Anna;
12
13                 provswprocess:isComposedBy :New_Resource_Specification , :Codification , :Test_Cases_Definition , :Test , :Deploy ;
14                 provswprocess:hasResponsible :Anna;
15                 provswprocess:hasResponsibleRole :Manager
16         .
17         :Anna a owl:NamedIndividual , provswprocess:Person_Stakeholder .
18         :Manager a owl:NamedIndividual , provswprocess:Stakeholder_Role .
```

Figure 3. Example

A similar work to the one proposed in this article is Blinker (Bose *et al.,* 2019), a framework that allows a hierarchical visualization of provenance graphs and query results. One difference between the model proposed in this article and Blinker is the number of tools and processes that would be necessary to adequately capture data provenance. Another related work that can be mentioned is DQProv Explorer (Bors et al., 2019), a system that captures provenance through conflicting data operations and allows them to be visualized in graph form. Both use extensions of the PROV model and assume forms of model validation test of different models than the proposal in this paper, where a validator from PROV itself is used.

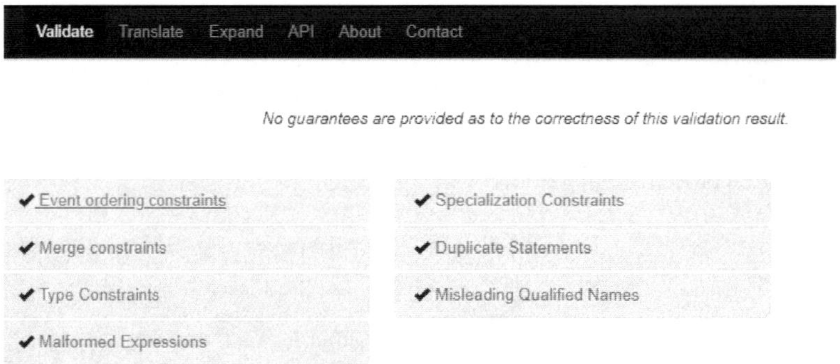

Figure 4. Validation Results Example

4. CONCLUSION

This paper details a systematics for capturing provenance data from the SDP, specifically regarding the validity checking of the captured data. It uses a tool called ProvValidator and shows how to check the validity of an example composed of a set of data from a real SDP. As a work in progress, our next steps mainly focus on improving the process to check the validity of provenance data with more automation of this process, obtaining the ontology with the data and performing its verification through a ProvValidator API, without the need to perform this task manually, accessing the tool via a web application.

ACKNOWLEDGEMENT

We want to thank CEFET-MG and CNPq for financial support.

REFERENCES

Bors C., Gschwandtner T., Miksch S., 2019. "Capturing and Visualizing Provenance From Data Wrangling", Publishing in *IEEE International Conference on Services, vol 39.*

Bose, R.P.J.C., Phokela, K.K., Kaulgud, V., Podder, S., 2019. "BLINKER: A Blockain-enabled Framework for Software Provenance". Asia-Pacific Software Engineering Conference (APSEC), *IEEE International Conference on Services* Publisher, Putrajaya, Malaysia.

Buneman P., Khanna S., Tan W., 2000. "Data Provenance: Some Basic Issues". *Foundations of Software Technology and Theoretical Computer Science (FST TCS)*, vol. 1974, Springer, Berlin, Heidelberg Publishers, New Delhi, India.

Costa, G. C. B., Dalpra, H. L. O., Teixeira, E. N., Werner, C. M. L., Braga, R. M. M., Miguel, M. A., 2018, "Software Processes Analysis with Provenance. Lecture Notes in Computer Science", *Springer International Publishing*,1ed. vol., pp. 106-122.

Lim, C., LU, S., Chebotko, A., Fotouhi, F, 2010, "Prospective and Retrospective Provenance Collection in Scientific Workflow Environments", *IEEE International Conference on Services Computing (SCC '10)*, Washington, DC, USA, pp. 449-456.

Moreau, L., Groth, P., 2013, "Provenance: an introduction to prov. Synthesis Lectures on the Semantic Web: Theory and Technology", v. 3, n. 4, pp. 1-129.

Moreau, L., Huynh, D, P., Michaelides, D. 2014, "An Online Validator for Provenance: Algorithmic Design, Testing, and API", pp. 1-15.

Pressman, R. S, Maxim, B., 2019. *Software Engineering: A Practitioner's Approach*, 9th ed., McGraw-Hill Education Publishers.

Wolf, A. L., Rosenblum, D. S. 1993, "A study in software process data capture and analysis. Software Process", *Second International Conference on the Continuous Software Improvement*. IEEE, pp. 115-124.

TOWARDS PROGRAMMING WITH FIRST-CLASS PATTERNS

Lutz Hamel[1], Timothy Colaneri[1], Ariel Finkle[2] and Oliver McLaughlin[1]
[1]*Dept. of Computer Science & Statistics*
[2]*Dept. of Life Sciences*
University of Rhode Island, Kingston, Rhode Island, USA

ABSTRACT

Pattern matching is a powerful programming paradigm which first appeared in functional programming languages to make data structure analysis and decomposition more declarative. Promoting patterns to first-class status does not increase the computational power of a programming language, but it does increase its expressiveness allowing for brand new ways of solving problems. First-class patterns were studied in the context of the lambda calculus. Today, almost all modern programming languages incorporate some form of pattern matching. However, with only a few exceptions, all programming languages we are aware of that support pattern matching stop short of treating patterns as first-class citizens. Consequently, many interesting use cases of pattern matching lie beyond the reach of those languages. We have implemented first-class patterns in Asteroid, a dynamically typed, multi-paradigm programming language, in order to assess and experiment with first-class patterns. Here we report some of our initial findings. The idea of first-class patterns is not new but we feel that the insights provided here are novel and highlight the impact that first-class patterns can have on programming languages and the discipline of programming itself.

KEYWORDS

Pattern Matching, First-Class Patterns, Programming Language Design, Programming

1. INTRODUCTION

Pattern matching is a powerful programming paradigm which first appeared in functional programming languages such as HOPE (Burstall, et al., 1980) in the 1970's and early 1980's to make data structure analysis and decomposition more declarative. It was adopted by functional languages such as Haskell (Peyton Jones, 2003) in the 1990's for similar reasons. Promoting patterns to first-class status does not increase the computational power of a programming language, but it does increase its expressiveness allowing for brand new ways of solving problems. First-class patterns were introduced into Haskell in the early 2000's (Tullsen, 2000), and formally studied in the context of the lambda calculus later in that decade (Jay & Kesner, D., 2009). Today, almost all modern programming languages such as Python (Kohn, et al., 2020), Rust (Matsakis & Klock II, 2014), and Swift (Apple Inc., 2020) incorporate some form of pattern matching. However, with only a few exceptions like Haskell, Thorn (Bloom & Hirzel, 2012), and Grace (Homer, et al., 2012), the programming languages we are aware of stop short of treating patterns as first-class citizens. Consequently, many interesting use cases of pattern matching lie beyond the reach of those languages.

Here we describe some of the insights we gained from implementing and programming with first-class patterns in Asteroid, a dynamically typed, multi-paradigm programming language. The idea of first-class patterns is not new but we feel that the insights provided here are novel and highlight the impact that first-class patterns have on programming languages and the discipline of programming itself.

In Asteroid, first-class patterns are introduced with the keywords 'pattern with' and patterns themselves are first-class values that we can store in variables and then reference when we want to use them. Like so,

```
let P = pattern with (x,y).
let *P = (1,2).
```

The left side of the second let statement dereferences the pattern stored in variable P and uses the pattern to match against the term (1,2) on the right side.

2. FIRST-CLASS PATTERNS: CASE STUDIES

Pattern Factoring. Patterns can become very complicated especially when conditional pattern matching is involved. First-class patterns allow us to control the complexity of patterns by breaking them up into smaller sub-patterns that are more easily managed. Consider the following function foo written in Asteroid that takes a pair of values. The twist is that the first component of the pair is restricted to the primitive data types of Asteroid's type system which we enforce with a conditional pattern introduced with the keyword '%if',

```
function foo with (x %if (x is %boolean) or (x is %integer) or (x is %string),y) do
  println(x,y).
end
```

The complexity of the pattern for the first component completely obliterates the overall structure of the parameter pattern and makes the function definition difficult to read. We can express the same function with a first-class pattern,

```
let TP = pattern with q %if (q is %boolean) or (q is %integer) or (q is %string).

function foo with (x:*TP,y) do
  println(x,y)
end
```

It is clear now that the main input structure to the function is a pair, and the conditional type restriction pattern has been relegated to a first-class sub-pattern stored in the variable TP. Thus, first-class patterns allowed us to factor the function parameter pattern into a main pattern, the pair, and a sub-pattern which expresses the type restriction.

Pattern Reuse. In most applications of patterns in programming languages, specific patterns appear in many different locations in a program. If patterns are not first-class citizens, the developer will have to retype the same patterns repeatedly in the various locations where the patterns occur. Consider the following Asteroid program snippet defining two functions,

```
function fact
    with 0 do return 1
    orwith (n:%integer) %if n > 0 do return n * fact (n-1).
    orwith (n:%integer) %if n < 0 do throw Error("negative value").
end
function sign
    with 0 do return 1
    orwith (n:%integer) %if n > 0 d return 1.
    orwith (n:%integer) %if n < 0 do return -1.
end
```

The first function is the classic recursive definition of the factorial, and the second function is the sign function which maps positive and negative values into 1 and -1, respectively. Here we use a multi-dispatch approach with the appropriate patterns restricting the values that each of the various bodies of the functions can receive. To write these two functions we had to repeat the almost identical pattern four times. First-class patterns allow us to write the same two functions in a much more elegant way,

```
let POS_INT = pattern with (x:%integer) %if x > 0.
let NEG_INT = pattern with (x:%integer) %if x < 0.
function fact
    with 0 do return 1
    orwith n:*POS_INT do return n * fact (n-1).
    orwith *NEG_INT do throw Error("negative value").
end
function sign
    with 0 do return 1
    orwith *POS_INT do return 1.
    orwith *NEG_INT do return -1.
end
```

The relevant first-class patterns are now stored in the variables POS_INT and NEG_INT. These are then used in the function definitions to select the appropriate values for the function bodies.

Running Patterns in Reverse. One of the challenges when programming with patterns is to keep an object structure and the patterns aimed at destructuring that object structure in sync. First-class patterns solve this problem by viewing patterns essentially as "object constructors." In that way, a first-class pattern is used to construct an object structure as well as to destructure it without having to worry about the structure and the corresponding pattern getting out of sync. In order to use a pattern as a constructor, we apply the eval function to it. This turns the pattern into a value from Asteroid's point of view. Free variables in the pattern are bound by the eval function. For example,

```
let P = pattern with ([a],[b]). -- first-class pattern
let a = 1. let b = 2.           -- define values for free variables of pattern
let v = eval P.                 -- use eval to construct a value from pattern
println v.                      -- print the value
(lambda with *P do println a. println b) v. -- first-class pattern to deconstruct value
```

The output of the program is,

```
([1],[2])
1
2
```

The first output line is the value computed by the eval function given the values associated with the variables a and b, and the first-class pattern P. The second and third lines of the output are generated by the lambda function, and are the result of destructuring the value passed to the function.

Notice that the whole program is essentially parameterized over the structure of the pattern. We could easily change the internals of this pattern without affecting the rest of the program.

3. CHALLENGES

Promoting patterns to first-class status brings with it some challenges. For example, when using patterns as constructors they turn out to behave like dynamically scoped functions. This is not very desirable due to the difficulty of predicting runtime behavior. Consider,

```
let P = pattern with (x,y).
let x = 1. let y = 2.
let z = eval P.
```

The evaluation of pattern P captures the variables x and y from the current environment and constructs the value (1,2). This has all the well-documented pitfalls of dynamically scoped functions, considering that x and y can be defined anywhere in the code. One solution we are contemplating is to provide an explicit initializer list to the eval operator for use in the constructor call,

```
let P = pattern with (x,y).
let z = eval P with (x=1,y=2).
```

where it would be an error to not provide an initializer for each free variable in the pattern. This extended eval operator is semantically equivalent to something like this,

```
let P = pattern with (x,y).
let z = (lambda with (Ptn,x,y) do return eval Ptn) (P,1,2).
```

where the pattern Ptn is evaluated in the context of the local scope of the lambda function.

Another challenge is the visibility of variables declared during a pattern match with a first-class pattern. In order to see this, consider a pattern match using a traditional pattern,

```
let (x,y) = (1,2).
assert(x==1 and y==2).
```

Here we can immediately see that the pattern match introduces x and y into the local scope. Now consider using a first-class pattern in order to accomplish the same thing,

```
let P = pattern with (x,y).
let *P = (1,2).
assert(x==1 and y==2).
```

Here it is no longer obvious that the pattern match introduces x and y into the local scope. This is especially true given that pattern definition and usage can be very far apart from each other, even in separate modules. A solution to this we are contemplating is explicit syntax for pattern match statements with first-class patterns such as,

```
let x,y in *P = (1,2).
```

indicating that the pattern match introduces variables x and y into the local scope. A variation on this might be,

```
let x as k in *P = (1,2).
```

This indicates that we are only using variable x from the pattern match, but introducing it as the variable k in the current scope. In this case, the variable y stays hidden and is not accessible in the current scope.

4. RELATED WORK

The work most similar to ours is the work by Homer et al. (Homer, et al., 2012) and Bloom and Hirzel (Bloom & Hirzel, 2012). In both cases first-class patterns are introduced into languages that are not strictly functional programming languages. However, our work differs from theirs in many details. For example, Homer et al. consider first-class patterns to be functions in the vein of (Tullsen, 2000) whereas we consider them to be structures. In our case, this allows us to view patterns as constructors. The Thorn language by Bloom and Hirzel has many similarities with Asteroid but also differs in its design philosophy, pattern sub-language, and its view of patterns as constructors. The insights and challenges we addressed here are novel and were not addressed in these works. Active patterns of F# (Syme, et al., 2016) are first-class elements of that language. However, active patterns in F# are essentially anonymous union discriminators and therefore differ substantially from the kind of first-class patterns we discuss here. Pattern synonyms in Haskell (Pickering, et al., 2016) allow the user to declare structural equivalences to a given pattern and use the declared equivalent pattern instead of the original one during pattern matching. Our first-class patterns seem to be more general than that, especially since we can also view our patterns as constructors.

5. CONCLUSIONS

Here we provided a snapshot of ongoing research with the Asteroid programming language in the context of first-class patterns. Promoting patterns to first-class status increases the expressiveness of a programming language and enables novel ways of solving problems. We have illustrated that with our use cases for the Asteroid programming language. First-class patterns also present a set of challenges which we outlined and proposed solutions for. The implementation of these solutions is ongoing research.

REFERENCES

Apple Inc., 2020. *Swift Language Reference.* [Online] Available at: https://docs.swift.org/swift-book/ReferenceManual/AboutTheLanguageReference.html

Bloom, B. and Hirzel, M.J., 2012. Robust scripting via patterns. *ACM SIGPLAN Notices*, *48*(2), pp. 29-40.

Burstall, R.M., MacQueen, D.B. and Sannella, D.T., 1980, August. HOPE: An experimental applicative language. In *Proceedings of the 1980 ACM conference on LISP and functional programming* (pp. 136-143).

Homer, M., Noble, J., Bruce, K.B., Black, A.P. and Pearce, D.J., 2012. Patterns as objects in Grace. ACM SIGPLAN Notices, 48(2), pp.17-28.

Jay, B. and Kesner, D., 2009. First-class patterns. *Journal of Functional Programming*, *19*(2), pp. 191-225.

Kohn, T., van Rossum, G., Bucher II, G.B. and Levkivskyi, I., 2020, November. Dynamic pattern matching with Python. In *Proceedings of the 16th ACM SIGPLAN International Symposium on Dynamic Languages* (pp. 85-98).

Matsakis, N.D. and Klock, F.S., 2014. The rust language. *ACM SIGAda Ada Letters*, *34*(3), pp. 103-104.

Peyton Jones, S. ed., 2003. *Haskell 98 language and libraries: the revised report*. Cambridge University Press.

Pickering, M., Érdi, G., Peyton Jones, S. and Eisenberg, R.A., 2016, September. Pattern synonyms. In *Proceedings of the 9th International Symposium on Haskell* (pp. 80-91).

Solodkyy, Y., Dos Reis, G. and Stroustrup, B., 2013, October. Open pattern matching for C++. In *Proceedings of the 12th international conference on Generative programming: concepts & experiences* (pp. 33-42).

Syme, D. et al., 2016. *The F# Language Specification.* [Online] Available at: https://fsharp.org/specs/language-spec

Tullsen, M., 2000, January. First Class Patterns?. *In International Symposium on Practical Aspects of Declarative Languages* (pp. 1-15). Springer, Berlin, Heidelberg.

Gap in pagination due to formatting issues.

Pages 245-246

PARTIAL RESULTS OF A REVIEW OF SURVEY METHODS MEASURING E-PRIVACY CONCERNS

Anders Matre, Magnus Englund and Vanessa Ayres-Pereira
University of Bergen, Christiesgt. 12, Bergen, Norway

ABSTRACT

We present partial results of a review of survey methods used to measure e-privacy concerns and discuss the validity of the privacy paradox. We analyzed the content of 246 questionnaire items used to measure privacy concerns in 27 papers. We conclude that privacy concerns have been operationalized as a heterogeneous construct and that the instruments may be partially responsible for varying conclusions about the paradox. We discuss the necessity to enhance content validity and investigate measurement accuracy.

KEYWORDS

Privacy Concerns, Privacy Paradox, E-privacy

1. INTRODUCTION

According to some researchers, measuring one's level of concern about the privacy of their digital data (e-privacy hereafter) is relevant to predict one's likelihood of engaging in privacy-protective behaviors (e.g., Malhotra et al, 2014). However, a body of research emerged contradicting this view and concluding that, despite reporting high levels of e-privacy concerns, users are likely to disclose personal information even for small benefits; this phenomenon was coined the privacy paradox (cf. Kokolakis, 2017, for a review). Kokolakis (2017) suggested that the contradictions across studies (sometimes supporting, sometimes refuting the paradox) could be, among other reasons, a function of the variability in the methods. Most surveys assess different aspects of the environment that people may be concerned about, however, the aspects can vary across studies. Therefore, researchers have been arguing for more work that helps to develop instruments to measure e-privacy concerns, especially in experiments (e.g., Buck et al, 2018).

Previous works have attempted to develop reliable and valid scales to measure privacy concerns (e.g., Buck et al, 2018; Malhotra et al, 2004; Smith et al, 1996; Stewart & Segars, 2002). The scales, however, vary in terms of scope and dimensions. While some assess privacy concerns in general (e.g., Stewart & Segars, 2002; Malhotra et al, 2004), other focus on specific sectors (Buck et al, 2018). Whereas some consider concerns for data collection, errors, unauthorized access, and secondary use (e.g., Smith et al, 1996; Stewart & Segars, 2002), others assess control factors, awareness of privacy practices (Malhotra et al, 2004), the type of data and benefits for disclosure (Buck et al, 2018).

Kokolakis (2017) noted that a common framework for measuring e-privacy concerns had not yet emerged. Therefore, the present paper aims to assess how researchers interested in the privacy paradox have defined and measured e-privacy concerns recently. This is a work-in-progress. And, while preliminary, our findings show trends in the operationalization of privacy concerns and provide parameters for item design considering current practices in the literature. We also discuss how some practices could be biasing and eliciting a higher degree of agreement towards privacy concerns.

2. BODY OF PAPER

2.1 Method

A systematic paper selection process was performed in several steps conforming to PRISMA guidelines for systematic reviews (Shamseer et al, 2015). A first set of papers (n = 40) was identified through the database PsycInfo and the second set (n = 62) through the reference list of the first set of papers. We selected the papers that were published within the last five years (2016–2020), involved the expression privacy paradox, used survey methods, included the entire questionnaire transcribed, and reported privacy concerns measures (inclusion criteria). We excluded literature reviews, papers about offline privacy decisions, and not peer-reviewed (exclusion criteria). Finally, we analyzed 246 questionnaire items measuring e-privacy concerns, published in 27 papers. We analyzed the content of the items using the content analysis technique (Hsieh & Shannon, 2005), that is, by determining the existence and frequency of several categories of analysis (see Results for details).

2.2 Results

2.2.1 General Trends Across Papers

Only four out of the 27 papers included a definition of the construct "privacy concerns". All definitions focused on the lack of control and/or potential misuse of one's data. Our sample of papers contained little to no discussion of potential questionnaire methodology shortcomings. All papers used closed-ended questions and a battery, rather than a single item, to measure e-privacy concerns. The number of items ranged between three and 25 ($M = 9.11$, $SD = 6.41$). No questionnaire was entirely identical, but, according to a text analyser tool, six studies used near-identical wordings in some items. These items could be traced back to Smith et al. (1996). Most studies used Likert scales (88.9%), 19 encompassed agree-disagree, mostly with seven or five points.

2.2.2 General Trends Across Items

The analysis of "e-privacy scenarios" typically involve the description of a) a technological context (e.g., social media), b) one or two actors—the user and a second agent, c) the type of information disclosed by the user (e.g., location), and d) an undesired consequence of data usage for the user (i.e., e-privacy risk). The user is any person who provides personally identifiable data for an audience. The second agent is anyone who acts upon the users' data (e.g., collects, accesses, shares). Considering this perspective, we determined the aspects of the "e-privacy scene" described in the items and their frequency. We also evaluated how many among the 246 items inquired about attitudes or beliefs.

Most of the items (58.1%) inquired about negatively valanced attitudes, often using literally the word "concern" (38.6%). Other items inquired about different types of attitudes (e.g., trust, importance) or beliefs. Most items regarded actions of a second agent upon the user's data (78.5%). The type of action varied: a quarter (25.2%) covered data access, usually unauthorized, and 19.9% addressed data collection. Although the majority inquired about the actions of a second agent, only 74.2% specified who the agent was. Those items that specified the agent, often treated of companies (e-commerce and social network sites, SNSs, 35.8%) or individuals (referred to as "people", "others" or "somebody", 11.4%). Nearly 60% specified the technological context (mostly SNSs, 42.3%). Only 24.8% referred to which type of data was processed, but it was often generally worded as "personal information". The items rarely specified actions taken by the users or personal negative consequences that could arise from data disclosure.

2.3 Discussion

Discussions on the privacy paradox usually assume that the different studies measure the same constructs. However, we found almost a lack of definition of the core construct and variations in the content of most of the analyzed measurement aspects. Still, the items do appear to have some commonalities. A typical privacy concern item will likely contain a reference to an attitude of concern, in a specific technological context, about an action of data collection of access to the user's data, and answers will be rated on an agree-disagree scale.

The superficial agreement across items increases the chances of replicability, but some of the current design practices, if overlooked, might leave questionnaires subject to measurement error and bias. Questions with unprecise information—that is, input information different from the one present when deciding whether or not to disclose data—can lead to a reduction in measurement accuracy and attitude-behavior consistency (cf. Schwarz & Bohner, 2001). The content of most items was general and rarely specified the type of data processed, how it could be misused, and who the second agent was. General terms can make respondents infer that the wordings refer to different objects or draw their answers on unintended contextual features. Also, vague information added to items framed with a focus on the presence of concern (and rarely on the absence of concern or both) could bias responses towards the selection of agreement rather than disagreement options. Our considerations call for future experiments to evaluate items' effects on responses and the instruments' ability to relate the construct to privacy-protective behaviors.

3. CONCLUSION

Our analyses, while preliminary, contribute to the literature by revealing recent trends on the operationalization of privacy concerns in the privacy paradox literature. In light of empirical discussions, we offer a brief examination of how some practices could be influencing agreement towards privacy concerns, reducing attitude-behavior consistency and, consequently, conclusions on the paradox. Our analyses are still in progress and must be expanded to evaluate associations between categories of analysis, as much as with the papers' varied conclusions on the paradox. While preliminary, the results can be applied to design items measuring e-privacy concerns considering current practices. The findings also reveal the potential to conduct studies evaluating contextual effects to enhance measurement accuracy and the value of privacy concerns in predicting privacy behaviors.

ACKNOWLEDGEMENT

A.M. and M.E. conducted the data collection, analyses, and drafted the first version of the manuscript. V.A.P. conceived and supervised the project; she also commented on the manuscript. This research is part of the scientific program of the ALerT project, supported by the Norwegian Research Council. We thank Dr. Gisela Böhm for comments and encouragement throughout the development of this paper.

REFERENCES

Buck, C., et al, 2018. An experiment series on app information privacy concerns. *Proceedings of the European Conference on Information Systems*. Portsmouth, UK, pp. 1-19.

Hsieh, H.F. and Shannon, S. E., 2005. Three approaches to qualitative content analysis. *In Qualitative Health Research*, Vol. 15, No. 9, pp. 1277-1288

Kokolakis, S., 2017. Privacy attitudes and privacy behaviour: A review of current research on the privacy paradox phenomenon. *In Computers & Security*, Vol. 64, pp. 122-134.

Malhotra, N., et al, 2004. Internet Users' Privacy Concerns (IUIPC): The construct, the scale, and a causal model. *In Information Systems Research*, Vol. 15, No. 4, pp. 336-355.

Schwarz, N. and Bohner, G., 2001. The construction of attitudes, in Tesser, A. & Schwarz, N. (eds), *Blackwell handbook of social psychology: Intrapersonal processes*. Oxford, Oxford, United Kingdom, pp. 436-457.

Shamseer, L., et al, 2015. Preferred reporting items for systematic review and meta-analysis protocols (PRIMA-P) 2015: Elaboration and explanation. In BMJ, Vol. 349, No. 1, pp. 1-25.

Smith, H. J., et al, 1996. Information privacy: Measuring individuals' concerns about organizational practices. *In MIS Quarterly*, Vol. 20, No. 2, pp. 167-196.

Stewart, K. A. and Segars, A. H., 2002. An empirical examination of the concern for information privacy instrument. *In Information Systems Research,* Vol. 13, No. 1, pp. 36-49.

AUTHOR INDEX